THE WORLD'S GREATEST HAND

Handloader's Digest

FROM THE EXPERTS AT
GunDigest
19TH EDITION

PHILIP P. MASSARO

Published by

Gun Digest® Books, an imprint of F+W Media, Inc.
Krause Publications • 700 East State Street • Iola, WI 54990-0001
715-445-2214 • 888-457-2873
www.krausebooks.com

To order books or other products call toll-free 1-800-258-0929
or visit us online at www.gundigeststore.com

Cover photography by J.D. Fielding Photography

ISBN-13: 978-1-4402-4531-2
ISBN-10: 1-4402-4531-2

Cover Design by Dave Hauser
Designed by Tom Nelsen
Edited by Chad Love

Printed in the United States of America

10 9 8 7 6 5 4 3 2 1

For more great Gun Digest titles on handloading and ballistics, go to the Gun Digest Store at www.gundigeststore.com

Suggested titles include:

Understanding Ballistics: Complete Guide to Bullet Selection

Cartridges of the World, 14th edition

Gun Digest Shooter's Guide to Reloading

Handbook of Reloading Basics

Introduction

Welcome back! It has been quite some time since a new edition of *Handloader's Digest* has graced the shelves, and it has been long overdue. The world of reloading has changed radically, and there are so many exciting things to discuss and share that I can't wait for you to delve into the meat of this tome. There have been many changes in products and tools on the market since the 18th Edition was published in 2003, so many, in fact, that sometimes it seems like the industry changes every couple of years, and while most of the old standbys are still with us, I've embraced some of the new designs and technologies that are offered.

The ammunition crunch of the last couple of years has brought many new people into the fold; an unavailability of ammunition has generated both a need and desire for shooters to roll their own, and as far as I am concerned, the more, the merrier! If you're completely new to reloading, you'll find a basic reloading sequence in this book, but it might be wise to pick up a more in-depth basic manual and spend some time with it, so you'll get the most out of the more detailed information here. While the products may have evolved, the basic principles are still the same. Still, there's something here for everyone.

As the President of Massaro Ballistic Laboratories, LLC, I am fortunate enough to create many different types of ammunition, from mild handgun loads for new shooters all the way up through the safari ammunition, firing bullets in excess of 500 grains. It certainly keeps me on my toes, and allows me to stay abreast of the newest products and techniques.

Within these covers, not only will you find a rather complex listing of the tools and products that we use during every reloading session, including those new developments on the market since last you cracked the binding of *Handloader's Digest*, but feature articles by names old and new. The names that you do recognize bring many years of field-proven knowledge to the table; those names that haven't graced your ears yet will prove themselves herein. If you're an old hand at the reloading press, you may enjoy the reviews of some of the new products available, and likewise, if you're relatively new to reloading, you may enjoy some of the older techniques and technologies reviewed herein. Traditionally, each edition of *Handloader's Digest* has become part of my reloading library, and I've often referred to the articles and reference material contained therein. I feel this edition is no different. Pistol or rifle, self-defense, targets, or hunting, it doesn't matter; we're all handloaders, and it's all good stuff.

In any manner, it's great to see a new edition of *Handloader's Digest* on the shelves and in your hands, and I am honored to be at the helm. For those of you new to the hobby, welcome to your new addiction.

Welcome, all, to *Handloader's Digest 19th Edition*, and I hope you enjoy!

Philip P. Massaro
Executive Editor

Contents

Section 1: Feature Stories

Section 2: Catalog

Metallic Handloading: The Tools

Metallic Handloading: The Components

Shotshell Reloading

Quick References

Book Excerpts

A NEWCOMER'S VIEW
ON RELOADING

By Carol Finnigan

Editor's Note: When I first met Carol Finnigan, she was in the unfortunate predicament of being in the company of one Mr. Bill Loeb, author of Gun Digest's The Custom 1911. You see, being wheelchair bound, and having to feign friendship with Mr. Loeb, she appeared to be trapped. I did my best to rescue her, at least in conversation. That conversation turned to shooting and reloading, and to my great surprise, Carol is not only a heck of a pistol shot, but also reloads her own ammunition. I immediately asked her to write a piece for HD19, about a new reloader's point of view. Sometimes, it pays to listen to those who see things with new eyes. Please allow me to introduce Carol Finnigan.

– Philip Massaro, Editor

Sitting down on the job

It's important to me to choose activities that I can do successfully while sitting down. I am largely confined to a wheelchair, so it would be frustrating and a wasted effort if I had to stand for long periods of time. I am also "vertically challenged," so for me too much walking is like reaching stuff on the top shelf; it just ain't gonna happen.

From an early age I had always wanted to learn how to shoot. When my dad caught me using my brother's BB gun to blast the vegetable cans off of a tree stump in the side lot, he would snatch the gun

from me, shake his finger and say, "Young ladies don't shoot guns."

Not exactly an enlightened outlook. Dad's disapproval or not, I never gave up on my dream. I wonder what he would think were he to know that I not only shoot and hunt, but also reload my own ammo? I would like to think that he would be proud of me.

So, why do I love reloading? There are several reasons. First off, it is a means to acquire a scarce product. In addition, I can control the quality of my ammunition, as well as customize it for me and my purposes.

I have to admit; the main reason that I love to reload is because I am all about saving money. If you see a penny with a bruise, it was probably me who pinched it. If there is a way to stretch my shooting budget, you can bet that I am going to find it. My only regret is that

Death to cardboard!

I didn't invest in reloading equipment earlier. Had I done so, I would be a much better shooter today because my shooting budget would have allowed me to practice that much more.

It wasn't that long ago when the price of ammunition, at least for the popular cartridges like 9mm, was quite affordable. Many people, myself included, didn't consider the cost of reloading equipment a worthwhile investment. Being a casual shooter who only shot a few thousand rounds a year, I couldn't justify it. That is, until the cost of ammo skyrocketed.

In addition to being expensive, ammo became hard to find. Since my entry into the gun culture was relatively recent, by the time I had gotten my first handgun we were on the cusp of an ammunition drought. Yeah, I know, great timing!

Between the federal government procuring billions of rounds of ammunition and the nervous public on a buying frenzy, it was almost impossible to find ammo in the stores. When you did, the price was often inflated. This forced my hand. If I wanted my gun to smoke, I had to roll my own.

Of course, thrift and availability isn't the only reason I love to reload. Dry firing is quite useful, and it drives my family nuts, which is another benefit. Still, there is no substitute for live fire. Pulling the gun out of recoil and back on target just can't be done in the living room. Well, it can, but the neighbors complain, the cops show up and it scares the cat.

Sure, I load a lot of my practice ammo light so that I can stretch my powder and it helps me not tire as quickly, but it is still shooting live ammo. My practice load is 4.1 grains of Hodgdon Titegroup pushing a 115-grain coated lead bullet from Donnie Miculek's company, Bayou Bullets.

This load cycles just fine out of a Springfield XDM 5.25 Comp, and I am getting 1000 fps. Of course, I do load my self-defense loads a lot hotter. A Barnes Tac/XP - an excellent copper projectile - scoots along at over 1250 fps when pushed by 5.1 grains of the same powder.

Typically, I keep a small amount of ammunition loaded and ready to go. Mostly I reload to replace what I use. Sometimes, if I am up to a big day at the range, I will load extra. By keeping my loaded stock of ammo to a minimum, it allows me to use my limited resources for my immediate needs, rather than have a lot of loaded ammunition that I might not need for months.

I try to keep in mind what I'm reloading for. Am I going to be shooting at paper targets at the range, or am I using this as my self-defense ammo? These are really my only two handgun shooting activities. Handgun hunting is not in my arena as of yet, although I

Resizing brass in fun

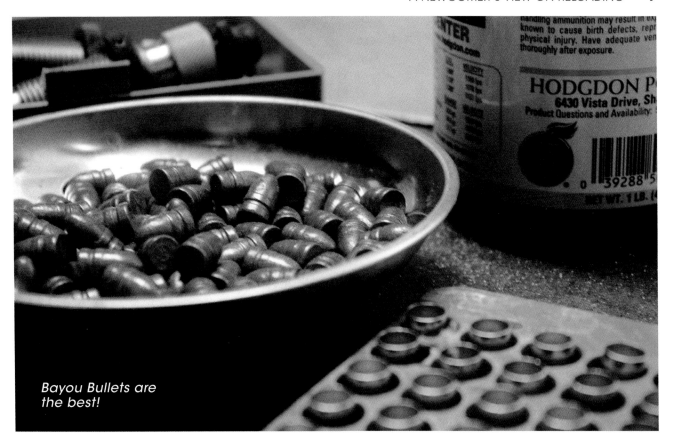

Bayou Bullets are the best!

have dispatched a deer with a rifle. Yes, I still fondly recall the beautiful doe that timidly came into view of the blind. She was delicious, by the way. Every hunter knows just how satisfying that first bite of their first kill is.

Since I do not have my own rifle yet, I have not invested in reloading anything except handgun ammo. Surely, that will be the next step for me.

I've come a long way from my primitive understanding of ammunition. I laugh now at how I used to think that gunpowder was a naturally-occurring product. Primers didn't scare me, though, because I didn't know that they were explosive. If I did, I would have been afraid of those, too. They don't look menacing at all. Plus, they are so cute lined up in those neat little trays.

The first time I was asked which bullets I wanted to reload, I wasn't even sure of which ones I had already used; other than they were copper-colored. Everyone was talking in abbreviations except me. I didn't know a JHP from a SWC. That day I wasn't just talking bullets; I was sweating them. I was embarrassed because I knew that they knew that I didn't know. Of course, it was all on me; they were being very supportive and just trying to help. I was always interested to learn how others reloaded and grateful for everyone's input.

Sorting brass "change"

Check and double-check your work!

Even though I have learned some terminology, seasoned reloaders speak a unique language, one that I haven't yet mastered. They can spout load data and ballistic statistics. It's going to take me awhile before I will be able join that conversation, so y'all better enjoy it now before you won't be able get a word in edgewise.

I don't try to memorize all of the information, but rather go through the ritual of looking it up each and every time. Heck, I don't even remember all of the different types of bullets and the variations of powder are mind numbing to me.

Still, I enjoy the process of "going to square one" and researching the load that I am going to produce, even if I have done it countless times before.

In the beginning, my best friend, Bill Loëb, author of *The Custom 1911,* gave me an overview of the reloading process. Being right there in his workshop as he explained and "air reloaded," demonstrating for me how it worked. At the time it all seemed so simple.

Until I grabbed the reigns for myself, I didn't understand the "feel" for the process. Like the way you can tell through the handle if you have a good crimp. How tight is too tight when setting up your dies. How often to check your powder throw. It took a while and

although I am not an expert, the satisfaction of doing it on my own is exhilarating.

In addition to all of the wonderful benefits of reloading, there is one that I didn't anticipate. You see, reloading is a great craft for the 'Obsessive Compulsive Disorder' in me. Learning good habits not only makes for consistent quality ammunition, but my OCD nature loves the repetition. Even when I get into the groove and go faster, it soothes me.

Of course "fast" is relative, as I use a single-stage press. The Redding Boss II is a beast. What it lacks in speed it makes up for with precision. Plus, the long handle gives lots of leverage. The press is amazingly smooth, so I can "feel" what is happening even if I'm not looking. Of course, OCD or not, I can think about other things while going through these simple steps. Usually I'm imagining I'm a specialized technician using futuristic equipment as a secret spy operative. It is all very "Manhattan Project"-esque.

While surely a unique view, I actually enjoy collecting spent brass. For me, it is like finding money on the ground in a dream. As I pick up one coin, I notice another, and then more and more, so I start picking up faster and faster, running out of room in my hands as I collect the change.

I can feel my adrenalin pumping and the excitement growing in my dream, and then I would wake up. I have to admit, I am a little sad when I do, because I had picked up a lot of cash in that dream! Well, the brass in a bay is just like that: 9mm cases are nickels and .45s are dimes. I have become an eagle eye expert spotting the telltale flickers of sunlight dancing on the spent casings. I quickly fill my hands and pockets, set them on my lap and in the tray on the back of my wheelchair. It only took a couple of trips to the range before I started coming prepared with empty bags to help the competitors collect the spent brass.

Certainly, most of the people that acquire this book are more expert than I am. Perhaps they are handloading for their African safari or their next I.D.P.A. match. Maybe they are planning a hog hunt or preparing ammunition as a military sniper. That in my small way I am linked to these other members of the gun culture is another reason why I love reloading: It is a way to connect to my people.

From my can-killing days as a child, I have always been drawn to firearms. I love being a part of the gun

Shagging brass is fun

Nickels
and
dimes

culture. Everywhere I've been people have been welcoming and helpful. Where else do world-class athletes treat novices like colleagues? At SHOT show, Brian Zins, Bruce Piatt, and BJ Norris treated me like one of them. The welcoming nature of the gun culture makes me want to do more.

So what does my future hold? I want to participate in shooting competitions like I.D.P.A. or U.S.P.S.A.

And I don't want to just shoot; I want to shoot well. I want to be able to overcome the struggles caused by the wheelchair, which would hijack my time in an emergency situation. I know that the shooting sports aren't "training," but the skills learned there would be very valuable.

In addition, I also want to become an avid hunter instead of just a novice, and provide game for my family's meals. I want to learn how to attract the deer and take the perfect shot. I also want to pay it forward. There have been so many people to help me as I learned to shoot and reload. I want to be there for the next person reaching out, to welcome them into our world.

THE .358 BLANDO: A SHORT SUCCESS STORY

By Philip P. Massaro

I was introduced to Dr. Tom Blando, better known as "Doc," through my good buddy Mike McNulty. Mike had told me much about Doc; his passion for shooting and reloading, and a bit about Doc's wildcat cartridge, the .358 Blando. When Doc and I finally had a chance to discuss reloading and ballistics, I knew I had found a guy who shared the love of the game. The wildcat that bears his name has been around for the better part of thirty years, and he's tweaked and honed it until it performs to the exact specification he had envisioned in the 1980s.

"I was intrigued by the silhouette pistol cartridges, particularly the .357 Maximum," Doc told me, "but I had a vision of a cartridge that would perform not only in the longer-barreled single-shot pistols, but one that would serve as a rifle cartridge as well. And, I wanted the cartridge to be as efficient as possible. I wanted all the powder to be burned in the barrel."

To make a long story short, Doc Blando achieved that vision, in a unique cartridge that is extremely efficient, especially for the size of the thing.

"I've always been a fan of the .35-caliber hunting cartridges, like the .358 Winchester and .350 Remington Magnum," he says. "They work very well for the whitetail deer and black bears here in the Adirondacks. I also love the fact that as a reloader I can use the lighter weight pistol bullets for the .38 Special and .357 Magnum as a plinking bullet for these cartridges. In a lot of ways it makes perfect sense."

Blando's guinea pig would be the famous .220 Swift case, a semi-rimmed affair with a very thick wall, and that thick wall, as well as the strength of the Swift case, was the reason for choosing it. Doc shortened the case carefully from the Swift's length of 2.205" to 1.560", a significant reduction in case length and one that left the thick part of the case wall to deal with.

J.D. Fielding photography

The body taper of the Swift design would be all but removed, using a shoulder with an angle of 22°-05' off centerline, and leaving a neck length of 0.245". Mind you, this was in the 80's, long before the short, stubby, fireplug cartridges that have been released in recent years were unleashed on the world.

While it would be easy to say that the neck length - being much less than the desired one-caliber dimension - is insufficient for proper neck tension, consider that the .300 Winchester Magnum sports a neck length of 0.264", so Doc Blando isn't all that radical with his design, especially when we consider that he uses the lighter bullets in .358" caliber for most of his local hunting.

Blando contacted RCBS, and once the cartridge dimensions were solidified on paper, he had a set of custom reloading dies built to order, including a set of two-step forming dies. The first step sets a rough

.220 Swift and .358 Blando

J.D. Fielding photography

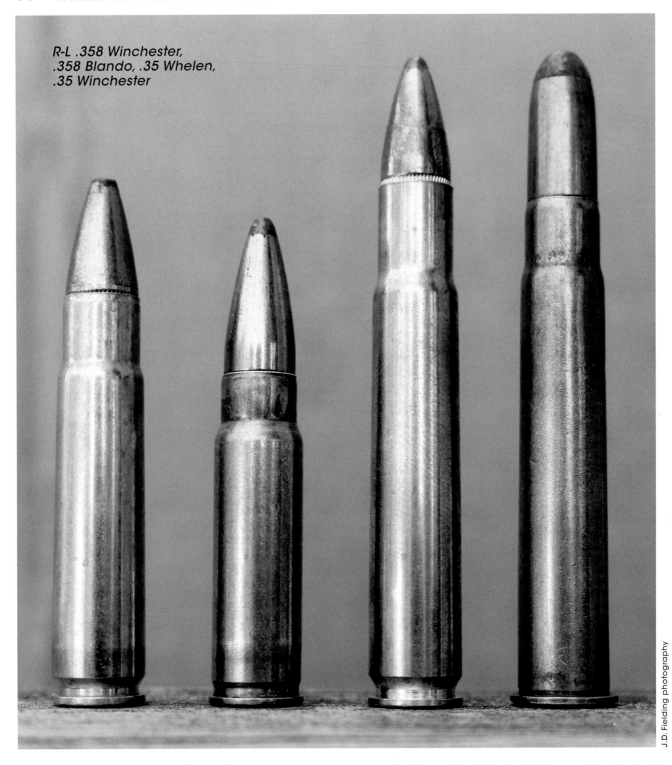

R-L .358 Winchester, .358 Blando, .35 Whelen, .35 Winchester

J.D. Fielding photography

shoulder into the cut-off Swift cartridge.

The neck must then be reamed to .358" inside-diameter, as the case wall portion of the .220 Swift case is much too thick to use as the case neck for the .358 Blando. The custom reamer cuts it to the proper dimension, and step two further refines the case shape and properly dimensions the case neck, getting it close enough to be loaded with a light charge for fireforming.

Doc fireforms his .358 Blando brass with a load of 20.0 grains of Hodgdon's Lil' Gun and a 158-grain .357" Speer pistol bullet.

Wait, what?! Hodgdon's Lil' Gun? Isn't that a powder normally reserved for pistol cartridges that run at lower velocities? Didn't you say that it was a rifle cartridge as well? Well, yes, you're right. But this cartridge will obtain rifle velocities using this powder. Bear with me for a minute…

Custom RCBS Dies

When Doc started the development of this cartridge, he was using H110 and W296 powders, both of which are well respected in the pistol community. Remember, he was initially inspired to create a silhouette pistol cartridge. But he found that he could push the rifle bullets to velocities similar to the .358 Winchester, and even approach the .35 Whelen, due to the strength of the case and the efficiency of the cartridge.

The Blando case creates a quick but safe pressure peak, and – even in a 14" barreled Thompson/Center Contender – will give very respectable velocities.

But how much was too much? How do you go about finding the limits of pressure in an unknown cartridge?

Well, he had to do some testing, to see where the limit of safety was. In a mechanical rest, with a means of firing the gun remotely, Dr. Blando pushed the pressure and velocity until he found mechanical failure: first cratered primers, then ruptured case heads, and ultimately a burst barrel [Editor's Note: DO NOT try this yourself without first becoming a student of pressure and the dangers of mechanical failure nor

*Dr. Thomas
Blando and
Author*

*Below: Author
shooting .358
Blando in
T/C Contender*

J.D. Fielding photography

J.D. Fielding photography

Chronograph reading
with 180-grain load

.358 Blando Rifle

J.D. Fielding photography

without the proper equipment and environment to test within; it can cost you your life].

This told him where the danger zone was. The powder charges were backed off, and several powders were tested to find the best combination of safe pressure, consistent velocity, and good accuracy.

Doc found that 31.0 grains of Lil' Gun under a 180-grain Speer flat-point bullet, sparked by a CCI200 large rifle primer, would easily achieve 2,550 fps from a long-barreled pistol, or short-barreled rifle; plenty enough velocity to take our local deer and bear. This would become his go-to hunting load for big game close to home.

But he wasn't satisfied with just a pistol in this cartridge; he knew it would work in a rifle as well. "With the mountains we hunt here, I envisioned a very petite rifle, with little recoil, that would effectively take the largest black bear you'd find in the Adirondacks," Doc explains. "I knew the .358 Blando would perform just as well in a short-barreled rifle, and with a short receiver, it would make carrying the rifle a dream come true."

Once I saw his prototype rifle, and had a chance to spend some time with it at the bench, I had to fully concur. It is a Ruger Model 77, born into this world as a .308 Winchester; perhaps not the ideal length action, but it was available. The action had a slim-contour barrel, 19 ½" in length, screwed to that action. The magazine, obviously long for the diminutive .358 Blando, needed a custom magazine reducer to get the cartridge to feed properly. It was set in a Ram-Line molded stock, with a recoil pad affixed to obtain the proper length of pull for Dr. Blando. At first handling, the rifle felt very light, like rimfire light. But once at the bench, I began to understand exactly what Doc was up to, and a broad smile began to form on my face.

The recoil, even with the 220-grain Speer bullet and 250-grain Hornady spire point, was more than manageable. To best describe it, I would say it has a recoil speed on the quick side, but not harsh at all. I would speculate that the recoil speed is attributed to the fast burn rate of the Lil' Gun powder. The recoil fits well with the light weight of the rifle, and from the offhand position, it was all but unnoticed.

However, it was the results displayed on the chronograph that really opened my eyes. Doc Blando just smiled. "I get an awful lot of cocked eyebrows when people actually see the groups and the velocities. I mean, it rivals some of the .35 Whelen loads."

Doc was correct; the tiny little cartridge with pistol powder produced some amazing results.

The light 150-grain Remington Cor-Lokt bullets, proven so effective in the .35 Remington cartridge of lever gun fame, run at a muzzle velocity of 2,770 fps from the Blando

Dr. Thomas Blando
Courtesy J.D. Fielding photography

.358 Blando & Diagram

case. This is a considerable advantage over the old lever classic; more than 400 fps.

I mentioned Doc's pet load, using the 180-grain bullets at a muzzle velocity of 2,550 fps that has accounted for so many deer and bear, but I like the Hornady InterLock 200-grain bullet tooling along at 2,505 fps on the chronograph. That Hornady bullet, especially at velocities below 2,800 fps, performs perfectly on game, holding together well and giving deep penetration.

A charge of 31.4 grains of Lil' Gun under a Speer Hot-Cor 220-grain flatpoint will leave the muzzle at 2,460 fps, and at this moderate velocity, the Speer bullets - that have been known to give rapid expansion when impact velocities are too high - should perform perfectly.

But the load that excited me the most, probably because I have been a long-time fan of heavy-for-caliber bullets at lower velocities, is the 250-grain Hornady spire point cruising from the muzzle at an even 2,300 fps when charged with 30.5 grains of Lil' Gun.

This load, when compared with the larger siblings of the .35-caliber clan, shows that the Blando cartridge is the equal of the near-obsolete .358 Winchester, and only 100 to 150 fps behind the .350 Remington Magnum and .35 Whelen. This is very impressive, especially when you consider that the .358 Winchester requires 15 more grains of powder to achieve the same velocities, but with considerably more recoil.

Author at bench with Blando rifle

This is a load that is worthy of the large bears, or the largest of plains game in Africa. All this from a cartridge that has an overall length of 2.326" - nearly ½" shorter than the .358 Winchester. What a fantastic ultra-light rifle this would make, for mountains or Alaskan streams. I immediately began to daydream about mountain hunts...

So, in all sincerity, do we need the .358 Blando? Is it the new face of the future of cartridge development? Anything is possible. At the very least, it could be considered as a light-recoiling, hard-hitting rifle/pistol cartridge that is highly effective on anything from varmints to big game. Even Doc Blando realizes that the shooting world has such a plethora of good cartridges to choose from that there is a large amount of overlap and redundancy. But wildcatters love to tinker, as a matter of fact that is sometimes the entire game. Oftentimes we feel a need to justify the very existence of a particular cartridge, due to the comparisons that we use to quantify things.

Dr. Thomas Blando saw the potential for a cartridge, and went through the trials and tribulations to bring that cartridge to light, just because he liked the idea. The idea was successful, if only to Dr. Blando. That sentiment, to me, is the spirit of wildcatting cartridges. The fact that he has used this cartridge in the game fields for over two decades makes it that much better.

Doc is in the process of building a new .358 Blando rifle, based on a Winchester Model 70 action. This rifle, soon to be sacrificed in the name of science, is chambered in the .22-250 Remington cartridge, so that magazine length will better serve the short cartridge than the .308 Winchester-length receiver does, and better feed the stubby little cartridge. He is ordering it with a 19" barrel, and that length will perfectly balance with the characteristics of the .358 Blando.

As Doc shares a love of Africa, I hope to soon share a campfire with him somewhere on that continent. The look on his face when he takes the first head of African game with the cartridge he designed, is something I want to see. Oh, did I mention that there is a .375 Blando in the works? Seems the tinkerer never rests for long, eh? More about that next time...

AUTHOR BIO:

Philip P. Massaro is the President of Massaro Ballistic Laboratories, LLC, a custom ammunition company, comfortably nestled in between the Hudson River and Catskill Mountains of Upstate New York. He has been a handloader for 20+ years, a veteran of five African safaris and dozens of North American hunts. He is a Licensed Professional Land Surveyor by trade, a musician by choice, and usually reeks of Hoppes No. 9.

HANDLOADING FOR THE AR

By Mark Nazi

The AR is a platform that I have had a love/hate relationship with ever since I picked up my first one, many moons ago. Most of my reloading experience with the AR platform has been trying to find a load that's accurate, uses components that are generally easy to obtain, cycles without fail, and uses bullets that I can seat deep enough so there is no fighting between the tip of the round and the wall of the magazine.

So when Phil tasked me with the project of using .308 and .223-powered ARs to disprove the popular notion that AR-platform rifles aren't as accurate as conventional rifles, I was extremely excited for the chance to develop a new load beyond my normal three gun / plinking load that I've used for many years.

But first a brief history lesson for those of you who may not know: Armalite is the original designer of the AR-15 and AR-10 rifles. Both were designed in the late 1950s. The "AR-15" was simply the 15th Armalite rifle project. During a tour of the Armalite factory in the late 1950s, Colt purchased the plans. Therefore, the only rifles that can bear the "AR-15" marking are ones that are manufactured by Colt or with a license from Colt.

Fast forward to present day, and of course you can now buy fully-assembled "AR-15" style rifles in just about every caliber produced, from .22LR all the way to the .50BMG. And when it comes to parts, I don't know of any other platform that has the amount of customization potential as the AR-style rifles. Recently, I actually saw a small chainsaw that attaches to the bottom of any Picatinny rail, as well as a number of knives, and just about anything else you can think of.

When it came time to pick my hardware for this project I knew I had the .223 end covered. With one phone call and a three-minute drive, I had my hands on a beau-

Mark Nazi at the bench testing .308 loads.

J.D. Fielding photography

tiful Rock River Arms rifle that had been outfitted with a full Krieger match-grade pipe, countless hours of stone work, and a trigger that breaks like an icicle.

Now all I needed was a .308. A quick call to a friend over at June Bug Customs and I had everything needed for the .308, including a beautiful, semi-heavy, 1:10 twist, 24-inch stainless steel barrel.

I decided to top these beautiful rifles with what I personally consider to be the top-of-the-line in rifle optics – Nightforce. The company provided a jaw dropping NXS 5.5-22 X 50 for the .223 and a monstrous NXS 8-32 X 56 for the .308, both equipped with the MOART reticles.

When these scopes arrived I bolted them up using the Nightforce 20 MOA one-piece ring and base. Having mounted countless scopes from every manufacture known to man, I must say that these Nightforce rings and bases are of the most unbelievable quality.

Normally I acquire my scope and mounting solution and then the lapping begins, but with these Nightforce products lapping the rings would be an insult.

After getting the scopes mounted and adjusted to my eye it was time to take them outside and get a look at the MOART reticle. The clarity of this glass is not something I can describe accurately in words. It is stunning.

Marty Groppi shooting the Rock River Arms EOP in .223

J.D. Fielding photography

J.D. Fielding photography

Premium Nightforce Optics

When I gathered my components I kept reminding myself that I was going for accuracy while being able to retain reliability. I knew off the bat that this was going to be a single-stage operation. When going for accuracy I personally prefer the single-stage method, as it allows me to walk my brass through each stage, keep a close eye on every process, and hand-check every step of every single cartridge.

I chose a Forsters Co-Ax B3 single-stage press. After the press had been decided, it was time to choose my options for everything else. First off was brass. I wanted something to hold everything together in a nice package., so I went with brand-new Norma .308 Winchester and .223 Winchester brass.

I figured that for what I was doing, 100 pieces of each would suffice. Next, I needed an ignition source. I've been a long-time fan of the Federal Gold Medal Match primers. Over the many years I've been using them, they have never given me anything but perfect performance.

After that it was time to pick some powder. For the .308 I picked Accurate Arms LT-30, IMR XBR 8208, Hodgdon Varget, and the classic IMR 4064. For the .223 I grabbed cans of Reloder #7, Varget, IMR 4198, and X-terminator by RamShot. After settling on my choice of brass, powders, and primers it was time to pick the projectiles.

Norma brass in .223 Remington and .308 Winchester

J.D. Fielding photography

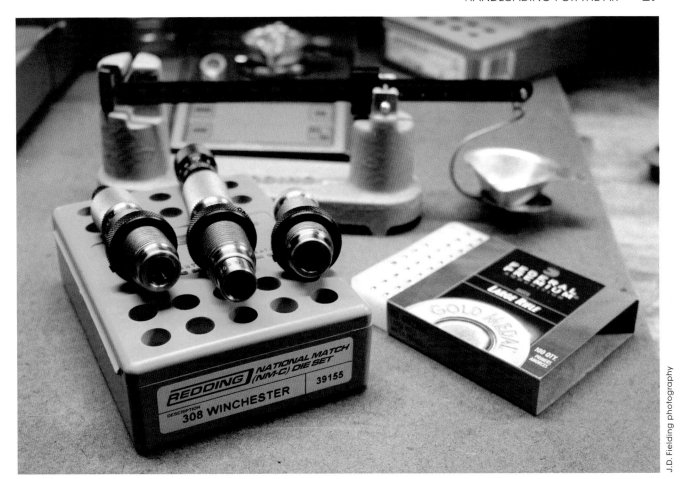

J.D. Fielding photography

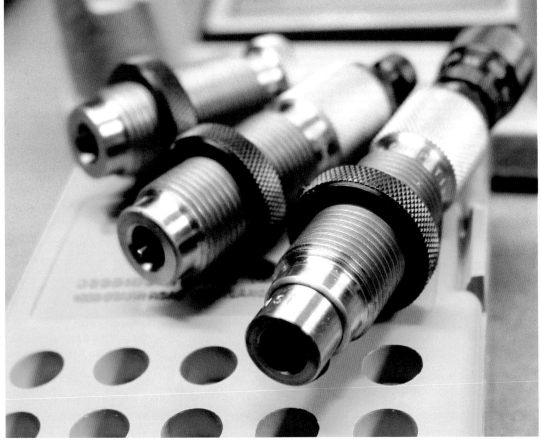

Redding National Match Dies in .308 – Redding National Match Dies in .223 Remington

J.D. Fielding photography

Redding small base dies

J.D. Fielding photography

Since I had been tasked with delivering accuracy, I decided to grab a few boxes of my favorite target bullets, the Match King hollowpoint boattail. This has long been one of my favorites. I was also able to acquire a few boxes of the brand new Tipped Match Kings, as well as a box of Nosler Ballistic Tips that I have also found to be flawless in performance.

Finally it was time to choose my dies. I tossed around a few ideas before deciding on Redding National Match dies in .223 and .308, with the added small-base sizing die included separately. Now that I had everything in front of me it was time to get to it.

I decided to start with the .308. After referencing a number of different reloading books as well as measuring the length of the magazines I had, I knew that my Cartridge Overall Length (C.O.L.) was going to be 2.800 across the board.

When I reload for accuracy I like to take all my components and lay them out, starting with the brass. I take my brass, and, one piece at a time, give it a good visual inspection before placing it into the loading block.

Once I've got my loading block filled up I begin my sizing process. First I'll take my tub of case wax and apply a little on my fingers. Next, as I grab each case to be sized, I rub the wax all over the case to insure that it will enter and exit the die smoothly.

With the semi-automatic AR-style rifles I ALWAYS use a small base sizing die as the first step. My reasoning for this is the rifles I am using - like most AR-style rifles - are a direct impingement system.

That means that as a round is fired gases from the explosion are recycled through the gas system to cycle the action, eject a spent casing, pick up a live round from the magazine, and chamber it.

After all my brass got the small base resizing it was time to run them through the full-length resizing die. Finally I had a full loading block of fully-sized brass. Normally I would say this is where I trim all my brass, but as I looked in my reloading manual to acquire the trim-to-length of this brass, I grabbed my digital calipers and started measuring. My trim-to length was 2.005. What I like to do is find a case in my lot that measures exactly 2.005 and set it aside. I refer to this casing as my "god case." I'll use it to set my case trimmer, set my die depth and height, and a number of other tasks.

What I found truly surprising when I started measuring was that was every single case I measured was exactly 2.005 exactly.

At first I was in disbelief. I asked my loading buddy to find me brass in this lot that did not measure 2.005. He was only able to find perhaps two pieces that measured either 2.006 or 2.004. I have to tip my hat to Norma; well done, boys.

I then fired up my Lyman case prep station and began looking and feeling for burrs left from the manufacturing process. Again, and to my delight, this Norma brass came out of the box ready to deliver.

With minimal chamfering and de-burring and now with all my brass to the proper size, length, and dimensions it was time to prime. I grabbed a fresh box of Federal GM 210 M large rifle primers which is Federal's match-grade large rifle primer, tossed them into my Lee auto prime XR, and began priming my cases. I was blown away how consistent the primer pockets of this brass were; they were tight but not too tight, and the pocket depth paired with the GM 210 M primers was right on the money.

I like to seat my primers a few hairs under flush with the bottom of the case. After I had my cases fully prepped it was time to start charging them, so I grabbed a one-pound can of XBR and a load data sheet.

For load development I went with the simplest form of testing the ladder test. A number of published loads for XBR paired with a 168-grain Match King bullet showed a starting load of 33.2 grains and a max load of 43.2 grains. With this data in hand I fired up my RCBS Chargemaster 1500.

With my process of ladder testing what I do is draw a diagram in my bench notebook and start with the lowest charge weight. I'll load five rounds at the start weight. In this case I started with 33.5 grains of XBR 8208. All five of these rounds will sit in row 1 of my ammo box.

From here I'll step up my charge weights in .5-grain increments. In other words; row two consists of five

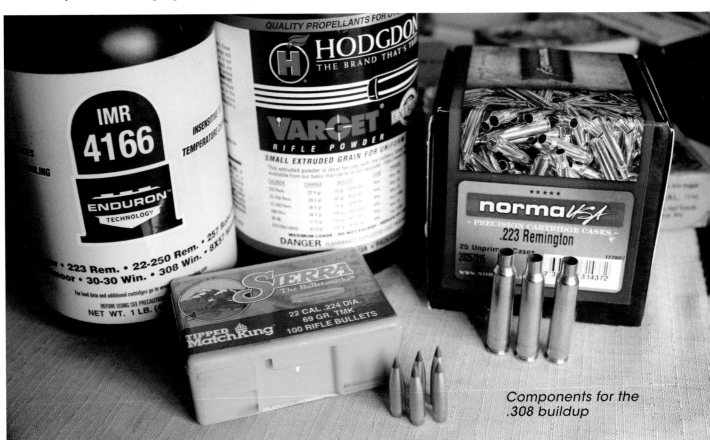

Components for the .308 buildup

rounds with a charge weight of 34.0 grains, and so on until I reach the maximum recommended weight.

If you do not have and live by the use of a reloading bench notebook I strongly recommend using one. I refuse to reload without my notebooks. If asked any questions regarding my load data for any particular rifle or cartridge, I will not attempt to remember off the top of my head; only after referring to my notebook will I give such data.

With the single-stage nature of loading for these rifles, my RCBS Chargemaster 1500 was the obvious choice for me.

For those who are not familiar with this extremely accurate, time-saving device, I highly recommend it. RCBS has taken a digital powder-dispensing system and paired it with a Chargemaster digital scale. You simply level the machine on a sturdy surface (I use a block of marble), calibrate it with the included weights, punch in your desired charge weight, press dispense, and away you go.

The scale and dispenser unit talk to each other until your desired weight has been reached, then the machine beeps and displays the actual charge weight as another check to insure you've reached your desired weight. It is a must-have for any single stage loader.

After getting all my cases charged it was finally time to break out the one die I had been drooling over since the beginning of this project, the Redding National Match Competition seating die. The micrometer adjustments were flawless, smooth and precise. The die uses a bushing system to seat the bullets, causing no deformity in the copper jackets.

I grabbed a box of .30-caliber 168-grain Tipped Match Kings, referenced as much published data as I could, and came up with a C.O.L. of 2.800. Setting my C.O.L. at 2.800 gave me enough room to be able to load in magazines and have them function properly. But what did worry me was not having much room to play with in the way of how far off the lands and grooves I was able to seat the bullet. Only time would tell if that adjustment was one that needed tinkering.

Seating the tipped 168-grain Sierra Match Kings was a dream, given the extremely high quality of the Redding dies coupled with the free-floating base plate of the Forster Co-Ax B3 press.

After getting all my bullets seated it was now time to discuss crimp. I've heard many schools of thought regarding crimping AR- style rifles, or even any semiautomatic rifle. What I do is make up a few extra rounds with no powder or primer in them, jot down my C.O.L., place two or three rounds into the magazine, then cycle the action as roughly as I can. I'll then take those rounds and take measurements again to see if the violence of the action is pushing my bullets deeper into the case.

If I do notice my C.O.L. getting shorter I know there is not enough neck tension holding the projectile to keep it in place. If a crimp is needed, I'll reset the test and apply the slightest crimp I possibly can, then re-test the rounds until my C.O.L. is the same going in as it is coming out.

Each rifle is different; some have military feed ramps and some do not. Some chambers are tighter than others. Always take some extra time to determine if a crimp is needed in your case.

One thing to keep in mind is how the feeding system in AR-style rifles works: the bolt pushes a round from the magazine into the feed ramps, the feed ramps then guide the round into the chamber. This is a very violent action and could potentially push your bullet too deep into the case, causing a catastrophic failure resulting in possible serious injury, death, and destruction of a very expensive set-up. After applying a wee

Sierra 168-grain Tipped Match King

J.D. Fielding photography

Measuring group size at the target

J.D. Fielding photography

bit of crimp to my rounds it was finally time to get behind this beautiful system.

I first loaded a few mags of factory-loaded ammo to get the rifle on paper. Again, the Nightforce scope was an absolute dream to work with. All the adjustments on the turrets were flawless and of the utmost precision. If you dialed up an inch adjustment at 100 yards, an inch is exactly what you ended up with. When you take the .308 out past 100 yards and really let it stretch its legs the zero stop feature of the Nightforce allows you to transition between what you are zeroed at and whatever distance you care to dope to quickly, efficiently, and with precision.

The way I run my ladder test is I will shoot from a bench with a rest on the front and rear of the rifle to take as much human error out of the equation as possible. I fire one round, then lock the bolt open to let

it cool back down to ambient temperature. I find the ejected brass and inspect it for any signs of high pressure; then I take the round that the rifle chambered and measure it to insure that my crimp and neck tension is holding the projectile in place properly.

Once the chamber and barrel have reached ambient temperature I'll fire my second round, repeating the process until my string of five rounds has been fired. After that I'll take a walk down to the target with calipers for my group measurements. After all my rounds have been fired I'll sit and compile my data.

Using the same chart for my ladder test, I'll write the group size in the corresponding row that already has the charge weight in it.

I was easily able to get five-shot groups under an inch at 100 yards at right around the 43.0-grain mark with the XBR powder.

IMR 8208 XBR &
168-grain Sierra
Tipped Match Kings

J.D. Fielding photography

Throughout my XBR testing I found the closer I got to the max load, the tighter my groups were getting. I finally settled on using 43.0 grains of XBR. This load was consistently between .5" and 1.00", cycled perfectly, and generally performed flawlessly. I also was able to find great accuracy with the other powders I tested but stuck with the XBR because I was happy with the results and it metered like a dream.

Now it was time to grab the .223 and basically duplicate the testing. For powder I grabbed cans of X-terminator, IMR 4198, and Reloder #7. After looking at bullets for a while and keeping in mind that I had to keep the C.O.L. less than the size of my magazine, and the fact that I was dealing with a tight Kreiger match chamber, I ended up grabbing a box of 40-grain Nosler Ballistic Tips and a box of 40-grain Sierra Blitz Kings.

I found that both of these bullets delivered five-shot, one-hole groups at 100 yards.

At the end of my load development 23.5 grains of Reloder #7 was the magic number when it came to the Nosler Ballistic Tips, delivering group sizes of under a half-inch at 100 yards. When I switched to the 40-grain Blitzkings it was 22.5 grains of IMR 4198 that delivered very similar results.

What I recommend, if tighter grouping is what you're after, is a second round of ladder testing. Let's take our .308 load of 43.0 grains of XBR and go back to the loading bench. Using the same diagram as we did before, let's load row 1 with 43.0 grain of XBR, row 2 with 43.1 grains, and row 3 at our max recommended charge of 43.2 grains.

What I also like to do in the second installment of ladder testing is go on both sides of the accuracy, so my 4th row will be 42.9 grains and 5th row of 42.8 grains. After that it's back to the shooting bench and let the fun data collection process begin. This second round of ladder testing will help you fine tune your load to the rifle and conditions you shoot in.

One last thing I'd like to touch on when it comes to reloading for the AR-style rifles is the endless ways to make cheap accurate ammo for them. Military brass is some of the most available brass out there but does require a little extra attention to bring it up to spec.

Military brass comes with a crimp applied to the primer pocket, as well as primer glue applied; this is to insure that water cannot enter the cartridge and that primers do not back out under fully automatic fire.

I've actually found that my loading buddies will normally just give away the brass they have acquired with the military crimp simply because they don't know how to or don't want to deal with it.

So let's talk about options: you can either cut the crimp from the primer pocket or you can swage the entire pocket back into spec. I've heard good and bad results about cutting the pocket, but after reviewing the data I decided to go with the swaging option. I called up Dillon and had them send me a primer pocket Super Swage 600. Let me tell you: this little device is a MUST HAVE if you deal with large quantities of military-primed brass. It chews through casing after casing without so much as a flinch, and with a little extra work you now have reloadable brass.

One other thing to keep in mind with military brass is that case capacity is slightly different from that of non-military brass. So keep this in mind if you've got a load worked up for your rifle using store-purchased brass, but discover a nice cheap lot of military brass.

Let's use our load from the .223 testing of 23.5 grains of Reloder #7 as an example. Say we want to transfer that load to the pile of military brass we have. What I would do is keep in mind your max load, then load a string of five rounds at 23.5 grains, then in the

This load showed excessive pressure signs – cratered primers and brass flowing into the extractor, so we had to back it down

following rows back your charge off .1 grains until you achieve the original accuracy.

As always practice safety with every step of reloading and never go above your skill level.

AUTHOR BIO:

Mark Nazi is a law enforcement officer and big game hunter who has been reloading for nearly a decade. He enjoys long walks at the rifle range and the sweet smell of burnt powder.

IMR4198 and Norma brass proved a winning combination

HANDLOADING FOR CLASSIC HUNTING REVOLVERS

By Martin Groppi

Modern reloading for hunting revolvers can bring newfound interest to old iron. I own a pair of classic revolvers; one is a 1979 Model 13 K-frame with a four-inch heavy barrel, chambered in .357 Magnum with Pachmayr grips. I inherited this gun, which was once my father's favorite pistol, and is now very dear to me.

My other favorite is a 1957 pre-model 29 N-frame with a 6 ½-inch barrel chambered in - of course - the classic .44 Remington Magnum. During the course of this exercise, which I am sharing with you, I had the pleasant opportunity to breathe some new life into these old guns by using some new bullet and powder combinations.

The .357 Magnum.

Though not looked upon by many as a hunting pistol, my old standby sidearm is the Smith & Wesson Model 13 chambered in .357 Magnum, with a four-inch barrel. Considered by many to be underpowered - and some have even called it "wimpy" - I have used this gun enough to know differently. Throughout my life I have tried to redefine the basic laws of physics, but have always failed miserably, usually resulting in broken bones, stitches, or some type of hard-learned lesson. I quickly learned that I cannot change these laws and that basic physics will always win.

Applying these pesky laws, I have found a 158-grain Hornady XTP with a muzzle velocity of 1,170 fps, when put in the right place, deals with all the critters I generally contend with here in Upstate NY.

Most of my data for the .357 may not be impressive in comparison to many reloading manuals or most of the Internet experts, but these loads were all derived from field testing in my four-inch-barreled Model 13 with many miles on it, not a Universal Receiver with

J.D. Fielding Photography

a 10-inch barrel, which will generate higher velocities and pressures that are not realistic from my handguns.

Here are the strengths and weaknesses of this pistol: First off, it's a pleasure to carry. It fits right on your belt and is easily concealed so you're not taking your gun off every time you go out. Here in Upstate NY we do not have laws that allow an open carry; it's concealed carry only.

One of my favorite things about this pistol is the fact that I can feed it .38 Special ammunition all day long and have a very accurate plinking gun. This is the pistol's usual diet, unless, of course, it's deer season. The recoil of this gun is. when compared to other hunting calibers, very manageable even with full-house loads. My wife shoots this gun regularly, and very accurately at that. When going out to do chores, this is the gun to wear. It doesn't get in your way on your belt and doesn't slow you down while working.

That's not something that can be said of carrying an X-frame revolver.

Secondly, when this little gun is off its diet of .38 Specials, it's fed with premium bullets, usually Barnes XPBs or Hornady's XTPs, and it's never had a problem putting venison in the freezer or exterminating any of the predators that always seem to be in my chicken coop.

One of the downfalls of this pistol is the effective range, as it is limited by its 4-inch barrel. It's a tradeoff that is offset by the handiness of this gun. I limit myself to a 50-yard shot at deer, and only if I have a clear shot at its vitals. At 50 yards I know I can shoot it accurately enough to make a solid hit and the bullet will still retain enough energy to get the job done cleanly. I don't consider myself to be a good enough shot to shoot any farther than this at

S&W Model 13 in .357 Magnum and Barnes XPB bullets.

J.D. Fielding Photography

any animal, as both accuracy and energies diminish to the point that I am not comfortable.

The limited sight radius on this short-barreled gun not only makes it less accurate than, for example, an 8-inch barreled gun, but once again those damned laws of physics rear their ugly heads; you don't have the velocity or energy generated by a longer barrel.

The .44 Magnum

One of my other favorite hunting pistols is my 1957 Smith & Wesson pre-29 .44 Remington Magnum with a 6 ½-inch barrel. I got lucky and found this gun at a local shop for a great price.

This gun seems to be capable of shooting better than I can, with just about any load. This gun has a great trigger and balances perfect for me. This pistol does not fit on the hip as well as my .357, but it is still much easier to carry than a rifle. With its 6 ½-inch barrel, the sight radius is much longer than the .357's four-inch barrel, thus making this pistol much more accurate to shoot.

I find this to be the optimal length for me when hunting with iron sights, but I still limit myself to 100-yard shots with this gun. I know there are plenty of people who can shoot an identical gun a lot farther, but this is my limit for iron sights.

In my neck of the woods most deer hunting is done within 100 yards or less. I find target acquisition to be very fast with this gun, when compared to a scoped pistol. Now I am not going to lie; usually a scoped single shot or a big X-frame in .460 or .500 will shoot a hell of a lot more accurately than my old .44, but this .44 Magnum is about as big a handgun as I can shoot accurately offhand. I stress "offhand" because I mean shooting it without a rest or fence post or anything to support the weight of the gun.

I can shoot my .460 Smith & Wesson at twice the distance and with twice the accuracy. But here's the kicker; I can't shoot it offhand, I can only shoot it well from a rest or supported position. It weighs too much for me to shoot accurately offhand. It also wears a 2.5x8 scope and has 12 inches of barrel. Is it still a handgun if you can't shoot it like a handgun? I will let you decide. I will also

The author's favorite .44 Magnum

J.D. Fielding Photography

include data for a couple of .44 Special loads because this is what I normally practice with. They are much easier on the gun and my wrist, not to mention cheaper to shoot.

Reloading

My reloading methods are not by no means considered the latest and greatest, or even advanced. Most anyone can replicate my loads with similar results. I am generally considered outdated by most of the people in the reloading crowd. I was even called a dinosaur this week because of some of the Winchester powder I was using. My gun/reloading room is a hodgepodge of reloading equipment, some of which are antiques, and some of my preferred powders have been around for over 50 years. I am generally of the mindset of "If it ain't broke, don't fix it" but I have started to use some of the modern products recently. Trying some of the new bullets and powders has given me some very impressive results that I did not think possible.

For this article I used all new dies, brass, primers, and bullets to take out some of the variables.

A .44 Magnum
case ready to load

J.D. Fielding Photography

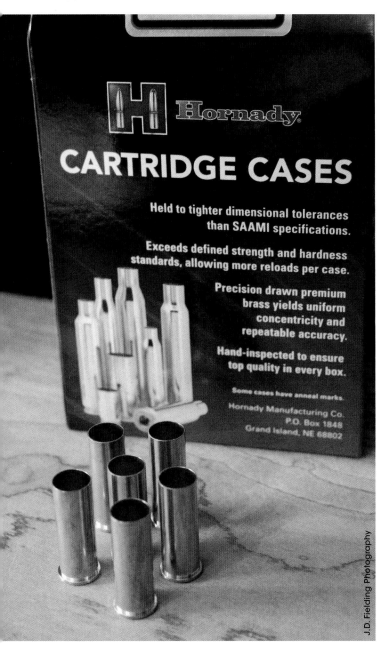

Hornady brass impressed with its consistency.

Don't get me wrong; I will always be the guy that saves all brass until it splits or the primers won't stay seated. But using some of today's new products has shown me that there are a lot more efficient ways to handload.

We will start off with the die sets. Most of my dies are yard sale specials, hand-me-downs, or bought off the clearance rack. I acquired new dies from Redding, to ensure there was no wear and tear. While using these new dies, in comparison to my old ones, all I can say is "Wow, these things are amazing!"

These Redding die sets feature micrometer-adjustable seating and crimping dies. The dies are fast and

easy to get set up and have given the best crimp I have ever achieved. Their ease of adjustment saves a lot of time when you're changing between different bullets. To be honest, I don't know how I am going to go back to using my old ones.

For this experiment I used brand-new Hornady brass cases. I spent the better half of a day measuring and weighing this brass, and did not find a single problem. I am a real stickler for trimming all pistol brass to get the perfect pistol crimp, but this brass is of such quality that trimming was not required. When the brass is of a uniform length, the crimping die will give an equally uniform crimp on the bullet's cannelure.

If your brass isn't trimmed to a uniform length, the resulting crimp will be all over the map, and can drastically affect the function of the revolver, as well as velocity and accuracy. All of the cases weighed and measured were well within all of my strict standards. All were of uniform weight and length. Hornady really impressed me with their product. If you have never used new brass before, you should definitely try it. You will be amazed!

For the primers, I used all Federal Gold Medal Match primers, small pistol primers for the .357, and large magnum pistol for the .44 Magnum. I have used them for years and found them to give the most consistent ignition, and I always keep a large supply on hand.

Now, on to the powders.

I wanted to use some old standby powders in order to compare them with some of the new powders on the market. I started off with some Hodgdon H110. I have used this powder often in the past, so I know how predictable the results are. I have also been happy with the accuracy of this powder, often giving me fantastic accuracy and consistent velocities. It meters very smoothly and consistently.

I also used some Alliant 2400, a top performer that I have been using for years. I wanted to try some new powders with this batch of premium bullets, so I grabbed some ACCURATE #9, and some Ramshot Enforcer, as these both work very well with the all-copper bullets I used for testing.

Despite my old-school mentality and utter reliance on my old standby loads, both of these gave top velocities and fantastic accuracy. I think the Enforcer might end up my new pet load for my .44 Mag., replacing my old standby loads of Alliant 2400 in the old gun.

Ramshot's Enforcer not only proved most accurate, but also gave among the highest velocities, something

Redding dies set up for the .44 Magnum in a vintage Red-ding Turret Press

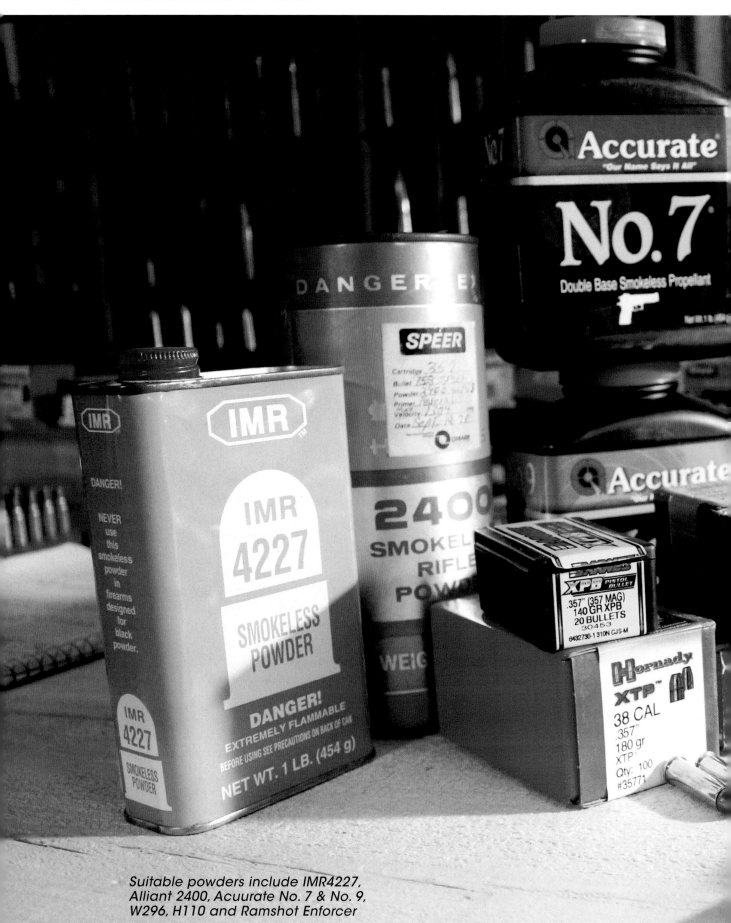

Suitable powders include IMR4227, Alliant 2400, Acuurate No. 7 & No. 9, W296, H110 and Ramshot Enforcer

J.D. Fielding Photography

that rarely happens.

This powder, made in Belgium, meters perfect and burns surprisingly clean. Enforcer seems to be made for the .44 Magnum. I like it so much that I will be stocking up on this powder. Enforcer also worked great in the .357 Magnum, being tied with the Accurate #9 for top accuracy.

The bullets I chose were all premium hunting bullets, as developing hunting loads was my goal, starting with the Hornady XTP.

The XTPs have always performed well for me; I have never had one fail me. They've been one of my favorite bullets, in many calibers, for a long time. They open up to at least 1 ½ times their original diameter for immediate energy transfer, but also penetrate very deep.

Any broadside shot I have ever taken with my .44 Magnum has resulted in a complete pass through; I have never recovered the bullet. Any deer I have ever hit with these XTP's hasn't taken more than a few steps before expiring. I prefer to use the heavier 300-grain bullets at a slower speed and I am amazed at their performance, whether the distance is 10 yards or 100.

The Nosler Jacketed Handgun bullet has long been a favorite in my .357, and the 158-grain slugs over a charge of Hodgdon's H110 has been a magic recipe for years. This has, and will continue to be, a go-to bullet for me.

Another of the premium bullets chosen was the Speer Gold Dot hunting bullets in .44 caliber, weighting 240 grains. These things are accurate and open up a huge hole. Although I have never hit a deer with one, I am sure they would be very effective. Penetration tests have shown me they would have no problem passing entirely through a deer. Two coyotes were taken with these bullets and that's how I know they open up so fast. They leave a Buick-sized exit wound. Most impressive! As far as a defensive bullet, they might be overkill but I would not hesitate to use them.

Ramshot's Enforcer is a very fine ball powder that will meter wonderfully!

J.D. Fielding Photography

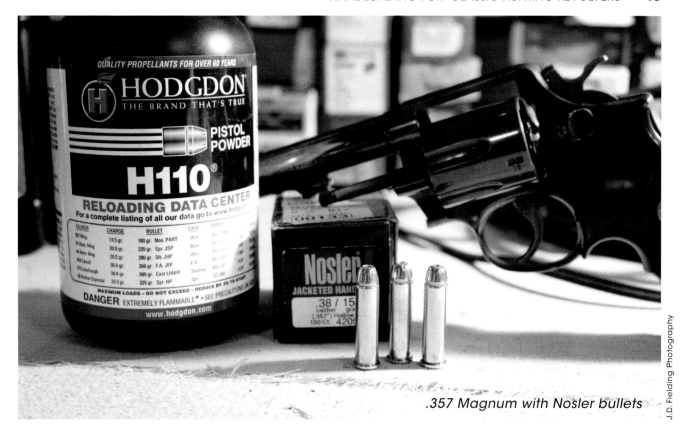

.357 Magnum with Nosler bullets

J.D. Fielding Photography

Whether you love them or hate them, the Barnes XPBs are the hot rods of handgun bullets. What I like about Barnes is that bullets are all that they make- just bullets. And they have been doing this for over 80 years. They seem to do a lot more research in the ballistic department than all the other companies. These bullets are an all-copper design with a massive hollow-point cavity, which upon impact forms the shape of a mushroom with razor-like pedals. These controlled expansion type bullets give devastating amounts of terminal damage when they hit flesh and bone. This is why deer never seem to take another step when hit correctly with one.

Barnes bullets deliver more energy within the game animal than any other bullets, in my opinion. I have heard people voice concerns about these large hollow-point cavities potentially becoming obstructed and not expanding. However, I have never had this problem. Now for the down side: these bullets cost more than most other brands, but you get what you pay for with Barnes.

Loading data is drastically different for these bullets than a lead-core type bullet, due to their all-copper construction. For example, a .44-caliber 225-grain Barnes is a lot longer than a bullet of the same weight that is jacketed lead. Therefore, they will leave less case capacity than lead bullets because they have to

Barnes 140-grain XPB and Hornady 158-grain XTB

J.D. Fielding Photography

Barnes 225 grain (L) has more bearing surface than the 300-grain Hornady XTP (Middle) or the 240-grain Speer Gold Dot (R)

J.D. Fielding Photography

Marty Groppi at the reloading bench

Caliber	Bullet	Powder	Charge	Primer	C L	Muzzle Velocity	Average Group Size 6 shots @ 15 yards
.357 Magnum	Barnes 140-gr XPB	H110	15.5 grains	Federal GM100M	1.590"	1,270 fps	2.0"
.357 Magnum	Barnes 140-gr XPB	Enforcer	14.5 grains	Federal GM100M	1.590"	1,390 fps	1.9"
.357 Magnum	Hornady 158-gr XTP	H110	15.5 grains	Federal GM100M	1.590"	1,230 fps	2.8"
.357 Magnum	Hornady 158-gr XTP	IMR4227	17.0 grains`	Federal GM100M	1.590"	1,293 fps	2.1"
.357 Magnum	Nosler 158-grain Jacketed HP	AA#7	11.0 grains	Federal GM100M	1.590"	1,149 fps	2.7"
.357 Magnum	Hornady 180-gr XTP	IMR4227	13.0 grains	Federal GM100M	1.590"	1,000 fps	2.4"
.357 Magnum	Hornady 180-gr XTP	AA#9	11.0 grains	Federal GM100M	1.590"	1,050 fps	2.3"
.38 Special	Cast 158-gr SWC	Alliant Bullseye	3.5 grains	Federal 100	1.455"	790 fps	1.7"
.38 Special	Cast 158-gr SWC	Hodgdon Trail Boss	4.0 grains	Federal 100	1.455"	740 fps	1.9"

Caliber	Bullet	Powder	Charge	Primer	COL	Muzzle Velocity	Average Group Size 6 shots @ 15 yards
.44 Magnum	Barnes 225-gr XPB	Enforcer	20.0 grains	Federal GM155M	1.604"	1,416 fps	1.5"
.44 Magnum	Barnes 225-gr XPB	AA#9	18.0 grains	Federal GM155M	1.604"	1,315 fps	2.1"
.44 Magnum	Barnes 225-gr XPB	H110	22.0 grains	Federal GM155M	1.604"	1,362 fps	2.3"
.44 Magnum	Hornady 300-gr XTP	Alliant 2400	17.0 grains	Federal GM155M	1.600"	1,106 fps	2.2"
.44 Magnum	Hornady 300-gr XTP	H110	19.5 grains	Federal GM155M	1.600"	1,142 fps	1.8"
.44 Magnum	Speer 240-gr Gold Dot	Alliant 2400	22.0 grains	Federal GM155M	1.600"	1,380 fps	2.0"
.44 Special	Falcon 240-gr SWC	Alliant Bullseye	5.0 grains	Federal 150	1.490"	815 fps	1.8"
.44 Special	Falcon 240-gr SWC	Alliant Unique	6.0 grains`	Federa; 150	1.490"	810 fps	1.9"

AUTHOR BIO:

Martin Groppi is a railroad man by trade and a lifelong firearm aficionado. In spring he can be found on the shore of various bodies of water, armed with rod and reel; in the fall you'll need to search the mountains to find him. He is allergic to a razor blade.

During the course of researching my handguns for this article, I called up Smith & Wesson for information and they transferred me over to Mr. Roy Jinks, their historian. This man is truly a wealth of knowledge in the firearms industry; this man is a legend and it was an honor to speak with him. All I had to do was give him the necessary numbers located on the bottom of the grip frame of my pistols, and he knew everything about them. I received quite the history lesson about these two revolvers. If you have a vintage Smith & Wesson revolver, don't hesitate to call Mr. Jinks and receive a history lesson of your own. For a nominal fee, S&W will send you a certified history of your firearm, to pass onto future generations.

J.D. Fielding Photography

be seated deeper in the case to maintain the same Cartridge Overall Length.

I ended up using some compressed loads with these, something I rarely do, but is common when using monometal bullets. I was also only able to find a limited amount of load data for Barnes, so, on a whim I just called them up.

The people at this company were very helpful, and more than willing to spend time with me discussing this project. I told them what powders I had and they gave me all the load data I needed, right over the phone. This was a big surprise to have customer service that was this knowledgeable and friendly. Barnes highly recommended using Ramshot's Enforcer as well as Accurate No. 9, as their laboratory testing found these powders to give the best results with their bullets.

This company has come a long way since 1932 when Fred Barnes started making bullets. They are definitely something all handloaders need to try.

I'm loading those Hornady XTPs for our local deer and bear seasons. The Gold Dot bullet will remain my favorite for the liberal coyote season we have here in New York, and the Barnes 225-grain XPB is getting the nod for an upcoming feral hog hunt. With this trio of bullets, I'm very well covered for anything smaller than coastal brown bears! I have really enjoyed the testing of these new powders and bullets, and it has truly brought new found interest to my pair of classic revolvers.

I am glad I knocked the dust off these two classics and tried modern loads through them. It has shown me how far reloading products have progressed and has given me new found respect for my old iron.

LIFE IN **THE .40s**

By Philip P. Massaro

Deep into the Nyaminga block of Zambia's Luangwa Valley, Professional Hunter Nicky Wightman gingerly spread the shooting sticks, eyeballing the Cape buffalo bull that was lying down 40 yards away. He and Lamec, his tracker and right-hand man, were silently communicating about the bull and whether or not he was old enough to take, while I stood by, with my Model 70 in .416 Remington, handloaded with 400-grain Swift A-Frames. Although every nerve stood on edge, I knew exactly what the rifle would do, as I had spent countless hours at the bench, and in practice from field positions. While the gun gave acceptable accuracy with factory ammunition, it shot sub-MOA with my handloads, and I knew that was the proper ammunition to use.

We sorted that bull out with a well-placed first shot, and a second A-Frame to 'pay the insurance', as the saying goes, and both bullets rested against the offside shoulder skin. They gave perfect performance, imparting all 5,000 ft.-lbs. within the bull, and killed quickly and humanely.

Fast forward almost four years and I stood with PHs Tim Schultz and Danie Wingard in Matabeleland North in Zimbabwe, with a huge-bodied bull elephant on the other end of the line. This time I carried a Heym Express in .404 Jeffery, handloaded with 400-grain Woodleigh Hydrostatically Stabilized Solids, at a muzzle velocity of 2,280 fps. It was a short hunt, and the bull was essentially gift-wrapped, feeding at 16 yards. The first shot nearly put the bull down on his haunches, and the second sealed the deal. My hunting buddy Dave deMoulpied had booked this hunt for me, and had come along as a camera man. After the bull was down, and the respects were paid, Dave showed me the footage. The Woodleigh solid had hit exactly where

Buffalo bull taken with .416 Rem handloads

Suzanne Massaro

aimed, and the video showed the effect of that well-designed bullet, a heart/lung shot which penetrated the entire elephant.

"Buddy, I'm glad you went with the Woodleigh," said Dave. "That hit was as impressive as the shots I've seen from .470s." Now, I know for certain that the .404 Jeff is not the equal of the mighty .470 Nitro Express, but it is a perfectly viable big game cartridge, suitable for absolutely anything on earth. That's what I want to discuss: the benefits of handloading rifles in the .410-

.423" calibers, and why they make so much sense for the traveling hunter.

Everybody who has hunted Africa is aware of the versatility of the famous .375 H&H Belted Rimless Magnum; there's simply no denying the fact that a good .375 H&H will get the job done, regardless of species. I've heard from more than one PH, "When in doubt, bring a .375 H&H."

That said, when it comes to the heavyweights like buffalo and elephant, there's no denying that the .40s hit harder, and the visible effect of the shot is plainly evident. However, the beauty of the .375 is its versatility; it can take the biggest elephant bull, but is also suitable for oribi, duiker and steenbok. I own a .375, I shoot it and I love it, but I'm also a huge fan of the .40s for reasons we'll outline shortly. What I like to do as a handloader, is to do my best to approximate the versatility of the .375s in the .40 calibers.

In this class of rifles, I like the following cartridges (in order of caliber) for a versatile hunting rifle: the .450/400 3" Nitro Express, the .416 Rigby, the .416 Remington, the .416 Ruger, the wildcat .416 Taylor, and the venerable .404 Jeffery. All of them have made their reputations shooting a 400-grain bullet of good sectional density, at muzzle velocities of 2,050 fps (for the .450/400), up to 2,400 fps for the .416s, with the .404 coming in somewhere in the middle, depending on how you load it. The classic recipe of the 400-grain bullets at 2,400 fps from the .416s will yield just about 5,000 ft.-lbs. of kinetic energy at the muzzle, yet is surprisingly easy on the shoulder, especially in comparison to the .458s pushing a 500-grain slug at 2,150 fps or so.

The .450/400 3" Nitro Express.

The .450/400 NE works well at the much lower velocity, being a perfect choice for the recoil-sensitive shooter to use against the heavyweights. The penetrative qualities of the .410" diameter bullet are legendary; flipping through John 'Pondoro' Taylor's classic African Rifles and Cartridges will yield the following comments:

"It's one of the grandest weapons imaginable for all big game hunting... ...I have used it extensively on all kinds of African game from elephant down with the greatest possible satisfaction."

That is what I would call a ringing endorsement from a man with decades of field experience. The bullets of today are much better than those of Pondoro's era, and the recent revival of this case is due to Ruger chambering their No. 1 single-shot rifle in this car-

The end result of a great elephant hunt with Woodleigh Hydro Solids in .404 Jeffery

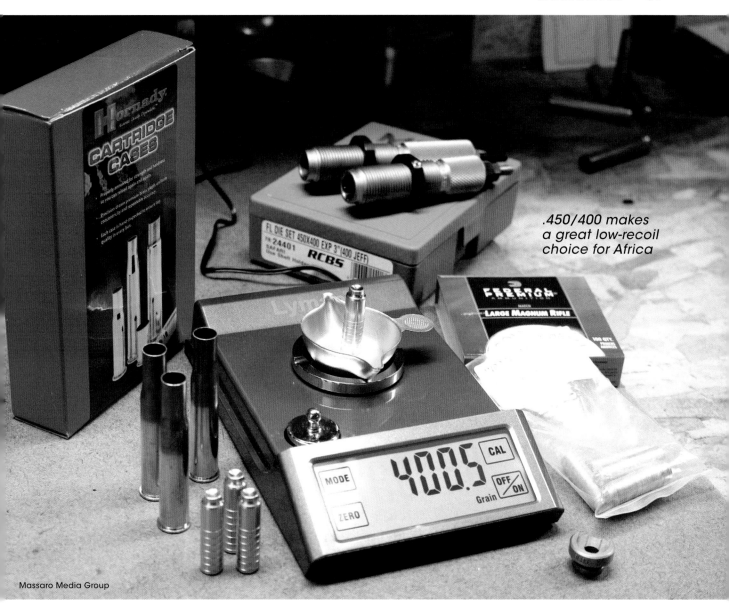

.450/400 makes a great low-recoil choice for Africa

Massaro Media Group

tridge, and Hornady's factory ammo available with the potent combination of DGX and DGS bullets.

My buddy Doug Giles, international hunter and author of Rise, Kill and Eat, is a huge proponent of the .450/400, and has both the No.1 and a sweet double in this cartridge. He asked me to handload some ammo for his upcoming safaris, which will include buffalo and big cats. I immediately recommended the North Fork trio of bullets: the semi-spitzer bonded core, the Percussion Point (similar to the semi-spitzer, but skived at the nose for greater expansion on cats), and the fantastic monometal Flat Point solid, all in 400-grain configuration. His double regulates well with the existing Hornady ammo, but Doug was after a custom ammunition experience.

I got my hands on some Hornady cases and a set of RCBS dies, and taking a long look at several reloading manuals, I settled on a load of 83.0 grains of Alliant's Reloder-19 and a Federal GM215M primer, which gave a muzzle velocity of 2,075 fps, in close proximity to the Hornady load, and (thankfully!) it shot just perfectly from Doug's rifles. He is now well equipped for any game animal on earth, including the dangerous stuff of Africa and North America.

The .416" rifles.

Undoubtedly, we owe the popularity of the .416" diameter cartridges to the writings of Robert Ruark, as he made both PH Harry Selby and the .416 Rigby famous in his classic safari book Horn of the Hunter. I, for one, am very happy he did that, because prior to that 1950s literary gem, the .416 was a proprietary cartridge that was little used.

Massaro Media Group

Accuracy of .404 Jeffery Heym rifle with Woodleigh Hydro solids

During the 1960s and 70s, as Kynoch faded away as an ammunition producer and supplies dwindled for the classic British rifles, an American PH named George Hoffman necked the .375 H&H case up to hold .416" bullets, resulting in the .416 Hoffman. Bob Chatfield-Taylor did a similar thing, but based his case on the shorter (2.500") .458 Winchester Magnum case, giving birth to the .416 Taylor. Remington saw the value of the Hoffman design, and modified their 8mm Remington Magnum case to cre-ate the .416 Remington Magnum, released in the year I graduated high school, 1988. The Hornady/Ruger team had great success with the .375 Ruger cartridge, and modified the beltless design to yield the .416 Ruger, fitting in a standard-length rifle action.

All these cartridges, generally speaking, deliver the wonderful 400-grain .416" caliber bullet at or near 2,400 fps, and this is a magic combination. For the handloader, there are many premium 400-grain bullets available that aren't commercially loaded. Remington did, at one time, load the 400-grain Swift A-Frame for the .416 Rem, but I don't find that in their catalogs any longer. I've said this before, but it warrants repeating: I feel that the Swift A-Frame, in a heavy-for-caliber weight, is the best Cape buffalo bullet on the market. It gives good expansion at a wide range of velocities, fantastic (90%+) weight retention, but most importantly it is strong enough to penetrate the biggest buffalo at any angle. I've used it extensively in my .416 Remington, not just on buffalo, but on a wide variety of plains game, from bushbuck and puku, to warthog and hartebeest, all with good results.

'Neighbor' Dave deMoulpied's AHR in .416 Rigby loves the 400-grain A-Frame, but at a reduced velocity

The .416 Remington Magnum and 400-grain Swift A-Frames and Hornady Solids

J.D. Fielding photography

deMoulpied's
.416 Rigby
with 325-grain
Cutting Edge
Safari Raptors

of 2,250 fps, because that's where we found the accuracy. Ninety grains of Reloder-19 prints three of them into sub-MOA groups at 100 yards.

Pair these A-Frames with a good solid and you've got the quintessential buffalo battery. While the Barnes Banded Solids, Trophy Bonded Sledgehammers and Hornady DGS are fantastic choices, for buffalo especially, I like a pair of 'new-wave' designs that have come along. The idea is this (although it is changing quickly): The first shot on buffalo should most definitely be a premium soft point, many of the older Professional Hunters demand a solid (read non-expanding) bullet for the follow up shots, to ensure penetration from any angle. The solids give exactly that; but offer no expansion at all to destroy vital tissue. Here's where the new-wave designs enter the mix.

The Woodleigh Hydrostatically Stabilized Solid, and the North Fork Cup solid, both have a small "dish" shaped meplat, enough to either create a shockwave of damage, or to give the slightest bit of expansion at the meplat for more tissue damage than traditional solids give. For buffalo, I like them both very much. Both shoot very accurately, and most importantly, to the same point of impact as most of the premium softpoints.

That idea of getting your solids to hit the same place as your softpoints, can be a bit of work for the handloader. The .375 is one of the most forgiving calibers in that respect, and I can say that my .416 Remington is as well.

My Model 70 .416 Remington likes just about any 400-grain bullet over a charge of 78.0 grains of IMR-4064 with the Federal GM215M primer. I use Remington nickel cases for the solids, and Norma brass cases for the softpoints, so I can easily distinguish one load from the other. If your rifle won't regulate softs and solids to the same point of impact, you'll have to tinker with the loads until you can find the best combination of individual accuracy for each load, and a common point of impact.

Generally speaking, I've found that backing off the load a grain or two for the solids can help bring them into line; in my experiences they tend to hit high.

Now, more about that versatility thing I mentioned early on. The .416s certainly shine when using the 400-grain slugs, and that weight makes a great all-around load. It's been my go-to choice for my .416 Rem. on two safaris, and it works well.

But maybe there are situations where you'd like to use a .416 with a lighter load, for a flatter trajectory. That very thing happened to me on my last safari. It was actually two safaris in one, as Dave deMoulpied and I were hunting for three days in the Waterberg District of South Africa for plains game, and then heading up to Zimbabwe for elephant near the Hwange National Park. I had the aforementioned Heym in .404 Jeffery, but I asked Dave to bring his .416 Rigby, in case some misfortune should befall the Heym. For plains game, we

Massaro Media Group

deMoulpied's Zebra

Massaro Media Group

*deMoulpied
with impala*

discussed some lighter bullets that would give suitable performance and a flatter trajectory, should a longer shot present itself.

Enter Cutting Edge Bullets, with their 325-grain Safari Raptor. These bullets are constructed of brass, with a deep hollowpoint. The walls of the hollowpoint are skived, so that when the bullet strikes flesh, the walls of the hollowpoint break into small blades, creating all sorts of impact trauma. The rest of the bullet remains at caliber dimension, to penetrate very deep into the vital organs, often penetrating the entire animal. Really cool concept, and I was eager to put them through field tests.

We pretty much nailed it on the first try. A mix of Hornady .416 Rigby cases, an even 100.0 grains of Reloder-22, Federal 215 primer and the CEB 325-grain Raptor printed groups of just under an inch at 100 yards. Dave made a few clicks of adjustment on his scope, and he was set. The Oehler chrony showed 2,550 fps, so longer shots wouldn't pose a problem.

The big cow wildebeest dropped to a frontal shot from 80 yards as if she were pole-axed; and Dave's impala didn't even have time to react. Both were one-shot kills, and while there may have been a bit of blood-shot meat, these bullets certainly did their job. It was Dave's zebra that impressed me most.

The striped horses of Africa have a reputation for being very tough, especially if hit improperly. Dave put that 325-grain Raptor right in the boiler room, a perfectly placed shot, from just under 200 yards away. The beautiful mare simply fell out of the scope. These lighter bullets do quite a bit for the versatility of the .416s, especially when hunting plains game. Other that the blades, there was nothing for the skinners to recover.

On the other end of the spectrum, there are some heavyweights available for the .416 rifles as well. Woodleigh's Weldcore and Solid bullets both come in 450 grains, and we can drive them to 2,150 fps. Those heavy 450s have a sectional density of 0.371, and should be fantastic for buffalo, elephant, hippo and other plus-size game animals. Another way to look at it is that you're only 50 grains lighter than the .458s, and while you'll be giving up a bit in frontal diameter, you gain in the SD figures.

The .416 Ruger case is, like the Rigby, a beltless case, but shortened to fit in a standard .30-'06 length action. My good buddy Tim Wegner absolutely loves this cartridge, and asked me to handload him some of the fantastic 400-grain Barnes TSX bullets.

While the factory stuff claims to reach the mystical 2,400 fps, even in the shorter Ruger African barrels (I haven't had an opportunity to test the factory stuff), according

.416 Ruger, Hornady cases, Barnes
TSX 400-grain bullets and Hodgdon's
VARGET powder

Massaro Media Group

to the manuals the handloads should run somewhere between 2,250 and 2,300 fps. I had the best blend of velocity and accuracy using 75.5 grains of Hodgdon's VARGET, in Hornady cases, fueled by a Federal GM215M primer. This gave 2,270 fps at the muzzle, and just over MOA accuracy – plenty enough for big bears, buffalo, or any other nasty worthy of a premium softpoint.

Among the .416s, I've found that the Rigby case gives the most severe recoil, due to the fact that the voluminous case (designed around the temperature sensitive Cordite) requires 90-100 grains of powder, depending on burn rate, while the Remington and Ruger cases run at 75-80 grains for most loads, albeit at a higher pressure. While I like the Rigby, and appreciate its place is

African cartridge history, I feel that the Remington case especially has been one of the most useful modern updates of a proven classic, offering all the same ballistics in a cartridge case and rifle that is smaller and handier in the field. The Rigby case will work best with powders on the slower end of the spectrum, like IMR4350, Reloder-19 and 22 and H4831, while the Remington and Ruger cases like a medium burning powder, like Reloder-15, IMR4064 and Hodgdon's VARGET.

The .404 Jeffery.

I feel like I've found a new old toy in the attic; the .404 Jeffery was always a cartridge that interested me, but until recently I didn't have an opportunity to experiment with it. My buddy Chris Sells, of Double Gun Imports, acts as the importer for Heym rifles of Germany. While Heym has a fantastic reputation in the double rifle community, their Express bolt-action rifle is a little-known gem. Stocked to feel like a fine British rifle of classic vintage, and using Heym's proprietary action, which they make differently for each individual caliber, this rifle is poetry in steel and walnut, balancing like a fine shotgun. When Chris offered the use of a .404 Jeffery for my plains game/elephant safari, I jumped at the opportunity.

The .404 Jeff has long been an African classic, being chosen as the standard issue rifle cartridge for most of Eastern and Southern Africa's game rangers, and its moderate recoil and striking power offer a fantastic balance of shootability and performance. Ruark's writing propelled the .416s to the forefront, but the .404 was truly the workhorse of Africa. Designed in 1909, the Jeffery case was intended to be the rimless equivalent of the .450/400; however the bullet diameter changed from .410" to .423", for reasons I can't explain. At any rate, the muzzle velocity of 2,150 fps with a 400-grain bullet generated just over 4,000 ft.-lbs. of energy, more than enough for the largest game,

but the sedate muzzle velocity is directly proportional to the moderate recoil. I will say that the felt recoil of a .404, with the classic loading, is less than that of the .375 H&H, especially in recoil speed. The older load's velocity is easy to attain as a handloader, and still works as well as it did in 1909.

The modern load is the 400-grain bullet, driven to 2,350 fps, putting it in the same league as the .416s. My own load for my safari was somewhere in the middle, and it worked out just perfect. I was using the 400-grain Woodleigh Hydrostatically Stabilized solids, over 80.0 grains of Reloder 15, sparked by the Federal GM215M primer, in Norma cases.

This combination yields 2,280 fps at the muzzle, for around 4,650 ft.-lbs. of energy, and will print MOA three-shot groups if I do my part. As I told you early on, this Woodleigh bullet gives fantastic penetration, and they worked well on both wildebeest and impala in addition to the huge-bodied bull elephant.

For a good all-around load, the Woodleigh Hydro solid is a fine choice. The other bullets I tried, like the 400-grain Hornady DGS and the North Fork semi-spitzer, liked the same load. While other powders will certainly work, I like Reloder 15 as a good medium burn rate choice.

Author's combination of 325-grain Cutting Edge Bullets and 400-grain Woodleigh Hydro Solids

Author's .404 Jeffery ammo

Being a curious creature, I wanted to see if that Cutting Edge Safari Raptor that worked so well in Dave's .416 Rigby would perform in the Jeffery. At 325 grains, it gave up a bit of the sectional density that the 400 grainers will give, but can be loaded to a higher velocity. The Heym liked them very much, putting them into MOA accuracy, and actually printing them to the same point of impact as the 400-grain Woodleighs. 85.0 grains of Reloder 15 gave a velocity of 2,560 fps, bringing the .404 into the realm of the .375 H&H, as far as decent trajectory goes. I brought that load over with me, with the intention of taking a bush pig with it. My PH, Cornus du Plooy made a great blind and set up, and while we put our time in, the bush pigs decided not to take part in our particular hunting adventure.

Norma has introduced a new load for the .404 Jeff, in their African PH line of ammunition. PH Kevin 'Doctari' Robertson has helped to shape the ballistics, and it is well thought out in addition to being very useful. Their factory ammo pushes a heavy-for-caliber 450-grain Woodleigh softpoint and solid at 2,150 fps, for 2,650 ft.-lbs. This makes good sense, especially for buffalo and elephant. The lower muzzle velocity has worked with the 400-grain bullets for over a century, but with an additional 50 grains of bullet, the sectional density figures

Author with Impala ram

Massaro Media Group

*Author
with Blue
Wildebeest*

increase considerably, which will make a cartridge that has a reputation for incredible penetration even better.

We can reproduce this formula at the bench. These Woodleigh bullets are available in component form for us handloaders, and if the heavyweights are on your list, there is no reason not to take advantage of them. I think that the 450-grain Woodleigh Weldcore would make a terrific bullet for big grizzly bears, interior or coastal. You'll definitely want a large rifle magnum primer, and I'd stick to powders on the faster end of the spectrum, as the longer bullets will start to eat up some of your case capacity.

With an effective bullet range of 325 grain up to 450 grains, and good cases produced by Norma and Hornady, the old Jeffery case should be seeing a revival in the next decade. Get a good set of dies from RCBS or Redding, and find a rifle that fits you well. After my safari, I called Chris Sells of Heym and asked him to hold on to the return shipping label for that Heym Express, and send an invoice in its place. I'll be hunting with this rifle for years to come.

In Conclusion

I've had people tell me that my sanity is questionable because I hunt dangerous game with handloaded ammunition. While I totally agree with the fact that factory ammunition is better than it's ever been, I feel that the diligence that I put into assembling the ammunition cannot be matched by the machines. I weigh the bullets, resize all the brand new cases, weigh every powder charge, and make sure that each and every round I intend to hunt with has been run through the rifle's chamber, to ensure that there will be no feeding issues. After five safaris, I can honestly say that with the exception of .22 LR ammunition, I've never pulled the trigger on factory ammunition in the game fields, and I'm totally OK with that!

AUTHOR BIO:

Philip P. Massaro is the President of Massaro Ballistic Laboratories, LLC, a custom ammunition company, comfortably nestled in between the Hudson River and Catskill Mountains of Upstate New York. He has been a handloader for 20+ years, a veteran of five African safaris and dozens of North American hunts. He is a Licensed Professional Land Surveyor by trade, a musician by choice, and usually reeks of Hoppes No. 9.

THE WAY OF
THE WILDCAT

By Bryce M. Towsley

"A wildcat cartridge, often shortened to wildcat, is a custom cartridge for which ammunition and/or firearms are not mass-produced. These cartridges are often created in order to optimize a certain performance characteristic (such as the power, size or efficiency) of an existing commercial cartridge."

- From Wikipedia

The word "wildcat" denotes something untamed, rebellious and maybe just a little bit dangerous. Just like the wildcat oil drillers who became legends, those gun guys who pioneered the wildcat cartridges were never afraid to ignore the naysayers. Wildcatters are the rebels, the guys who refuse to accept the status quo. They are the pioneers who stretch the boundaries to prove that there can be something more, something better.

Like most pioneers they rarely get the credit. Take for example the .22-250 Remington. Popular cartridge, right? How many of you ever heard of guys named Harvey Donaldson, Grosvenor Wotkyns, J.E. Gebby, John Sweany, or J.B. Smith?

Remington didn't develop the .22-250; those guys did. They pioneered the early high speed .22 cartridges. The Wotkyns version was called the .220 Wotkyns

Original Swift (WOS) and was the forerunner to the .220 Swift, later introduced by Winchester. Gebby and Smith are most often credited with the version we call the .22-250 Remington today. They named it the .22 Varminter. Gebby even obtained a copyright on that name, but Remington took the design, added their name and got all the glory.

It's the same with the .204 Ruger, 7mm Remington Magnum, .257 Roberts, .35 Whelen, the Winchester Short Magnums and a very long list of other popular cartridges. They were all developed by independent wildcatters and then "claimed" by a gun company as its own, often with the blessing of the wildcatter, but sometimes not. For the most part the guys who developed the cartridges expected - and got - nothing. The exception might be the WSM cartridges, which are his-

Above: The 416 UMT rifle on shooting sticks, cape buffalo in background. Selous Reserve in Tanzania. Scope is a Swarovski a 1.25-4X24 Habicht model in Warne mounts. A dangerous game rifle will be used at close range and a low power, wide field of view scope is the best choice. I must be reliable and tough enough to endure the high recoil of big game cartridges.

Left: RCBS .416 UMT dies with cases and lube. One pass over the tapered expander in the RCBS resizing die will neck the .375 RUM up to .416. To increase neck tension polish a small amount of material off the neck sizing button. Lubrication is important for sizing cartridge cases. But, it requires just the right amount.

torical as the wildcats that ended up in court. It's also what is slowly killing these cartridges.

But that's OK. Wildcat cartridge designers are not in it for the glory or to get rich. They do it for a love of guns and cartridges and for the challenge of doing something that's never been done. Just like mountain climbers, they do it because "it's there."

For as long as I can remember I have been handloading and shooting many popular wildcats, like the .357 Herrett, 7mm TCU, .243 AI, .280 AI, .300 Whisper, .375 JDJ, and several others. I learned about case forming and load development by working with these cartridges, often in the very early years when there was little available data.

But like a lot of hard-core gun guys with a technical mind and a love of pushing the edges, I felt the need to create wildcats of my own.

Nobody ever called me a conformist in anything I do, and I found the inspiration for my wildcats hiding that part of my rebel brain. I love .35-caliber rifle cartridges, even while the public does not. There has really never been a hugely successful .35-caliber cartridge. The .35 Remington probably comes the closest, but it's been dying a slow death for decades. So of course that's where I went for my first wildcat cartridge.

.358 UMT

Remington showed a select group of gun writers their new .300 Remington Ultra Mag in the fall of 1998, and the first thing I thought was that that big case would be awesome with a .358 bullet.

After considering a lot of case design possibilities I decided to keep it simple and necked the .300 Remington Ultra Mag case up to .358 with no other changes. It maintains the same body taper, the same 30-degree shoulder and the same datum line for headspacing. The only difference is a larger neck and the resulting

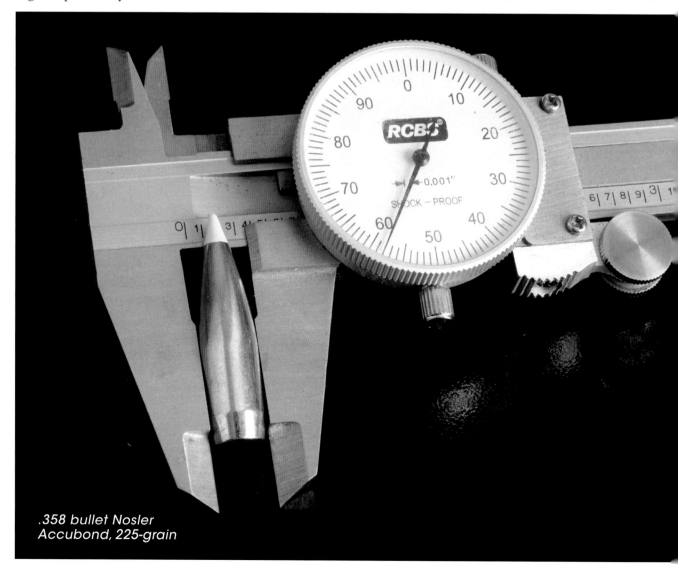

.358 bullet Nosler Accubond, 225-grain

shorter shoulder. I called the new cartridge the .358 Ultra Mag Towsley (UMT).

One pass of a well-lubed Remington case through the RCBS sizing die's tapered expander button takes the neck from .30 to .35. Case loss during forming is all but non-existent. The expanding process shortens the case by about .018-inch, so I square the new case mouths and trim to 2.820-inch.

The rifle started as a stainless steel Remington Model 700 chambered for .300 RUM, but only the action remains. I ordered a Krieger barrel with a 1:14 twist rate to stabilize 250-grain bullets. The barrel proved accurate and the bore is remarkably smooth and is easy to clean. Gunsmith Mark Bansner turned the 24-inch barrel to a taper that measures .675″ at the muzzle and then added six longitudinal flutes.

The limiting factor in overall cartridge length with any of the Ultra Mag cartridges is the rifle's magazine. I knew the maximum workable cartridge length in this gun would be 3.675-inch. I made up some dummy cartridges with Nosler 250-grain Partition bullets and shipped them to Dave Manson Precision Reamers. I asked Manson to configure the chamber reamer so it would provide a .010-inch jump to the rifling with the Nosler bullet seated to 3.675-inch. My other bullet choice at the time was a Barnes 225-grain X-bullet and because of the difference in bullet profile, it would have a jump of about .030-inch when seated to the same overall length. This is fine because the Barnes X-Bullet requires a larger gap for peak performance.

Bansner chambered the barrel and installed it on the action, which had been polished and tuned. The entire barreled action

.358 UMT

was then bead-blasted for a matte finish.

I had him install a trigger from Timney Manufacturing Inc. and adjust it for a crisp three-pound pull. I also asked him to change the safety so it will lock the bolt down when it is on (eliminating my pet peeve with current Model 700 rifles.)

Bansner then added one of his High Tech synthetic stocks, which proved to be one of the keys to making this rifle so user friendly. The stock is designed so the butt is 90 degrees to the bore, which directs recoil straight back and helps to eliminate muzzle rise. As a result, the shooter's face is not beaten up by the rifle's comb, as often happens with hard-recoiling rifles. The stock has a wide butt and a Pachmayr Decelerator recoil pad to further reduce felt recoil.

I conceived this to be a gun that would be lugged for miles up steep elk mountains or through the muskeg of Alaska. The weight needed to be balanced between

.358 UMT (.300 Rem. Ultra Mag)
225-grain Barnes Triple Shock

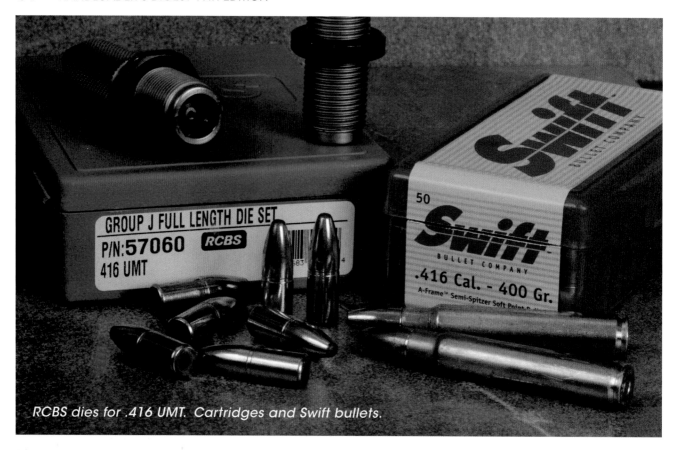

RCBS dies for .416 UMT. Cartridges and Swift bullets.

heavy enough to shoot well under field conditions and light enough to not be hateful at the end of a long day. When fitted with a Leupold Vari-X III 3.5-10 scope in Leupold two-piece mounts, the rifle weighs eight pounds. This is on the light side for a rifle chambered in so powerful a cartridge, but the recoil is very manageable for an experienced shooter. Most people who shoot the rifle for the first time remark that the kick was a lot less than they anticipated.

I wanted a rifle suitable for hunting elk, big bears, moose and the larger African plains game in all the differing terrain they live in. I wanted it to shoot flat so it could handle long shots, but also to hit hard and penetrate deep for big and tough game. This calls for heavy bullets with high sectional density and ballistic coefficient numbers. Bullets weighing 225 to 250 grains were the obvious choice. With a large case capacity, heavy bullets usually call for slow-burning powder to push them and that proved true with the .358 UMT. It is not a particularly fussy cartridge to load for, except that it does favor specific powders. I initially thought it would work best with powders like 4350 or 4831, but they actually proved to be a bit too fast. IMR-7828 was by far the best powder tested, but H-1000 also works very well in some loads. With big charges of any powder, a hot primer is important; I used only Federal 215 primers.

The SAAMI spec for the .300 Ultra Mag cartridge is a mean average pressure of 65,000 PSI, which I used as a guideline.

Some interesting things happened when I started shooting this cartridge. Most .358 bullets are designed for a much lower velocity and some of the best big game bullets that work so well in my .350 Rem Mag and .35 Whelen turned into varmint bullets with this cartridge, often fragmenting on impact. The Barnes bullets were an exception. I started with a 225-grain XLC Coated X-bullet. Barnes didn't make that one, but coated some for me as a favor. After I wrote about it they got so many requests that they added it to their line. The XLC bullets are gone now, replaced by the Triple Shock. Today my preferred bullet in this cartridge is the Barnes TSX 225-grain loaded with IMR-7828. This produces 3,165 fps and sub-inch groups.

Another bullet that proved to work well is the Swift 250-grain A-Frame. When teamed with IMR-7828 it spits out the muzzle at 3,114 fps Accuracy is nearly one hole for the best three-shot groups and always averages under minute-of-angle. The steep ogive profile of this bullet allows it to be seated out close to the rifling lands, while the cartridge length remains short enough to fit in the magazine. The bullet expands very rapidly and very big, so penetration is not as good as expected. But for elk-sized or smaller game this bullet does a great job.

I have used the .358 UMT while hunting a diversity of big game from springbuck to brown bears. It's been to Africa with me twice and has accounted for a lot of African game, including a waterbuck and a diminutive red duiker that both made the record book. I have used it a lot in North America as well while hunting game as diverse as mule deer to brown bears. The odd thing is that while I developed the gun for elk, I have not shot an elk with it! It's been elk hunting, but never when the elk got the memo and remembered to show up.

The .358 UMT shoots flatter than a .300 Winchester with a 180-grain bullet and has more energy than a .416 Remington at any range.

With a 250-yard zero the 225-grain Barnes TSX is 2.24 inches high at 100 yards and 3.26 inches low at 300 yards.

With the 250-grain bullet the .358 UMT produces 5,384 foot-pounds of muzzle energy. At 100 yards it still has more energy than the .375 H&H has at the muzzle and at 200 yards it retains 3,676 foot-pounds, almost as much as the .338 Win Mag has at the muzzle.

.416 UMT

A few years later, I decided that if big is good, bigger is even better and I designed another cartridge in the UMT family; the .416.

The .416 UMT is not a complicated wildcat. It is simply a .375 Remington Ultra Mag necked up to take a .416 bullet. The shoulder angle, base to shoulder length, and datum line are all maintained the same as the .375 RUM. One pass of a well lubricated .375 RUM case over a RCBS resizing die equipped with a tapered neck expander forms the case. The only other thing I do is to square up the case mouth with a case trimmer. This results in a case that is 2.825-inch, or about .025-inch shorter than the .375 RUM.

The case holds 120.2 grains of water to the top of the neck. The most popular .416 cartridges and the closest "competitors" are the .416 Remington, which holds 103.4 grains of water and the .416 Rigby which holds 129.6 grains. The Ultra Mag class of cartridges were all designed to operate at a maximum average pressure of 65,000 psi, which is the same as the .416 Remington. The larger case capacity with equal pressure will result in higher velocity with a given bullet weight. The .416

Rigby runs at about 52,000 psi, which keeps the performance lower when compared to case capacity.

Alliant RL 15 and Hodgdon H4350 are two of the best powders tested, and accuracy is excellent with groups averaging just over one inch with the best loads. With 400-grain bullets and RL15, velocity runs a bit over 2,500 fps

There are actually a couple of boxes of this unique ammo someplace in the Dar es Salaam airport, as I was greeted on my way home by a Nazi masquerading as a KLM airline ticket agent. She would not let my bags on the plane because they were a few pounds overweight, even if I paid. I was headed home, the ammo was disposable, and the last time I saw it some guy was carrying it at arm's length like it was a nuclear bomb.

A muzzle velocity of 2,500 fps is a considerable increase over the .416 Remington and .416 Rigby, which are cataloged at 2,400 fps but rarely have shown it on my chronograph. The realistic "real world" gain in velocity for the .416 UMT is about 150 – 200 fps over those two rivals when compared with guns of equal barrel length.

The performance on game is outstanding. The first shot of the safari dropped a warthog like he was hit

L to R: .416 Remington, .416 UMT and .416 Rigby.

Above: .416 UMT rifle built on a Remington Model 700 by Mark Bansner. Swarovski scope. 400 grain Swift A-Frame.

Right: Bryce M. Towsley with a cape buffalo taken in the Selous Reserve in Tanzania. Taken with the .416 UMT. 400 grain Swift A-Frame. Dangerous game is hunted close and bullet placement must be precise. A 100 yard zero works well.

with Thor's hammer. My buffalo was hit with three Swift A-Frames and two Barnes Banded Solid bullets. All but the first shot exited and they all went through the vitals, including the first shot which traveled end for end. It hit him in the ass and stopped under the skin on his neck. (Yes, I was aiming there. Don't ask, it's a long story.) This buffalo had just been part of a very nasty and bloody encounter, so I didn't go gently with him. While any one of the shots would have killed him, as long as he was on his feet, I kept shooting as fast as I could. He took the five hits in much less than a minute. A year or so later my son Nathan shot a moose with this gun, with very impressive results and a lot less noise.

Mark Bansner built the gun on a Remington Model 700 action and fitted it with a 24-inch Lilja barrel. The extractor was changed to a larger design for a more positive grip on the case during extraction. I had Mark replace the safety with one that would lock the bolt shut. Mark coated the metal with his proprietary Ti-K-Cote polymer based finish and fitted the barreled action to one of his High Tech Specialties Stocks. We added a staggered-feed magazine with a single-stack, center feed system from H. S. Precision so that the gun would feed Barnes Solids reliably.

When I received the rifle from Mark it only weighed 8-1/2 pounds with a scope. With a brake it was a beast, but it was manageable. I took the brake off and this gun became a detached retina in waiting. I could shoot it, but it wasn't fun. It also ate high quality scopes like they were snacks. So I had Mark install three mercury recoil suppressors, two for the butt and one in the forend. The result was a gun that comes in at a comfortable 10-1/4 pounds when equipped with a Swarovski 1.25-4X24 Habicht scope in Warne detachable mounts. Unlike some others, this scope has stayed together through several hundred shots.

The rifle weight is just about right for this type of gun. It's still light enough to carry well on those long tracking jobs, but is heavy enough to allow the recoil to be manageable. The biggest advantage of that in a dangerous game rifle is to be able to control the rifle for fast follow up shots. With this gun I was now able to fire repeated shots very quickly.

.358 WSM

I have no doubt that I was the first person to conceive this wildcat and make plans to build one. I was there

.358 WSM wildcat.
225-grain Trophy Bonded
bullet. 75 grains of RL17.
Fed 215M primer.

Bryce M. Towsley shot this Colorado elk at 248 yards with a .358 WSM wildcat. 225-grain Trophy Bonded bullet. 75 grains of RL17. Fed 215M primer. Nitrix scope.

when Winchester launched the .300 WSM and my first thought was to neck it to 35-caliber. In fact, I ordered a "donor" rifle that day. But due to some uncontrollable issues the project stalled for a couple of years and by the time I got my rifle somebody else had already done the cartridge and called it the .358 Sambar.

My rifle is based on a Winchester Model 70 short action rifle. Mark Bansner built the gun as he has several other custom rifles in the past, including both of my UMT wildcats.

The brass is easy to make by simply running .300 Winchester Short Magnum cases into a RCBS die with a tapered expander. I have tested several powders, but of those I tried, Aliant RL 17 is by far the best. It was developed for the short magnums and has certainly lived up to that in this cartridge. It gives me over 100 feet per second more velocity with a 225-grain bullet than any of the other powders I have tried to date.

With a 225-grain bullet this cartridge easily produces 2,950 fps on my chronograph. That's the same "advertised" velocity of a 180-grain bullet from a .300 Winchester Magnum. The 225-grain loads pro-

.358 WSM

duce 4,400 foot-pounds of muzzle energy, which is almost 1,000 foot-pounds more than the .300 Winchester.

Rifle is Bansner build on M-70. Nitrix scope. .358 WSM wildcat. 225-grain Trophy Bonded bullet. 75 grains of RL17. Fed 215M primer.

Right: The .416 UMT is a wildcat made from .375 RUM cases. It demands the hottest primers and the best bullets.

Below: Bryce M. Towsley with a whitetail taken with Bansner Custom Model 70 in .358 WSM.

Left: The .416 UMT is shown with a .30/06 cartridge for size comparison. Middle: The parent cartridge .375 RUM 300-grain A-Frame on right, .416 UMT 400-grain A-Frame on left. Right: The parent cartridge .375 RUM is flanked by .416 UMT cases. The left case is loaded with a 400-grain Barnes Banded Solid and on the right is a 400-grain Swift A-Frame.

I have used Trophy Bonded 225-grain bullets to shoot elk, whitetails, and even antelope. The first was a bull elk at 250 yards. The bullet broke both shoulders and exited. You can't ask for more than that.

The Barnes 225 TSX shoots close to one-half MOA in my gun and is deadly on any game I have shot. The last one was a big whitetail buck that was facing away from me at 15 yards. I caught the last rib and the bullet exited out his neck. To say the results were spectacular would be an understatement; it captures the concept, but not the magnitude.

The 200-grain Barnes Tipped Triple Shock X bullets have a muzzle velocity of 3,100 fps and average .73 inches in my rifle at 100 yards. With a 250-yard zero this load is 2.55 inches high at 100 yards and 3.67 inches low at 300 yards.

This cartridge is not fussy and is very easy to handload for. Recoil is very manageable. This is an extremely versatile cartridge that is good for hunting any big game in North America. It's not out of place for deer, and I would not hesitate to use it to hunt brown bear. It's also a good choice for African plains game, including the huge and tough to kill eland.

I don't kid myself that my wildcats will ever achieve commercial success like the .22-250 or 7mm Remington Mangum and that's OK. I like that they are a bit oddball. While their level of performance is outstanding, the huddled masses will never recognize that. But a gun guy will see the truth and that's what matters most to a wildcatter.

AUTHOR BIO:

Bryce M. Towsley is an award-winning writer and photographer whose work covers a wide diversity of subjects, but none more than the field of hunting and the firearms. Towsley published his first article in 1980 and in the time since has published thousands of articles and photos in most of the major outdoor and gun magazines. He has worked as a full time writer and photographer since 1993. Towsley is an admitted gun buff and is an avid hunter with almost 50 year of experience. He has hunted extensively throughout the United States and Canada, as well as in Mexico, South Africa, Zimbabwe, Tanzania, Argentina, Russia and Europe for a wide variety of game. Check out his website at www.brycetowsley.com

HOW STRONG A BULLET DO I NEED?

By Craig Boddington

When I was a kid our bullet choices were a lot more limited. In factory loads we had Remington's Core-Lokt and Bronze Point; Winchester's Power Point and Silvertip; and Federal's Hi-Shok. For handloading we had Hornady's InterLock, Speer's Hot-Cor, Sierra's GameKing, and of course, Nosler's Partition. Designed by John Nosler in 1948, it was the first commonly available "premium bullet," and we knew that it was pretty much the toughest of the bunch. We also knew that it often wasn't the most accurate bullet.

So even among such a limited selection we were already making decisions—and compromises—between accuracy and terminal performance. Today we have dozens of bullets to choose from, including a number of greatly improved designs. So selecting the exact "best" bullet for a given application can be confusing and difficult. Let's start by confusing things even more:

There are several bullets that we expect great accuracy from, and several others that usually don't produce the smallest groups but perform like gangbusters on game.

However, there is absolutely no telling exactly which bullet a given rifle will shoot best, so if optimum accuracy is the goal it's best to let your rifle tell you what it likes rather than make assumptions. Now let's make the difficult a little bit easier: There are lots of great bullets today. In any given application there are plenty of good options, and while some choices are more suitable than others, it's almost impossible to identify just one "perfect" bullet for any given purpose.

WHAT IS "STRONG ENOUGH?"

Well, in essence, you need a bullet strong enough to penetrate into the vitals of the game you are hunting. In most cases you want the bullet to expand as it penetrates,

because expansion creates a larger wound channel, resulting in greater damage to vital organs, more rapid blood loss, and a quicker and more humane death.

Some hunters are not satisfied with this; they want a bullet to penetrate completely and exit the off side. Their theory is that, at least with expanding bullets, the exit wound will be larger than the entrance wound, thus leaving a better blood trail for easier tracking. This is absolutely true, and for many years I followed this school: I wanted through-and-through penetration.

The opposite viewpoint is that, if the bullet is placed correctly in the first place there will be no need for tracking. Yes, that's true...but we all mess up now and again. A more compelling argument, at least to me, is that a bullet that expands fully (meaning as much as its design allows) and remains in the animal also expends all of its energy inside the animal. A bullet that exits has retained energy, which is wasted on rocks and trees on the far side.

All bears require strong, tough bullets...and the bigger they are, the more bullet you need. This bear was taken with a 250-grain Nosler Partition from a .340 Weatherby. Introduced in 1948, the grand old Partition is still a good choice for tough game.

These days, in a perfect world I tend to prefer bullets that penetrate into the vitals, expand and do damage, and remain inside the animal. Obviously our world is not perfect. Animals are not created equal, nor are the shots we take. There is a big difference between a broadside shoulder/heart shot that is certain to encounter bone, and a behind-the-shoulder lung shot that just might catch a rib, but might also slide between the ribs and encounter nothing but soft tissue.

Most of us who hunt big game are primarily deer hunters. On deer I have no problem with a bullet that, on a broadside shoulder shot, enters and wrecks the vitals but does not exit the off-shoulder. However, if I take the behind-the-shoulder lung shot and don't get an exit, I'm nervous about that bullet: Will it reliably penetrate the shoulder, or might it expand too much too fast and splatter on the outside? And would penetration be adequate if I needed to take a quartering shot? I would also submit that any bullet that fails to exit on a broadside deer isn't strong enough—tough enough—to use reliably on larger game such as elk!

EXPANSION VERSUS PENETRATION

The jacketed bullet was a parallel and enabling development to smokeless powder. Lead and lead alloy bullets used for centuries were too soft to "take" the rifling at the unprecedented velocities of the new nitrocellulose propellants. Enter the jacketed bullet, a lead core surrounded by a jacket of harder metal. The first such bullets, designed for military use, had "full metal jackets," a complete covering from nose to base. Unless they came apart, which happened (and still does), they penetrated like gangbusters, especially at the new smokeless powder velocities.

The Barnes X-Bullet was the first successful homogenous alloy expanding bullet. Expansion is not radical, so this type of bullet tends to penetrate deeply. The standing bullet is the TSX; lying down is the tipped version, the TTSX.

Such bullets are still with us. Many match bullets and - in accordance with the Geneva Convention - all military bullets, have full metal jackets. There are also non-expanding hunting bullets, called "FMJs" or "solids." Some of these have a full covering of copper jacket, often plated onto a second coating of mild steel ("steel-jacketed 'solids'"); others are homogenous alloy bullets of copper, copper alloy, or bronze. The point is they are designed not to expand at all, and to deliver maximum penetration. These are the "strongest" of all bullets…but their utility on game is very limited.

Although they provide the ultimate in penetration, non-expanding bullets are actually illegal for big game in many North American jurisdictions. In Africa they are essential for elephant, rhino, and hippo, because only non-expanding bullets can be counted upon to penetrate deeply enough. With buffalo there are still a few professional hunters who recommend "solids only," but this is a throwback to the time when expanding bullets were much less reliable than today.

The toughest expanding bullets are plenty strong enough, especially on broadside, facing, and slightly quartering shots. Most hunters recommend hedging the bet a bit, using a tough expanding bullet for the first shot, then backing it up with solids. After the first shot the angles often get bad, and only a solid penetrates enough reach the chest of a northbound buffalo from the southern side.

This is true due to one simple fact: Expansion is the great enemy of penetration. Shortly after the success of the first full-jacketed military bullets it was learned that a bit of exposed lead at the nose caused the bullet to upset or expand as it penetrated, the jacket peeling back and the lead core flattening. The effect was obvious: Larger wound channel, greater tissue damage, and more rapid energy transfer. However, expansion increases resistance. Resistance causes the bullet

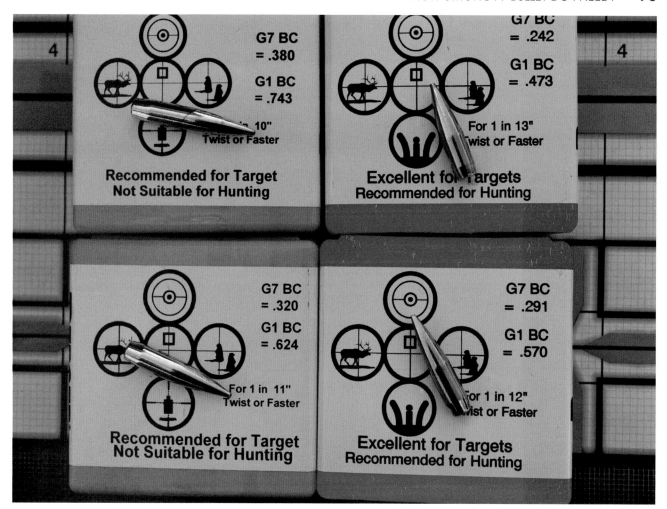

to slow down and eventually stop. Velocity obviously helps overcome resistance, but velocity is an enemy to bullet performance: The faster the bullet, the stronger it must be to stay together. More about that later, but for now please accept that you simply cannot have expansion and penetration in equal measures. The more a bullet expands the less it can penetrate. The less a bullet expands, the deeper it can penetrate.

ACCURACY VERSUS PERFORMANCE

American riflemen have at least two strange obsessions: We crave accuracy, which does help if we're among the relatively few who actually shoot game at long range. For the majority who rarely shoot at game beyond 200 yards there is little practical utility between a 1.25-inch group and a .25-inch group. Accuracy does build confidence, but it's still the bullet that does the work. We also crave velocity, but few game animals can tell the difference between impact velocities varying by a few hundred feet per second—more about that later.

The Berger bullet is legendary for accuracy, but only recently has their VLD, right, entered the field as a hunting bullet. Berger boxes are clearly marked as to whether the bullet is intended for hunting or target use.

As I said earlier, there's no telling exactly which bullet will shoot best in a given rifle, but I submit that, for field shooting, it's always the bullet that does the work. So for almost all field shooting, terminal performance is more important than raw accuracy. Although almost never described as "the most accurate bullets," there are rifle that will shoot tougher, stronger bullets like Nosler Partitions, Swift A-Frames, and the homogenous alloy bullets better than anything else. This may be a serendipitous coincidence, or it may not. Read on! However, we can say there are trends.

The most accurate bullets are generally "match bullets" designed for optimum accuracy. Legendary names include Berger, Hornady Match, and Sierra MatchKing. Some hunters do indeed use them, and in some cases they may be appropriate, but these bullets are generally thin-jacketed bullets designed to punch paper and ring steel, not to provide ideal terminal performance on game. The same can said of all bullets described as "varmint bullets." They are designed not just for accuracy, but also for maximum explosive expansion on impact, both to reduce chances of ricochet and also for decisive results on smaller varmint like prairie dogs and woodchucks.

In varmint hunting you need all the accuracy you can get, and terminal performance is not critical. So you can start with the bullets designed for accuracy, rapid expansion, or both. Somewhere in that group you'll probably find something you like. Otherwise you may have to make compromises between the velocity you would like to have and the terminal performance you need. But, in the thirst to discover what bullets shoot best in your rifles, you can have some interesting surprises. I have seen .375s and .416s that are most accurate with steel-jacketed or homogenous alloy solids, understanding that I would not use such bullets on bears, and also understanding that accuracy is not the first criterion for selecting bullets for large, tough game.

I've seen other rifles that prefer seemingly obsolescent round-nose designs to bullets with aerodynamic shapes. Regardless of accuracy, a round-nose is a poor choice in open country because it sheds velocity like a thrown rock…but also regardless of accuracy, if you don't really need range, a good-old round-nose may be a great choice because blunt-shaped bullets transfer energy much more quickly than sharp-pointed bullets, thus delivering a much heavier initial blow.

VELOCITY AND RANGE

Now we are actually, and finally, getting down to the real business of selecting bullets that deliver the performance needed for the game you are hunting. Like most of us, I always want more accuracy than I really need, and I also want more velocity than actually makes a difference. Both build confidence, and confidence cannot be overlooked. But let's get real. In 1915 the .250 Savage or .250-3000 was the first commercial cartridge to produce 3000 fps. In big-game cartridges 3000 fps is still considered "fast." A 180-grain .30-06 bullet is "standard" at 2700 fps. That is only a 10 percent difference.

With equally aerodynamic bullets and a 200-yard zero, the difference in drop is less than 1.25 inches at 300 yards. Bullet drop obviously increases along with range, but here's the point: No matter what you're shooting at whatever velocity you have to work with, at some point you must start to hold over (whether by guesstimate, dialing the range, or using extra aiming points in your reticle). At this point trajectory is just a number, and you must know it.

African buffalo are both large and very strong, but today's strongest expanding bullets are very much up to the task. Most professional hunters today recommend expanding bullets for buffalo, at least for the first shot.

A more significant advantage to velocity is that it yields more energy. This is important, especially at longer ranges, because energy, along with velocity, drops as range increases. Generally speaking, velocity increases bullet expansion. Early expanding bullets worked pretty well at, say, .30-30 velocities in the low 2000s, but when velocities crept up significantly, as in the .250 Savage (3000 fps) bullet performance became schizophrenic. Sometimes animals dropped as if hit with the hammer of Thor, and sometimes premature expansion caused only nasty surface wounds. Today we have many great bullets that, through various design and construction features, manage to effectively slow, retard, or control expansion.

Please keep two things in mind: First, no bullet can expand the same across a wide velocity spectrum. The .30-30 Winchester uses the same diameter bullet as the .300 Weatherby Magnum, but the velocity difference between the two cartridges is 1000 fps. Bullets designed for the .30-30 expand quite reliably at .30-30 velocities, but would become unreliable bombs if unleashed from a .300 magnum. The converse is also true: Tough bullets intended to expand at magnum .30-caliber velocities aren't going to expand very much when fired from a .30-30. Second, regardless of bullet design it is inevitable that expansion will be reduced as velocity drops.

Modern bullets are designed to perform across a considerable velocity spread, but there are limits. A strong bullet fired at high velocity should be expected to hold together at close range, but it might not expand much if the impact is out at 500 yards. So maybe you don't want the toughest bullets for shooting in open country. However, if it's long-range shooting you're doing, if you choose the softest, quickest-expanding bullet you could well get into trouble if you draw a very close shot. Now let's look at some popular bullet designs.

The polymer-tipped bullet is now offered by most manufacturers. It won't batter in the magazine and improves aerodynamics...but upon impact the tip is driven into the bullet, initiating expansion, so absent additional design features to counter this, polymer-tipped bullets expand quickly.

TIPPED

Regardless of nose shape, common problems with traditional lead-tipped bullets include battering (flattening) in the magazine, and also the fact that, at very high velocity, an exposed lead tip can melt away, leaving you with a bullet that is actually less aerodynamic than it appears. Putting a harder tip on a bullet is not new. Remington's old Bronze Point and Winchester's (old) Silvertip used metal tips. The real forerunner of today's polymer-tipped bullet, however, was the old Sabre Tip from Canadian Industries Ltd. (CIL). Today's polymer-tipped bullets are all the rage, and almost every manufacturer offers them. Some companies use specific colors (Swift's Scirocco is black; Hornady's are all red; Nosler's are color-coded by caliber except for their ho-

Bullets recovered from game aren't always testing-lab pretty, but no matter the appearance two things should be obvious: First, they didn't exit. Some folks like this and other don't. Second, since they were recovered they obviously did their work.

There are dozens and dozens of great bullets on the market today so choices can be confusing. Add a grain of salt to advertising hype, but pay attention to the purposes the manufacturer suggests for any given bullet.

mogenous alloy E-Tip, which is green; and so forth).

The polymer tip allows a sharp, aerodynamic tip that remains constant throughout flight, and it precludes battering in the magazine. However, it has another function: Depending on bullet design and material, the tip is underlain by the lead core or a cavity. Upon impact the tip is driven into the bullet, initiating and expediting expansion. Polymer-tipped bullets with no design features to slow or control expansion are thus bullets that expand very rapidly. These include the original Nosler Ballistic Tip, the very similar Winchester Ballistic Silvertip, and the Hornady SST.

This does not make them "bad" bullets, as bullet expansion is not a bad thing. In fact, I like them on the deer/sheep/goat class of game…but you won't get many exit wounds, and up close at extreme velocity expansion can be explosive.

BONDED

Bill Steigers' Bitterroot Bullet, though only made in small quantities, was probably the first commercially available bonded-core bullet. "Bonded" means that the jacket is chemically affixed to the core, so weight loss is minimal even if expansion is radical. In other words, bonded-core bullets tend to hold together, and even with extreme expansion more bullet weight driving forward enhances penetration. Jack Carter's Trophy Bonded Bearclaw was much more available than the Bitterroot, and was a landmark bullet, made under license by Federal for many years.

Perhaps the toughest lead-core bullet out there is the Swift A-Frame. It combines a wall or partition of jacket material (like the Nosler Partition) with a front core bonded to the jacket. It is just about the only lead core bullet I know of with average retained weight as high as a homogenous alloy bullet, usually at least 97 percent and often more.

TIPPED AND BONDED

Many hunters found the simple lead-core tipped bullets a bit too soft, especially for larger game and higher velocities. I believe Nosler's AccuBond was the first to combine a polymer tip with a bonded core. The AccuBond is a great bullet, but now there are more. Hornady has their InterBond, an equally good bullet; and Swift has the Scirocco, which probably offers the greatest weight retention in this type of bullet. Federal now has a tipped version of the Bearclaw, the Trophy Bonded Tip.

The "tipped and bonded" bullet is the great compromise. It has the aerodynamics of the polymer tip, good weight retention, and excellent expansion. They have become among my favorite "all around" bullets. They are strong enough for fairly large game, tend to be accurate, and expand radically enough that they don't over-penetrate.

Penetrating an elephant's skull to reach the brain is asking a lot of any bullet. This is a job for a full-metal-jacket or homogenous alloy "solid" designed for the purpose; no expanding bullet is strong enough.

Boddington used a 150-grain Sierra GameKing in a .300 H&H to take this desert bighorn in Sonora with a 340-yard shot. The Sierra isn't a fancy bullet—but it's extremely accurate and, in caliber and weight appropriate to the game, it performs well.

A really great mule deer from the Alberta prairies, taken with a 130-grain Barnes TTSX from a .270 Winchester. The homogenous alloy bullet will usually exit on deer-sized game, and it certainly did on this buck.

HOMOGENOUS ALLOY

In the beginning there was Barnes X...I actually helped name that bullet. Barnes' Randy Brooks was in my office at the old Petersen Publishing Company, showing me laboratory expansions of this new whiz-bang all-copper bullet he'd invented. He had already done his homogenous alloy "Super Solid," so he was thinking of calling the expanding version the "Super Soft." I protested, suggesting that it sounded too soft. We turned it one way and saw the petals peeling back made a cross. We turned it a bit and, presto, there was the X!

Today the original X has been improved with driving bands to reduce copper fouling, the TSX; and a polymer-tipped version, the TTSX. Today, too, there are others: Hornady's GMX, Nosler's E-Tip, the North Fork, and more. Average accuracy is good, and in some rifles fabulous. The way they work is they are essentially hollowpoints, with a nose cavity surrounded by a skived meplat that creates petals. Upon impact the petals peel open, but since there is no core, expansion is limited to the depth of the cavity. Weight retention will approach 100 percent unless a petal breaks off, which happens occasionally. Please understand one thing: These are strong bullets. If you want exit wounds, you should love them! If you don't, you will curse them.

I live in the "Condor Zone" in California, where lead-free bullets are required for hunting. So, for deer, pigs, tule elk, and whatever, we use these bullets. I have also used them by choice in Africa and elsewhere. They are marvelous...but they are "penetrating bullets" more than "expanding bullets." Expansion is never radical, and at longer ranges (lower velocities) more limited. Given a choice I would not use them at long range, where softer bullets expand more...but man, do they penetrate! If you use them, consider the shoulder/heart shot rather than the behind-the-shoulder lung shot.

PLAIN OLD BULLETS

Traditional jacketed bullets are called "cup and core" because a "cup" of jacketing metal is drawn and filled with the more malleable lead core. Simple jacketed bullets like this are inexpensive and tend to be accurate. In the 1890s performance was inconsistent, but we quickly learned that both jacket thickness and the amount of lead exposed at the tip retarded expansion. Later some manufacturers added mechanical features to help contain the core within the jacket, such as Remington's Core-Lokt and Hornady's InterLock.

Another way to do it is to leave a hollow cavity at the nose, the hollowpoint bullet. Although often very accurate, this is a design that tends to expand quickly; many match and frangible varmint bullets are hollowpoints because rapid expansion is either desirable or doesn't matter. Very few bullets designed for big game (other than the homogenous alloy bullets) are hollowpoints, but Walt Berger's VLD is an exception. It does expand rapidly, but as we've seen this is not always a bad thing: The VLD is a great long-range hunting bullet.

Because we have so many more advanced designs the plain old "cup and core" bullets are often maligned. This is actually silly.

Plain old bullets like the Federal Hi-Shok, Hornady InterLock, Remington Core-Lokt, Sierra GameKing, and Winchester Power Point have been taking game effectively for decades, and still do. Such bullets are less expensive than more complex designs (so you can shoot more!), and will often (not always) be the most accurate choices. Maybe they aren't the best for close range at extremely high velocity, but in non-magnum cartridges good performance is routine. Let me give you a little secret: Bullet weight matters. If you want to shoot elk with a 130-grain .270, 140-grain 7mm, or 150-grain .30-caliber bullet because you can get more velocity, then you'd better pick (and pay for) really good bullets. If, instead, you choose a 150-grain .270, 165-grain 7mm, or 180-grain .30-caliber then it doesn't matter nearly so much which bullet you choose. Our plain old bullets are still wonderful deer bullets. On larger game, or at higher velocities, just add a bit of bullet weight!

ENOUGH BULLET...BUT NOT TOO MUCH

I was a child of the first magnum craze of the late 50s and early 60s. Although I've toned it down a bit today, with this background I've been "overgunned" for much of my life. What I see out there today is that, rather than too much gun, a lot of hunters are using "too much bullet." Obviously you should choose a bullet that shoots well (enough) in your rifle and gives you confidence. There is no huge sin in using a bullet that is tougher, stronger, and more expensive than you really need, no more than there is a huge problem in being "overgunned." The greater sins lie in using a caliber too light or an inadequate bullet.

Even so, let's keep in mind that it's penetration through the vitals that kills game...but it's bullet expansion (in the vitals) that kills more quickly and re-

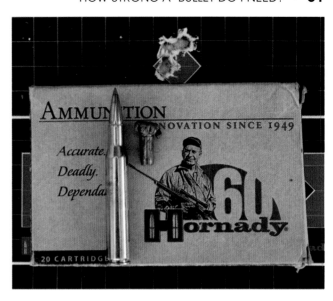

The homogenous alloy bullets penetrate well and usually shoot well enough, but in some rifles they're very accurate. Hornady's 130-grain GMX .270 groups extremely well in an MGA .270...and also performs. The recovered bullet dropped a big red stag at 400 yards.

duces tracking. You absolutely must choose a bullet that will penetrate deeply on the game you intend to hunt. Elk are bigger than deer; bears, though not necessarily bigger than elk, are absolutely tougher.

So you must keep the game you're hunting in mind, but also factor in your conditions. Nobody in their right mind shoots bears at long range, so that's simple: Choose a tough, heavy-for-caliber bullet. With elk, well, are you hunting in thick timber where your shot will be close...or up in the high Alpine where you expect to reach several hundred yards? The solution isn't always simple, but let's back to the good news: No matter what hunting application you have in mind there are lots of great choices. Give it some serious thought and choose wisely!

AUTHOR BIO:

Craig Boddington is one of today's most respected outdoor journalists. He spent the past forty years exploring our natural world as a hunter and sharing his knowledge and experiences in dozens of books and through thousands of published articles and essays. He's a decorated Marine, an award-winning author, and continues to be a leading voice for conservation and ethical hunting around the world.

THE CASE FOR
SELF DEFENSE
HANDLOADS

By Brianna Loeb

Many people can't leave home without the security of certain items. Maybe it's their cell phone – that extension of their hand that connects them to the globe. Maybe it's the comfort of a pocket knife, tucked into a convenient pocket or a purse. Or, as I'd suspect is the case with us, we wouldn't leave home without a dependable and concealable sidearm.

When I slip on my carry gun in the morning, I feel the serene confidence which comes from being prepared to deal with the worst that my day could ever throw at me. Knowing that I'm securely armed allows me to proceed with assuredness.

However, what good is your cell phone without a full charge? What good is your utilitarian pocketknife with a dull edge? If you can't depend on these items to do their minor jobs, what happens if you can't depend on your sidearm to do the major job of self-protection

when you really need it? Just like your cell phone is useless without a charger, so too is your handgun without reliable ammunition.

Why Handloads for Self-Defense?

When I first started carrying daily, I figured that grabbing a box of the best ammo I could buy would be "good enough." And to be fair, factory ammo has gotten so good in recent years that the argument could be made for it being "sufficient." The obvious benefit of handloading your own ammo is that with a little care and knowledge, it will surpass "sufficient." I realized I didn't have to settle for sufficiency, but rather I could have increased precision and reliability of the device with which I would be willing to defend my life. Why choose "one size fits all" when you can tailor the recipe of your cartridge for maximizing your desired velocity

Anh-Viet Dinh

Brianna at the loading bench.

and accuracy to your exact specifications. How is that a bad thing?

Actually, how is it a bad thing? Though convinced that this is a good idea, I wanted to know if there are any downsides at all. I immediately turned to one of my long-time idols, Massad Ayoob, to see what he thinks about it. To my surprise, I learned that he does not condone putting handloads in a concealed carry weapon. In Combat Shooting with Massad Ayoob, he addresses the question of ammo and legal defensibility:

"Anti-gun types have attacked our ammo as well as our firearms since long before I came on the scene. It happens in the press, it happens in State Houses, and yes, it also happens in the courts. "Ladies and gentlemen of the jury, he established malice when he loaded his gun with hollow-nose dum-dum bullets, designed to rend and tear brutal wounds and cause horrible pain and suffering and ensure the agonizing death of his victim!"

So he is saying that legal defensibility should be enough to deter you from carrying the best you can get. While that certainly sounds foreboding, Ayoob doesn't present any actual case in which this has happened, merely that it could. I cannot find any documentation that such a circumstance has arisen. If you are justified in shooting, reloaded ammo shouldn't make much difference. Whether a zealous attorney could incite a jury's concern or not, forensics can tell the powder, primer, and bullet – and beyond that, wouldn't it be irrelevant? As my father would say, "It's better to be judged by twelve than carried by six." This "what if," while certainly notable, is merely hypothetical.

However, Massad is correct that the attack on gun rights has permeated the court system. Prosecutors can make the aftermath of the unthinkable even more unthinkable with criminal charges disputing your use of deadly force and then the inevitable civil cases for

Why choose "one size fits all?"

wrongful death that follow. And even if all cases end in your favor, the legal bills can be suffocating.

So legal gun owners are put in the position of choosing between becoming the victim of violent crime or the possibility to becoming a victim of the entire legal system. That is why there are firearm-based legal defense programs specifically designed to help gun owners with coverage against all legal predators. I proudly use Texas' Law Shield to have my back, legally speaking. It's just another resource to ensure your personal defense. So if you're of the mind that you should

control every aspect of your personal protection, you should certainly look into tailoring every aspect of your concealed carry lifestyle. Where better to start than at your reloading press?

Choose Your Caliber

Before delving into the fun bits, it's important to decide what you're going to reload! I chose 9mm for a few reasons. Everything is a compromise: A less powerful round, like the .380, is more easily concealed, but doesn't have enough "horsepower" to give me confidence. 40 S&W and .45 ACP are great rounds, and certainly one is not undergunned with one on their hip. However, that hip carries a high burden, and recoil in a small package is an issue for me.

For me, the 9mm is the perfect round for concealed carry. The 9mm allows a defender to get off more shots more quickly with less recoil and the ability to get back on target swiftly when compared to more powerful rounds. Add the fact that the higher capacity of ammo is potential benefit. After all, no one ever wished they had less ammunition when the lead is flying.

The already prevalent 9mm pistol is rising in popularity as a daily sidearm, as well as for duty carry among law enforcement, and with good reason. Bigger isn't always better. Remember when the FBI adopted the outstanding 10mm? No matter how great the

The Redding Turret Press is built for the ultimate perfectionist

round is, if the agent can't hit the target, the sidearm is a paperweight, albeit a loud one.

The 9mm also seems to appeal to women, the fastest growing segment of handgun owners. With less upper body strength, we gals often prefer the light recoil of 9mm, especially in a small concealable package. This means that we are more likely to practice with it, and so, should we ever need to employ it for self-defense, will increase the chance we'll hit our target.

Of course I hear that a 9mm is not a reliable man-stopper and that might have been the case in years gone by, but no more. With modern propellants, the 9mm can scoot along at .357 velocities. Current self-defense bullets are nothing short of amazing, getting full expansion at even moderate velocities. All of these attributes make the 9mm the best choice to slip into my Flashbang Bra Holster.

Components

Once you've established the cartridge you'll be using, you need the foundation. Or rather, the press. No one argues that Redding makes the most precise dies on the market, but I wish more people would look at the amazing Redding Turret Press. It's probably going to last longer than I will. It is mega-solid and built for the most obsessed perfectionist. Frankly, I think it is the best press on the market. It has the strength of a single stage and I believe that since you don't have to change dies, you create more consistent ammunition.

So now for the actual components. As someone who was raised and trained to retain all spent cases, it is certainly a strange sensation for me to purchase new brass for reloading purposes. As I'm developing rounds specifically for carry and defense rather than target practice, it only makes sense to use virgin brass.

I chose Starline as my high-quality brass case because they make the most precise brass on the market. When crafting your ammunition for self-defense, it is a challenge to set aside our habits of comparing the costs of the components. The goal is to develop an accurate round that has the potential to defend your life. The value of the lives that you protect with your defensive handgun will always be greater than the cost of the ammunition, no matter what.

For me, choosing primers is never difficult. Admittedly I haven't done a ton of testing because I found something that works and stuck with it. Winchester primers have never failed me. Actually, CCI primers have never failed me in a pistol, but I can't say that such is the case in my revolvers. This is not to say that they are not a quality product. There are

I prefer to seat the Winchester Small Pistol Primers by hand

Anh-Viet Dinh

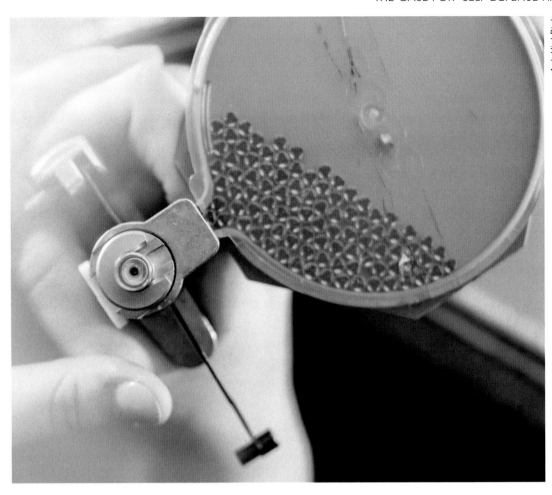

Anh-Viet Dinh

The RCBS hand tool is portable and reliable.

a few thousand CCI primers in my stack of components, and they do have a very important advantage. CCI primers have a larger area of reliable ignition, or "sweet spot," than other primers. With this in mind, always look at your spent shells and see where your firing pin is hitting. If it is considerably off center, a CCI might be the perfect choice. With a burn rate that is almost identical to Winchester and my firing pin, actually a "striker" hitting dead center, I chose the softer option.

One thing that I find helpful is using a hand primer tool. There is more sensitivity and control when you feel the process in your hands as opposed to the lever of the press. I use my RBCS tool to seat the primers properly. It's also portable, and aside from the fact that you really do have to pay attention, it's definitely convenient during March Madness. Thank goodness for commercial breaks!

As far as powder goes- I'm amazed at how great modern powders are. Most powders have become resistant to dampness because they're greatly gelatinized. Additionally, the stabilizers added allow for a long shelf life. Smokeless powders are also not sensitive to shock,

so as long as your powder stays at a consistent temperature, they are increasingly safer to work with.

I went through many types of smokeless powders to test for my load recipe. Some factors to consider are the burn rate, shape, and density. The burn rate will affect the pressure and should be directly correlated to the bullet weight you choose. Since I carry a sidearm with a short barrel, I needed a powder with a fast burn rate. The shape of the powder is important- ball powder, or spherical, usually is very consistent. Flake powder can stack up and be a lot less uniform. This could allow it to dispense improperly, leading to inconsistent dispense and charge. The density will determine how much bulk, and if it's bulkier, it can prevent double charges.

I have had great experiences with Winchester, IMR, Alliant, but I am a fan of Hodgdon Powder, and this one is a spherical propellant specifically formulated for accuracy. Hodgdon Titegroup Smokeless Powder is my go-to, and has delivered consistently flawless performance for me. One reason is that it meters so well. When I get my powder throw dialed in, I get virtually identical powder drops. Out of 100 cases there is virtually no variation. While this may not be of paramount importance with some guns, my everyday sidearm is the Springfield XD-S 9mm, with a 3.3" barrel and it is sensitive to variations in velocity. That short barrel requires a fast burning powder like Titegroup.

In addition, Titegroup is very clean. While this is not a huge factor for self-defense ammunition, it is a nice attribute. It is also economically efficient. In fact, I use it for my practice rounds. Since I'm used to working with Titegroup, and have always had excellent results, I'm inclined to use it for whatever I can. A little goes a long way, I'm familiar with it, and it meters uniformly. At 4.3 grains, I'm getting 1178 fps, and as the name implies, very accurate hits.

Choosing the right bullet weight is, perhaps, the most important decision that you will face when creating your perfect self-defense cartridge. Sadly, most people don't pay very much attention to the grain of their bullets, yet there are a lot of choices. Within each caliber, there is a range of common bullet weights that will fit different needs, and oddball amounts that you can occasionally find when needed. For 9mm, you're generally looking at 115, 124, or 147 grain. (Again, these are just typical ranges, you can find as light as 95 grains if you know where to look.)

Velocity is required for reliable bullet expansion and penetration. Everyone seems to have an opinion on the matter, but there are a lot of factors to consider when making your selection. First of all, your gun might perform differently with different weight bullets. Experiment with the available options to see what your sidearm "prefers."

Additionally, find out what has worked for other people with the same gun as you. If they've had a lot of time on the trigger, they might have some helpful suggestions with the behavior they've seen from the same firearm. Some factors that will affect the accuracy include the barrel length, the twist rate, bore diameter, and velocity.

I've found that my handgun tends to do very well with the midweight 124 grain bullets. Lighter projectiles do not seem to be as consistent, and 147 grain are never as accurate. This surprised me as the moderate twist rate of 1:10 should be fine with the heavier round, but my target says otherwise. Go figure. It must not have enough time in the 3.3-inch barrel to stabilize. In addition, I lose enough velocity that I am concerned about reliable bullet expansion. The key is to aim for both expansion and penetration in a light jacketed hollowpoint. It's like they say, "Sticks and stones may break my bones, but hollowpoints expand on impact."

I chose Hornady XTP 124 grain for a dense bullet that expands with satisfaction at an ideal velocity. With impressive penetration from a light jacket and a dense core, Hornady XTP products are THE products for accuracy. Not to say that they are only good bullets, but they seem to do everything well out of my XDS. Barnes XPB is one of my favorites and the Speer Gold Dot also performs well out of my gun, but for carrying daily, I think Hornady is the pick of the crop, with accuracy. Like most self-defense bullets, they are designed to perform when pushed over 1000ft/sec, but research suggests that they don't ex-

Hodgon Titegroup Smokeless Powder is a spherical propellant specifically formulated for accuracy

Anh-Viet Dinh

Anh-Viet Dinh

pand too rapidly when over 1100. The same can be said for the Speer and the Barnes. The Speer is just as accurate but doesn't seem to expand as much. The Barnes expands beautifully, but my gun isn't as accurate…So it is Hornady for me. But of course, I encourage you to explore all the different flavors to see what works best for you and your handgun.

I have been working up my load, and it is important to remember that since the 4.3 grains of Titegroup is more than Hodgdon suggests, my editor and this publication cannot recommend that you follow my lead. That said, I am getting close to 1200 feet per second with my Hornady XTP. It does seem to be sensitive to the crimp, and so I keep it tight. 1.150 is the recommended overall length and it is not something that I have adjusted as I am happy with the velocity and recoil.

If you're going to construct your own ammunition for any purpose, the most important part is to test drive everything. Head out to the range to test your handloads for accuracy. Anything you're going to be carrying to protect yourself should be as dependable as possible. It comes down to finding what's right for you and the sidearm for which you are building your

ammo. Ultimately, your sidearm will pick the weight and speed of the ammunition that you build, so invest in a chronograph, and take some much-deserved time at the range to learn what works best for you.

When done properly, your handloads should be superior to generic factory ammunition. You should be able to leave your home carrying the best you can get for your personal safety and the safety of your loved ones. When you face the evil in this world, you can do so with confidence and empowerment. But be wary. If you're worried about the defensibility of your choice to carry at all, nonetheless to carry handloaded ammunition, invest in a legal protection program.

AUTHOR BIO:

Briana Loeb is a lifelong reloading enthusiast. She began shooting at age six and has never stopped. A passionate believer in personal empowerment, she is a women's self-defense instructor and concealed carry advocate.

P.O. ACKLEY'S IMPROVED CARTRIDGES

By Fred Zeglin

P.O. Ackley passed away in 1989. His career as a barrel maker, gunsmith and writer lasted more than fifty years. All that has been long since overshadowed by his work with "Improved" cartridges.

Improved cartridge designs are a class of custom cartridges with a very important characteristic: it is possible to utilize factory ammunition in an improved chamber without first modifying the brass in reloading or form dies. Ackley Improved cartridges are not true wildcats, because no forming of the brass is required to make them fit the chamber before firing.

According to Ackley, "An improved cartridge is a factory cartridge that has been fired in an improved chamber and thus has its form changed. In other words, a rifle made to handle an improved cartridge. For example, the Improved .257 (Roberts), will still handle factory ammunition, but the fire-formed cases can be reloaded, or handloaded, to considerably higher velocities without danger to the shooter."

There are two important points when it comes to the higher velocities and safety that Ackley mentioned above:

1. More powder capacity is the reason for more velocity.
2. There is no need to go beyond safe pressure limits to get the improved results.

Ackley was not the first gunsmith to try to improve cartridge designs by fire-forming, but he was the most successful at marketing them. His name has become so synonymous with the improved chamber concept that when a new factory cartridge comes to the market, reamer makers and gunsmiths quickly offer "Ackley Improved" versions.

There is always a learning curve when you're working on a new concept. Ackley started his work with im-

The .280 Ackley Improved (AI) is not as well known as the time-honored .30-06, but perhaps it should be. Here is a custom-made .280 Ackley Improved rifle built on the CZ-550 action and fitted with a Montana Rifleman barrel.

proved cartridges using rimmed cartridges. We know from his letters to author Richard F. Simmons that his earliest improved designs were on the 22 Savage Hi-Power, and then the 219 Zipper.

Rimmed cartridges have a huge advantage for a gunsmith or reloader learning about fire-forming brass. Because the rim sets the headspace, the chamber can take nearly any form that will still extract. So working with rimmed cases first is a natural building block for a knowledge base.

Winchester introduced the 219 Zipper in 1937. In less than a year after the appearance of the Zipper, Ackley had an improved version of the case and was marketing it. Ackley had already cut his teeth on the 22 Hi-Power, so the 219 Zipper arriving on the scene on the heels of Ackley's first experiment with fire-formed wildcats in the 22 Hi-Power. It was a natural progression to do the same thing with the Zipper and grab the

Author Fred Zeglin and Mike Bellm. Mike was the last guy to buy out P.O. Ackley rifle barrels. Mike is also one of the few guys who really spent time with P.O. that is still alive.

attention of shooters playing with a new cartridge.

In the pre-war years rimmed cartridges were designed for the transition period from black powder to smokeless powder. Most of these early factory brass cases had a large amount of taper to facilitate both feeding and extraction. Large amounts of taper were valuable when cases were loaded with black powder, as it helped deal with the powder fouling so that the gun would feed and fire reliably. Because these early brass cases were low pressure, the tapered case did not create any problems.

But when it came to "Improving" cartridges, the tapered designs of these older factory rimmed cases had the most to gain from being improved. Often, not only is the shoulder blown out, but also the neck is shortened by moving the shoulder forward to increase case capacity substantially. Case capacity is increased and therefore velocity increased dramatically in these early experiments. Shooters then as now were interested in more velocity, and the cartridges in the chart below delivered in a big way.

Factory Cartridge	Bullet Weight Grains	Factory Velocity	Ackley Improved Velocity	Percent Increase of Velocity
219 Zipper	55	3110	3450	10.9
25-35 WCF	117	2230	2579	15.7
30-30 WCF	150	2370	2535	6.8
30-40 Krag	180	2445	2740	12.1
348 Winchester	250	2297	2470	7.7

This chart compares published factory velocities with tested loads from Ackley Improved chambers.

The primary reason for the desire to fire factory ammunition in an improved chamber is to allow for easy fire-forming. No need for expensive dies to form the brass and no specialty tools are needed. By extension, the shooter need not learn to form brass in dies. In short, it's easy. The secondary argument in favor of improved designs is that if you somehow ended up on a trip and lost or forgot your ammo you could still buy factory ammo and be able to hunt.

True wildcats require special form dies to prepare the brass for the new wildcat chamber. Often, large cases are cut down to make a wildcat, requiring form and trim dies to accomplish the new shape of the case. Wildcatters must also gain knowledge and experience in these specialty operations, something that not every

shooter desires to do. But nearly anyone can handle an Ackley Improved case and gain a unique gun for their collection.

Getting Technical

Naturally, both Ackley and his customers were interested in expanding this concept to other types of cartridges. This is where Ackley's true genius came to the surface. When he started working with rimless bottleneck cases, Ackley came up with a simple and reliable way to headspace them so that factory ammunition could safely be fired in his improved chambers.

Sadly, this is where gunsmiths, both professional and hobbyists, often make a mistake. The concept is so simple that folks simply try to make it harder.

P.O. Ackley said of his Ackley Improved case designs for rimless bottleneck cases, "When checking the headspace, a standard "Go" gauge with .004" ground off the head is the proper one to use. In other words, the headspace has to be minimum-minus .004" in order to prevent case head separations." The standard "Go" gauge for the caliber becomes the "No-Go" gauge for the Ackley Improved chamber. Of course, this method is in reference to rimless or rebated cases only. Most reamer makers offer "Ackley" gauges today.

To be clear, these traditional gauges will have the shoulder angle of the factory cartridge. When placed in an improved chamber a factory cartridge will actually headspace then on the junction of the neck and shoulder, rather than on a datum point down the shoulder. This is probably what confuses most novice gunsmiths and shooters.

In recent years reamer makers have begun making headspace gauges for Ackley Improved chambers with the correct shoulder angle to match the chamber. For this to work correctly the tool maker must calculate the correct location of the shoulder so that factory cartridges can still be safely fired. There is no difference in the dimensions of the reamers in such cases, only the gauge is being modified.

Most of the Ackley Improved cartridges have 40-degree shoulders. When gauges are made to match this angle the reamer maker does the math to set a datum line on the shoulder to keep the tooling in line with existing SAMMI methods. These gauges produce the same length chamber as the traditional method used by Ackley, if made correctly. Making gauges specific to the cartridge allows the toolmaker to standardize the tooling and by extension sell more tools. In all fairness, I suspect the toolmakers are tired of explaining Ackley headspace, so making specific gauges eliminates many hours on the phone.

Ackley Improved Velocity

Over the years I have heard clients complain that they don't like Ackley designs because their factory ammo is actually lower velocity in the Ackley chamber. I have even seen this repeated in articles from time to time. Shooters who say this do not understand the simple facts of fire-formed improved cases. To attain the increased velocity in the Ackley Improved case you will have to burn more powder than you did in the parent cartridge. It's as if you have bored an engine over-sized; it will then burn more fuel to produce more horsepower. An Ackley Improved chamber is like boring out the cylinder; it will burn more fuel and deliver more energy to the bullet (the piston). The increase in case capacity is a primary factor in just how much more velocity is possible.

When using factory ammunition to fire-form Ackley Improved cases it is common to see a drop in velocity as compared to a factory chamber. This is because energy is being utilized to form the brass as well as the fact that there is a larger volume in the improved chamber. The increased chamber volume lowers pressure, therefore lowering velocity.

Once you have fire-formed your factory cases you're ready to load them to their new potential with their increased case capacity. Starting loads are easy for Ackley Improved designs. You can simply go to your favorite loading manual and take the top load listed for the parent cartridge, i.e., if you have a .257 Roberts Ackley Improved, simply use 257 Roberts data as your starting point. Then work up loads as you would for any new rifle.

You will note in the following chart that some Ackley Improved cartridges have very little increase in capacity. Let's focus on the .270 Winchester. Ackley was not a fan of the .270 Ackley Improved or the .25-06 Ackley Improved. He offered them because clients asked for them, since after all a guy has to make a living. In checking case capacity by water weight I found that a factory .270 Winchester has a water weight capacity full to case mouth of 67.5 grains. The .270 Ackley has a water weight capacity of 68.6 grains, an increase of only 1.6 percent in capacity. Powder makers will tell you that it's possible to have that much

variation in load density when using a powder measure to drop loads.

Factory Cartridge	Bullet Weight Grains	Factory Velocity	Ackley Improved Velocity	Percent Increase of Velocity
22-250 Remington	50	3719	3947	6.1
6mm Remington	75	3400	3553	4.5
243 Winchester	100	2960	3089	4.4
250 Savage	100	2820	3129	11
257 Roberts	117	2780	3120	12.2
25-06	117	2990	3051	2
6.5-06 A-Square	140	2954	3095	4.8
270 Winchester	150	3010	3048	1.3
7mm-08	150	2823	2865	1.5
7x57 Mauser	160	2690	2791	3.7
280 Remington	160	2795	2988	6.7
30-06 Springfield	150	2900	3117	7.3
30-06 Springfield	180	2690	2865	6.7
300 H&H	220	2565	2835	10.5
35 Whelen	250	2400	2575	7.4
375 H&H	250	2690	2940	9.2
375 H&H	300	2600	2800	7.7

This chart compares published factory velocities with tested loads from Ackley Improved chambers.

Another reason that the .270 Winchester gains very little from being improved is the fact that its case capacity is about maximum for the .270 bore. We know this to be true because you must add large amounts of powder to gain small increases in velocity. There is a maximum bore capacity for all calibers, once you exceed that capacity, you're adding heat, noise and recoil to the system with little to show for it, except possibly shorter barrel life.

Small wonder, then, that cartridges with tiny increases in capacity show meager improvement in velocity. When choosing cartridges from the Ackley Improved list the best results for improved velocity will come from cartridges that offer increased capacity of three percent or more in case volume.

Most newer cartridges that have come to the market from the factories have employed most of the principles incorporated in Ackley Improved cartridges. In short, they have relatively minimum body taper and sharper shoulders than in those prior to around 1970. P.O. Ackley and the shooting public proved these de-

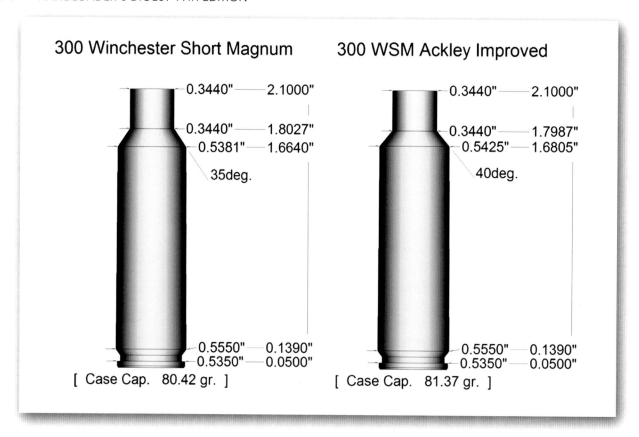

sign concepts and the factories followed suit by adopting them. With these newer cartridges, there is little to be gained from "Improving" them.

Compare the factory 300 WSM with what you would get from an Ackley Improved version of the cartridge. Essentially a one-grain increase by water weight.

I checked the Ackley Improved dimension for the 26 and 28 Nosler cartridges, and the case capacity would only increase by 2.6%. In short, modern case design has caught up to Ackley, it just took about 40 years.

Now you're probably asking, "Why would Ackley Improved cartridges live on, if the newer cases follow Ackley's designs?" Good question, but the answer is different than you might expect.

Today we have a trend toward large magnum cases that have a lot of recoil and a very loud report. Adding insult to injury, many shooters feel the need to add a muzzle brake which increases noise and concussion at the firing line. It's no fun to be at the shooting bench next to a guy with a muzzle brake, especially if your range has a roof over the firing line.

Consequently, non-magnum cartridges start to be considered more fun to shoot, with less recoil and better accuracy because the shooter is less recoil conscious. If you shoot a lot you will learn that heavy recoil wears you out. It's just like any activity that requires muscle control and mental concentration; you can only do it so long. Non-magnum cartridges have much less recoil, so they simply do not wear you out at the firing line the way a magnum will.

Brass Availability

We have already established that anyone can easily fire-form Ackley cartridges. So you can easily make your own brass.

If you're going to fire-form your own brass there is one detail that you should pay attention to. When you load factory brass to fire-form Ackley Improved cartridges, choose a load with enough pressure so that the brass will fully form. Let's say you're working with a .257 Roberts: don't select a light starting load from the .257 Roberts tables. Because of the increased size of the Ackley chamber, such a load will have trouble fully forming the brass with nice crisp shoulders, and might even fail to fully set the new shoulder.

Instead, choose a load from the top end of the table. You want your brass to fully form on the first shot. Trying to save a penny or two on powder will only mean you might have to fire-form twice. Remember, a top-end load for the parent cartridge is a starting load for an Ackley Improved chamber.

Some guys worry about mixing their Ackley brass with standard brass. This is not a problem because you cannot fit Ackley formed cases into a standard chamber, and if you put standard factory cases in an Ackley chamber you will simply fire-form them.

If you're still worried about keeping your brass separated, there are a few things you can do to make it easy to differentiate the cartridges. Many shooters use nickel brass for certain cartridges to make them easy to spot. Some shooters will only have the Ackley chambering in their collection and not own the factory counterpart chambering; i.e. they will have a 30-06 Ackley Improved but not a 30-06.

My personal favorite is to buy headstamped brass. Quality Cartridge of Hollywood, MD offers a lot of Ackley Improved cases fully formed and headstamped so you can keep them separate from regular factory headstamps. Obviously, they don't have every cartridge, but it's a pretty strong sampling. They also offer a number of Ackley's true wildcat cases fully formed and headstamped.

17-223 Ackley Improved	270 Ackley Improved
22-250 Ackley Improved	280 Ackley Improved
243 Win. Ackley Improved	7-08 Ackley Improved
6mm Rem Ackley Improved	7x57 Ackley Improved
6mm-06 Ackley Improved	30-06 Ackley Improved
25-06 Ackley Improved	8mm-06 Ackley Improved
250 Savage Ackley Improved	338-06 Ackley Improved
257 Roberts Ackley Improved	35 Whelen Ackley Improved
260 Ackley Improved	375 H&H Ackley Improved
6.5-06 Ackley Improved	375 Whelen Ackley Improved
6.5-257 Roberts Ackley Improved	

A quick perusal of the reloading dies available on the market proves that you can buy dies for most of the above listed Ackley cartridges and many more for pretty reasonable prices. Keep in mind there are no form dies needed for improved cartridge designs.

Accuracy

Naturally once you have the extra 50 or 100 feet per second, accuracy is the next thing the shooter and reloader start to look for.

Over the years I have probably chambered for most of the Ackley Improved cartridge that you can name and a few more. To my pleasant surprise it's not unusual for factory ammo to shoot very well during fire forming.

I have never done testing to prove it, but, I suspect that the reason for the fine accuracy I've experienced during fire-forming is because the cartridge has less contact with the chamber than it would normally. The brass is touching the bolt face and the junction of the neck and shoulder; the body is not touching at all at this point. In fact, sometimes the reloaded ammo requires some tweaking before the accuracy returns to fire-forming levels. For me this is the proof that less contact with the chamber is actually an advantage.

If Ackley chambers have any accuracy deficiencies, they are related to the 40-degree shoulder. The sharper the shoulder angle, the more important that the length of the case matches the chamber, because the contact area is reduced as compared to a longer shoulder. Ackley himself pointed out, and I am paraphrasing here, that in his experiments 40 degrees was as far as you could push the shoulder angle and avoid real accuracy problems. Once you exceed 40 degrees, holding proper headspace becomes difficult.

On average, Ackley Improved cartridges are no more or less accurate than any other cartridge. Think about it: the bullet has no idea what the cartridge looks like. Bullets are not intelligent, they simply react to the circumstances and energy applied to them.

Bottom line: if the gunsmith does a good job of assembling the rifle for accuracy and the barrel is of good quality then you should be able to get all the accuracy you desire.

Ackley continued to produce Improved designs as often as the factories brought out new brass to work with. With a career that lasted so long, it's no surprise there are so many Ackley Improved cartridges. P. O. Ackley has been gone for over 25 years and his designs are more popular than ever. It's safe to say, "They're here to stay."

Headspace and Ackley Cartridges

Not too long ago we rented a 30-30 Ackley Improved (AI) reamer to a hobby gunsmith so that he could rechamber his NEF single shot rifle. Soon the gentleman called me with some concerns about doing this job on his own. Now, don't get the idea that we offer a free education with every reamer we rent: on the contrary, it's not unusual for us to tell a guy he should go to a competent gunsmith. But this situation got my attention because he was active on an online discussion

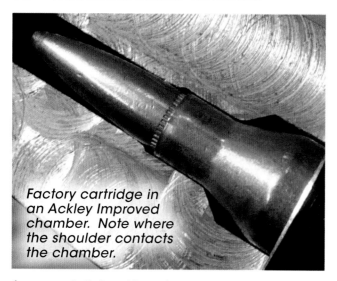

Factory cartridge in an Ackley Improved chamber. Note where the shoulder contacts the chamber.

forum, and all the self proclaimed experts were scaring the pants off this poor guy.

It seems that many shooters - and some gunsmiths - are confused about the proper way to headspace an Ackley Improved cartridge. They were telling this would-be gunsmith that he had to set the barrel back to get a true "Ackley" chamber. The problem is, that with rimmed cases this is not true, as long as the headspace for the parent case is correct. Rimmed cases are headspaced by the rim being trapped between the bolt-face and the breech or rim-cut of the barrel. So the shape or length of the chamber are almost immaterial with rimmed cases. As long as the case design will allow the case to be extracted, the case can be much smaller than the chamber and it will fire-form just fine. Again, this goes back to the fact that the rim is the headspace limit for such cases.

In the photo of the 30-30 AI chamber (below), you will note that the rim is solid against the back of the barrel. Imagine if you will, that a breech block with the weight of a locomotive has been locked into position against the back of the cartridge. Now that rim is

Fully formed case in the same chamber as in the figure above.

totally trapped with nowhere to go. A standard 30-30 Winchester is in the chamber so you can see the difference in shape from the original, to the AI. Clearly there is no reason that the barrel would need to be set back to get the chamber correct. This photo should make that easy to see, however later in this article we will discuss some of Ackley's other designs and show where the confusion comes from.

Similar in headspacing are belted magnum cases. The case is designed to headspace with the distance from the bolt-face to the front edge of the belt, in the same way that the rimmed case is trapped. The 375 H&H AI is a good example of this. Just as the rim above holds the case during forming, here the belt holds the case while the body and new shoulder are formed in the improved chamber. Most of our magnum cases are modern enough designs that they do not benefit greatly from being "Improved".

Truthfully, most of the AI chamberings that clients request are either rimmed cases or rimless cases. The basis for most of the confusion about head spacing for Improved cases comes from the fact that the rimless cases DO require that the barrel be set back to get a proper new chamber. The reason for this is really very simple. Ackley was a pretty smart guy, he figured out that by shortening the chamber by .004" you would still be able to chamber factory loads, but with his sharp shoulder and expanded body the only place the case would touch in the new chamber was the bolt-face and the junction between the neck and the shoulder of the case. By holding the case tightly against the bolt-face in this way, the cartridge could be fired safely, allowing the brass to fire-form into the unsupported areas of the new larger than original factory chamber.

So the proper headspace gauges for a rimless Ackley Improved chamber are a "go" gauge made for the specific caliber, and a "go" gauge from the factory caliber becomes the "no-go". This works because the Ackley gauge is .004" shorter than the standard "go" gauge for the given caliber. Because such a small portion of the shoulder will actually be in contact with the shorter chamber, the resistance one might expect is almost nonexistent.

In order to make a perfect headspace job with a rimless Ackley Improved chamber you will have to set the barrel back one thread. There are added advantages to this process. You can offer your client some accuracy work on the action at the same time, truing the receiver

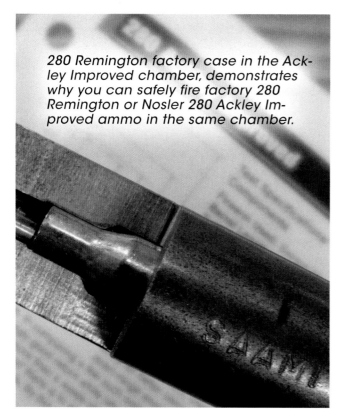

280 Remington factory case in the Ackley Improved chamber, demonstrates why you can safely fire factory 280 Remington or Nosler 280 Ackley Improved ammo in the same chamber.

Above: Quality Cartridge is a reliable source for properly headstamped and form cases for many Ackley calibers.

Left: Scratches at the junction of the neck and shoulder demonstrate where the factory cartridge headspaces prior to fire forming.

face, lapping lugs, and squaring the bolt face are all items that will improve accuracy.

Since you will be resetting the headspace this is a great time to offer these modifications to the action. Factory chambers are often out-of-round, off-center from the bore line, or oversized. As a result of the set-back you can often clean up most of these problems and improve the accuracy of the finished rifle. Most important of all for the re-chamber job to the Ackley design, the set-back and re-chamber will allow you to shorten the chamber to get the correct headspace measurement.

If the barrel has no sights you can set if back a partial turn, in some cases the client will like this because it will hide the factory markings under the wood line, then you just engrave a new caliber marking. Be sure to set the barrel back far enough so that you will actually be cutting a new chamber with your reamer, otherwise you might end up with a chamber with multiple steps, this is unsightly and unprofessional, the client will notice it when they reload, causing you much embarrassment.

Here is a 22-250 in an AI chamber (top left). Headspace is achieved when the junction of the neck and the shoulder of the case contacts that same junction in the chamber. Note the open area around the shoulder, when the case if fire-formed the brass with expand to

fill all that space. Subsequently when you reload the brass you will have the added case capacity that makes "Improved" cartridges desirable.

If a rimless case is rechambered using an Ackley Improved reamer without setting the barrel back the result is an undesirable wildcat. Factory ammo will have an excessive headspace condition in such a chamber. Firing factory ammo in such a chamber will result in case head separations, misfires, or at the very least short brass life. Such a chambering should be considered unsafe as well as poor quality.

AUTHOR BIO:

Fred Zeglin has been building custom rifles for over 30 years and specializes in wildcat designs for his clients. He is currently the Firearms Technology Coordinator and the NRA Short Term Gunsmithing Program Coordinator for Flathead Valley Community College in Kalispell, MT. He owns 4D Reamer Rentals Ltd. so he deals with more reamers and headspace gauges than any other gunsmith you will ever meet. Fred has published two books, "Hawk Cartridges Manual" and "Wildcat Cartridges, The Reloader's Handbook of Wildcat Cartridge Design."

SHOULDER POSITION, SHOULDER BUMP AND ACCURACY

By Robin Sharpless

The cartridge case which is most conformal to the chamber is one which would yield the greatest accuracy potential with all other variables being equal. We neck size our fired cases in an attempt to maintain a cartridge case that is as dimensionally equivalent to the internal configuration of the chamber as is possible to provide for the best bore axis alignment. Neck sizing is a very good way to enhance accuracy but can only be used so many times, until the cartridge case itself is fully obturated or fully expanded.

We use brass for cases due to its ability to obturate, ie. expand, under pressure to fill and seal the chamber and then spring back to allow for ease of extraction once the pressure has dropped. At each subsequent firing the case begins a bit larger than the last and therefore springs back less and less until the case is so formed to the internals of the chamber that it becomes difficult to extract. This is the point when the case is fully obturated. It is also the point where neck sizing alone will not fill the requirement for creating a useful case.

At this point we must fully size once again to allow the cartridge to freely chamber in the rifle. In general, full-length sizing dies are designed to produce a finished cartridge case - after spring back - that will fit a SAAMI or equivalent minimum chamber.

This is not simply in terms of body and neck diameters but also by bumping the shoulder back to below minimum chamber datum line headspace dimension. Here we run into some difficulty, as nearly all chambers are not cut at minimum for the datum line headspace dimension. The SAAMI specification for this dimension is Minimum + 0.010" and that does not make for an accurate or precise case to chamber fit. So what is our answer to this dilemma?

Research the Chamber Dimensions

The first step is to determine exactly what the datum line headspace is in your existing chamber. To do this we can use a fully obturated case to create a fingerprint of the chamber in which it was fired. The easiest way to do this is to neck size and fire a case until extraction becomes sticky. It may take a few firings to complete the task but it is simple enough.

Once done, we have the "tool" to derive the needed measurement. In an industrial setting this would be done on an optical comparator with machinists gauge blocks, but even for the serious handloader this would be a big piece of equipment and a serious investment.

Luckily a great tool to do this with is Redding's instant indicator. This device is a very unique reloader's measuring instrument, which does a variety of comparator tasks on bullets, cartridge cases and loaded

The SAAMI spec reference headspace gauge in .308 Winchester.

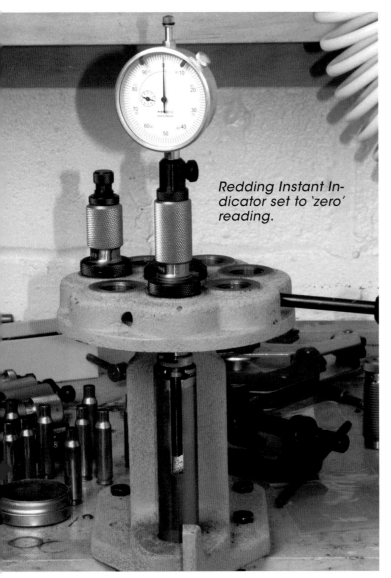

Redding Instant Indicator set to 'zero' reading.

308 & set up.

rounds. In our use we would use the datum line head-space feature incorporated in the tool. This is a true datum line device, as it does not measure the surface of the entire shoulder but measures from a sharp, machined surface that contacts the shoulder at the specific datum line diameter. I like to use this in a Redding T7 turret press so that I can move from my sizing die to my instant indicator simply by rotating the turret head.

The Redding Instant Indicator is shipped with a SAAMI minimum set up gauge for the specified chambering. We set the device so that the included dial indicator to reads "0" when the shellholder is in solid contact with the bottom of the Indicator's die body. Using this method we can see that our fully expanded case gives us a dimension of +0.008. Therefore we will work to produce a sized and shoulder-bumped case that is 0.0015 to 0.002" shorter than this dimension.

In this case, we wish to produce a case with a bump of -0.006". This will leave enough space to allow for free chambering but still maintaining a very conformal fit to the chamber for improved accuracy potential. Additionally, it will reduce the amount of sizing to a minimum and limit the imposed stresses on the case, adding to its useful life.

Fitting the case to your chamber, not a Minimum Chamber

Simply, this knowledge allows us to size the case only enough to fit the chamber in question. To control the amount of shoulder bump or set-back as is necessary to allow a free, but still very close dimensional fit to the chamber is a great goal, but not so easily achieved.

Many believe they can simply set the die "out" a bit to accomplish this, but testing has shown a considerable flaw in this practice. First, the thread pitch of 1 in 14 as most dies have today leads us through some simple math to calculate 1" divided by 14 revolutions, as one revolution of the die moves the shoulder position by 0.071428571".

Just under 72 thousandths and we wish to move our shoulder by somewhere less than 10 thousandths. So to say move it 2 thousandths of an inch (0.002") we would need to accurately rotate the die by 1/36 of a turn.

As you can quickly see this is not a task for mere mortals. A 7/8 by 14 Class 2 UNF thread pitch is used to make die changes quick and to provide a strong thread-mating surface for the loads a sizing die can come under.

Moreover the die threads are of a class designed for ease of installation, not one for tight precision. Where is this all leading to? It leads to the inherent movement (compression) and reduced precision in the die threads under load. All threads have some, and the lower the class number, the more space between the mating surfaces and a greater potential for compression (movement) under load.

There are a few thousandths of compressibility built into the mating of press and die. And the greater the load, the greater the compression, hence variability in the datum line position of the sized case.

The press also has built in attributes, which, while they are necessary for it to do its work, also diminish its ability to reproduce a true Top Dead Center on each stroke with varying degrees of induced load, like that of sizing a case and bumping a shoulder.

Clearly, a repeatable TDC has a great deal to do with precisely setting a shoulder position accurately from one case to another. All modern presses (other than arbor presses), single stage and turret, as reflected by the catalog listings of the various makers, have in

common a form of linkage at the base of the ram which uses various shafts or pins on which the individual parts rotate to create the increased pressure generated through the compound leverage cycle.

To turn these shafts and pins they each need clearance to rotate. There is also lubricant in the spaces as well. As the press goes through its cycle and these spaces or clearances diminish through induced pressure of say, full-length sizing a die.

The true Top Dead Center of the press changes by as many thousandths as are available based on the given force. As all cases have slight difference in their metallurgy, wall thickness, and degree of hardness, use each will create a slightly different induced force on these various pins and shafts. Each will compress or bottom the part on the shaft in a slightly different way. Like the thread issue, this part of the process too leads us to a variability of true Top Dead Center and creates a second issue with the shoulder position location due to inherent mechanical variabilities.

Cam Over is a Solution and a Problem

To gain the full mechanical power of the press and eliminate the indicated issues with the detailed vari-

Instant Indicator gauge, Competition Shellholders and .308 case

abilities, we need to put the press into a state of "cam over." Simply put, we drive the die a bit deeper into the press and cause the pressure or force exerted to be maximized and thereby mitigate the issues of thread compression and mechanical compression of the shafts and pins with their mating parts.

This is generally accomplished by turning the die in ⅛th to ¼ turn deeper into the press after it contacts the shellholder at apparent TDC. This is done easily by backing off the ram and making the adjustment.

When this is done correctly the ram stroke will stack pressure and them "cam over" the top releasing that pressure as the ram drops slightly at the end of its

.308 Winchester case about to measured for headspace

stroke. With this method we remove the issues previously indicated; we set a die squaring between the base of the die and the top surface of the shellholder. We also control force through the maximum the press can mechanically provide at the "cam over" moment.

All that is great, but we know sizing dies operating at their full potential create a shoulder bump sufficient to fit a minimum chamber even after springback. We also know from our measurements with the Instant Indicator that our chamber is longer than SAAMI minumum.

A Solution With Cam Over

A considerable issue for sure, but not one which cannot be overcome. Enter Redding Competition Shellholders, set of shellholders that allow for the modification of Datum Line headspace on the cartridge case in increments of 0.002" with the ability to use the full cam-over advantages with all the consistency the press and die combination can offer in that mode.

They are offered in a cased set of five shellholders which can create a case that is correct for a +0.002, +0.004, +0.006, +0.008 and +0.010" chamber covering the SAAMI specification for minimum chamber plus 0.010". Since we look for a 0.0015 to 0.002" clearance these increments work out very well.

Unique in their design, they actually have all of the same external dimensions of a standard shellholder. This allows you to change the shoulder position without resetting the die each time, making set up easy. They are polished and blued to quickly differentiate them from standard shellholders with each being engraved with the amount of change its use offers.

Where they differ from standard shellholders is in the depth at which the key seat cut is made. This is the portion of the shellholder on which the case head rests.

By precisely cutting this dimension deeper in the body of the shellholder. we cause the interference of the shellholder with the base of the die to occur at a point where the case is effectively shortened in the die. This interference is how we generate cam over, with all of its positive attributes.

So this means the case cannot travel as far into the die body and the case shoulder is pushed back by a specified lesser amount resulting in a case with the shoulder position longer than that needed to fit the SAAMI minimum chamber for which the die was designed. These shellholders allow us to override the intended design of the dies internals and let us determine the shoulder position with a full cam over.

From our data derived from the fully obturated cases in the Instant Indicator we can determine our start point to make the more perfect full-length resized case. If we have a +0.007chamber fingerprint from our cases per the dial indicator on the properly adjusted Instant Indicator, we would start with the +0.008 Competition Shellholder.

We always should strive to work with the largest number, which will produce a case that freely chambers in the rifle. Set the die up with this shellholder, lube the case, and with a full cam over size the case.

Now clean the sized case and try it in the rifle. As we know cases spring back after firing, the chamber is likely slightly larger or in terms of datum line headspace longer than what we can record from the case. If the case chambers freely we have completed our task. If it does not we simply replace that shellholder with the +0.006". As the external dimensions are the same no additional set up of the die is needed. Now repeat the lube, size, test process and we have a free chambering with the knowledge that we are within 0.002" of the chambers shoulder dimension with a fully resized case allowing longer brass life and a higher degree of accuracy potential.

Proof of Concept

Experiment #1

Process complete and cases sized to the correct dimensions for the chamber in question, but now let's look at the proof of consistency. A good friend and local deputy sheriff provided me with a quantity of once-fired Federal Match .308 brass from their precision marksman unit training. All one lot and all fired from very similar rifles. This will be a good start for our testing to illustrate the flaws in backing out a die to set shoulder position and the need for cam over to gain the level of consistency in shoulder position we desire for our precision hand loads.

The Instant Indicator, T-7 Turret Press and our full-length sizing die speed this testing as we can rotate the turret head to verify datum line on the case after sizing quickly and accurately. I have randomly selected 20 cases for this first test. We will first check the current datum line, choose a point we wish to size to, and then check to see if by backing out the die we

can achieve the desired dimension and do it repeatably using this process. The large dial on the indicator makes photos easy and so the proof will be yours to see.

The average datum line on these cases is +0.008" over the minimum chamber set up gauge. As we are loading these for a personal hunting rifle which we have a datum line dimension for, we want to be -0.002" shorter than max fired case length to assure fast clean cycling for a follow up shot if needed.

So we begin with the first case and starting long, we slowly screw the die down in a series of steps to set the datum. It is accomplished fairly quickly as we can

Dial reading +0.002"

Dial at Zero

rotate the turret head from sizing die to instant indicator and back again after each adjustment. Through a series of cycles we have found the datum, which we have indicated for. At this point we should lock down the die and make one final test to see that the datum line headspace has not moved. This complete, we can move on to additional cases from our lot of the original 20.

Now we will simply quickly size each case as would be done in normal reloading operations by first lubing them and running them through the full-length sizing die. With this complete we will now use the instant indicator to check datum line headspace on each of the cases and they will be indicated on the chart below.

As you can see there is considerable variance in datum line headspace this is a function of the necessary tolerance, which the press and the die must have to

Case Number	Datum Line Dimension	Variance
1	+0.006	Set up no variance
2	+0.003	-0.003
3	+0.004	-0.002
4	+0.002	-0.004
5	+0.004	-0.002
6	+0.004	-0.002
7	+0.003	-0.003
8	0	-0.006
9	+0.002	-0.004
10	+0.004	-0.002
11	+0.003	-0.003
12	+0.002	-0.004
13	+0.004	-0.002
14	+0.004	-0.002
15	+0.004	-0.002
16	+0.005	-0.001
17	+0.004	-0.002
18	+0.002	-0.004
19	0	-0.006
20	+0.003	-0.003

properly operate. While this is a simple test it does prove the fallacy of backing the die out to set the repeatable custom datum line headspace. We may assume that the set-up piece of brass was harder and provided greater resistance to setting back the shoulder since no other cases hit the +0.006" number. We had an average variation of -0.00285" and a standard deviation of -0.00149".

Experiment #2

Now using an additional 20 cases from the same lot as provided for use in the first experiment, we will use Redding competition shell holders to accomplish the same task. We will select the proper show holder as indicated by the stamp on it and insert it into the press. We will lube and size one case, check it on the instant indicator and find that we have in fact selected the proper shoulder for the desired datum line. Using the exact same methodology as we used the first time. The reason for this check is that different cases have different spring back and from lot to lot that variability may affect short position. Of course we have set this show holder up with a sizing die that makes full contact and cam over with its upper surface, thereby eliminating the tolerance inherent in the press and the die threads.

Now we will continue the experiment with the remainder of this lot of 20 cases. Lube and size each one, as we normally would do, but now utilizing the competition shellholder and the full cam over capability of the press. The chart below and readings taken

Case Number	Datum Line Dimension	Variance
1	+0.006	Set up no variance
2	+0.006	0
3	+0.006	0
4	+0.006	0
5	+0.006	0
6	+0.006	0
7	+0.006	0
8	+0.006	0
9	+0.006	0
10	+0.006	0
11	+0.006	0
12	+0.006	0
13	+0.006	0
14	+0.006	0
15	+0.006	0
16	+0.006	0
17	+0.006	0
18	+0.006	0
19	+0.006	0
20	+0.006	0

from the instant indicator show that we have accomplished our task of producing cases with datum line headspace showing very little if any variance. This is shown clearly in the chart above.

While it may seem a bit anti-climactic, the proof coupled with the ease-of-use shows the validity of Redding's concept in creating the competition shell holder system that makes a task that was formerly very difficult simple, effective, fast and highly precise. We had an average variation of -0.000" and a standard deviation of 0.000".

I will be honest and say that the dial indicator may have rubbed the top or bottom of the line but the variance amount did not even warrant attempting to interpolate a plus or minus ½ thousandth of an inch.

+0.008"
Dial reading

AUTHOR BIO:

Robin Sharpless is a lifelong professional in the shooting industry and the current Executive Vice President of Redding Reloading Equipment, one of the most respected brands in handloading equipment.

THREE **SIXES**

By Philip P. Massaro

I was raised in a household where money was tight, but hunting was a part of our family's culture. When a firearm was purchased, it was not a frivolous decision; it had to fill many roles and suffice for many different hunting situations. Hunting in Upstate New York, we certainly had the opportunity for whitetail deer, and black bear in the Catskill and Adirondack Mountains were a bonus.

As a result, I was taught to hunt with a .30-caliber rifle, as that bullet diameter would proficiently handle both species, and I had good success with the .30/30 WCFs, .308 Winchesters and .30-'06s that I either owned or borrowed. Coyotes were virtually non-existent, or better put, we did not have the liberal season for them that we now have. The summer woodchucks were usually dispatched with a .22 Long Rifle, as the thought of a dedicated varmint rifle was out of my financial means.

Although any deviation from .30 caliber was considered blasphemy and would earn you the cold shoulder at summer picnics, I dreamed of other calibers. Many hours poring through reloading manuals revealed that more than just the .30 calibers that I've mentioned could have performed the job we were trying to achieve, though there's no denying that the three I've mentioned are among the classic deer/bear cartridges.

Things have changed these days, and the coyote and fox populations have exploded, to the point where a sportsman who ignores the furbearer seasons is missing much of the valuable time afield. It is also undeniable that the whitetail deer is pursued more than any other game animal on the continent. I can therefore see why a hunter would want a combination deer/varmint rifle, as it will be so useful for the lion's share of hunting here in the Northeast, perfect for the smaller deer

J.D. Fielding Photography

of the South, and flat-shooting enough for the prairie of the West.

Allow me to say that the .30-caliber rifles I've mentioned will always work, but sometimes there are better tools for the job that don't require the heavier bullets and heavier recoil associated with them. I will further say that a 6mm cartridge is just about perfect for that combination of game animals.

Let's take a look at three of them: The uber-popular .243 Winchester, the lesser-known .244 Remington/6mm Remington, and that new kid on the block, the .243 Winchester Super Short Magnum.

The last, although the newest, suffers from the loss of a popularity contest, and I feel that the only way to keep the WSSM alive is via handloading. All of them have their good points and bad points, so let's take a further look at how to use each of them for double-

The .244 Remington left, and the .243 Winchester, right

J.D. Fielding Photography

duty, and the trials and tribulations involved in getting the results we're after.

First a bit of history, so we can get a better grasp of the nature of things. The 6mm bullets have a weight range of 55 grains, up to 115 grains for the heavyweights. This makes for a very useful menu, as the lightest of the bunch can and will generate all kinds of hydraulic shock, in addition to giving a very flat trajectory, making the distant targets (smaller than those of whitetail or antelope) easier to connect with.

Perhaps we should also briefly discuss the cases themselves, so as to have a better grasp on how to handload for them. The .243 Winchester is simply the .308 Winchester, necked down to hold 6mm bullets. It has all the 'inherently accurate' qualities of the .308, and the case capacity makes it perfect for 6mm bullets. It makes a fantastic choice for a short-action rifle.

The .244 Remington/6mm Remington – they are the same cartridge, but more on that later – is based on the classic 7x57 Mauser case, necked down to 6mm,

and, in theory, should offer a considerable advantage over the .243 Winchester.

The .243 WSSM is a severely shortened .300 Winchester Short Magnum (which in turn was derived from the venerable .404 Jeffery), and is a squat fireplug of a cartridge, designed to give very high velocity from a short-action rifle. Each has its own little quirks, and if you're a 6mm fan, I feel those quirks are worth discussing.

The .243 WSSM

Let's start with the newest, and most obscure. The .243 WSSM was Winchester's attempt to get maximum velocities from a short-action rifle, and (in theory) it worked. I have always had a major issue with both the WSM and WSSM cartridges: the way they feed. In a rifle that is even remotely finicky, feeding can become a nightmare. But, if you have a rifle that feeds well, like our Browning A-Bolt test rifle, the cartridges make a neat choice.

Yes, they look a little radical, or should I say stumpy, but the velocities are certainly delivered in a small package. The design is far from what I'd call 'classic', but I'm of the age where I am coming to terms with embracing new and radical designs.

I decided, for this piece, to mate the .243 WSSM with a pair of newer bullets from a newer company: The 55-grain Cutting Edge Raptor and the 88-grain Cutting Edge Match/Tactical/Hunting. These Cutting Edge Bullets are a horse of a different color; they are all-copper hollowpoints, and upon impact the ogive of the bullet breaks in to little 'blades', causing all sorts of impact trauma, while the 'blunt trauma base' remains at caliber dimension and drives deep into, if not fully through, the animal's vital organs.

These bullets have performed flawlessly in the safari calibers, but the timing of this piece precludes me from being able to test the 6mm bullets in the hunting fields. I have no doubt that they will deliver the goods.

For a powder, I chose IMR4350 for both bullets, because it is on the slow end of the burn rate spectrum for the lighter bullets, and on the faster end of the spectrum with the heavier bullets. I've had very good luck with the 6mm cartridges with powders in the IMR4350/Reloder-19/H414 range, as they will give good velocities and little deviation in pressure. I had some once-fired Winchester nickel plated cases, Federal GM210M primers, and a good set of RCBS dies.

The .243 WSSM and its short, fat case, loaded with the 55-grain Cutting Edge Raptor

J.D. Fielding Photography

243 WSSM and 88-grain Cutting Edge MTH.

After trying several charge weights, the load that gave the best accuracy with the 55-grain Raptors was 49.5 grains of IMR4350, set at a C.O.L. of 2.350", just behind the first groove on the bullet shank. Many times, these monometal bullets will show that they are very sensitive to seating depth, not liking a whole lot of bullet jump. I set these bullets out as far as the Browning's magazine would handle them, and that worked fine.

Even with a pencil-thin barrel that heats up in a hurry, three of those Cutting Edge Raptors printed a group measuring under an inch at the 100-yard mark. The Oehler 35P chronograph spat out a receipt showing an average velocity of 3,710 fps; giving a trajectory flat enough to hit any target within sane shooting distances, with enough energy to create the 'red mist' that the varmint cartridges are famous for.

The 88-grain MTH bullet would serve the big game hunter well in any of the 6mms. Unlike the Raptor, it has smooth sides, lacking the grooves, but instead uses a driving band to best seal the gases, and at 88 grains is as long as some of the 100+ grain bullets.

.244 Remington, left and its parent, the venerable 7x57 Mauser.

This bullet liked a load of 42.5 grains of IMR4350, again with the Federal GM210M primer (for some reason, although heavy, most loads for the .243 WSSM shun the magnum primers), set to a depth of 2.330", with the case mouth just behind the driving band.

Velocities averaged 3,210 fps, and group size was just over an inch. Again, we had a pencil-thin barrel that showed heat rather quickly, but cool shots, spread out over time, tightened things up. I firmly believe that this pair of bullets will readily handle any game you'd use a 6mm bore to hunt. I can easily see this combination working very well for pronghorn antelope and whitetail deer, as well as coyotes in a very windy situation.

I also tried one of the old standby bullets in the .243 WSSM. The Nosler Partition has long been relied upon to give hunters the performance they desire. The 95-grain 6mm Partition we loaded worked wonders in the .243 WSSM over top of a load of 46 ½ grains of Hodgdon's RETUMBO, set to a COL of 2.270". The chrony showed us muzzle velocities averaging 3,260 fps – a load that would handle the largest deer the Lord has ever put on earth.

The .244 Remington, better known as the 6mm Remington.

Noted cartridge guru Fred Huntington designed the .243 Rockchucker wildcat in the early '50s, with visions of the ultimate predator cartridge in mind. Mr. H took the wonderful .257 Roberts case as a starting point, and necked it down to hold 6mm bullets, using a 32-degree shoulder angle.

The cartridge did exactly what it was asked to do: the 75-grain and 90-grain bullets made short work of the largest of the furbearers, and was absolute hell on ground hogs and prairie dogs. Remington legitimized the cartridge, but using a 26-degree shoulder on the same case platform, releasing the .244 Remington.

All was well in the Remington camp. Until, that is, the shooting world realized how well the equally new-fangled .243 Winchester could push the 100 and 105-grain bullets. You see, the standard-issue Remington barrel in the Model 722 had a 1:12" twist rate, while the .243 Winchester used a 1:10". This prevented the .244 from stabilizing bullets heavier than 90 grains. None of this would be a big deal, except for the fact that hunters quickly picked up on the fact that the 100+ grain 6mm bullets from the .243 Winchester worked very well on big game, and the 75 and 90-grain bullets loaded in the .244 left a bit to be desired when it came

I even have a set of period specific RCBS dies in .244 Remington!

J.D. Fielding Photography

to deer and bear-sized game.

Twist rate killed another cartridge, and spurned countless campfire debates. But gun marketing is as fickle as the marketing in any other industry, and once the rot was in it was nearly impossible to fix it.

When comparing the cases, the .244, being the spawn of the 7x57 Mauser, has a slight advantage in powder capacity advantage over the .308-based .243 Winchester, and therefore a slight velocity advantage.

On all planes, the .244, when barreled with a 1:10" or 1:9" twist rate, should've won the 6mm popularity contest, and that's exactly what Remington was banking on in 1963. Big Green renamed the .244, giving it the alias of 6mm Remington, and changing the twist rate to an appropriate 1:9", but alas it was too late. The .243 Winchester had become the apple of many hunters' eyes, and had the firmest of footholds.

Now, for the owner of a modern 6mm Remington, the full range of modern bullets can be utilized with-

out much trouble, and there are some good ones out there. But it just so happens that Mr. Martin Groppi, whose work you'll be reading in another part of this tome, owns a 1958 Remington Model 722, chambered in nothing other than .244 Remington. He needed a load for this particular rifle, something that would agree with that tighter twist rate, so we chose some of the more potent, yet lighter bullets.

The 55- grain Cutting Edge ESP Raptor, which worked so well in the .243 WSSM, showed wonderful potential in the .244 Remington. Hornady's 65-grain V-Max was a logical choice for the coyotes that haunt our New York woods.

It was the Cutting Edge 77-grain Match/Tactical/ Hunting bullet that really piqued my curiosity, as this bullet would satisfy all the hunting requirements anyone could place on the vintage .244 Remington.

The 55-grain CEB gave us best accuracy when using a full-house load of 46.0 grains of VARGET,

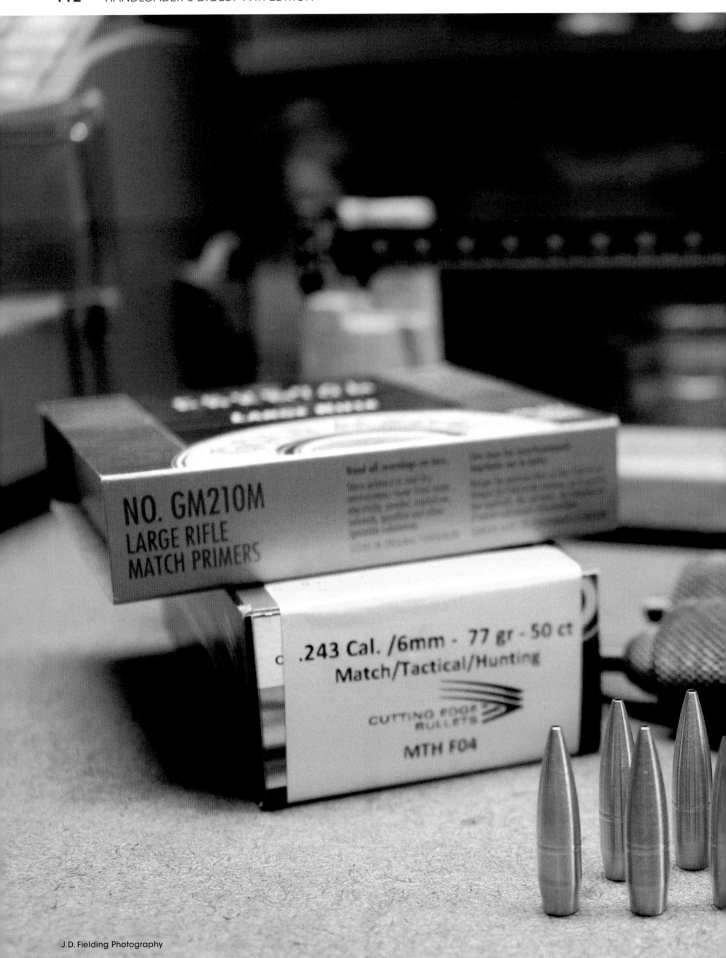

The 77-grain Cutting Edge Bullets MTH, propelled by Hodgdon's VARGET powder gave the best results in our rifle.

with the polymer tip inserted, sparked by a Federal GM210M primer and seated to a COL of 2.830" gave 3,875 fps, and sub-MOA accuracy. If you're serious about hunting fur, those same 55-grain ESP Raptors can be turned around and loaded as a solid, having the same nose profile (BBW#13), and will do very little damage to the pelt.

The 65-grain V-Max, seated over a charge of 49.0 grains of H4831SC and a CCI 200 primer gave 3,525 fps and will absolutely smoke the largest coyote ever born, out to any sane distance.

The 77-grain CEB MTH bullet was the best of the lot, giving the best accuracy and the lowest standard deviation on velocity. We cobbled together the following load: R-P cases, 40.0 grains of VARGET over a Federal GM210M primer, giving 3,340 fps on the chrony and ½ MOA at 100 yards. This combination will get the nod for deer season this fall.

Irrespective of bullet weight, the modern construction of these bullets enable the hunter suffering from a twist rate handicap to confidently hunt any animal worthy of a 6mm rifle. When it comes to the .244 Remington, bullet construction trumps 10-20 grains of extra weight, in modern bullets.

The .243 Winchester

The .308 saw the light of day in 1952, and while the gun writers were obsessed with the comparisons between it and the .30-'06 Springfield, the wildcatters immediately headed to their respective laboratories, and the tinkering began.

Three years later, in 1955, the world was introduced to the .243 Winchester. The .308 has been necked up and down in bullet diameters from 6mm up to .358", but the .243 Winchester has proven to be the most successful of the offspring. It will, in reality, come so close to the performance of the .244/6mm Remington that game animals most likely won't be able to tell the difference. In my experiences, the .243 Winchester is easier to load for, and has that nagging 'inherent accuracy' thing that the .308 possesses.

I have found that the .243 makes a great deer round when using a cup-and-core bullet of 100 or 105 grains, or one of the monometals weighing 85 to 90 grains.

Matter of fact, I killed my biggest whitetail, a very tall seven-point Texas buck, with a .243 and a factory Federal Trophy Bonded 85-grain all-copper bullet, and killed him very dead. The .243 is, in my opinion,

The 77-grain Cutting Edge MTH, perfect for the slow twist rate of the .244 Remington.

J.D. Fielding Photography

much like the 6.5mm cartridges, in that it kills much better than the paper ballistics would suggest.

My handloading experiences with the .243 have usually been centered around the heavier cup-and-core bullets, which work so well on our bigger-bodied whitetails here in New York.

I have had great success loading the Hornady 100-grain boattail spire point, over a charge of 43.6 grains of Alliant's Reloder-19, sparked by a CCI 200 large rifle primer. Velocities run at 2,925 fps at the muzzle, and accuracy was less than MOA. This combination has accounted for many deer, and based on the bullet performance, I might even venture to say that this load might handle black bear, but I'd still maintain that there are better tools for that job.

For a modern update of the .243 Winchester, we got the 85-grain Barnes TSX to shoot well over a load of 53.0 grains of Accurate's Mag Pro powder, giving 3,310 fps and ¾" groups at 100 yards, and that would handle all sorts of big game.

Berger's 105-grain VLD made, what I feel to be, a fantastic long range load in the .243 Winchester. This sleek bullet, with its long boattail and slowly tapering ogive, shot best when coupled with 43 ½ grains of Reloder 22, with a Federal GM210M primer.

I seated these bullets a bit longer than the SAAMI maximum length, but at 2.700" there were no problems feeding them through the magazine. At 2,825 fps, they should have no problems bucking the wind for those shots out past 250 yards. Group size was routinely ¾ MOA.

The 100-grain Speer Grand Slam gave decent accuracy with my older load of 43.6 grains of Reloder 19, but worked much better over 44.0 grains of Hodgdon's H4831SC, still sparked by the Federal GM210M primer.

At 100 yards, three-shot groups averaged 7/8", and the flat-base bullets were happily cruising along at 2,940 fps. This would make really nice woods load for whitetail deer.

I hope you're looking at the 6mm cartridges in a new light, As handloaders, we can take full advantage

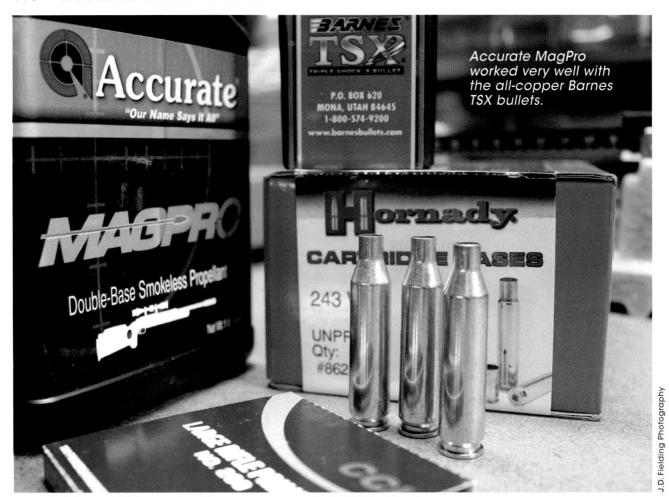

Accurate MagPro worked very well with the all-copper Barnes TSX bullets.

Hornady Interlock 100-grain boat tail spire point has worked well for years.

Above: The 105-grain Berger VLD is a nasty bullet!

Right: The 100-grain Speer Grand Slam flat base makes a good choice for a woods bullet.

of some of the newer, innovative bullet designs available today, as well as rely on some of the older, industry standard bullets that have proven themselves over the years.

With the ability to handload so many different bullets, we can take a bore diameter that already gave quite a bit of flexibility and really make it shine.

AUTHOR BIO:

Philip P. Massaro is the President of Massaro Ballistic Laboratories, LLC, a custom ammunition company, comfortably nestled in between the Hudson River and Catskill Mountains of Upstate New York. He has been a handloader for 20+ years, a veteran of five African safaris and dozens of North American hunts. He is a Licensed Professional Land Surveyor by trade, a musician by choice, and usually reeks of Hoppes No. 9.

PARENT CASES &
POWER POTENTIAL

By Andrew Chamberlain

For many of us in North America, our shooting and hunting world revolves around five to eight primary cartridges. We readily use these as a reference to new cartridges that enter into our world. We might be aware of another eight to 10 cartridges, but they are outliers with perceived levels of performance that render them impractical for our personal requirements. One might describe these outlying cartridges as "So light and so fast it's like shooting a laser. But it will disintegrate in the rain!" Another could be "That thing throws so much lead it kills on both ends! It might as well be an anti-tank cannon."

In North America we have access to over 200 standardized, mass-produced rifle cartridges. When I illustrate this fact with the American Standard Cartridge Poster (which displays every standardized rifle, handgun and shotgun cartridges mass produced in the U.S.A, full color & life size), many people exclaim, "I had no idea that many existed!"

For many, getting their head around the 200-plus cartridges (over 500 if you consider European-Metric and SAAMI-Proprietary cartridges) can seem to be mission impossible. The difficulty can intensify when one considers the tens, if not hundreds, of unique loadings available for every cartridge.

However, in the next few paragraphs I will explain a few simple concepts that, when understood, will show you how to simplify the masses of cartridges. The key is to understand the fundamentals of parent cases, and the inherent power potential governed by a parent case. This will help you place any cartridge into an orderly, easily understood and easily organized array of cartridge groupings.

In my work as an author and lecturer (as well as a hunter, conservationist and outdoorsman), I have studied, shot, reloaded, hunted with, made comparisons of, documented, and written about the vast world

of cartridges. I should point out that any particular cartridge is typically loaded with anywhere from four to 20 different bullet weights. And these bullet weights are loaded with very distinct velocities from one manufacturer or handload source to the next.

For example, the 30-06 Springfield can be loaded with at least 19 unique bullet weights that span from 100 grains to 220 grains. Furthermore, within one bullet weight group, the velocity can vary as widely as 100 to 300 fps depending on the source. That amount of variability can make the vastness of cartridges exhaustive, which is why I wrote "The Cartridge Comparison Guide the ultimate hunting and ballistics manual" to clearly and simply categorize cartridges and their ballistic potential. It displays the best loads for each bullet weight available to each cartridge. It then compares that cartridge against any other with a comparable characteristic.

AUTHOR BIO:

Andrew Chamberlain is known as a ballistics expert but prefers to be called a Ballistics Enthusiast. He has published three books and has written many articles for hunting magazines and blogs. He has produced ten unique cartridge posters. Each one features life-sized images of cartridges that pertain to a specific theme. Professionally Andrew has earned a Bachelor of Science/Engineering degree as well as a Project Management Professional (PMP) certification and is a Board Member of P.O.M.A. (Professional Outdoor Media Association). Andrew grew up in a small town, working, taking care of animals, hunting, fishing, and camping. He loves all things American especially the ability to feed one's self and family.

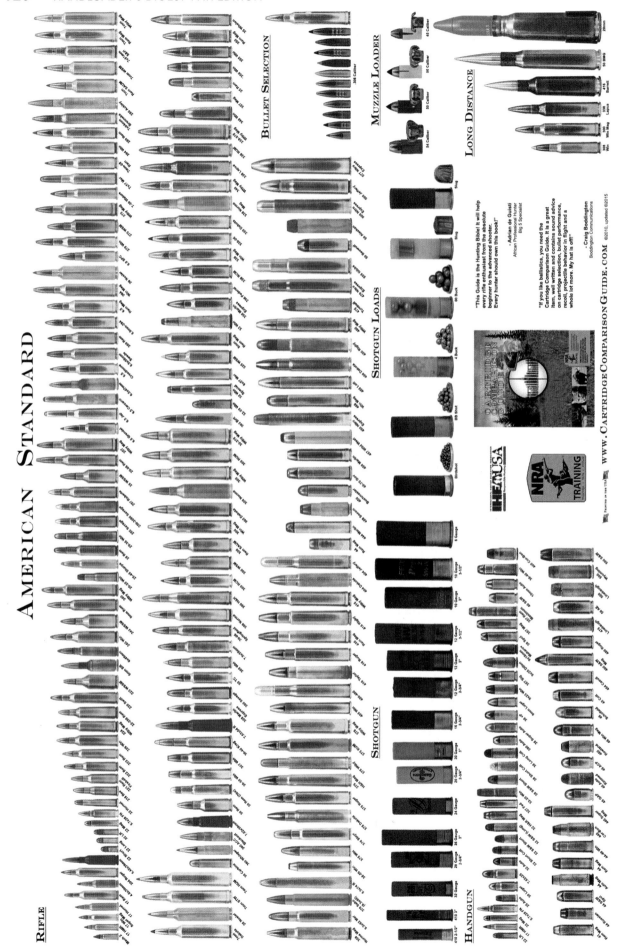

AMERICAN STANDARD

RIFLE

BULLET SELECTION

MUZZLE LOADER

LONG DISTANCE

SHOTGUN LOADS

SHOTGUN

HANDGUN

WWW.CARTRIDGECOMPARISONGUIDE.COM

Oftentimes in an effort to understand or categorize how one cartridge might compare against another (but only adding to the confusion), people will present two cartridges and ask "Which is better?" They are asking which cartridge is better but only considering one load from each. For instance, many people ask, "Which is better, a 30-06 Springfield or a .270 Winchester?"

I usually tell them that the .270 is based on the 30-06, but the 270 is 0.046 inches longer. They look at me confused. (The mechanics of the 270 vs. 30-06 question, and others, will be answered as this discussion continues.)

I gave the example of the 30-06 load variations and the 270 vs. 30-06 comparison to present the idea that understanding the concept of *Parent Case* and its *Power Potential* is a very powerful tool. It allows you to take the vastness of all the loads available to a particular cartridge and condense them down into three sub categories: Max Velocity, Max Energy, and Max Power (a combination of maximum momentum & maximum Energy).

These three categories combine to describe what I call the cartridge's power potential. Therefore, understanding which loads in a particular cartridge produce the maximum velocity, maximum energy, and maximum power is the key to understanding Power Potential.

Understanding power potential is the fundamental first step to understanding and simplifying the world of cartridges. The next step is to understand how power potential is affected, as well as limited, when that same case (or parent case) is manipulated to propel projectiles that are either smaller in caliber and inherently lighter, or larger in caliber and inherently heavier.

A parent case is exactly what it sounds like; it is the original & unique case from which new cartridges are built. For example the 30-06 Springfield is one of the earliest mass-

270 Win   30-06 Springfield

30-06 PARENT CASE

25-06 Rem   270 Win   280 Rem   30-06 Springfield   338-06   35 Whelen

produced big game cartridges. The 30-06 Springfield is also the parent case for many popular hunting cartridges. A small sampling of these include the: 25-06 Remington, 270 Winchester, 280 Remington, 338-06, and 35 Whelen.

A given cartridge has a perceived range of capabilities (or perceived power potential). New cartridges can be built from the existing cartridge to accomplish a new set of capabilities. This is done by simply changing one or more of the case's three main physical characteristics. These are: 1-the neck diameter, 2-the case length, and 3-the shoulder height & angle. A fourth could be body taper, but that is much less common than the first three.

1. Neck Diameter: Reducing the neck diameter allows the cartridge to fire a smaller caliber bullet. Enlarging the neck diameter allows it to fire a larger caliber bullet. Manipulating the neck diameter tends to either increase bullet velocity or increase overall power potential (*not both*)

2. Case Length: Lengthening a parent case increases its powder capacity and increases its overall power potential. Shortening a case provides a smaller powder charge. This reduces recoil and overall power potential. But this can also increase powder efficiency. Manipulating the length of the parent case usually occurs in the draw process (when mechanically forming the case from a piece of brass). New improved powders occasionally allow a new cartridge to use a smaller case capacity and maintain a similar power potential as an older established cartridge that has a noticeably larger case capacity.

3. Shoulder: Manipulating the shoulder height and its angle can change how the burning powder builds pressure in the cartridge. This manipulates how the bullet is propelled out the barrel. "Improved" shoulders can increase velocity, powder charge, and overall power potential.

The power potential of a parent case is governed by the fact that it has a fixed maximum powder load. As discussed above, power potential can be utilized to maximize velocity by propelling a lighter projectile. Or this power potential can be utilized to maximize energy & momentum by propelling a heavier and or larger caliber bullet.

Let us explain this in a bit more detail. As gunpowder burns it produces gas pressure within the barrel. When the barrel is built, its metal has specific yield strength. Therefore a maximum threshold of gas pressure is set. This maximum pressure and the powder charge controls power potential.

Two basic equations describing the gas pressure and power potential relationship are; PxA=F & F=MxA.

PxA=F (Gas Pressure multiplied by the bullet's cross sectional Area equals the Force applied to the bullet) & F=MxA (the sum of all Forces equals the Mass of the bullet multiplied by its Acceleration).

So with a relative maximum peak gas pressure, the primary variable in force is the area (or caliber) of the bullet. When a larger-caliber bullet is used in a parent case, the maximum pressure is applied to a larger area. This yields a greater force. BUT, as the caliber gets bigger, the mass of the bullet tends to increase. As mass goes up acceleration goes down. As mass goes down acceleration tends to go up. If caliber goes up, but mass maintains the same, acceleration also tends to go up.

Understanding the mechanics of the force equation is important. (Powder burn rate and pressure curve is also very important. But PxA=F & F = MxA is generally the primary controlling factor, especially if similar powders are used.)

To give an example of parent case and power potential, let's look at the .270 Win. and 338-06. Both are based on the 30-06 but the .270 Win. is smaller in caliber and the 338-06 is larger in caliber.

The 30-06 can push a 180-grain projectile (bullet) at a velocity of 2,880 ft/sec, producing 3,314 ft-lbs of energy & 74.1 lbs-ft/sec of momentum.

A .270 Winchester can push a 150-grain bullet at 2,950 ft/sec, delivery 2,898 ft-lbs of energy & 63.2 lbs-ft/sec of momentum. It can also push a 130-grain bullet at 3,200 ft/sec delivering 2,955 ft-lbs energy & 59.4 lbs-ft/sec momentum.

A 338-06 pushes a 180-grain bullet at 2,950 ft/sec delivering 3,477 ft-lbs energy &76 lbs-ft/sec momentum. It can also push a 250-grain bullet at 2,600 ft/sec delivering 3,752 ft-lbs energy and 93 lbs-ft/sec momentum. As caliber gets smaller and bullet weight decreases, velocity increases. But in contrast as caliber and bullet weight increases, energy and momentum also increase. This example illustrates PxA=F & F=MxA, Power potential & Parent Case.

We have just illustrated how parent case and power potential tie together. It shows how understanding one parent case, and the group of cartridges built from it, can simplify and categorize a certain amount of cartridges. Now, if the right progression of parent cases is chosen, they will form an outline. It will outline a minimum to maximum power potential, with enough granularity to accommodate the hundreds of cartridges the world has to offer. I propose this can be done by using just eight parent cases, their power potentials, and that of the cartridges built from them.

The proposed eight parent cases are: 223 Remington (222 Remington Magnum), 30-30 Winchester, 308 Winchester, 30-06 Springfield, 300 Winchester Magnum (300 Holland & Holland Magnum), 300 Remington Ultra Magnum, 404 Jeffery, and 378 Weatherby Magnum.

For clarity and accuracy of this list, the 222 Remington Magnum is actually the parent case of the 223 Remington, but most will recognize the 223 Remington much more easily. So for ease of recognizing these parent case groupings and their power potential

5-8 PRIMARY CARTRIDGES

8-10 REFERENCE CARTRIDGES

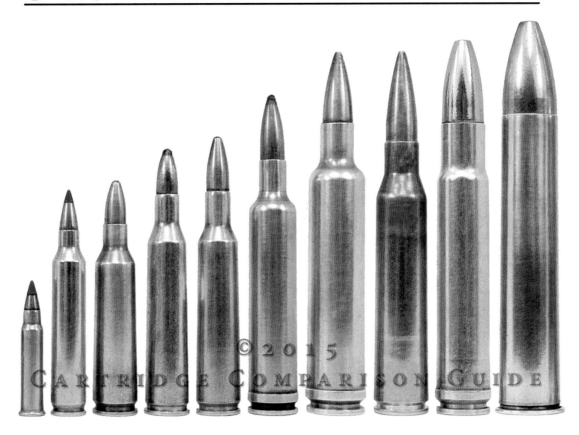

grouping (the purposes of this narrative), this group will be referred to as the 223 Rem group. The same is true for the 300 H&H (Holland & Holland) Magnum. It is the parent case of the 300 Winchester Magnum and all standard belted magnum cases. But most will identify with the 300 Winchester Magnum and not the 300 H&H Magnum.

Additionally, some will argue that because the 308 Winchester was created from the 30-06 Springfield all cartridges built from the 308 Winchester are really built from a shortened 30-06 Springfield. But for simplicity and clarity of recognition we will call the 308 Winchester a parent case and the 30-06 a parent case.

Now using this list of 8 parent cases, we can quickly produce a list of recognizable cartridges that are formed from these cases. These cartridges are as follows:

223 Remington; 17 Remington, 204 Ruger, 221 Rem Fireball, 222 Remington, 6x45mm, 25x45 Sharps, 300 ACC Blackout.

30-30 Winchester; 7-30 Waters, 32 Win Special, 356 Winchester, 375 Winchester. (219 Zipper - based on 25-35 WCF very similar to the 30-30 Win)

308 Winchester; 22-250, 243 Winchester, 250 Savage, 260 Remington, 7mm-08, 300 Savage, 338 Federal, 35 Remington, 358 Winchester.

30-06 Springfield; 25-06 Remington, 270 Winchester, 280 Remington, 280 Remington Ackley Improved, 338-06, 35 Whelen. (22-06), (6mm-06 or 240 Hawk), (6.5-06 or 264 Hawk), (8mm-06 or 3200 Hawk), (9.3mm Hawk), (375 Hawk/Skovill), (411 Hawk).

300 Win Mag (Belted Magnums); 257 Weatherby Magnum, 6.5 Remington Magnum, 264 Winchester Magnum, 270 Weatherby Magnum, 7mm Remington Magnum, 7mm Weatherby Magnum, 7mm STW (Shooting Times Westerner), 300 H&H Magnum, 308 Norma Magnum, 300 Winchester Magnum, 300 Weatherby Magnum, 8mm Remington Magnum, 338 Winchester Magnum, 340 Weatherby Magnum, 350 Remington Magnum, 358 Norma Magnum, 376 Steyr, 375 H&H Magnum, 375 Weatherby Magnum, 416 Taylor, 416 Remington Magnum, 450 Marlin, 458 Win Magnum, 458 Lott, (470 Capstick).

404 Jeffery; 26 Nosler, 7mm Dakota, 28 Nosler, 300 Dakota, 330 Dakota, 375 Ruger, 375 Dakota, 416 Ruger, 404 Dakota, 450 Dakota.

300 R.U.M. (Remington Ultra Magnum); 7mm R.U.M., 300 R.U.M., 338 R.U.M., 375 R.U.M. (416 UltraCat), (458 UltraCat)

378 Weatherby Magnum; 30-378 Weatherby Magnum, 338-378 Weatherby Magnum, 378 Weatherby Magnum, 416 Weatherby Magnum, 460 Weatherby Magnum, (500 A-Square).

(Cartridge names in parenthesis are proprietary or custom cartridges of that parent case grouping. *Hawk and UltraCat cartridges are a product of Z-Hat customs Inc.)

These eight parent cases, and the cartridges built from them, create a very useful outline under which the remainder of the cartridges can be organized.

It is worth noting that because of relative power potential I have omitted the Winchester Super Short Magnums (WSSM), the Winchester Short Magnums (WSM), the Remington Short Action Ultra Magnums (RSAUM) and the Ruger Compact Magnums (RCM) from the parent case list. This is because these cartridges produce a similar power potential to their traditional cartridge counterparts. This streamlines the discussion and further supports the eight parent case outline.

There are other cartridges like the 6mm Navy, 7x57 Mauser, 416 Rigby, 45-70 Government, even the 22 LR, 22 Magnum, and several others that could be considered important parent cases. These have also been omitted from the list of eight parent cases because they (and their few offspring) fall into the granularity of power potential listed by the eight traditional cases. Again, because of power potential and in interest of keeping a streamlined list, these cartridges can be placed within the outline of these eight parent cases.

Now that I have explained my logic (and bias) for choosing these eight parent cases, let me show ballistic data that supports these choices. First, let us pick a caliber that is common to all 8 parent cases. By examining a common caliber cartridge from each parent case, we can more easily see the increasing power potential (the granularity) in the parent cases. It appears that .30 caliber is the only/best common cartridge in all eight parent cases. (The 300 ACC Blackout represents the 223 Remington Parent case and the 300 Dakota represents the 404 Jeffery Parent case. The others carry the name of their parent case.) Notice the ascending order of power potential (bullet: weight, velocity, energy and momentum).

COMMON CALIBER
PARENT CASE

300 ACC Blackout:	125 grains, vel = 2,215 ft/sec, energy =1,361 ft-lbs & 39.6 lbs-ft/sec momentum
30-30 Winchester :	150 grains, vel = 2,390 ft/sec, energy =1,900 ft-lbs & 51.2 lbs-ft/sec momentum
308 Winchester:	168 grains, vel = 2,700 ft/sec, energy =2,720 ft-lbs & 64.8 lbs-ft/sec momentum
30-06 Springfield:	180 grains, vel = 2,850 ft/sec, energy =3,315 ft-lbs & 74.1 lbs-ft/sec momentum
300 Winchester:	180 grains, vel = 3,130 ft/sec, energy =3,914 ft-lbs & 80.5 lbs-ft/sec momentum
300 Dakota:	180 grains, vel = 3,100 ft/sec, energy =3,840 ft-lbs & 79.7 lbs-ft/sec momentum
300 R.U.M.:	180 grains, vel = 3,250 ft/sec, energy =4,220 ft-lbs & 83.6 lbs-ft/sec momentum
30-378 Weatherby:	180 grains, vel = 3,420 ft/sec, energy =4,674 ft-lbs & 87.9 lbs-ft/sec momentum

Using a common caliber one can quickly see the granularity and increasing order of power potential. This establishes a framework that other cartridges can quickly and cleanly fit into.

We can now use this same method to look at specific categories within Power Potential. Let's look at Velocity Potential. This will remove the constraint of a common caliber or common bullet weight. The Velocity Potential shows how cartridges formed from a parent case can maximize bullet velocity (ft/sec). It also illustrates that particular cartridge's bullet weight (grains) and the resulting bullet energy (ft-lbs).

MAX VELOCITY
PARENT CASE

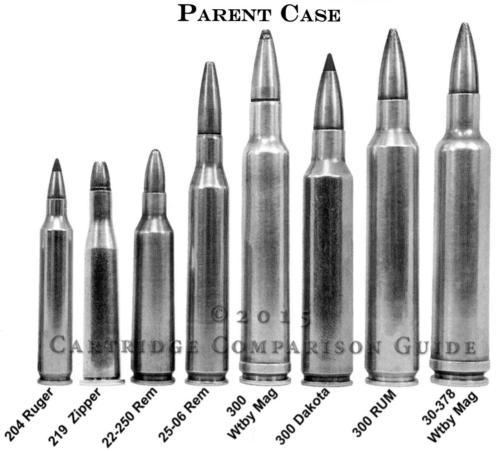

204 Ruger (from 223 Rem):	24 grains @ 4,400 ft/sec, energy =1,031 ft-lbs
219 Zipper (from 30-30 Win):	50 grains @ 3,500 ft/sec, energy =1,360 ft-lbs
22-250 Rem (from 308 Win):	36 grains @ 4,420 ft/sec, energy =1,561 ft-lbs
25-06 Rem (from 30-06):	75 grains @ 3,700 ft/sec, energy =2,279 ft-lbs
300 Weatherby (from Belted Mag):	110 grains @ 3,900 ft/sec, energy =3,714 ft-lbs
300 Dakota (from 404 Jeffery):	110 grains @ 3,800 ft/sec energy =3,526 ft-lbs
300 Rem Ultra Mag (from R.U.M.):	110 grains @ 3,900 ft/sec energy =3,714 ft-lbs
30-378 Weatherby (378 Weatherby):	125 grains @ 3,835 ft/sec energy =4,084 ft-lbs

This shows that reducing the neck diameter of a parent case to propel a smaller caliber or simply using a lighter bullet can significantly increase velocity. However, the resulting velocity and energy may not be what one expects. Also, not all parent cases are necked down to the same minimum caliber. Nor are they loaded with identical bullet weights, nor do they include the same assortment of calibers.

Now let's look at Maximum Power Potential. This will remove any constraint of caliber or velocity. This will show the raw granularity of power (energy & momen-

tum) as we progress through the cartridges formed from a parent case. Seeing Max Power Potential alongside of Velocity Potential and Common Caliber power potential will very clearly illustrate why these eight parent cases and the cartridges formed from them set such an effective outline with which all the other cartridges can be organized.

These eight parent cases set a progressive scale within the framework of power potential. These eight (and the cartridges built from them) provide baseline reference points as caliber increases or decreases. This scale and its

MAX POWER
PARENT CASE

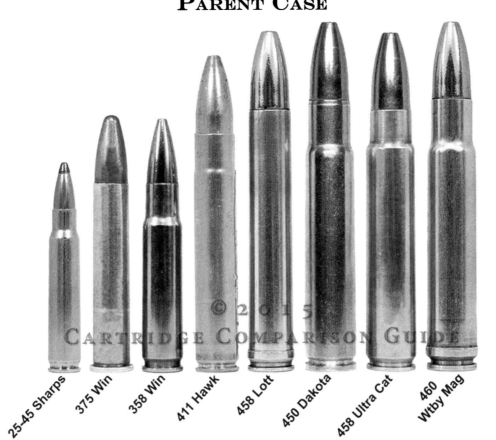

25x45 Sharps (223):	87 grains, vel = 3,000 ft/sec, energy =1,738 ft-lbs & 37.3 lbs-ft/sec momentum
375 Win (30-30 Win):	220 grains, vel = 2,300 ft/sec, energy =2,584 ft-lbs & 72.3 lbs-ft/sec momentum
358 Win (308 Win):	250 grains, vel = 2,330 ft/sec, energy =3,013 ft-lbs & 83.2 lbs-ft/sec momentum
411 Hawk (30-06):	350 grains, vel = 2,415 ft/sec, energy =4,532 ft-lbs & 120.8 lbs-ft/sec momentum
458 Lott (Belted Mag):	500 grains, vel = 2,300 ft/sec, energy =5,872 ft-lbs & 164.3 lbs-ft/sec momentum
450 Dakota (404 Jeff):	500 grains, vel = 2,450 ft/sec, energy =6,662 ft-lbs & 175.0 lbs-ft/sec momentum
458 UltraCat (R.U.M.):	500 grains, vel = 2,500 ft/sec, energy =6,938 ft-lbs & 178.6 lbs-ft/sec momentum
460 Weatherby Mag:	500 grains, vel = 2,600 ft/sec, energy =7,503 ft-lbs & 185.7 lbs-ft/sec momentum

reference points can position any cartridge within a relative threshold of Power Potential.

This allows you to consider the power potential of any cartridge the world has to offer. You simply need to consider which parent case it comes from and how that case sits among the eight listed here. You can then estimate where a cartridge should fit (within, above or below) in this framework. Then, if you wish, you can find enough ballistics data to fine tune where the cartridge actually falls in reference to any other cartridge. (This is one reason the Cartridge Comparison Guide was written).

Understanding Parent Case & Power Potential and how this affects cartridges formed from a parent case allows you to quickly sort and organize any cartridge in the world. There may be hundreds of cartridges and literally thousands of unique loads available to us as sportsmen and shooters. But by utilizing parent case and their inherent power potential (PxA=F & F=MxA) you can identify how these cartridges compare and which particular cartridge provides that special niche that will make it a best fit for your hunting or shooting needs. Be safe, shoot straight!

SHOTGUN RELOADING

By Dave deMoulpied

I was asked by my good friend Phil Massaro to write this chapter on basic shotshell reloading to appeal to the person who's thinking about getting into this type of reloading, but doesn't know what goes on "behind the curtain" so to speak. As I sat down to write this, I pondered the obvious question, why reload shot shells at all?? I mean with 12-gauge reloads, you are saving less than a buck per box of 25 shells.

If you're shooting some of the less popular sizes such as 28-gauge and .410, then I understand that. Availability for those two can be hit or miss. Also it's pretty economical to make those yourself. The answer is, it comes down to control. I want to control the quality of the shells produced, and the quality of the components that go into them.

And if that may seem a little odd to some, think about this: There is a huge market for premium rifle projectiles right now. A lot of whitetail deer hunters, myself included, are spending a lot of money and a lot of time developing loads for these premium bullets that will not only penetrate a deer from stem to stern, but hammer bears and some large African critters as well in their "made for deer" configuration.

I'll bet you that more deer have been killed with old cup-and-core bullets than with all of these newer bullets put together. But for some reason, I can't bring myself to buy off-the-shelf cartridges, the vanilla-grade ammo that my father and his generation hunted with (with great success I might add). It's the whole "what if" question that drives reloaders such as myself to have as much say in what comes out of their barrels.

With that being said, remember this: everyone who loads their own ammo has an opinion; and usually a strong one. What I will be discussing in this chapter is based on my own experience; my likes and

dislikes. To you newer reloaders, experiment with the published data, and find out what works for you, and what shoots well out of your shotgun.

So let's break down a shot shell, look at its components and talk about each of them.

Hulls

The quality of the shotshell hulls you start with will dictate how many times you can reload them. Don't skimp on these! My two favorite hulls are the Remington STS and the venerable Winchester AA. I have been able to get up to 10 reloads out of the STS, but that's pushing the envelope. There are basically two things to make hulls "go bad": The first is cracking of the hull walls, the other is the inability to get a good tight crimp on a finished shell. It is very important to visually inspect each of the hulls before putting them into your reloading queue. It doesn't take long, and it

will save you headaches when pellets start falling out of an open, poorly crimped shell. I know, I've done it myself.

If you're just starting out, you have a few options in obtaining your hulls. You can buy brand new, or save a few dollars and buy once-fired hulls. I've found at the sporting clays club I shoot at they have huge clear garbage bags of empty hulls they've picked up around the course. They give these bags away for free. So if you are watching your pennies, you could easily pickup a few boxes of once-fired shells for nada. Just remember to stick with the hulls I mentioned earlier.

Powder

Veteran reloaders have their favorite powder, or powders that they use based on experience. As someone new to this endeavor, choosing a powder can be overwhelming! Alliant, for example, offers 14 different powder choices for shotshell reloading alone! It behooves you to go online to Alliant or Hodgkin's websites, and go through their online loading data. I really like the look of Alliant's 2015 Reloader's Guide. Load data is up to date and very well laid out for the novice or expert alike.

More empty hulls ready for reloading.

LET'S LOOK INSIDE A SHOTSHELL...

CRIMP
Seats all components tightly inside the hull. May be 6 or 8 point.

SHOT
Comes in a variety of sizes for different shooting situations.

HULL
The outer case that holds the components. May be plastic or paper.

SHOT CUP
Plastic cup holds shot in the pattern as it leaves gun muzzle.

WAD
Confines powder for uniform ignition and separates powder from shot. (Most commonly used is a combination shot cup and wad — called a "wad column.")

POWDER CHARGE
When ignited by primer powder charge burning at a controlled rate generates gas pressure which with the aid of a wad column propels shot out of gun barrel.

BASE
Holds primer and securely anchors shell in gun breech. May be brass or steel.

PRIMER
Gun firing pin detonates component in primer, which ignites main powder charge.

PRIMER POCKET
Opening in metal base into which primer is inserted.

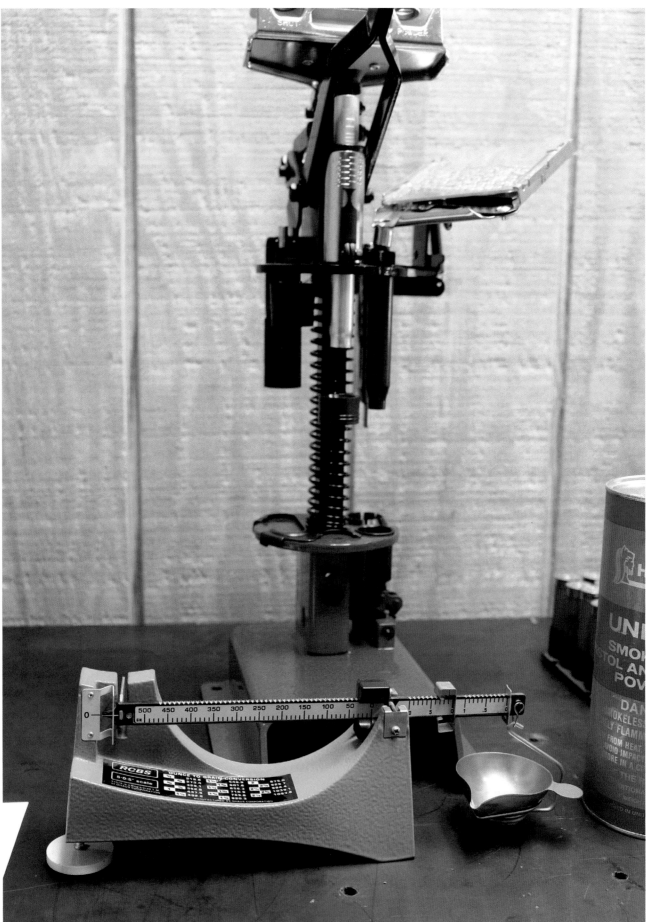

*Winchester 209
Shotshell Primers*

J.D. Fielding Photography

If you shoot skeet, trap or clays and are a member at a club, find out who reloads, and talk to them about what powder they use. There's no sense reinventing the wheel here, getting a good starting point on what powder to use for busting clays will not only put your mind at ease, but will give you confidence as you delve into this new hobby of yours.

For me I like a starting point of 1150-1200fps which is essentially 2 ¾ and 3 dram equivalents. SAAMI (which is an abbreviation for the Sporting Arms and Ammunition Manufacturer's Institute) says that a 2 ¾ dram equivalent load with 1 1/8 oz of shot will travel approximately 1150ft fps; 3 dram with 1 1/8oz will travel 1200 fps. You can't go wrong with either of these velocities. Let me state that 2 ¾ dram shells will break any clay you can hit. For longer crossing shots on the clays field, 3 dram shells will give you that little extra you're looking for on those types of shots.

If I was starting out, I'd pick one of the popular powders, like Green Dot, pick a velocity of 1200 fps, then see how it feels to shoot. Remember, shooting 100 rounds on a Saturday afternoon with an O/U, running 3 dram, 1 1/8 loads can be tough on some. You can always go down to 2 ¾ dram, 1 oz loads, and not give much away. There isn't a target out there that 1oz of #8s at 1200fps won't break! Find what you're comfortable with, and then pattern your gun on paper with your load(s) and see how they look.

Primers

Primers are the little caps in the base of shotshells that are struck by the shotgun's firing pin and explode, thus igniting the powder. Important Note: Not all 209 primers are the same! Some burn hotter than others, and care must be taken when putting together a reloading recipe. Pay close attention to the primer brand. Don't assume 209 means Remington, or Winchester or CCI. Loading data tables are very specific about which brand primer to use in any given recipe, so please play close attention!! Also make sure to put primers left over from your loading session into their original labeled box.

Wads

Wads are what hold the shot in the shell and help cushion it from the exploding powder. This cushioning helps minimize deformed pellets, meaning fewer "flyers", and tighter, more consistent shot patterns. If you think one size fits all for wad selection, you're sore-

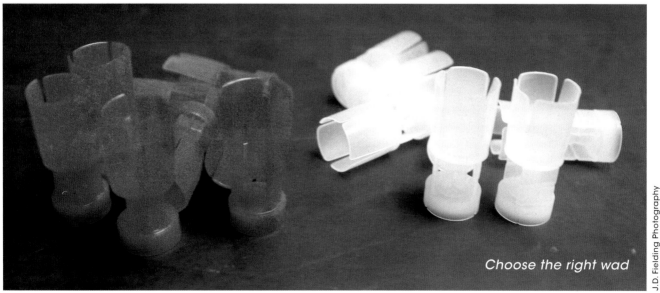

Choose the right wad

J.D. Fielding Photography

Finished Shell

ly mistaken. Go on any of the big company sites like Remington or Winchester, and you will see how there are specific wads for different shooting applications, be it hunting or clays. They are probably the most overlooked component in shotshell reloading, but there is a lot of science behind every design out there.

And speaking of designs, you can save quite a bit on buying wads that are clones to the ones made by the big guys. Companies such as Claybuster and Downrange are two fine examples of this. If you look at the Alliant Reloader's Guide, you'll see wads from these companies suggested in a lot of the shotshell recipes for clays shooting.

Shot

There's more to shot than just size alone. Basic rule of thumb here is: For target shooting you want to keep sizes from #7 1/2 to #9. I shoot skeet with 9s. For sporting clays I'll use 7 ½, same for trap.

One point I do want to talk about is pellet hardness. Antimony is added to lead when making shot to make the pellets harder. It's obvious to everyone that harder shot makes breaking clays easier to do, and that's correct. But the part that some people miss is that harder pellets mean less pellet deformation, and therefore fewer flyers, tighter shot strings, and more uniform patterns. This is very important for clay busters and bird hunters alike.

Chilled lead shot is slightly softer than magnum lead shot. Magnum shot has been alloyed with higher concentrations of antimony. A lot of shooters prefer harder magnum shot for its ability to retain a spherical form better. Conversely, chilled lead shot contains lower concentrations of antimony, which is lighter than lead, so the chilled shot pellet is slightly denser than magnum shot. I know this sounds confusing, but it's just a matter of preference.

There's also copper and nickel-coated shot to consider. I've gone to the sporting goods store to pick up four boxes of shells to shoot clays when there was no time to reload, and there were no target loads available. My only choice was the bargain dove and quail-type loads. It must be psychological, but in those few situations, my confidence going into my round was low, and my shooting suffered. I was shooting soft lead and crummy wads, and it got in my head. Don't settle for cheap shells with cheap components. I buy hard (magnum) shot for all of my clays and bird shooting, and I feel better about things right out of the gate! That's why we're doing this in the first place, right?

Now that we've looked at what goes into a shotshell, let's look at types of presses and setting up a press.

Types of Presses

There are two types of presses; single-stage and progressive. A single-stage press requires the user to work the press handle while manually moving the shotshell through the different stages. Progressive reloaders allow the user to work on multiple shells simultaneously using features such as auto priming. These loaders turn out large volumes of shells in a short amount of time. That being said, it's imperative to pull shells along the way to check charge weights and crimps. This is always paramount to production volume.

Mounting Your Loader to the Bench

Ideally, if you have the available space, you should bolt your loader securely to a bench top. If you don't have that luxury, then you can mount it to a piece of ¾-inch plywood. Make sure to measure approximately 4-5 inches wider than the loaders base, and about 7-8 inches longer. This will give you the room you need to properly clamp it to your work surface. Make sure to use a large, wide-mouthed C- clamp for holding your loader securely in place. After mounting, try working the handle of the loader up and down a few strokes to see if it's moving about.

The beauty of this arrangement is that someone with limited space can use their loader when needed and then have the space available for other projects when they're finished reloading. One word to the wise: progressive reloaders take longer to set up and can be finicky at times compared to the simpler, single-stage press.

Setting Up Your Reloader

Now that your loader is securely mounted, the next step is setting up the charge bar. Most loaders come with multiple bushings that allow you charge different weights of both powder and shot. A side note here, MEC (Mayville Engineering Company) makes an adjustable "universal charge bar" that allows the user to create any size powder/shot load combination. I've used one on my MEC Sizemaster and 650 for years, and love it! Once your charge bar has the correct bushing in place, it's time to fill and attach the powder and shot bottles the unit.

MEC Sizemaster assembled and mounted on bench

Charge bar showing that it's for a single stage press (#302), and that it delivers 1 1/8oz of shot(118).

J.D. Fielding Photography

Two types of charge bars: A bar that uses interchangeable bushings for different weight powder charges, and an MEC Universal Charge Bar.

J.D. Fielding Photography

Once you've filled them for dispensing, make absolutely sure that you label each bottle with what's inside. This is extremely important! If you are, for instance, using Green Dot powder, write it on a label and put it on the powder bottle. This attention to detail will be invaluable as you acquire different powders and sizes of shot.

I purchase extra powder and shot bottles for each type/size that I'm going to use. When not in use, they are capped tightly and kept on a shelf, ready to go when I need them. At this point I like to take an empty hull with a used primer in the bottom to throw powder charges to weigh for accuracy. Never, ever trust what's written on the bushings for charge weights. Environmental conditions like humidity or a nearly empty powder bottle will give you different weights per charge volume. Make the investment in a good balance, too. I use the same balance that I use for rifle reloading, and that's an RCBS 505.

I usually throw four powder charges (the first charge always being culled from the group), record the weights and see if they are close to the desired weight. With an adjustable bar, I'll tweak it until it delivers what I need,

charge-wise. Reloading is all about R+R; Repeatability and Reproducibility! And that's why after you've verified your charge weights, you still pull a sample every 6-8 rounds just to make sure things are staying the same, and that the crimps are looking OK.

Now is the time to date and document your load in your notebook and make sure you detail what type and how much powder and shot you are charging into your hull, the make of the hull, the primer type, and wad information. Make sure you write down the bushing numbers, or charge bar settings as well. This sounds like a lot to do, but believe me, if I walk away from my reloader for 4-6 weeks, and sit down and try to remember what I loaded last on it from memory, I'd be lost.

Another point I want to stress is always keep your reloading components, such as primers and wads, in their original container. Believe me, you don't want to mix up primers; they all look the same! Attention to the smallest details, and reloading without distractions are two of the key points in working safely. And that's the most important part of reloading - WORKING SAFELY!

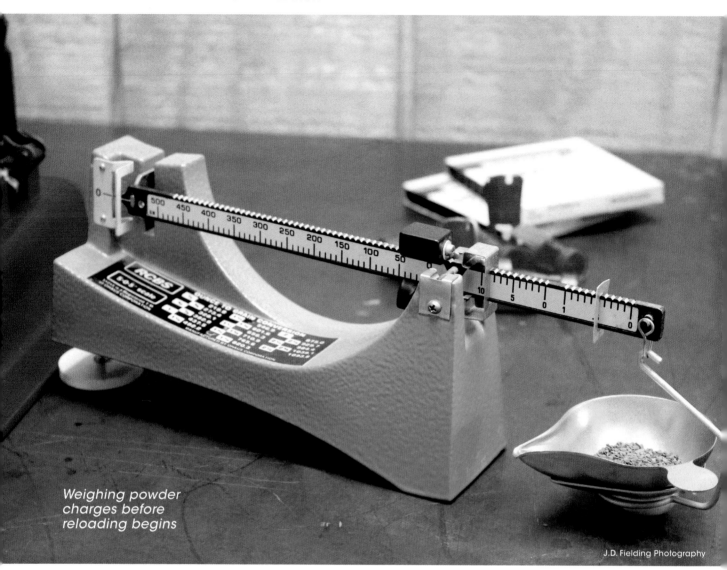

Weighing powder charges before reloading begins

J.D. Fielding Photography

Powder and shot in bottles

J.D. Fielding Photography

To start the reloading process itself, grab your empty hull, and move to the first stage. Pulling down on the handle removes the old primer. Then a new primer is pressed into the primer pocket at the base of the hull. Note: With progressive loaders, and some single stage, an auto feed primer tray is filled with primers and then attached to the reloader. These are automatically dispensed at one particular station as each shell rotates through.

The second stage requires sliding the charge bar to one side to dispense the powder charge into the hull. A wad is then pressed into the shell at this time. With the handle still down, the charge bar is slid to the opposite side and the shot charge falls into the wad. The shell is sent to the next station where the first crimp is started, and finally the last station is where the final crimp is applied.

For those of you shooting autoloading or pump shotguns, it makes sense to add the extra step of resizing. What happens is after the final crimp, shells are collected and then a resizing die is put in place. (In some loaders the brass is

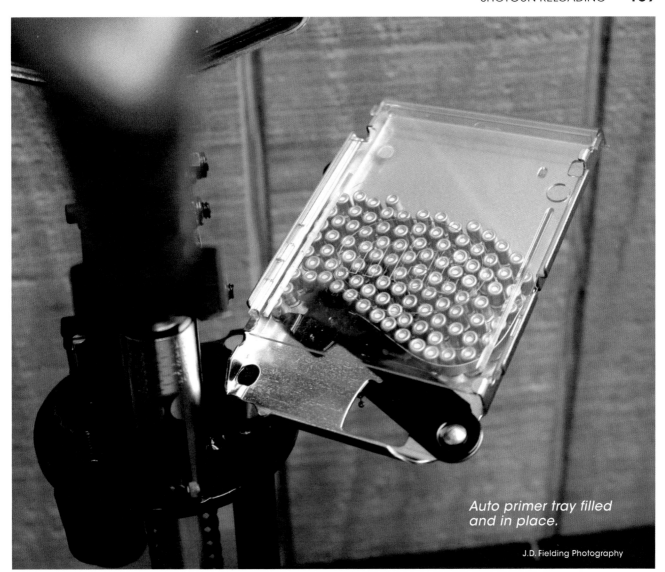

Auto primer tray filled
and in place.

J.D. Fielding Photography

resized simultaneously as you remove the old primer). The handle is pulled down, resizing the brass base, and adding a slight taper at the end of the shell. This allows for slick feeding into the chambers of autos and pump guns.

The good thing about some progressive loaders, such as the MEC 650, is that they can be used as a single-stage press as well. Just unhook the auto primer feed, and you're all set. This is good for someone just starting out, who wants to get the feel of the basic reloading stages. Once you're comfortable with the process, they can easily convert to the progressive setup and start cranking out high volumes of loaded shells in much less time!

Favorite Loads

I find that the loads I've developed for my clay bird shooting translate very well to the upland fields here in the Northeast. Our quarry runs from the diminutive woodcock, to the ruffed grouse and the hearty pheasant. Now our season opens on Oct. 1st for partridge

and pheasant, with the woodcock following a few days later. Early season hunts for grouse and timberdoodle take place with a lot of foliage still in place.

In my 12-gauge Browning Superposed I'll have the first barrel choked skeet with 1 1/8oz of 7 ½s and the second barrel chocked IC with 1 1/8oz of #6s. Since I hunt over a pointing dog (my drathaar, Magnus), my opportunity for a close first shot is good. But as you well know, partridge are often unpredictable and will bust before the dog locks on point. With the 7 ½s and an open choke, I have my best opportunity of getting part of the pattern on that bird. If I've missed, which is a good possibility, I have the larger shot size of the #6s with more retained energy to get through the foliage and drop the bird.

Pheasants on the other hand are a tough, unpredictable bird that will run one day, and hold tight the next. I have taken birds with shells from size 7 ½ down to #4s. My preference though is for 1 1/4oz of #5s at around 1300-1350fps, especially in that second bar-

*Stage 1-
Depriming and
resizing the shell.*

*Stage 2-
Priming the shell.*

*Stage 3a -
Charging powder
to shell.*

Stage 3b -
Putting wad
into shell

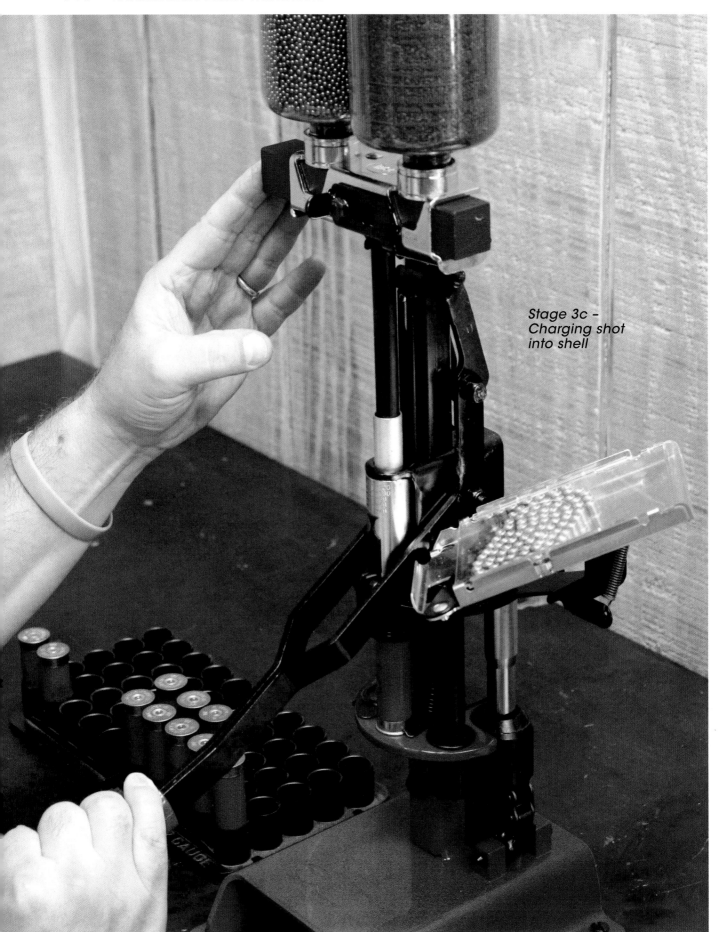

*Stage 3c –
Charging shot
into shell*

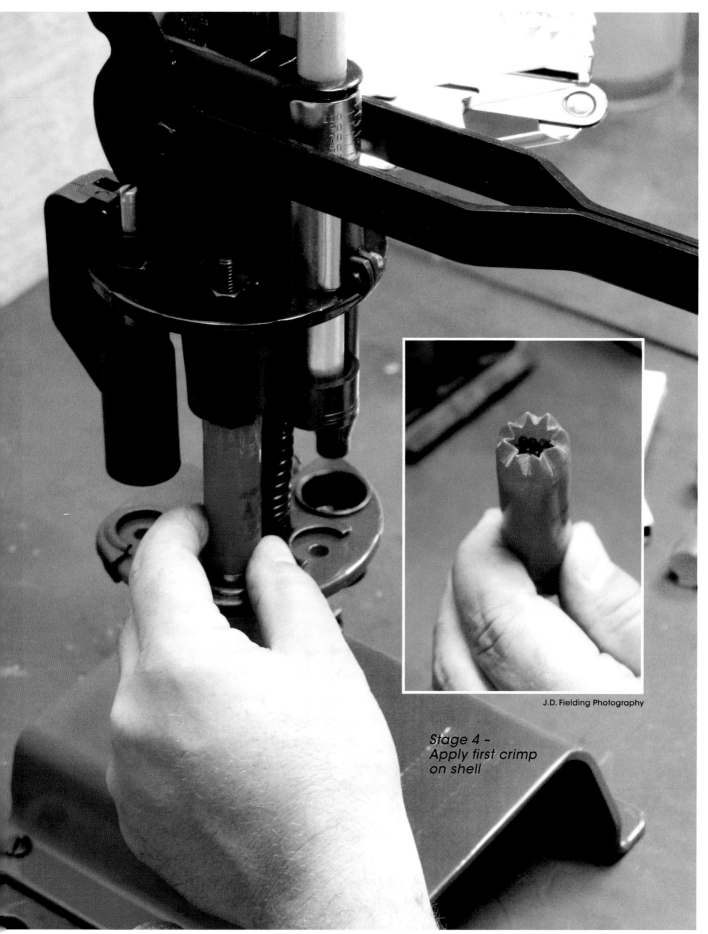

J.D. Fielding Photography

Stage 4 –
Apply first crimp
on shell

Stage 5 –
Finished crimp
applied

Finished shells checked for fit in Browning Superposed

J.D. Fielding Photography

rel when the cock bird turns on the afterburners after you've missed that easy first shot!

I've found that #5s give you a little more oomph on the longer 35-40-yard shots than the same load of #6s. And there are more pellets in that same charge as in the same load of #4's. So to me it's the best of both worlds.

Depending on what type of clay busting I'm doing, I have a few pet loads that have served me very well over the years. For skeet, I'm a #9 shot guy, shooting 1 1/8oz at 1200fps all day long in my Remington 1100. I know a lot of guys as well,who swear by #8s. Either is fine; it's simply a matter of personal preference. I haven't shot a lot of trap, my friends who do say 1 1/8oz of #7 ½s is the ticket. For sporting clays I'll bring a mix of #7 ½'s (1oz and 1 1/8oz) and 9's. For longer targets and a when I'm shooting a fixed choke, say IC, I like the extra pellets in the heavier 7 1/2 load for good shot density at those longer birds.

So there's a snapshot of what makes up a shot shell, and how to take those components, and turn them into a fine finished product. Once you get through making your first box, you'll realize how fun and easy it is to do. So get yourself a press, a reloading guide or two, and start cooking up some great loads for yourself!

J.D. Fielding Photography

AUTHOR BIO:

Dave deMoulpied is an avid upland bird hunter. He spends every fall traipsing the hills and fields of the Northern Catskill Mountains in search of woodcock, partridge, and pheasant with his drathaar, Magnus.

He is president of "deMoulpied and Son Outdoor Adventures", and when not bird hunting, or hunting the bushveldt of Africa, he dreams of both to the point of distraction. Just ask his wife!

www.dnsoutdooradventures.com

CASE PREPARATION
SOME TIPS TO MAKE LIFE EASIER

By Philip P. Massaro

Having brass cases that are properly prepared for loading is a huge part of the accuracy and reliability equation, and taking the proper steps to get them there can make a reloader's life much easier. Even if you're dealing with a good bunch of brand-new component brass, there are some steps you can take to improve the end result. Whether you're mass-producing pistol ammunition for an IDPA match, or making the most accurate ammunition you can for the hunt of a lifetime, you should follow a routine that will help avoid the pitfalls that can cause frustration or a dangerous situation.

I'd like to walk you through the process of taking spent brass, and working our way up to the stage that the cases are ready to be primed and loaded, including cleaning, depriming, resizing and trimming.

Visual Inspection - Sort 'Em Out, Brother

Let's assume that you're starting with a nice pile of once-fired brass for your chosen caliber. The first thing I do is take a good look at each case to see if there is anything wrong with it that would prevent me from wanting to reload that case. Any and all steel cases, or aluminum in some cases, are removed for the pile, and I prefer to crush the case mouth with a pair of pliers to prevent them from sneaking back into the game.

If you have trouble telling the difference, a small magnet will quickly identify the steel cases.

I like to inspect the cases for splits in the brass, especially in the neck and mouth area.

Any cases that have split face the same fate as the steel and aluminum cases: crushed by the pliers of doom. I also take a good look at the area of the

J.D. Fielding Photography

case body just above the rim; if a bright, shiny ring is present, it may mean that the case wall has stretched to the point that the wall is beginning to get dangerously thin.

If that ring is present, I use a 'feeler' to examine the case. I will straighten out a paper clip, and bend a 1/8" to ¼" section at right angles, so I can scrape the bent end of the clip up and down the interior of the case wall. If I feel a severe dip in the interior of the wall, I will discard that case. Reloading a case with that thin spot in the wall can lead to the case pulling itself apart upon being fired, and things can get very, very ugly should that happen. The scenario is known as 'case head separation', and it is the stuff of nightmares and

This Blazer ammo, while inexpensive and wonderful to practice with, uses aluminum cases and can't be reloaded.

Massaro Media Group

disintegrating rifles. Case head separation is usually not a problem with pistol cartridges, and is much more prevalent in the higher-pressure rifle cases.

Another area that I pay special attention to is the primer. There are a few instances where a cartridge case may use more than one primer size, and if the cases are not properly sorted, things can get messy. The .45 ACP, .454 Casull and .45-70 come quickly to mind. While most of these cases use a large primer, there are instances where a small primer has been used, and trying to jam a large primer into a small primer pocket can cause detonation. This is espe-

cially dangerous if you're loading on a progressive press, where large quantities of primers and powder are present. So I give them a good sorting, putting anything with an oddball primer pocket into a separate bag or coffee can.

With my rifle cartridges, I also like to sort the cases by brand, and also segregate any of the nickel-plated cases. I've found that while the nickel cases can produce very good accuracy, the point of impact has been different in some of my rifles, so I usually separate them for a different bullet or load altogether. I like to load the same brand of rifle case for my loads, to

Case split in the neck.

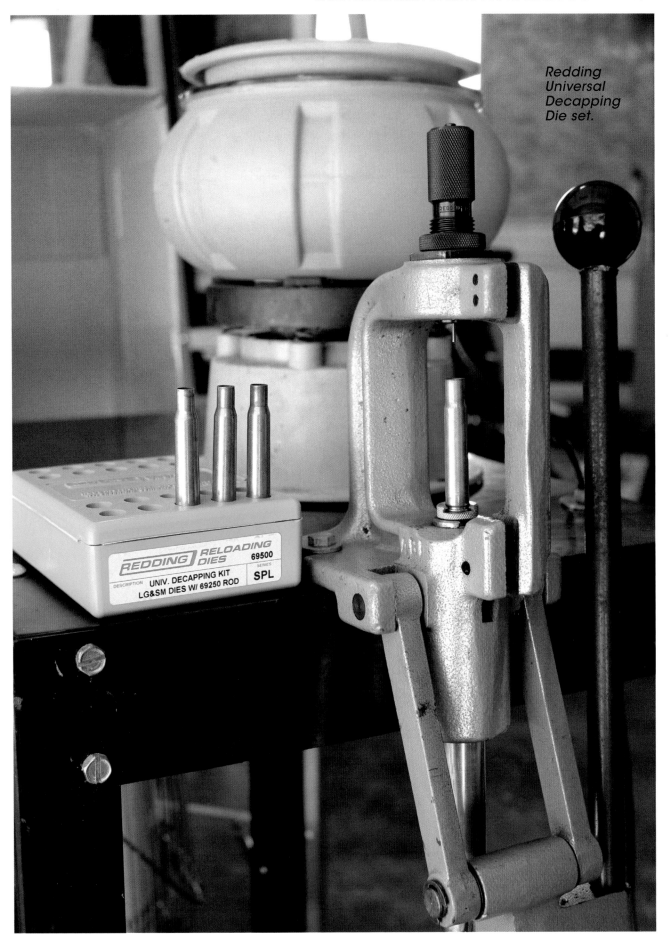

Redding Universal Decapping Die set.

keep things as uniform as possible. Within the different brands, there are minute case thickness differences which will affect the performance of your handloads.

In the pistol realm, I also like to sort them by brand, as the thickness of the brass can affect the crimp applied to the cartridge. With my pistol cases segregated, I can stop the crimping process when I switch brands of brass to make sure the crimping die is properly adjusted.

Ok, now that we've got them inspected and properly sorted, let's clean them.

Cleanliness is Next to Godliness.

The nickel-plated brass cases don't need to be cleaned – on the outside at any rate – but the traditional brass case most certainly does. Unless you're using a progressive press, we are at a crossroads, and need to make a decision: You can opt to clean your cases with the spent primers still in place – you don't want to run dirty brass into your resizing dies – and clean the primer pocket after, or you could very easily setup a small press with a universal decapping die, so you don't resize anything, just pop the old primer out so you can clean the primer pocket before resizing.

I like the latter idea for a couple of reasons. First, and most obvious, you get a chance to clean the primer pocket before resizing, and you can avoid having all that spent primer dust getting up into your dies. Secondly, you don't run the risk of breaking the decapping pin and the rod that holds the expander ball in the resizing die if the primer is already out. As a matter of fact, if you opt for the universal decapping die, you don't need to use a pin in your resizing die.

Either way, it's time to remove the filth. There are two main types of case cleaners: the vibratory cleaner and the ultrasonic cleaner.

The vibratory cleaners use some sort of abrasive media to put a good polish on your cases. Crushed walnut shells, ground corn cobs, even stainless steel; all of the available media will scour the brass cases

The Vibratory Cleaner.

Massaro Media Group

Midway Sifter will remove most of the media.

clean. I have a couple of vibratory cleaners I have used and love: a Midway model and an RCBS model. Both are effective and work rather quickly. I like to throw my cases in the tub of the cleaner with a bit of Lyman's Turbo-Brite brass cleaner and let them enjoy the ride for a couple of hours while I attend to something else. The vibratory action of the motor-driven cleaner acts much like beach sand; it gives a good polish to the out-side of the cases, but the cleaning on the inside of the case is less than perfect.

That's why I love the ultrasonic cleaners so much. They use a cleaning solution along with ultrasonic vibration to really get rid of all that grime and burnt powder residue. The ultrasonic cleaner will definitely do a good job cleaning the inside of your cases, and that's a good enough reason to own one. I own two, and like them both: The Lyman 2500 and the RCBS Ultrasonic Case Cleaner.

Within the ultrasonic cleaner, an element heats the solution to clean more effectively, and the buzzing sound is the small bursts of high-frequency vibration, which will loosen all the caked-on gunk and break it away from your cases. I'd like to note that ultrasonic cleaners can be used to clean reloading dies, gun parts, and even entire handguns if you'd like. The ultrasonic cleaners do their job in a short period of time, usually ten to twenty minutes.

The one drawback to the ultrasonic cleaners is that they don't polish the cases like the vibratory cleaners do, so I really like to use the two in tandem. Give 'em a bath in the ultrasonic to remove all the dirty stuff, and once they're dry, send 'em into the vibratory cleaner for a bit to get a nice polish. When I'm reloading those nickel-plated cases I mentioned before, I just give them the ultrasonic treatment, so as to get all the dirty stuff out of the inside of the case, there's really no need for any further treatment.

RCBS Dies.

Once the cases have been polished in the vibratory cleaner, I use the RCBS Rotary Case and Media Separator to take all of the media out of the cases. This simple device uses a basket with external handles – resembling the pedals on a bicycle – housed within a plastic container. Sift the cases out of the media in the vibratory cleaner, place them in the Media Separator's basket, give it a couple of cranks and most of the little granules of media will fall away from the polished cases.

Now mind you, I said most of the granules will come away. One word of warning about the media used in the vibratory cleaners: even with RCBS's Media Separator, some residual media will tend to stick to the inside of the cases. This gets even more interesting if you've removed the old primer; those little grains can stick in the flash hole of the cleaned case. Give your cases a really good inspection, again, to make sure that none of the kernels remain within the case, or are obstructing the primer pocket and/or flash hole.

Resizing Your Cases.

Now that the cases are sorted and cleaned, it is time to put them back into shape.

We'll need to set up your resizing dies to reduce the expanded brass back to the SAAMI specified dimensions. You see, upon firing a cartridge in your firearm, the brass case expands to the chamber dimensions, which is slightly larger than the case (that's the only way a cartridge will feed into the chamber). The job of the resizing die is to squeeze that brass case back to the proper dimension; brass is used because it is a malleable metal that can be worked and reworked without coming apart.

So after inserting the proper shellholder for your cartridge into the ram of the press, extend the ram all the way upward. Take the resizing die, with the lock ring loose, and screw the die into the top of the press until the bottom of the die body makes contact with the top of the shellholder.

Once you've felt it make contact on the shellholder, lower the ram and screw the die body down one-quarter to one-third turn, lower the lock ring down onto the surface of the press, and lock down the set screw (if your die doesn't have a set screw, turn the ring down until you feel it make positive contact on the top of the press).

The press can now use its mechanical advantage to cam-over into the die, giving you a consistent point

Screw the resizing die into the press.

The inner working of a resizing die.

Massaro Media Group

of reference for resizing your brass cases. Adjust the decapping pin to protrude 3/16ths to ¼ inch below the bottom of the die body.

If you're loading rifle cases, you'll definitely need to lubricate your cases before running them into the resizing die. Most pistol cartridges can be worked in a carbide steel sizing die, which does not require lubrication. Be sure and verify that your dies are carbide before trying to resize without lubrication.

The lubricants available to reloaders take many forms. There are gels, sprays, waxes, and powders. Which you choose will depend on your particular loading style. For years, I used RCBS Case Lube gel, spread on a lube pad, and that worked very well for me, although I constantly had sticky hands.

I have come to love the Redding Imperial Sizing Wax, because when used in conjunction with Redding Dies, the risk of hydraulic dents in the shoulder area is greatly minimized. Simply apply a tiny bit of Imperial wax on your forefinger and thumb, and rub it along the case body. I lubricate the case mouths and necks with Imperial's Dry Neck Lube, a gray powdery substance that works very well on the expander ball for consistent neck concentricity.

Some guys like the sprays, like the Hornady One-Shot, with which you can lubricate many cases at once. While too little lubrication can cause your cases to become stuck in the resizing die (we'll discuss how to remove a stuck case a bit later), too much lubricant can cause hydraulic dents in the shoulder area. If the dents are minor, they will shoot out upon the next firing, but if they are huge I generally don't load the case. You'll quickly develop a feel for how much lubricant is required.

At any rate, once your cases are lubricated, you must send them up into the resizing die. If you haven't popped that old primer out yet, you'll be doing that when the case is pushed into the die.

Here's exactly what's going on when you pull the handle and push that case up into the resizing die: The case - which after being fired is larger than it should be - is pressed into the die. Having smaller dimensions, the die and the force of the press squeeze that brass case down to a dimension that is compliant with the SAAMI specifications. In a bottle-necked rifle case, the neck portion of the case is brought down to a dimension 0.003" to 0.004" below bullet diameter, and when the press' ram is

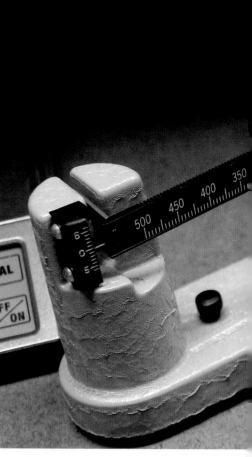

Massaro Media Group

Above: *Redding Resizing Die set up properly to remove primers.*

Below: *Shell holder making contact with bottom of die.*

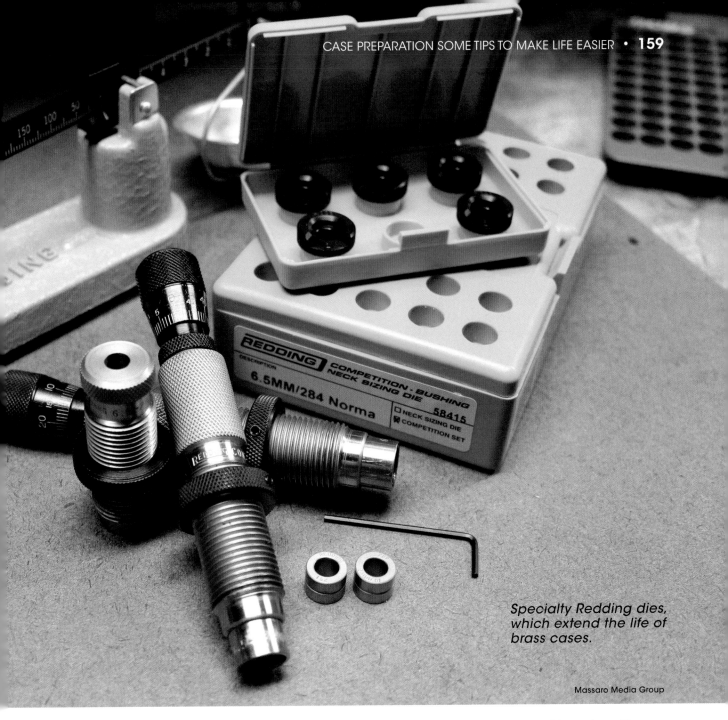

Specialty Redding dies, which extend the life of brass cases.

Massaro Media Group

lowered, the case neck is drawn against the expander ball within the die body to a dimension 0.002" smaller than bullet diameter, to ensure good neck tension when the bullet is seated.

If you've decided to use a neck sizer – usually reserved for the bolt-action crowd - you don't need to lubricate the case body, but some of that Dry Neck Lube would go a long way. The case body and shoulder will remain a mirror image of your rifle's chamber, and only the neck portion will be worked to assure proper bullet tension. Although I'm sure that you're already aware, I'll feel better reiterating the point that neck sized brass can only be used in the rifle that it was fired in initially.

Manscaping Your Brass - Keeping it Neat and Well Manicured.

Now that the case has been cleaned and reformed to the proper specifications, it's time for the last few steps to prepare them for reloading.

We need to check the length of the cases, to see it they need to be trimmed. You see, that brass case - with all of its malleable properties that allow us to reuse them - also stretches when you fire them.

So, you'll need a good set of calipers to measure the length of the cases after resizing, and compare that length to the maximum case length as published in your reloading manual. You'll need a means of

Imperial Sizing Wax and Dry Neck Lube.

Imperial Dry Neck Lube.

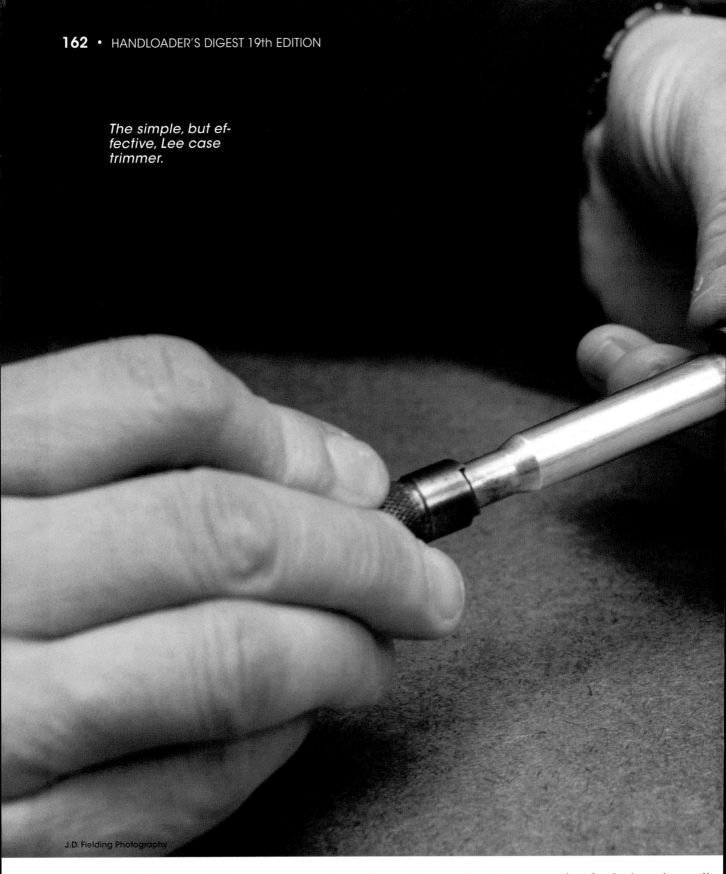

The simple, but effective, Lee case trimmer.

J.D. Fielding Photography

trimming that brass, and there are many tools available to neatly trim the case to length. Whether it's a manual 'crank' type trimmer, or my own personal favorite, the RCBS Universal Case Prep Station, trimming the brass to the SAAMI-specified length is very important.

Proper trimming assures that the final product will feed into the chamber properly, allowing the case to headspace on the shoulder and not hang up on the case mouth, which can cause dangerously high pressures. If too long, the rifle will force the case mouth to 'bite' down on the bullet, and that can be detrimental.

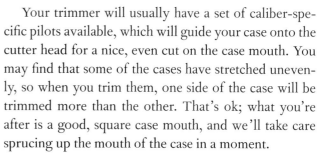

Your trimmer will usually have a set of caliber-specific pilots available, which will guide your case onto the cutter head for a nice, even cut on the case mouth. You may find that some of the cases have stretched unevenly, so when you trim them, one side of the case will be trimmed more than the other. That's ok; what you're after is a good, square case mouth, and we'll take care sprucing up the mouth of the case in a moment.

At this stage of the game, we have a clean, resized, and properly trimmed brass case. We need to dress up that case mouth for two reasons: one, so the bullet may be seated cleanly into the case, and two, so that the case has no burrs or jagged brass on the outside of the mouth from the trimming process. You'll need a chamfer/deburring tool to clean up the case mouth. There are many on the market, but their function is the same.

The chamfer side of the tool puts a nice bevel on the inside of the case mouth, so that when the time comes to seat the bullet, it will slide neatly into the case

Digital calipers make measuring cases a breeze.

J.D. Fielding Photography

RCBS Universal Case Prep Station.

The RCBS Universal Case Prep Station trimming .308 Winchester brass.

*Chamfering the
case mouth.*

*Deburring the
case mouth.*

The primer pocket scraper.

New component brass.

J.D. Fielding Photography

without scraping or scratching the shank of the bullet during the seating process. The deburring tool works on the outside of the case mouth, cutting away any of those annoying little pieces of brass that can appear on the mouth during trimming.

Both functions only require a few twists of your wrist to clean the mouth up. If you haven't cleaned that primer pocket yet, now is the time to do so.

There are steel brushes, or steel scrapers that will remove the burnt primer residue quickly. I also like to take a good look at the flash hole, and if it looks less than perfect, I use a small drill bit specifically designed to clean the hole, assuring that the primer spark reaches the powder charge.

The last step in this process is reserved for the straight-walled cases only. Before loading the straight wall case, the mouth of the case must be slightly flared, and the reloading die set for any straight walled case usually comes with a special flaring die. You don't need to flare the mouth too radically, a flare about 1/8th inch deep will provide enough room to prevent the case from crumpling when the bullet is seated. Don't worry, the seating die will put the flared mouth back where it belongs.

In Conclusion.

When I'm loading new component brass, I don't clean them, but I do complete all of the other steps, including trimming and resizing, so that I have a nice, uniform product to start with when I'm loading cartridges.

While it can seem like a lot of tedious work, thorough case preparation will allow you to make the best ammunition you can, and you'll be able to rely on your stuff for many shooting sessions or hunting seasons.

AUTHOR BIO:

Philip P. Massaro is the President of Massaro Ballistic Laboratories, LLC, a custom ammunition company, comfortably nestled in between the Hudson River and Catskill Mountains of Upstate New York. He has been a handloader for 20+ years, a veteran of five African safaris and dozens of North American hunts. He is a Licensed Professional Land Surveyor by trade, a musician by choice, and usually reeks of Hoppes No. 9.

MODERN SMOKELESS
PAPER PATCHING

By Marty Longbottom

When talking to my friend and editor Philip Massaro about the preparation of this article, we discussed the many facets of how to approach this topic. What we decided on was a beginner's guide, written by someone who has progressed from a babe in the woods to a novice. In this article, I hope to impart my knowledge of the basic concepts of smokeless paper patching and help you avoid my pitfalls as well as avoid re-inventing the wheel.

First a little background is in order. The paper patch cartridge was developed during the black powder era, and used by target shooters and militaries around the world. The idea was that if you kept the bore clean of lead and fouling, then more shots could be fired.

For target shooters, that meant being able to shoot longer and more accurate strings between cleaning. For the foot soldier, easier cleaning and the ability to shoot more before moving into hand-to-hand combat

was a great improvement. The most common use here in America was by the buffalo hunters. A man could shoot all day without much fouling between shots.

The paper patch bullet was loaded by most of the ammunition makers of the day, and even sold as ready-patched bullets for shooters in the field to load themselves. Eventually we would see the invention of smokeless powders that produced less fouling and the transition into that modern full metal patched bullets, or as we know them 'jacketed'.

Let us jump ahead 130 years. By now you are probably asking why does this guy cast his bullets and wrap them in paper? Wouldn't powder coating be easier? Yes powder coating would probably be easier, but I would not have the satisfaction of having made something myself that in itself is unique. It is also my stress buster. The advantages are that I clean less with easier cleaning and shoot more for my dollar. Isn't that what

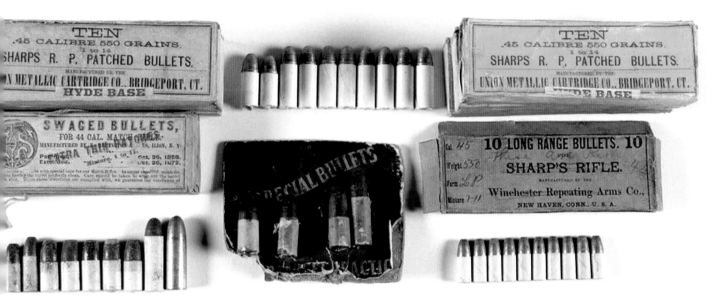

we are all trying to do nowadays?

Be honest with yourself here: If you were at the range and saw a box of ammo that had bullets wrapped in paper, would you not be asking what are those and what cannon are you shooting?

Let's get started: The first thing is to gather materials, supplies and equipment. If you are a cast bullet shooter most of this will be on hand.

Start with paper: The caliber of the bullet and how much you are patching the bullet up will determine the type and thickness of your paper. I use several types of paper from a 9lb. onionskin to a 24lb. bond tracing paper.

One example is the 450-400 3" I have patched for this project. The tracing paper dries at a .4135" and I can size that bullet to .413, which fits the throat perfectly. On the other side I tried several types of paper

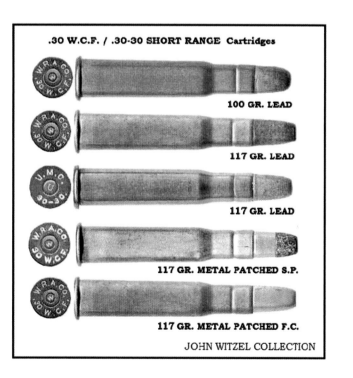

.30 W.C.F. / .30-30 SHORT RANGE Cartridges

100 GR. LEAD

117 GR. LEAD

117 GR. LEAD

117 GR. METAL PATCHED S.P.

117 GR. METAL PATCHED F.C.

JOHN WITZEL COLLECTION

and found that the 20lb graph paper is what works best for my 45-70. Just try to avoid the papers with high clay content, as they are more abrasive than anything else you will shoot from your rifle.

A paper cutter is next on the list. I like to use a photo cutter. This type has a bar that holds the paper in place and cutters that slide. Also, the angles are marked for a quick reference. The other option is a standard paper cutter, which works well for high-volume cutting.

For the rolling board I like a plastic textured cutting board. The textured board allows the paper to be stretched slightly when wet and also holds it in place while rolling the bullet, another tool for this function is a cigarette roller.

You'll also need a small container to wet the patches with; I use one of those cheap reusable types. Next are templates for marking your patches to cut. Some can be store-bought from Buffalo Arms, but they are fairly easy to make, and I will discuss this later on.

To round out the shopping list we need beeswax and Vaseline to lubricate the patch and provide some waterproofing, egg-shaped lead sinkers in several sizes for slugging your bore, and sizing dies for getting your bullet to the correct starting diameter and to size after patching and lubing.

And finally, of course, the most important item: your bullets. If you do not cast your own bullets, don't worry, store-bought are good as well, and I tend to use them as I do not cast in high volume for some bullets. When buying store-bought bullets make sure to get some that are soft, I like to use a 20:1 or softer.

Everything on this list is fairly inexpensive. You might see a bit of cost with the sizing dies, but that is really the only place. Everything I do is on a budget so I can enjoy more bang for the buck.

Now that you have gathered everything it is time to get started. We are going to take this step-by-step.

Measure Your Bore

The first thing that needs to be done is to measure the bore of your barrel, the goal being a bullet .001" or so above the bore diameter. There are several ways to do this. The easiest way for me was to slug the barrel.

This is accomplished by driving an egg-shaped sinker larger than the bore through the barrel. I use a long brass rod to do this. You can either go from the breech or the muzzle. Some people do both. I usually tap in from the muzzle and then drive it home gently

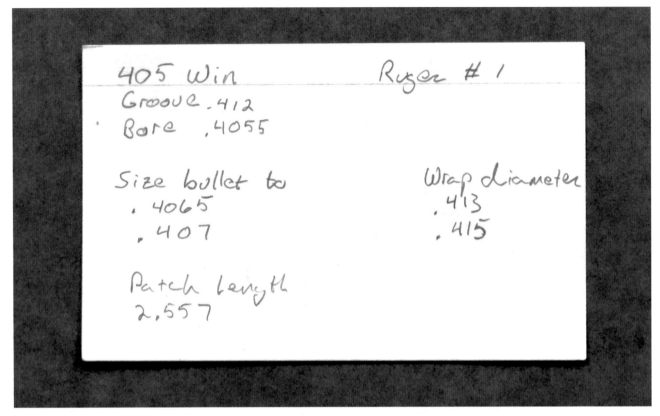

with my brass rod and hammer.

If you have a set of pin gauges, they are more accurate than pounding the sinker through. The best options though, are either a chamber cast with Cerosafe, or a pound cast using soft lead and a plugged case. If you do not feel comfortable doing this, I recommend finding a competent gunsmith to do this for you. Not only will you get the bore and groove size, but you will have the throat dimension. This allows you to determine the maximum throat size as well as your chamber in relation to the cartridge case. The goal from all of this is to have a patched bullet that will slip-fit into a fired case. Some rifles will allow this and others won't.

Now with a slug in hand it is time to measure for the bore and groove. I use both calipers and a micrometer. The part inside on the slug will give you your bore, and the raised part will be the groove size.

Getting these as close as possible is very important, as it will determine both the size for your bullet before wrapping and the size after wrapping. You will want to size your bullets to .001" or .0015" above bore diameter before wrapping, and the ideal size after wrapping is .001"/.003" above the groove after patching.

Ideally, we want the bullet to fit in the throat and chamber and engage the rifling without being oversized. This will determine the dimensions of the sizing

dies needed. This is where keeping good notes comes into play. I use a 3x5 card for each rifle I shoot patched through.

This is one I made for my 450-400 3" that is used in this article. It shows the groove and bore size. I used a spreadsheet program to make a fast calculator to determine the bullet size and the final wrap diameter. The final diameter will be different with every paper. You will need to play with the paper a bit to see how much it will add.

Bullet Prep

Now that we have the proper sizing dies, it is time to get started. You will need un-lubed bullets, plain base or gas check will work. I like the gas check design as it seems to hold the paper on the base better. If you have purchased lubed bullets you can use those, or just use what you have on hand.

I would also like to note that it is common for some to use smooth-sided bullets as well. Some like to knurl them very lightly to get the paper to hold in place when rolling, but this sometimes does not work. Rolling the slick side on a file is the best way to do this.

If you have lubed bullets, with or without gas checks on them, you will need to remove the lube. If not, the paper will not come off when being shot, and tight shotgun-type patterns will occur. That is my ex-

perience in the learning process.

I have found the easiest way for me to remove lube and gas checks is a pot of boiling water. I purchased a hot plate from a garage sale, and a cheap non-stick pan and strainer from one of the many local dollar stores.

At this point it is time for a life lesson or friendly warning: Do not at anytime use your better half's cooking utensils, or any other kitchen aid in this hobby!

Two or three trips into boiling water should remove the lube. I change the water after each hot bath and a quick wipe of the pot gets the lube residue out. If you have to remove the gas checks, be very careful as the bullets will be extremely hot. Just a quick wipe down with a paper towel and they are ready.

Sizing Bullets

With clean bullets in hand it is time to size them. At this point I want to stop you from making some of my mistakes. I have both the Lee push-through sizers and a Lyman 450. Both worked for me in the beginning, but they were not my best option.

Let's address the Lyman first. I found out quickly that you have to size the bullets with the nose down to prevent any sort of deformation, and also to make sure to change out the nose punch-out. I turned some 113-grain .309" bullets into some rather impressive wad cutters. Those were patched to fit a CZ527 in 7.62X39 and shot rather well.

Now for the Lee dies. With these you are pushing the nose through and avoiding any damage to the bullet. The drawback is that the Lees tend to need to be polished, and a new pusher made for them to work properly. I have had one altered from .410" to .413" to size the patched bullets for two of my rifles.

Another option and probably the best is to just have a custom Lee-style made for sizing down and for the final patched bullet. Before you size your bullets down you will need to lube them with a water soluble lube

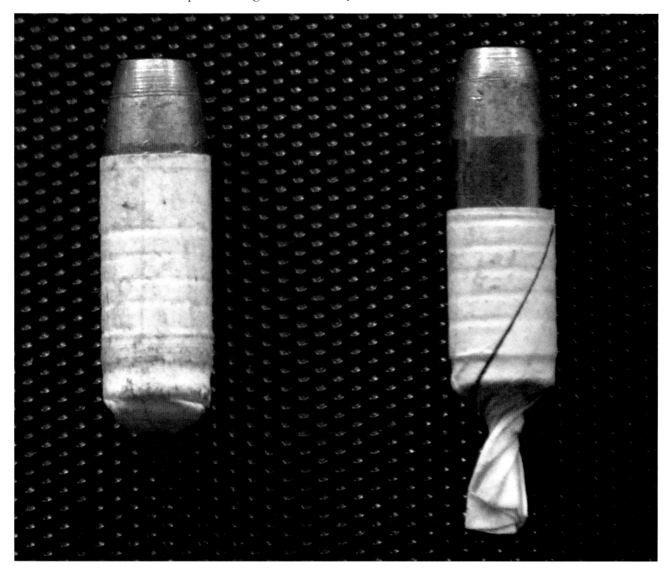

like dish soap or RCBS case lube. You will be taking the bullet down sometimes as much as .007" and the lube will help. Just a quick rinse after will have them all clean.

The second die is for after the bullet has been patched and lubed. Just push the patched bullet through, making sure to not get the lubricant on the base. We will discuss this further later on.

Templates

Depending on the caliber you have chosen to patch, you have either a store-bought template, or have to make one. To be honest you do not have to even make a template, but I do for a quick reference. If you have to make your own template it is rather simple once you get the hang of things. My first few attempts were rather bad, either they were way too short or long.

All we need for this is a calculator and calipers. The formula is; Core Diameter * Pi * 2 = patch length plus or minus a few thousandths. For example, on my 45-70 the core is .457 *3.14*2= 2.87" for my patch length. I like to cut mine short to allow for the stretch of wet paper. My end goal is around .010" from the ends meeting. Once you have your patch length where you want it just cut the template to size. Since I am a frugal person I saved several strips from an old mini blind. These

are very easy to cut and adjust.

We are getting closer now to wrapping those bullets, just one last measurement to determine the patch width. This is to decide if you want to twist the tail or go tailless. I have done both and for me it depends on the bullet. Place the bullet next to a ruler, and then measure from where the patch is going to stop and how far past the base you want to go. Remember you need to cover the base to protect it. I had to play around with this before I found what worked for me. This is the main reason I made my templates for a quick reference.

Cutting Patches

Let's get to work now and cut some patches. The first thing I do is cut several strips of my paper the same width as my template. Some people say to cut with the grain, other say against. For me at my skill level there has not really been a huge difference. See what works best for you.

Once you have your strips ready, mark one with your template, or with your calipers from the earlier measurements recorded. I usually put three or four strips together and clip one end to keep them from moving. This is why I like my photo cutter, as it has an arm that rises up and will hold the paper in place, as

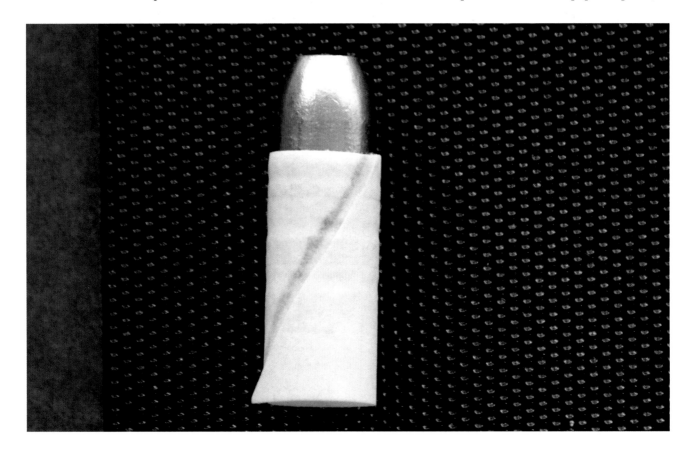

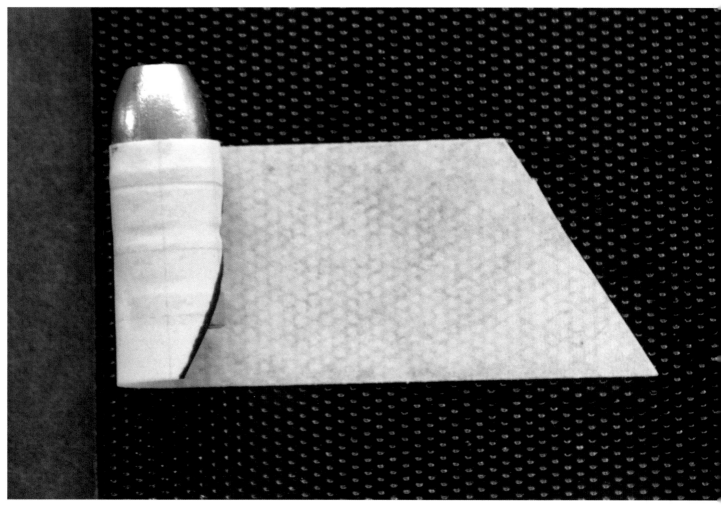

well as the angles marked.

You will want to cut the angles at 60 degrees. Several quick cuts and you will have a handful of patches. A standard paper cutter is also great for this and I do have one handy for cutting large quantities. Having a good supply of zip locks will make storing them handy. You can just use your sharpie to make the patch and what bullet it is for.

Rolling Patches

Now we're ready to start rolling the patches on. What you will need here is a container with some warm water, and the cutting board. Again I would like to warn against using anything from the better half's kitchen, we do not want anyone getting lead in their food or you sleeping on the couch.

At this point I like to mark the leading edge of the patch with a sharpie. This helps me see if I am getting too much stretch on the paper and any overlap on the edges. What works best for me is to set up an assembly line at my work station. First take a patch and dip it in the water and place it on the rolling board with the top corner hanging over about ¼ of an inch, then place the bullet on the patch with the ogive just at the top edge. The ogive is the point where the straight side starts a radius to the nose.

Keeping the top edge straight, roll the bullet away

from your body with a little pressure. When the patch is on, I roll it across the board a couple of time and then give a slight twist to the tail, being careful not to tear it off, or fold it under if going tailless, and press the base on the cutting board with a twisting motion.

A side note here about the success of your first patching session; it might require a cursing jar and a pre-paid donation. My first ten or so attempts were very discouraging. The patches tore, the tails twisted off, I missed even getting close to the ogive, and probably a dozen other stupid mistakes in between. Do not give up here, as with any hobby it takes time and practice.

After I have the bullet patched, I place them nose-down in a loading block to dry overnight.

Some people use other methods like placing them in an oven on warm, or a space heater blowing on them. One of my mentors and a guy who has been a good sport about helping me likes to fold under and twist the base in a warm pan on a hot plate. He gets a fast dry from this. I like to just put them aside so that I can focus on case prep. When they are dry you can snip the tail off, lube them and size them.

This is where I really like the push-through dies from Lee, as you can modify them or even get a custom-made one to the size you need. Using a 50/50 mix of Vaseline and bees wax is the best choice. There are other options out there, just make sure that they will not soak through the paper and stick to the bullet, as this degrades accuracy.

Lube the sides of the bullet to cover the paper, but try to avoid getting any on the base to prevent contamination of the powder. After lubing and sizing, I like to put them nose-down in my loading block to keep them ready for loading.

Case Prep and Loading

Getting your cases ready is just like any other loading session, with a few exceptions. If you are loading for a lever action, you will still need to do a neck sizing like normal if shooting from the same rifle, usually no sizing at all if the bullet will slip fit with the neck tension holding it in.

For bolt actions and single shots you can either just neck size or used fired brass from that rifle. Most of the target shooters I know use the un-sized brass and just press fit the bullet into the neck and let the action seat the bullet so that the paper is touching the rifling.

Remember the cases are full from either a full charge of a slow burning ball powder or a reduced charge using a filler to keep the bullet from setting too far back into the case.

Since I set mine up for hunting I either use an unsized case or one that has been barely neck-sized. Before I seat my bullet to depth, which is usually close to the rifling or just touching to start the paper, I use an expander die to open the neck just enough for seating. The only neck tension used is what is there when the seater die takes any flare from the case.

The main school of thought is to use a slow-burning powder of a ball type, which fills the case 100%. Since we are focusing on loading for hunting and using a soft expanding alloy, I like to keep my bullets in the 1800-2000 fps area, as this is more than enough to take anything we go after in North America.

Before I knew anything, I started with the upper-end loads from Lyman's Fourth Edition For Cast Bullets, or the lower-end loads from one of my many

AUTHOR BIO:

Marty Longbottom was born and raised in Southeast Texas, where he grew up hunting small game in the big thicket, and learning his love of shooting and collection firearms from his father. His main interests are falling-block rifles, U.S. and Japanese military, and loading and shooting obsolete cartridges.

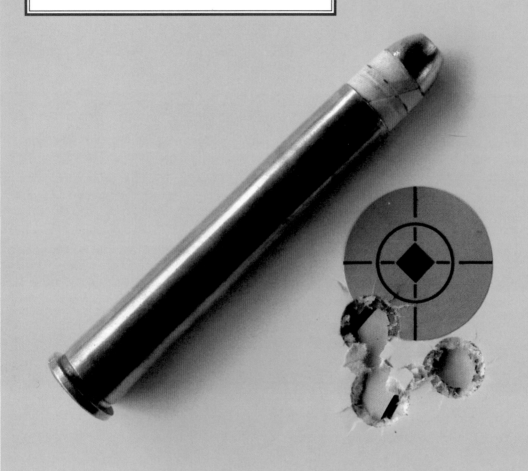

load manuals. Again, I got rather sad results, then started to research and ask for advice from people who know more than me. Soon I had my .45-70 shooting 10 shots into a three-inch group, plus or minus, at 100 yards.

You will need to develop your load data for a compressed load of powder, either with an inert filler such as PuffLon, or a 100 percent charge of powder.

Shooting Your Loads

Now that everything is assembled, get out to the range and make some confetti. Here are a few tips from my range trips.

Check your bore after each shot to make sure nothing is left in it. You might see some powder, but that happens with any firearm. Just run a dry brush or swab down the barrel after each shot as this will help keep accuracy consistent.

Start at 25-50 yards, and use a large sheet of paper for the target. Do not let a tight shotgun-type group discourage you. My first time out I was not even able to keep them inside of 15 inches at 50 yards. The cause was that I did not know enough to take the lube off of the bullet before I wrapped it, making the paper stick to the bullet, and had too much

crimp. You want just enough crimp so the bullet does not fall out and you can twist the bullet slightly and chamber. I fixed these problems and started getting the kind of hunting accuracy I wanted, and even some groups that were pushing MOA for five shots from a 45-70.

A few more tips to consider:

Use a large-bore cartridge to start off with as they tend to be easier to get to shoot, and a straight wall is even better. At this point I am getting good results with my .40-caliber rifles and larger. As for the smaller bores, the .30WCF and .308 Marlin Express are improving to acceptable hunting accuracy. I made a rookie mistake the first time I patched for them; the patch did not go all the way to the ogive.

This dramatically affected the accuracy. After correcting that and playing with it for a year or so things are looking better for hunting. There is no definitive correct way to paper patching, but there are some basic rules in the article, so find what works for you.

Remember, I am just an average shooter, and anything we do gets better with practice and the more we refine our methods. Happy shooting and good hunting!

A PROGRESSIVE PRESS ROUNDTABLE

By Philip P. Massaro

In this modern era of readily available information, there are many resources that a customer can use to obtain a review of the particular product they are interested in; YouTube, reloading forums, product websites; there are plenty of places to find good information.

However, if you hang around a gun shop that sells reloading supplies, you'll invariably hear those "real world" discussions; the ones that give the unsolicited good and bad points that we all want to hear. Rather than pick a press or two, and review them, I felt that a roundtable discussion of experiences – good and bad – and perhaps some helpful advice to avoid pitfalls and problems, would best serve those who have an interest in obtaining or better using a progressive press.

So, three friends sat down in what we call "The Parlor", the Headquarters of the Handloaders Syndicate, among some progressive presses, and began to banter and pontificate, about the finer points of loading with a progressive press.

Mr. Jeff Koonz, proprietor of Coxsackie Gun & Bow, has been handloading his own ammunition for forty years, and has owned many progressive presses. His handloads have been used to train numerous new shooters.

Marty Groppi, whose work appears here, has been an avid collector of firearms and a handloader of the finest degree for decades. He shoots IDPA as well, and has spent more time behind the trigger of a 1911 than anyone else I know.

And me? As the President of Massaro Ballistic Laboratories and a handloading junkie, I've had the opportunity to use and experiment with many different pieces of gear, from many different manufacturers, and while I don't participate in the gun games, I do produce quite an amount of handgun ammunition for those that do.

J.D. Fielding Photography

What follows is a collection of ideas and experiences, and I hope it aids you in your choice of, or use of, a progressive press.

PM: "Ok, boys. Tell me about your favorite progressives."

JK: "I grew up using a turret press, due to financial constraints, but when I finally could afford a Dillon 450, my eyes were opened. Eventually I progressed to the Dillon XL650, and though I still use the 450, I think the 650 is a better machine."

MG: "My Dillon 550 was my first progressive, but the Square Deal Press came first, and I still use that as my backup. That said, the Dillon XL650 has been a pleasure to use."

PM: "Like Jeff, my experiences began with a turret press, but the RCBS Pro2000 Auto-Index was the first progressive I ever owned. I like the design; it's simple and effective."

PM: "What is it about those Dillons that you guys like so much?"

MG: "The assembly is a piece of cake. The instructions are clear, simple to follow, and to the point. Once assembled, they stay in tune, deliver a consistent product, and the "No B.S." warranty is unprecedented."

JK: "They're pretty much bullet-proof. They are very easy to operate, and work as advertised. In all these years, I've never had a single problem with my Dillon."

PM: "Having spent some time with the XL650, I have to agree that the press works very well. The .45ACP ammo we've produced has been amazing."

MG: "The Dillon powder thrower is a very accurate design. Time after time, I've weighed the charge

The Dillon XL650

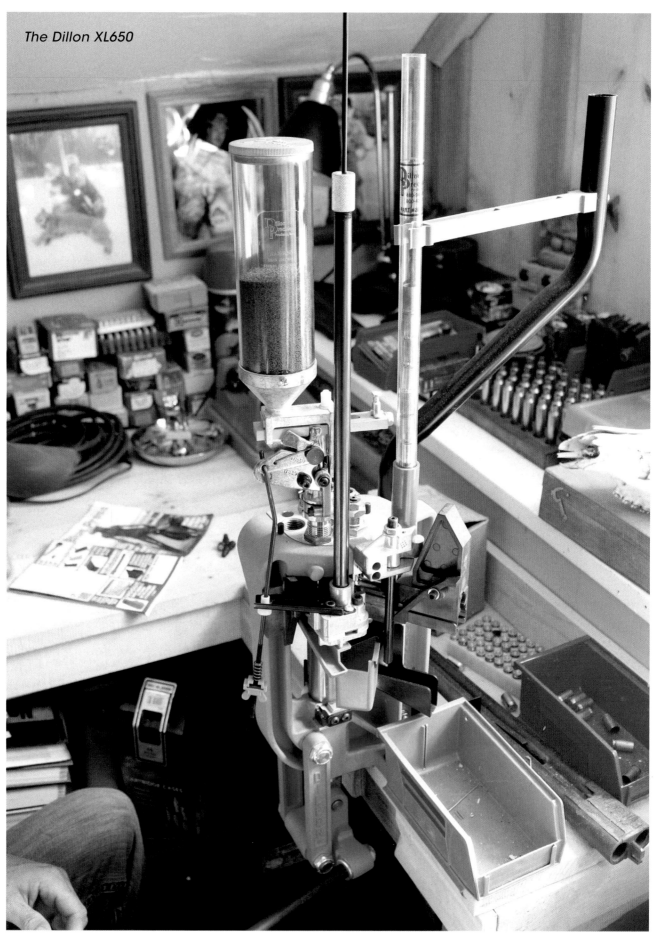

J.D. Fielding Photography

thrown and it measures exactly where I need it to. The all-steel linkage on the powder thrower has a very smooth feel, which is important when operating a progressive. Any slight variation is easily felt."

JK: "I use my Dillon for many different pistol calibers, and the adjustment between calibers is easy. Just remove the two pins, change out the tool head and shellplate, and you're back in business. That is an appreciable feature, especially when you own as many different pistol calibers as I do."

PM: "I like the Dillon dies. Once the cotter key is removed the internal assembly comes right out without removing the die body, and that assembly can be cleaned to remove all the gunk that builds up when loading lead bullets. That feature makes the Dillon dies well worth the investment. The fact that they stay in adjustment is an added bonus."

MG: "I like the floating decap assembly; it seems to throw old primers out of the case. Even if the primer is sealed into the primer pocket, these dies send them south without any issue."

JK: "The two-sided seater plug makes it a joy to switch between semi-wadcutters and roundnose bullets. Simply put, you pull the cotter key, pop the retainer pin and flip the bullet seater around to change it. Easy-peasy."

Dual-sided Dillon bullet seater

J.D. Fielding Photography

MG: "Dillon's Powder-Check System is a life saver. When you're shooting IDPA, you're so concentrated on the target, that a squib load could end your day, in addition to ruining your handgun. The Dillon system detects and warns of both no-powder present or over-charged loads."

Dillon .45ACP Dies

J.D. Fielding Photography

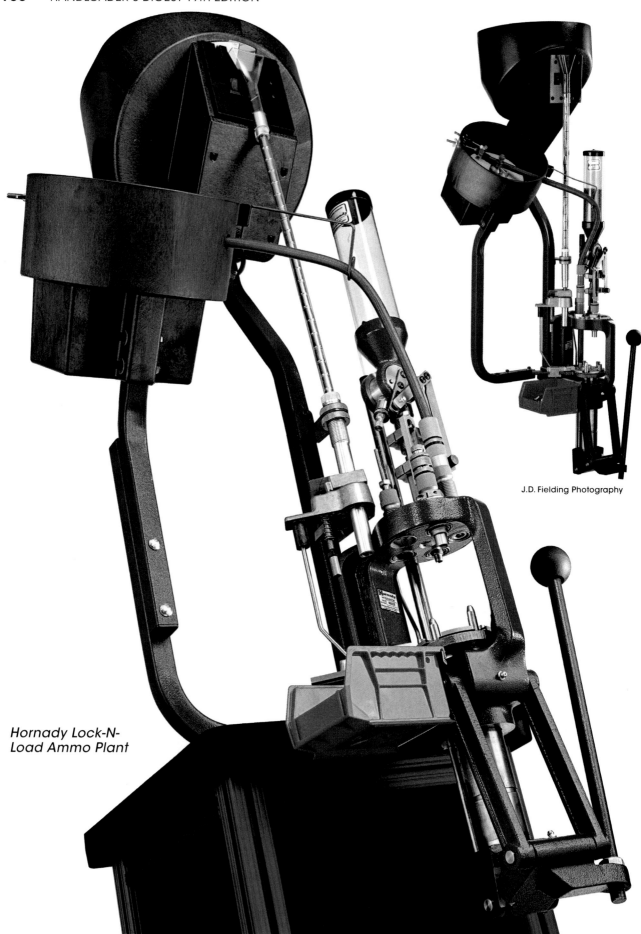

J.D. Fielding Photography

Hornady Lock-N-Load Ammo Plant

J.D. Fielding Photography

J.D. Fielding Photography

Left: Hornady AP under construction

Hornady Lock-N-Load Bushings

STEP 3
③

STEP 1
①

STEP 2
②

JK: "Wow, that's an awesome feature. I really wish we had that years ago!"

PM: "What are your thoughts on this Hornady Lock-N-Load Ammo Plant?"

JK: "I like the feel of the 2" diameter ram, each pull of the handle gives a positive touch, especially during the priming phase. Even though the press is rather tall, and takes up a bit of space on your bench and in your room, the overall package is a solid design. "

MG: "Even though the assembly of the Hornady progressive is more difficult and time consuming than the Dillon, once the Hornady is assembled, it is a pleasure to use. The bullet and case loaders are a bit noisy, but they make ammo production quite faster. The

DVD was a huge help, but I still had to make some phone calls to Hornady for assistance. Good customer service."

PM: "I'll have to agree with the noisy part; it kind of reminds me of the New York State Lottery drawing!"

MG: "The grease fitting is an awesome feature."

PM: "I like any press with a zerk fitting. I even like saying zerk fitting."

JK: "What's a zerk fitting?"

MG: "Not only does the ram have a grease fitting, but the linkage does as well. Properly cared for, this Hornady press could give a lifetime of service."

JK: "The Lock-N-Load bushings are a great design. Once the dies are adjusted, you can easily switch out calibers in a quarter turn. Nothing comes out of adjustment, nothing changes at all."

MG: "That design is one that really works well. Setting up your dies can be a chore, and the Hornady design lets them stay where you set them. The dies snap in with a 1/8 turn twist, and there's no question of resetting the dies."

PM: "The fact that the cases are dropped mechanically, as well as the bullets, makes ammo production increase significantly."

MG: "Indeed. The Hornady powder drop is easy to adjust, and more than accurate. I've used Hornady's powder thrower in the past with fantastic results."

The APS priming system that gives the author fits.

J.D. Fielding Photography

JK: "Many people really like the floating bullet seater in Hornady, and I'm among them. I like the way they center the bullet during the seating process. "

MG: "I'm OK with them, but not entirely impressed. I've used them, and they've made good ammo, but I've also used others with equal results."

PM: "I do like the Hornady shellplates, they seem to be well constructed and very consistent."

MG: "The whole Hornady package seems to be over-built, and I say that in a good way. The shellplates are thicker than normal, which won't deform under extreme stresses."

PM: "Do you guys have any thoughts on the other presses? I like my RCBS Pro2000 Auto Index and all of its features, excepting the APS priming system. Those plastic strips

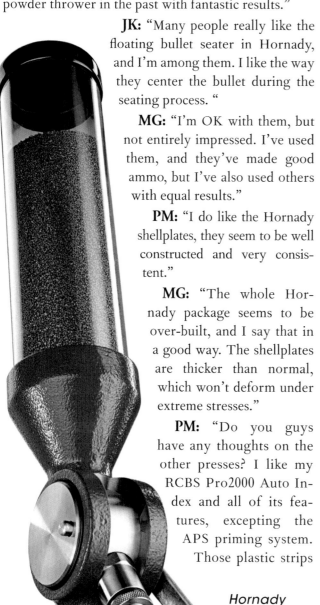

Hornady Powder Dispenser

The Pro2000 Auto Index at work

J.D. Fielding Photography

drive me insane when they jam up in the press. You have to dissemble the whole damned shellplate assembly to clean it out."

MG: "I've only used your RCBS machine, but I like it. It indexes really well, and the RCBS dies are good too. I don't mind the APS system; it seems to be a safer design than the standard primer tube."

PM: "I completely agree about that, if a primer were to pop you probably wouldn't set the whole strip off. I'm often concerned about primer detonation on a pro-

*The RCBS
Pro2000
Auto Index*

J.D. Fielding Photography

Above: *Falcon Bullet Company .45 caliber 200-grain Semi-WadCutter.*

Right: *Rainier 230-grain copper plated roundnose*

J.D. Fielding Photography

gressive, especially with a hopper full of powder. Even thought that APS system is a bit more time consuming to load, I feel better about it."

JK: "I've always liked the RCBS stuff. Have you seen the new ProChucker?"

PM: "I saw it at the SHOT Show last January. Seems to be an amazing press, and they've gone back to the primer tubes. The ProChucker 7 would probably be the way to go; the extra stations would be perfect to run an extra crimp die, powder check die or whatever you'd like. Plus the ram has a zerk fitting."

JK: "What's a zerk fitting?"

MG: "What do you guys like to use for bullets? I like to run cast, especially in the progressives. They're cheap, accurate and easy to load. Perfect for IDPA."

PM: "I like them too. Falcon Bullets makes a good, affordable bullet for most pistol calibers. The 200-grain .45 caliber semi-wadcutter is a really cool bullet, especially the coated version."

JK: "You mean the lipstick-red ones? What's the deal with those?"

PM: "Exactly. Falcon uses a proprietary coating called FalCoating. It cuts down the leading in your barrel significantly, as well as in the dies."

MG: "My 1911 loves those things. They load very well in the Dillon; accurate as all hell."

PM: "I also like the Rainier bullets. They're completely copper plated, no exposed lead at all. They are another affordable option, and the roundnose Rainiers feed like a dream in just about any gun.

PM: "OK, gents- let's talk about some pitfalls while using a progressive press. What tricks do you use, what advice can you give?"

JK: "You've got to pay strict attention to the way you work the ram. Every stroke should be the same, so you get a good seat on your primers, and the powder dumps the same way every time. Also, it helps to weigh a powder charge every so often to make sure nothing comes out of adjustment with your powder drop."

MG: "Always walk away from your press at a known point, that is, at a point where you know what the next step is. I like to leave my press with a primed round in the appropriate stage, and a bullet, loosely seated in the bullet seating stage. That way, I know exactly what is going to happen when I work the press handle at the next session."

PM: "I try to keep a close eye on the powder supply and the primers as well. If you run out of either, you end up with a non-primed case and powder all over the shellplate. That usually results in me having to take the machine apart to clean things up. A real pain in the arse."

MG: "When you do make a mistake, the best remedy, in my opinion, is to start all processes from the beginning, to avoid the possibility of a double charge or a squib load. I don't ever want that to happen."

PM: "One last question: do you guys ever use your progressive for making rifle ammunition? Personally I don't, I prefer a single-stage or turret press."

JK: "I tried it once, to make some 7.62x39 ammo. I didn't work out so well. Never went back."

MG: "Nah, when it comes to rifle ammo I'm a single-stage or turret guy, like Jeff. Pistols, absolutely. Rifles, no. "

PM: "I appreciate you guys sitting down with me for this. Anything else to add?"

JK: "Will somebody please tell me what a zerk fitting is?"

Editors Note: We'll let Jeff Google zerk fittings...

HANDLOADING
CATALOG

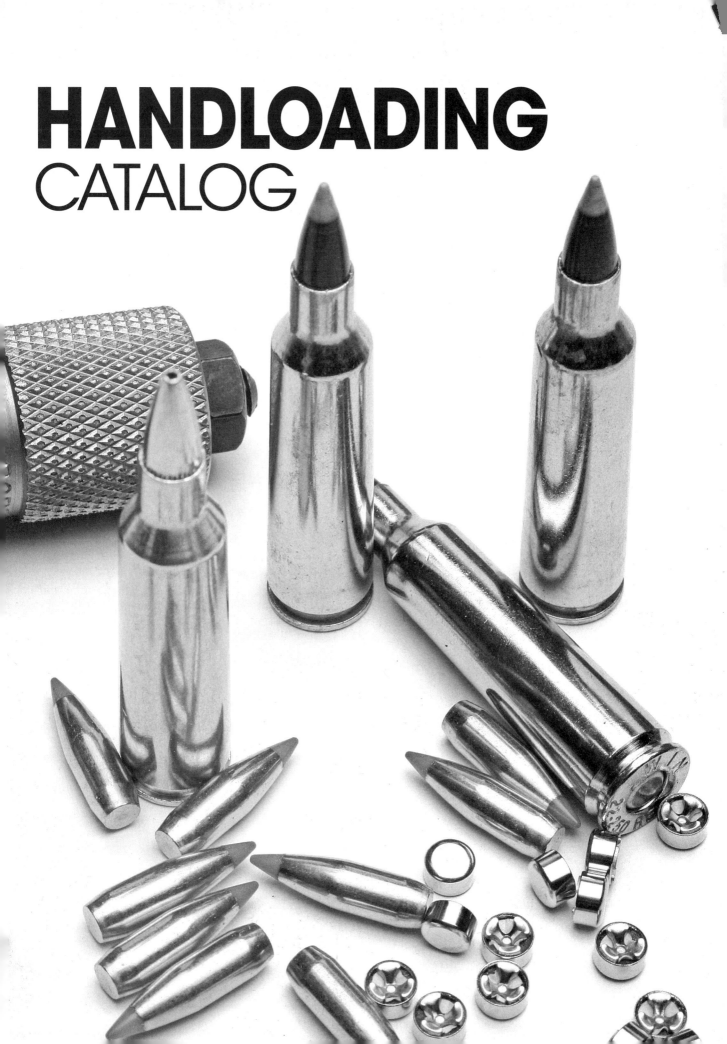

METALLIC HANDLOADING TOOLS:
PRESSES

Reloading Presses

The reloading press is, without a doubt, the single piece of gear that we reloaders are going to use the most. There are many makes, models, colors, shapes and sizes available today, and different applications for each type. Depending on your reloading style and objectives, there may be more than one type of press that will get the job done, and I'd be willing to bet that if you reload for long enough, you'll end up owning more than one model, and probably more than one type of press. Single-stage, turret, progressive, shotgun, there's all kinds of stuff out there, and it warrants taking a look at.

Single Stage for Rifle/Pistol

The single-stage press is the simplest machine, performing a single operation at a time, having a threaded hole for a single reloading die. They are (usually) the most rigid, and can deliver the tightest tolerances available. The single-stage presses come in two main types: a "C" press and an "O" press, named after the shape of their frame. The "C" presses leave one side of the press open – hence the "C" moniker – and while strong, can leave room for a bit of unwanted flexure. The "O" press, in which the frame is a solid mass, cannot flex, and (again usually) gives the most uniform results.

The classic single-stage press, the RCBS RockChucker, is a great example of an "O" frame press. I own a couple, and they are a good value. Mine have given me years of good service, cranking out tens of thousands of rounds.

Turret Presses for Rifle/Pistol

The turret press, having threaded receptacles for holding multiple reloading dies simultaneously, can make the reloader's life a bit easier. The top of the press, or turret, can be rotated manually, to allow, for example, resizing, flaring and seating dies, so the reloader can switch between them quickly when the need arises. The turret can, in some instances, have a bit of play in the press, and some reloaders find that unacceptable.

The better quality turret presses have very little or no play in them at all. I have a Redding T7 turret press that holds up to seven dies at once and it is one of the nicest presses I've ever used. It handles most of my daily duties as a reloader, and handles them well.

I also have used a Lee Turret press, with the interchangeable aluminum heads, that has produced an obscene amount of ammunition, fueling dozens of rifles and pistols, and supplying ammunition for a half-dozen African Safaris. Play aside, if you keep a good eye on the tolerances, you can use many different tools to achieve the same goal.

Progressive Presses For Pistol/Rifle

The progressive presses are invariably the fastest means of producing large quantities of ammunition, especially for the pistols calibers. They perform multiple operations with each push/pull motion of the press handle, including resizing, priming, flaring, powder charging, bullet seating and crimping. They can be a hefty investment, and a bit difficult to setup and keep running, but when you've finally got the hang of things, you can make hundreds of rounds of ammunition per hour.

The complicated manner in which these presses operate requires the handloader to have a complete knowledge and vast experience with the processes involved, and I'd feel safe saying that the progressive isn't the best choice for the beginner or novice. The differences in progressive presses can huge, as can the price tags, and they can be outfitted with many bells and whistles (sometimes literally), that can help to keep things safe.

If you shoot IDPA, USPSC, or any of the other gun games, a progressive press will keep you well supplied with ammunition. I haven't had the best of luck producing rifle ammunition on a progressive press, as the shell plates can give flexure when resizing the longer rifle cases, which take more pressure to properly resize. I do enjoy their convenience for pistol ammunition.

Editor's Picks:
Single-Stage Presses

Without a doubt, the single-stage press has been what I've used to produce most of my ammunition. It is the most economical of choices, and a great tool to have on hand even if you decide that the turrets or progressives are for you. I keep an inexpensive Lee "C" press on the bench, just for decapping brass.

1. The RCBS RockChucker Supreme- Part No. 9356

This is the latest variation on the RockChucker series, featuring the famous cast-iron "O" frame, and an arm for priming cartridges from the press. The slot in the press ram will work with most major brands of shell holders, as well as with most brands of reloading dies.

It's really difficult to wear out a RockChucker, as they are built like a small tank. My main reason for picking the RockChucker is its value. For a minimal investment, you can produce amazing ammunition, pretty much anything smaller than the .50 BMG, and do it for a lifetime. The ⅞"-14 standard die thread that most dies use is provided, but can be changed to 1 ¼"-12 by removing the bushing, for the big, fat safari calibers if you so choose. From the smallest pistol caliber to the largest safari caliber, a RockChucker can handle it. Lifetime warranty for home reloaders.

2. The RCBS Summit Press – Part no. 9290

This is a horse of a different color. The Summit press is a new design for RCBS, and a pretty cool one at that. Instead on having the ram move the shellholder and cartridge case up into the stationary die, on the Summit press the case and shellholder remain in place at the lower portion of the press and the die is lowered onto the case.

The mechanical advantage comes from the steel linkage and a huge 2" ram, which features a Zerk fitting that you can grease like your truck. The "frame" of the press is made from cast iron, for a lifetime of service, and the handle can be moved from right to left without trouble. The only feature that I wish would have been included in the Summit design is a means of priming cases from the press; it isn't offered (many of the good folks at RCBS believe we should be priming by hand, anyhow), but the press is a sound design that I've used for the last couple of years. I especially like it for the bullet seating process; it gives all sorts of "feel", especially when seating longer bullets. Comes with RCBS Limited Lifetime Warranty.

3. Forster Co-Ax Press – Part No. 028271

C-frame, cast iron and steel construction, features dual floating guide rods for perfect alignment. Proprietary 'jaw' shellholder design doesn't require the use of traditional shellholders. Dies snap into a slot, and are held by the lock ring rather than by threads. Fully-adjustable primer seater. Right or left-hand operation.

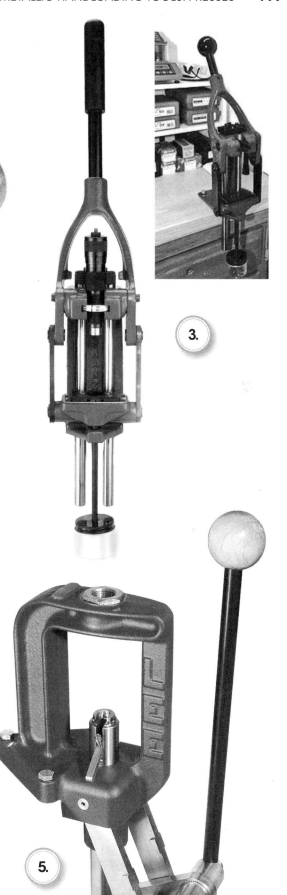

3.

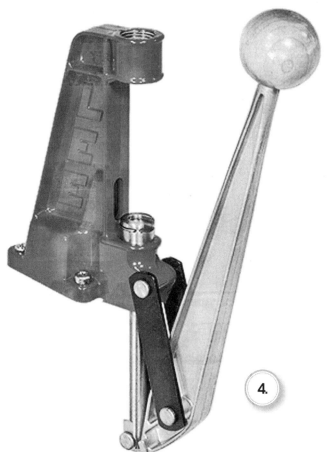

4.

4. Lee Reloader Press – Part No. 90045

C-frame, cast aluminum construction, bottom-center positioned handle for ambidextrous use. 3 ¼" ram stroke. No priming system included, optional Ram Prime Unit available.

5. Lee Classic Cast Press – Part No. 90998

O-frame, cast iron construction, 4" ram stroke. Left or right-hand operation, steel compound linkage. Accepts ⅞"-14 threaded dies, and 1-¼"-12 dies when the thread adapter is removed. Ram diameter 1 ⅛", includes spent primer tube that can be directed to trash can. Primer arm operates at bottom of ram stroke.

5.

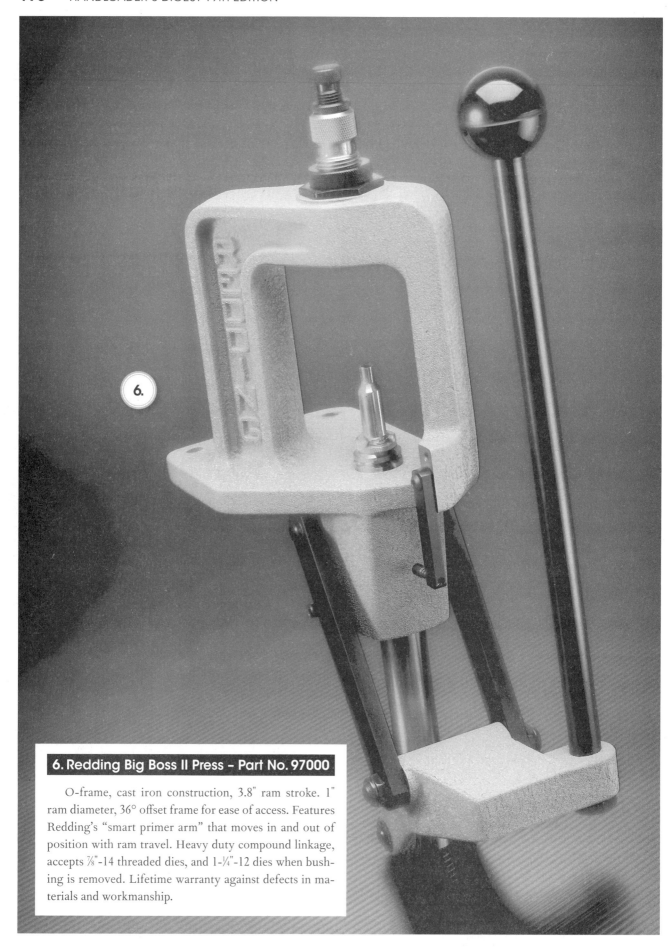

6. Redding Big Boss II Press - Part No. 97000

O-frame, cast iron construction, 3.8" ram stroke. 1" ram diameter, 36° offset frame for ease of access. Features Redding's "smart primer arm" that moves in and out of position with ram travel. Heavy duty compound linkage, accepts ⅞"-14 threaded dies, and 1-¼"-12 dies when bushing is removed. Lifetime warranty against defects in materials and workmanship.

7. Lyman Crusher 2 Press –Part No. 7726300

O-frame, cast iron construction, 4" ram stroke. 1" diameter ram, priming arm included with large and small primer cups. Left or right-hand operation, press handle attaches at bottom of compound press linkage. 4.5" opening for loading of large cases. Silver hammertone powder coat finish. One year manufacturers warranty.

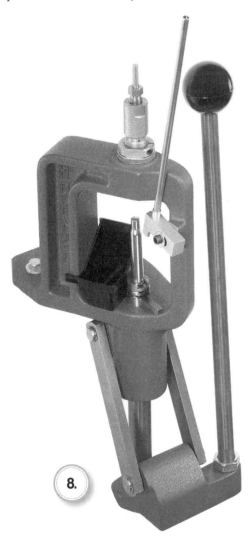

8. Hornady Lock-N-Load Classic press – Part No. 085001

O-frame, cast alloy construction. 30° offset frame, 3.75" ram stroke. Hornady Positive Priming System, large and small primer cups included. Three Hornady Lock-N-Load bushings included, for quick change of dies. Standard ⅞"-14 threads only. Lifetime warranty.

9. RCBS AmmoMaster – Part No. 88703

Cast aluminum construction, this press uses long columns for a very long ram stroke of 6 ¾", perfect for loading the longest of cartridges. The 1" ram is steel constructed, and the press comes with a ram prime unit. Accepts both standard ⅞"-14 thread dies, remove the bushing to use larger 1 ½"-12 thread dies. Lifetime warranty for personal use.

10. Sinclair Benchrest Press

Designed for use at the bench or at the competition. Machined from a solid billet of aluminum, heavy duty linkage is covered for protection. 2.5" opening will handle cartridges of .308 Winchester length and smaller. Spent primers exit through the bottom of the ram, keeping any primer debris away from the linkage.

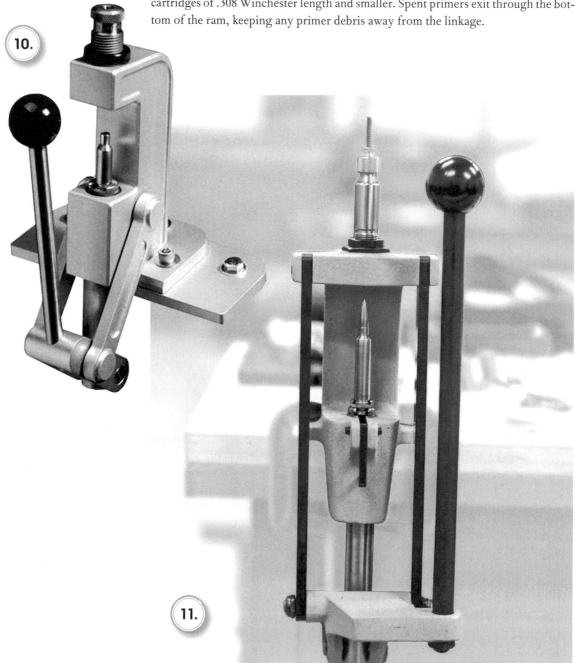

11. Redding Model 700 Ultramag Press – Part No. 70000

O-frame press, cast iron and steel construction. Designed for the longest cartridges, this press has a huge 4-¾" opening. Its compound leverage system generates all sorts of mechanical advantage over the entire travel of the ram. Smart primer arm, large and small primer cups included. Uses standard ⅞"-14 dies with supplied adapter, remove adapter to use 1-¼"-12 dies. Perfect press for the longest Nitro Express cartridges, as well as older black powder cartridges over 3" in length.

Editor's Picks:
Turret Presses

These multi-die wonders are the in-between development of the single stage presses and the progressive presses, allowing the reloader to keep multiple dies on the press at once. I especially like them for pistol reloading, as I can switch between flaring dies, seating dies and resizing dies without having to screw/unscrew each one when a change needs to be made.

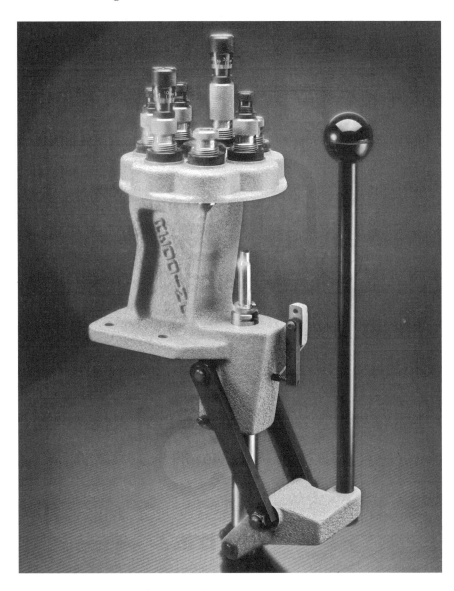

1.

1. The Redding T7 Turret Press – Part No. 67000

This is a well-built and well-thought out reloading press. The tight tolerances engender all kinds of confidence, even when priming from the press. Like all Redding products, the threads are cut perfectly, and the hardware is over-designed, to give you a lifetime of good service.

Couple this with some of Redding's fantastic dies, and you've got a recipe for success. I even like the little details, like the spent primer tube that prevents the shiny little dead guys from spilling all over the floor. This is a cast-iron behemoth, which is good for generating all kinds of pressure while resizing, as once bolted securely to your bench, there's no movement whatsoever.

Switching between stations is just a simple turn of the handle, and you can fell the detent 'click' into place. I've not experienced any flexure in the top, as I have with some others, and my buddy Marty Groppi has one that is older than he is and still produces fantastic ammunition. This is well worth the investment.

2. The Lee Classic Four Hole Turret Press - Part No. 90064

If you're on a budget, and you want an affordable option, look long and hard at the Lee Classic Turret press. It was the press that I learned on when Dad taught me how to reload, and the model that we had, which Dad purchased in the early 70s, has made tens of thousands of rounds of ammunition, including the big safari cartridges like the .416 Remington and .458 Lott.

Yes, when compared to the Redding T7, you'll find a bit of play in the aluminum head, but if you keep an eye on things you can produce very good ammunition on a tight budget. The frame is cast iron, and the columns are steel. A reversible lever-style priming system, with large and small primer cups.

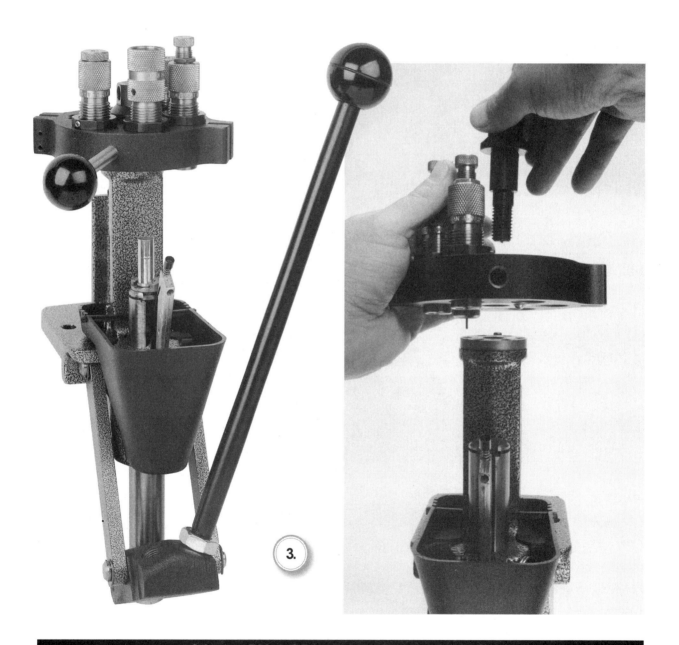

3.

3. Lyman T-Mag 2 Turret press- Part No. 7040781

Cast iron construction, six station turret head. Uses standard ⅞"-14 thread dies. 4" ram stroke, on press priming with spent primer catcher. Right or left hand operation – handle can be moved to either side.

Press head is detachable for changing die sets without removing dies – dies and extra heads sold separately. Handle for switching between stations, turret head can be replaced so you can leave your dies set up. 1 year manufacturer's warranty.

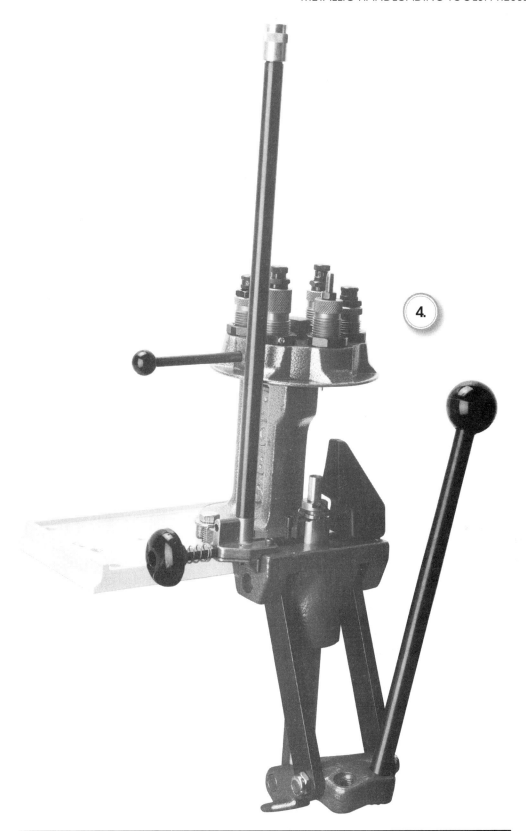

4. RCBS Turret Press – Part No. 88901

Cast iron construction, six station turret head. Uses standard ⅞"-14 thread dies. 4" ram stroke, automatic priming system included. Includes primer tube, primer plugs, and sleeves for large and small primers. Handle is moveable for right or left hand use. Replaceable turret is held in place with one bolt, for quick changeover. Extra turret heads sold separately.

Editor's Picks:
Progressive Presses

The wise choice for seasoned reloaders who need to generate a great volume of ammunition; the progressive press is a very useful tool when it's set up properly and running right. Getting those presses into that condition can be a bit of a chore, but the reward is worth the investment.

Take the time to watch some of the promotional videos, as well as some of the independent reviews to get a feel for the level of difficulty of assembly as well as maintenance.

The progressive presents a unique situation, in that you have an appreciable store of powder in close proximity to a large supply of primers. While a very rare instance, there are examples of primers detonating in the primers tube, and frankly that scares me. The possibility of injury from the primer detonation is enough to worry about, and the thought of that happening next to a hopper full of powder gives me the willies.

That aside, my own actual production numbers usually run shy of the advertised figures, more than likely because I take my time to ensure each stroke of the press is executed consistently, giving as close to the same pressures as I can. I want the primers to be seated uniformly (that's on the downstroke) and I want to make sure the powder dispenser gets the same stroke as well, to keep everything on the level.

Many of the progressives have different levels of upgrades; things like electronic bullet and case feeders, and powder check devices that deliver an audible beep when there is an excess (double) charge, or no powder present at all.

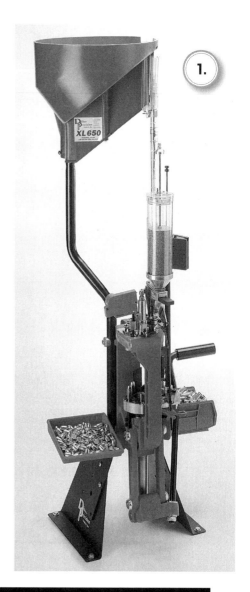

1.

1. The Dillon XL 650

Dillon has, in my opinion, the most straightforward design among all the progressives. Well-constructed, with all-steel linkages; this auto-indexing progressive is easy to use and makes some great ammunition. Large and small primer tubes are included, and a powder thrower of appropriate volume for the case you intend to reload. Dillon's customer service is impeccable, and they are readily available to assist the reloader should he or she have any questions.

Their "no BS" lifetime warranty is another added bonus in choosing this company's product.

While some of their other models, like the big honkin' Super 1050, will give features like a primer pocket swager and auto case feeder, I feel the XL 650 represents one of the best values on the market. Dillon's powder drop funnel doubles as a flaring die, leaving four others stations for resizing, seating, and crimping. The last stage of the XL 650 has an auto eject feature, which kicks the completed cartridge out into a plastic bin. Some of the upgrades available for the XL 650 are worth the expense.

The powder check system indicates an over charge or under charge (or no charge at all), and occupies its own station in the tool head. Speaking of the tool head, it can be quickly changed out if you'd like to change calibers, and Dillon offers some color-coded anodized aluminum replacement tool heads for easy identification of differing calibers.

Although the XL 650 works with any standard die set, Dillon offers a good set of proprietary dies that work very well with the progressives; they are very easy to clean and disassemble by means of a cotter key. You'd be doing yourself a favor by requesting a copy of "The Blue Press", Dillon's catalog, to discover all the possible options for their reloading machines.

2. The RCBS Pro2000 Auto Index Progressive Press – Part No. 88882

Cast iron frame, five station, 3.5" ram stroke, auto-indexing progressive. The Pro2000 uses APS priming strips to minimize the potential of primer tube detonation. The RCBS Die plate is held in by means of two pins, and be easily removed to change calibers. The included RCBS Uniflow Powder Measure comes with a micrometer adjustment screw, to dial in exact powder charges. Requires dies and shellplates, sold separately. Uses standard ⅞"-14 threaded dies. Right hand operation.

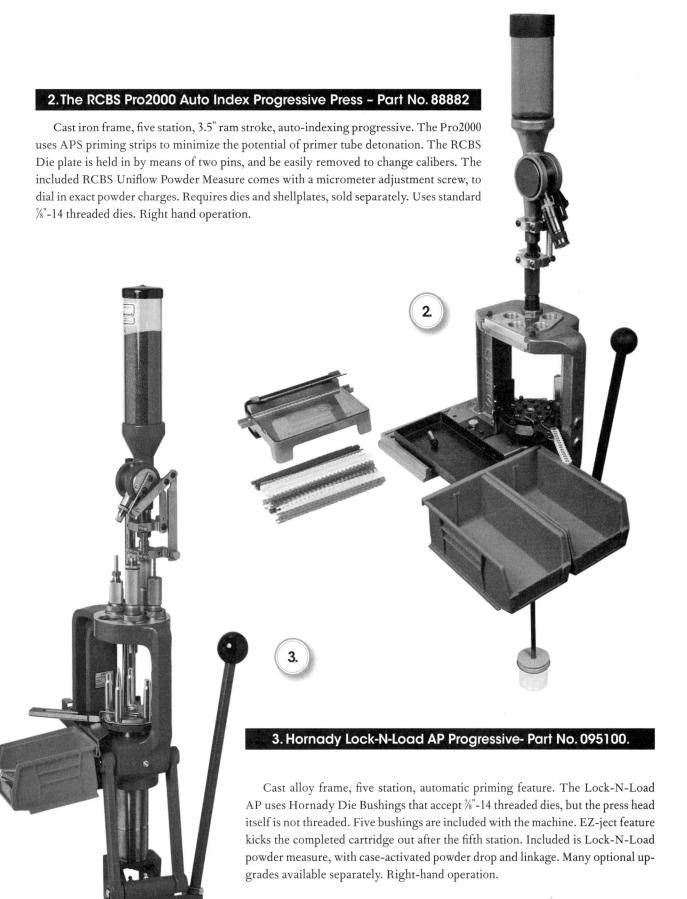

3. Hornady Lock-N-Load AP Progressive- Part No. 095100.

Cast alloy frame, five station, automatic priming feature. The Lock-N-Load AP uses Hornady Die Bushings that accept ⅞"-14 threaded dies, but the press head itself is not threaded. Five bushings are included with the machine. EZ-ject feature kicks the completed cartridge out after the fifth station. Included is Lock-N-Load powder measure, with case-activated powder drop and linkage. Many optional upgrades available separately. Right-hand operation.

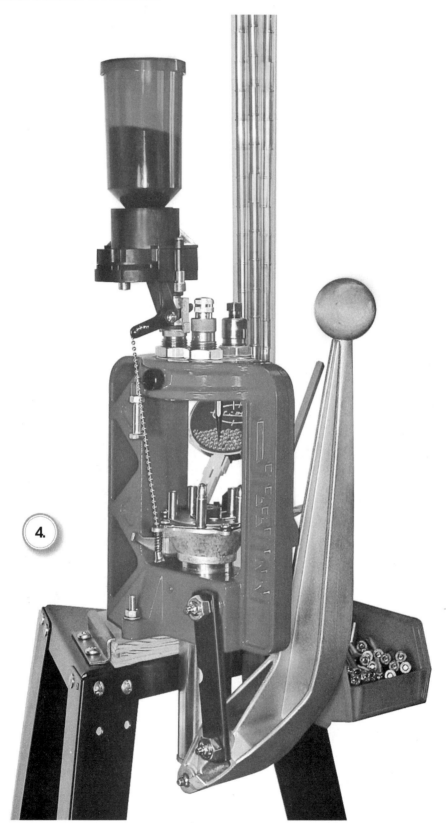

4. Lee Load-Master Progressive Press – Part No. 90183

Frame constructed of steel, cast aluminum and polymer. Five station detachable turret, auto-indexing, accepts ⅞"-14 thread dies. Press doesn't come with priming capability or powder thrower; they are available separately, or as a Lee caliber-specific kit. Turret head is easily removed so dies do not need to be adjusted. Right hand operation. Lee recommends only CCI or Remington primers for use with this press; to use other primers you must purchase the Lee 'explosion shield.'

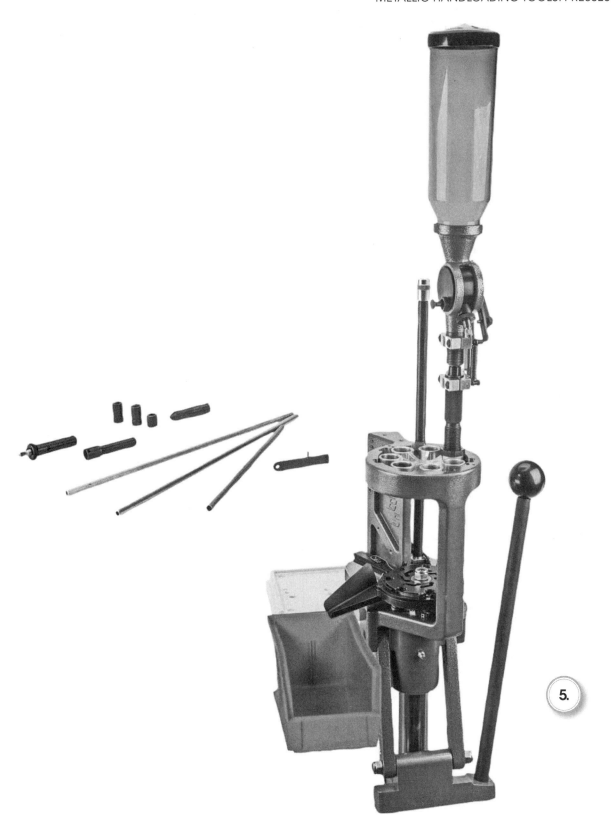

5.

5. RCBS Pro Chucker 7 Auto Index Progressive Press - Part No. 88911

RCBS's new flagship of progressives, this cast alloy frame seven-station press gives the reloader a whole bunch of options. Seven-stations allow the use of separate seater and crimp dies, as well as a bullet feeder or other options. The Pro Chucker 7 uses a standard primer drop tube, as opposed to the APS strips used by the Pro2000. Powder measure features a quick drain tube for changing powders without removing the measure from the press. Right hand operation.

METALLIC HANDLOADING TOOLS: RELOADING DIES

Reloading Dies

There are many makes, models, colors, shapes and sizes available today, and different appliThe ability to accurately and reliably resize and reload centerfire brass cartridges falls to a good set of reloading dies. The reloading dies are the nucleus of the reloading procedure, allowing us to turn expanded brass into perfectly resized cases, and giving us the capability of pressing our new bullets into the resized case.

The basic set of dies consists of a full-length resizing die, and a bullet seating die, with a flaring die thrown into the mix if you're loading for a straight-walled cartridge. However, there are specialty dies available: dies that only resize the neck portion of the cartridge, to enhance accuracy in the bolt-action rifles, dies that resize the case all the way to the base to best cycle through the autoloading rifles, competition-style dies with micrometer adjustments for ultra-precise bullet seating depths, pistol does made form carbide steel so you don't need to lubricate; the list goes on and on.

With few exceptions, each set of dies are caliber-specific – some die sets can do double duty - so you'll need to purchase a set for each of the cartridges that you intend to reload (Certain cartridges may share the same die set, for example .38 Special/.357 Magnum, .44 Special/.44 Magnum, .45 Colt/.454 Casull – they simply require a spacer for the longer cartridge).

They must be properly adjusted to the proper depths to work in your press, and as each reloading company offers a detailed set of instruction with their product, I highly recommend you spend some time reading the literature to save yourself some headaches.

Redding .45 Colt/.454 Casull dies

The basic concept of reloading dies remains relatively unchanged, and I still use dies that are older than I am. If you keep your dies well maintained and clean, they should give you a lifetime of use.

Not all dies are created equal, and there are quirks to each brand. That's not to say that one brand is necessarily better than another, rather say they do different things. I've used just about every brand of reloading die at one point in time or another, and I've been successful using all of them.

Obviously there is a logical correlation of quality and ease to price of product, but there is good value in the inexpensive dies as well, as long as you keep a strict eye on subtle variances in finished ammunition.

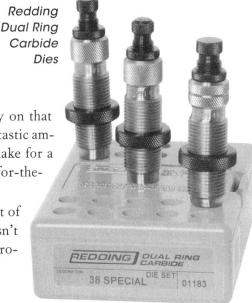

Redding Dual Ring Carbide Dies

Put more plainly, a Redding Competition seating die, armed with a micrometer-adjustable seater plug, will give the consistent results much easier than, say, an entry level Lee seater die.

Please keep in mind I own and use both, and while I can rely on that Redding die to maintain a consistent dimension, I've produced fantastic ammunition with many sets of Lee dies. RCBS and Hornady dies make for a good middle-of-the-road choice, giving perhaps the best 'bang-for-the-buck' (pun fully intended) to a reloader on a budget.

If you load for your pistol and participate in the gun games, a set of dies with a carbide resizing die is a smart choice, as lubrication isn't necessary, and it's nice to be able to skip that step, especially on a progressive press.

Some die sets include multiple bullet seating plugs, for different meplat profiles.

It requires some homework on your part to investigate which dies offer this in your chosen caliber, and an Internet search will quickly reveal the options offered to you. Some companies - Redding and RCBS come quickly to mind - offer a 'custom die' service. If you're into wildcatting cartridges, this is a great resource for you, as they can help bring your dream cartridge to fruition.

From Hornady's floating bullet seater, to the rust preventative that Redding uses which must be removed prior to use, each set of dies has its own personality, if you will, and it will take some experimentation for you to find what works best for you.

RCBCS Bullet Seater Plugs in 416 Rigby, for roundnose and spitzer bullets

Editor's Picks:
Reloading Dies

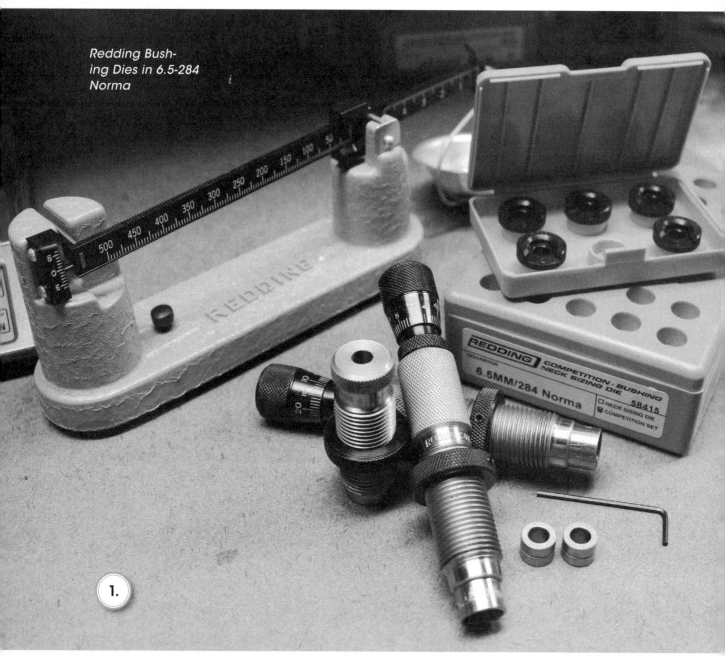

Redding Bush-
ing Dies in 6.5-284
Norma

1.

1. Redding Match Bushing Full Die Set

I've fallen deeply in love with these dies. The resizing die uses a bushing, which will work best with your brand of brass, to minimize the stress on the case mouth. You see, a standard resizing die will shrink your case mouth down to an inside dimension .002 or .003" below caliber dimension, so the case may drawn over the expander ball, leaving it .001" below caliber for good neck tension during bullet seating.

If your brass is thick, it will be over-worked and become brittle prematurely. By using a bushing that matches the O.D. of your particular brass, you will extend case life significantly. The Competition Seating die uses a micrometer adjustable seater to give repeatable seating depths time after time. The adjustment is held in place by a coil spring, and as a result shouldn't be used with compressed loads. I've used these dies in several calibers for my rifles, and the resulting ammunition is very accurate.

2. RCBS Safari Series Dies

If you love the big guns –as I do- you know that as the cartridges get more obscure, the dies can get really, really expensive. But RCBS offers the Safari Series dies at a reasonable price, so we can fuel the big guys.

My own .404 Jeffery falls into this category, and the RCBS dies work perfectly. RCBS provides a full-length resizing die (you don't want to neck size for dangerous game rifles, as positive feeding and extraction are paramount) and a bullet seating die. Some of the larger cartridges require a different thread (other than ⅞"-14) and may require a bushing to operate in your press. If you need to fuel the .500 Jeffery of your dreams, look at the RCBS Safari Series.

RCSB Safari Dies
in .450/400 NE

Other Die Sets

Lee Precision, Inc

Lee offers a great value, especially to a beginning reloader on a budget. Their Pacesetter 3-die sets give just what is needed: A full-length resizing die, a good bullet seater, and the Lee Factory Crimp die to hold the bullet firmly in the case. These dies also come with a proper shellholder for the cartridge you're loading, as well as a load data chart.

The Ultimate Four Rifle Die Set features the same trio of dies as the Pacesetter 3-die set, but includes a collet neck sizing die, for those who find neck-sized ammunition to give better accuracy.

I like the 4 Die Deluxe Pistol Set from Lee, as it includes the Carbide Factory Crimp Die. I know many reloaders who purchase a Lee Crimp die, irrespective of the brand of the resizing, flaring and seating dies they own. The Powder Through Expanding Die makes perfect sense for those who like to use a turret press instead of a progressive; you can flare the case and charge it in the same step.

My own pet peeves with Lee dies? The lock rings don't lock. They are held in place with a rubber O-ring, and they can come out of adjustment if you're not careful. The seater adjustments can befall the same fate. That said, I have used – and still use – Lee dies to make good ammunition, and will continue to do so.

Lee .45ACP Dies

Hornady Dies

Hornady has been in the reloading game for quite a while now, first as Pacific Dies (I still use some old Pacific sets), but in recent years they have expanded the product line under their own name.

I like Hornady dies for several reasons: One, I've always found them to be consistent, delivering a good product every time. If you've ever caught a bad set of dies, you'll appreciate the good ones (I had a bad set of .300 H&H Magnum dies, from a now defunct company, that made me question my own sanity).

Two, the floating bullet seater aligns the bullet to the center of the case mouth for consistent loading, and that helps to keep bullet runout to a minimum.

Thirdly, and it's a little thing, they place the lock ring tightening screw so it fights against itself, instead of acting like a set screw against the threads.

I also like the concept of Hornady's elliptical expander ball, which seems to be easier on the brass, as well as making it easier to 'neck-up' brass if you're using one caliber to form brass for a larger caliber.

Hornady offers a set of dies for most every caliber, as well as blank dies for forming your own wildcat calibers. They have a great taper crimp die for the pistol calibers that headspace off of the case mouth. These are well made dies that will offer a lifetime of service.

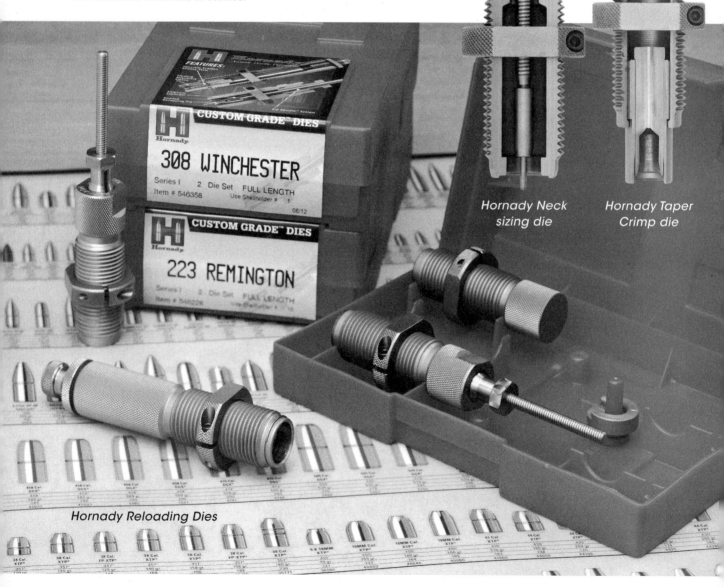

Hornady Neck sizing die

Hornady Taper Crimp die

Hornady Reloading Dies

Rifle Dies & Reloading Essentials

SERIES I: The most popular bottleneck rifle cartridges. Two die set: size die and bullet seater die.

SERIES II: The most popular handgun cartridges. Three die set: size die, expander die, seating die.

SERIES III: A second tier of bottleneck rifle cartridges. Two die set: size die and bullet seater die. For slightly less popular cartridges.

SERIES IV: Another tier of bottleneck rifle cartridges, obscure, almost semi-custom. Two die set: size die and seater die. Very low volume. Includes the Nitro Express cartridges.

SERIES V: The magnum handgun cartridges, and straight-wall rifle cartridges that require a special crimp (i.e. 450 Bushmaster is the only one). Four die set: size die, expander die, bullet seater die, and a special taper crimp die.

Rifle Cartridge	Bullet Diameter (inches)	Die Set	Die Series	Full-Length Size Die	Seating Die	Expander Die	Taper Crimp Die Only	Neck Size Die	Shell Holder # / Item No.	Shell Plate # / Item No.	Case Feeder Plate Size / Item No.	Bullet Feeder Die	Trimmer Pilot # / Item No.	Primer Punch	Bullet Puller Collet # / Item No.
HORNET	.172	546118	I	046202	044101	—	—	—	#3/390543	#3/392603	Sm Rfl/095314	—	*/390942	Small	#1/392154
REM FIREBALL	.172	546117	I	046200	044101	—	—	—	#16/390556	#16/392616	Sm Rfl/095314	—	*/390942	Small	#1/392154
REM	.172	546200	III	046201	044101	—	—	—	#16/390556	#16/392616	Sm Rfl/095314	—	*/390942	Small	#1/392154
222	.172	546202	IV	—	—	—	—	—	#16/390556	#16/392616	Sm Rfl/095314	—	*/390942	Small	#1/392154
223	.172	546204	IV	—	—	—	—	—	#16/390556	#16/392616	Sm Rfl/095314	—	*/390942	Small	#1/392154
VT	.204	546205	III	046206	044139	—	—	046038	#16/390556	#16/392616	Sm Rfl/095314	—	#22/390940	Small	#14/392167
TACTICAL	.204	546209	III	046208	044139	—	—	046038	#16/390556	#16/392616	Sm Rfl/095314	—	#22/390940	Small	#14/392167
4 RUGER	.204	546201	I	046590	044139	—	—	046038	#16/390556	#16/392616	Sm Rfl/095314	—	#22/390940	Small	#14/392167
HORNET	.224	546212	I	046213	044102	—	—	046066	#3/390543	#3/392603	Sm Rfl/095314	—	#1/390943	Small	#2/392155
K-HORNET	.224	546214	IV	—	—	—	—	046066	#3/390543	#3/392603	Sm Rfl/095314	—	#1/390943	Small	#2/392155
7x28 FN	.224	546203	III	046212	044136	—	—	—	#37/390577	—/—	Sm Rfl/095314	—	#1/390943	Small	#2/392155
8 BEE	.224	546206	IV	—	—	—	—	046066	#7/390547	#7/392607	Sm Rfl/095314	—	#1/390943	Small	#2/392155
1 REM FIREBALL	.224	546210	III	046211	044102	—	—	046040	#16/390556	#16/392616	Sm Rfl/095314	—	#1/390943	Small	#2/392155
2 REM	.224	546224	I	046225	044102	—	—	046040	#16/390556	#16/392616	Sm Rfl/095314	—	#1/390943	Small	#2/392155
3 REM	.224	546228	I	046229	044102	—	—	046040	#16/390556	#16/392616	Sm Rfl/095314	095340	#1/390943	Small	#2/392155
3 REM MATCH	.224	—	—	544229	044102	—	—	544227	#16/390556	#16/392616	Sm Rfl/095314	095340	#1/390943	Small	#2/392155
PPC	.224	546216	IV	—	—	—	—	046053	#6/390546	#6/392606	Sm Rfl/095314	—	#1/390943	Small	#2/392155
6x50 MAG	.224	546234	IV	—	—	—	—	046040	#16/390556	#16/392616	Sm Rfl/095314	—	#1/390943	Small	#2/392155
9 ZIPPER	.224	546208	IV	—	—	—	—	046040	#2/390542	#2/392602	Lg Rfl/095316	—	#1/390943	Large	#2/392155
5 WIN	.224	546232	III	046233	044127	—	—	046040	#4/390544	#4/392604	Lg Rfl/095316	—	#1/390943	Large	#2/392155
4 WBY	.224	546230	IV	—	—	—	—	046040	#17/390557	—/—	Lg Rfl/095316	—	#1/390943	Large	#2/392155
/250 REM	.224	546220	I	046221	044102	—	—	046040	#1/390541	#1/392601	Lg Rfl/095316	—	#1/390943	Large	#2/392155
/250 ACKLEY IMP	.224	546219	IV	—	—	—	—	046040	#1/390541	#1/392601	Lg Rfl/095316	—	#1/390943	Large	#2/392155
0 SWIFT	.224	546222	I	046223	044127	—	—	046054	#4/390544	#4/392604	Lg Rfl/095316	—	#1/390943	Large	#2/392155
x57	.224	546236	IV	—	—	—	—	—	#1/390541	#1/392601	Lg Rfl/095316	—	#1/390943	Large	#2/392155
3 WIN SS MAG	.224	546223	I	046558	044707	—	—	—	#35/390575	#35/392635	Lg Rfl/095316	—	#1/390943	Large	#2/392155
6MM	.224	546249	III	046238	044127	—	—	046054	#1/390541	#1/392601	Lg Rfl/095316	—	#1/390943	Large	#2/392155
SAV HP	.227	546240	IV	—	—	—	—	—	#2/390542	#2/392602	Lg Rfl/095316	—	#2/390944	Large	#2/392155
x52R	.227	546238	IV	—	—	—	—	—	#2/390542	#2/392602	Lg Rfl/095316	—	#2/390944	Large	#2/392155
M/223	.243	546248	IV	—	—	—	—	046047	#16/390556	#16/392616	Sm Rfl/095314	—	#3/390945	Small	#3/392156
M TCU	.243	546256	IV	—	—	—	—	046047	#16/390556	#16/392616	Sm Rfl/095314	—	#3/390945	Small	#3/392156
47 REM	.243	546258	IV	—	—	—	—	046047	#16/390556	#16/392616	Sm Rfl/095314	—	#3/390945	Small	#3/392156
47 LAPUA MATCH	.243	—	—	—	—	—	—	—	#1/390541	#16/392616	Sm Rfl/095314	—	#3/390945	Small	#3/392156
M PPC	.243	546254	IV	—	—	—	—	046052	#6/390546	#6/392606	Sm Rfl/095314	—	#3/390945	Small	#3/392156
M PPC MATCH	.243	—	—	544255	—	—	—	544253	#6/390546	#6/392606	Sm Rfl/095314	—	#3/390945	Small	#3/392156
M INT	.243	546252	IV	—	—	—	—	046041	#1/390541	#1/392601	Lg Rfl/095316	—	#3/390945	Large	#3/392156
M REM BR	.243	546432	IV	—	—	—	—	046047	#1/390541	#1/392601	Sm Rfl/095314	—	#3/390945	Small	#3/392156
M REM BR MATCH	.243	—	—	544251	—	—	—	544259	#1/390541	#1/392601	Sm Rfl/095314	—	#3/390945	Small	#3/392156
M HAGAR	.243	546303	IV	—	—	—	—	—	#12/390552	#12/392612	Sm Rfl/095314	—	#3/390945	Large	#3/392156
M CREEDMOOR	.243	546295	IV	—	—	—	—	046041	#1/390541	#1/392601	Lg Rfl/095316	—	#3/390945	Large	#3/392156
3 WIN	.243	546244	I	046245	044103	—	—	046041	#1/390541	#1/392601	Lg Rfl/095316	—	#3/390945	Large	#3/392156
4/6MM REM	.243	546246	I	046247	044103	—	—	046041	#1/390541	#1/392601	Lg Rfl/095316	—	#3/390945	Large	#3/392156
M/284	.243	546250	IV	—	—	—	—	046041	#1/390541	#1/392601	Lg Rfl/095316	—	#3/390945	Large	#3/392156
0 WBY	.243	546242	IV	—	—	—	—	046041	#1/390541	#1/392601	Lg Rfl/095316	—	#3/390945	Large	#3/392156
3 WIN SS MAG	.243	546225	I	046557	044104	—	—	—	#35/390575	#35/392635	Lg Rfl/095316	—	#3/390945	Large	#3/392156
/20 WIN	.257	546264	IV	—	—	—	—	—	#7/390547	#7/392607	Sm Rfl/095314	—	#4/390946	Small	#4/392157
6 WIN	.257	546272	IV	—	—	—	—	—	#6/390546	#6/392606	Sm Rfl/095314	—	#4/390946	Large	#4/392157
/35 WIN	.257	546266	IV	—	—	—	—	—	#2/390542	#2/392602	Lg Rfl/095316	—	#4/390946	Large	#4/392157
REM	.257	546260	III	046276	044104	—	—	—	#12/390552	#12/392612	Lg Rfl/095316	—	#4/390946	Large	#4/392157
0 SAV	.257	546270	IV	—	—	—	—	046042	#1/390541	#1/392601	Lg Rfl/095316	—	#4/390946	Large	#4/392157
7 ROBERTS	.257	546274	III	046275	044104	—	—	046042	#1/390541	#1/392601	Lg Rfl/095316	—	#4/390946	Large	#4/392157
WIN SS MAG	.257	546263	IV	—	—	—	—	—	#35/390575	#35/392635	Lg Rfl/095316	—	#4/390946	Large	#4/392157
06 REM	.257	546262	I	046263	044104	—	—	046042	#1/390541	#1/392601	Lg Rfl/095316	—	#4/390946	Large	#4/392157
/284	.257	546268	IV	—	—	—	—	046042	#1/390541	#1/392601	Lg Rfl/095316	—	#4/390946	Large	#4/392157
7 WBY	.257	546276	III	046277	044104	—	—	046042	#5/390545	#5/392605	Lg Rfl/095316	—	#4/390946	Large	#4/392157
MMx47 MATCH	.264	544650	—	—	—	—	—	—	#1/390541	—/—	—/—	—	#5/390947	Small	#4/392157
5MM TCU	.264	546296	IV	—	—	—	—	046048	#16/390556	#16/392616	Sm Rfl/095314	—	#5/390947	Small	#4/392157
GRENDEL	.264	546291	I	046598	044164	—	—	—	#6/390546	#6/392606	Sm Rfl/095314	—	#5/390947	Large	#4/392157
JAP	.264	546290	III	046291	044106	—	—	046043	#34/390574	—/—	Lg Rfl/095316	—	#5/390947	Large	#4/392157

cal. trimmer pilots include a cutter for the Hornady® Cam-Lock™ Trimmer.

Rifle Cartridge	Bullet Diameter (inches)	Die Set	Die Series	Full-Length Size Die	Seating Die	Expander Die	Taper Crimp Die Only	Neck Size Die	Shell Holder # / Item No.	Shell Plate # / Item No.	Case Feeder Plate Size / Item No.	Bullet Feeder Die	Trimmer Pilot # / Item No.	Primer Punch	Bullet Puller Collet # / Item No.
6.5 JDJ	.264	—	—	—	—	—	—	046043	#4/390544	#4/392604	Lg Rfl/095316	—	#5/390947	Large	#4/39215
6.5 MANN/SCH.	.264	546292	IV	—	—	—	—	046043	#20/390560	—/—	Lg Rfl/095316	—	#5/390947	Large	#4/39215
6.5x55/SCAN.	.264	546282	I	046283	044106	—	—	046043	#19/390559	#19/392619	Lg Rfl/095316	—	#5/390947	Large	#4/39215
260 REM	.264	546269	III	046441	044106	—	—	046043	#1/390541	#1/392601	Lg Rfl/095316	—	#5/390947	Large	#4/39215
6.5 CREEDMOOR	.264	546289	I	046596	044106	—	—	046043	#1/390541	#1/392601	Lg Rfl/095316	—	#5/390947	Large	#4/39215
6.5 CREEDMOOR MATCH	.264	544655	—	—	—	—	—	—	#1/390541	#1/392601	Lg Rfl/095316	—	#5/390947	Large	#4/39215
6.5x57	.264	546284	III	046285	044106	—	—	046043	#1/390541	#1/392601	Lg Rfl/095316	—	#5/390947	Large	#4/39215
6.5/284	.264	546301	III	046443	044106	—	—	046043	#1/390541	#1/392601	Lg Rfl/095316	—	#5/390947	Large	#4/39215
6.5/06	.264	546280	III	046281	044123	—	—	046043	#1/390541	#1/392601	Lg Rfl/095316	—	#5/390947	Large	#4/39215
6.5 REM MAG	.264	546294	IV	—	—	—	—	046043	#5/390545	#5/392605	Lg Rfl/095316	—	#5/390947	Large	#4/39215
264 WIN MAG	.264	546278	III	046279	044123	—	—	046043	#5/390545	#5/392605	Lg Rfl/095316	—	#5/390947	Large	#4/39215
6.5x68	.264	546286	III	046287	044123	—	—	046043	#30/390570	#30/392630	Lg Rfl/095316	—	#5/390947	Large	#4/39215
26 NOSLER	.264	546279	III	046280	044191	—	—	046043	#5/390545	#5/392605	Lg Rfl/095316	—	#5/390947	Large	#4/39215
6.5 CARC	.268	546288	III	046289	044134	—	—	046043	#21/390561	—/—	Lg Rfl/095316	—	#5/390947	Large	#4/39215
6.8MM REM SPC	.277	546299	III	046711	044713	—	—	—	#12/390552	#12/392612	Lg Rfl/095316	—	#6/390948	Small	#5/39215
270 REN	.277	—	—	—	—	—	—	—	#3/390543	#3/392603	Sm Rfl/095314	—	#6/390948	Small	#5/39215
270 WIN	.277	546300	I	046301	044107	—	—	046051	#1/390541	#1/392601	Lg Rfl/095316	—	#6/390948	Large	#5/39215
270 WIN SHORT MAG	.277	546297	I	046450	044161	—	—	046055	#35/390575	#35/392635	Lg Rfl/095316	—	#6/390948	Large	#5/39215
270 WBY	.277	546298	III	046299	044107	—	—	046051	#5/390545	#5/392605	Lg Rfl/095316	—	#6/390948	Large	#5/39215
7MM/223 INGRAM	.284	546318	IV	—	—	—	—	046049	#16/390556	#16/392616	Sm Rfl/095314	—	#7/390949	Small	#6/39215
7MM TCU	.284	546328	IV	—	—	—	—	046049	#16/390556	#16/392616	Sm Rfl/095314	—	#7/390949	Small	#6/39215
7x47 HELM	.284	546306	IV	—	—	—	—	046049	#16/390556	#16/392616	Sm Rfl/095314	—	#7/390949	Large	#6/39215
7MM REM BR	.284	546324	IV	—	—	—	—	046049	#1/390541	#1/392601	Sm Rfl/095314	—	#7/390949	Large	#6/39215
7x30 WATERS	.284	546304	IV	—	—	—	—	046049	#2/390542	#2/392602	Lg Rfl/095316	—	#7/390949	Large	#6/39215
7MM MERRILL	.284	546322	IV	—	—	—	—	046044	#4/390544	#4/392604	Lg Rfl/095316	—	#7/390949	Large	#6/39215
7MM/08 REM	.284	546316	I	046317	044108	—	—	046044	#1/390541	#1/392601	Lg Rfl/095316	—	#7/390949	Large	#6/39215
7x57-7MM MAUSER	.284	546308	I	046309	044133	—	—	046044	#1/390541	#1/392601	Lg Rfl/095316	—	#7/390949	Large	#6/39215
7x57R	.284	546311	I	—	—	—	—	046044	#13/390553	#13/392613	Lg Rfl/095316	—	#7/390949	Large	#6/39215
284 WIN	.284	546302	III	046303	044108	—	—	046044	#1/390541	#1/392601	Lg Rfl/095316	—	#7/390949	Large	#6/39215
280 REM/7MM EXP	.284	546320	I	046321	044133	—	—	046044	#1/390541	#1/392601	Lg Rfl/095316	—	#7/390949	Large	#6/39215
280 ACKLEY IMP	.284	546321	III	046304	044133	—	—	046044	#1/390541	#1/392601	Lg Rfl/095316	—	#7/390949	Large	#6/39215
7x65R	.284	546314	IV	046315	044133	—	—	046044	#13/390553	#13/392613	Lg Rfl/095316	—	#7/390949	Large	#6/39215
7x61 S&H	.284	546310	IV	—	—	—	—	046044	#35/390575	#35/392635	Lg Rfl/095316	—	#7/390949	Large	#6/39215
7x64	.284	546312	IV	046313	044133	—	—	046044	#1/390541	#1/392601	Lg Rfl/095316	—	#7/390949	Large	#6/39215
7MM REM SA ULTRA MAG	.284	546309	III	046452	044108	—	—	046056	#5/390545	#5/392605	Lg Rfl/095316	—	#7/390949	Large	#6/39215
7MM REM MAG	.284	546326	I	046327	044133	—	—	046044	#5/390545	#5/392605	Lg Rfl/095316	—	#7/390949	Large	#6/39215
7MM WIN SHORT MAG	.284	546327	I	046451	044108	—	—	046056	#35/390575	#35/392635	Lg Rfl/095316	—	#7/390949	Large	#6/39215
7MM WBY	.284	546330	III	046331	044133	—	—	046044	#5/390545	#5/392605	Lg Rfl/095316	—	#7/390949	Large	#6/39215
7MM STW	.284	546440	IV	—	—	—	—	046044	#5/390545	#5/392605	Lg Rfl/095316	—	#7/390949	Large	#6/39215
7MM REM ULTRA MAG	.284	546307	III	046454	044133	—	—	046056	#5/390545	#5/392605	Lg Rfl/095316	—	#7/390949	Large	#6/39215
7.35 CARC	.300	546332	IV	—	—	—	—	—	#21/390561	—/—	Lg Rfl/095316	—	#8/390950	Large	#7/3921
30 M1 CARB	.308	546503	II	046504	044142	044505	—	—	#22/390562	#22/392622	Sm Rfl/095314	—	#9/390951	Small	#7/3921
30 REM	.308	—	—	—	—	—	—	046050	#12/390552	#12/392612	Lg Rfl/095316	—	#9/390951	Large	#7/3921
300 BLACKOUT (WHISPER)	.308	546349	I	046459	044165	—	—	—	#16/390556	#16/392616	Sm Rfl/095314	—	#9/390951	Small	#7/3921
30 HERRETT	.308	546334	IV	—	—	—	—	046050	#2/390542	#2/392602	Lg Rfl/095316	—	#9/390951	Large	#7/3921
30/30 WIN	.308	546342	I	046343	044111	—	—	046050	#2/390542	#2/392602	Lg Rfl/095316	—	#9/390951	Large	#7/3921
30-30 ACKLEY IMP	.308	546345	IV	—	—	—	—	046050	#2/390542	#2/392602	Lg Rfl/095316	—	#9/390951	Large	#7/3921
303 SAV	.308	546354	IV	—	—	—	—	046050	#33/390573	—/—	Lg Rfl/095316	—	#9/390951	Large	#7/3921
300 SAV	.308	546348	III	046349	044111	—	—	046050	#1/390541	#1/392601	Lg Rfl/095316	—	#9/390951	Large	#7/3921
30 MERRILL	.308	546338	IV	—	—	—	—	046050	#4/390544	#4/392604	Lg Rfl/095316	—	#9/390951	Large	#7/3921
308 MARLIN EXP	.308	546357	I	046358	044111	—	—	046045	#27/390567	#27/392627	Lg Rfl/095316	—	#9/390951	Large	#7/3921
307 WIN	.308	—	—	—	—	—	—	046045	#33/390573	—/—	Lg Rfl/095316	—	#9/390951	Large	#7/3921
7.5 SWISS (7.5X55)	.308	546360	III	046361	044111	—	—	046045	#2/390542	#2/392602	Lg Rfl/095316	—	#9/390951	Large	#7/3921
7.5 SWISS K31	.308	546361	III	046362	044111	—	—	046045	#2/390542	—/—	Lg Rfl/095316	—	#9/390951	Large	#7/3921
308 WIN	.308	546358	I	046359	044111	—	—	046045	#1/390541	#1/392601	Lg Rfl/095316	—	#9/390951	Large	#7/3921
308 WIN MATCH	.308	—	—	544359	—	—	—	544357	#1/390541	#1/392601	Lg Rfl/095316	095345	#9/390951	Large	#7/3921
7.62 RUSS	.308	546362	III	046363	044111	—	—	046050	#23/390563	#23/392623	Lg Rfl/095316	—	#9/390951	Large	#7/3921
30/40 KRAG	.308	546344	IV	—	—	—	—	046045	#11/390551	#11/392611	Lg Rfl/095316	—	#9/390951	Large	#7/3921
30 TC	.308	546335	I	046336	044111	—	—	046045	#1/390541	#1/392601	Lg Rfl/095316	—	#9/390951	Large	#7/3921
30/06	.308	546340	I	046341	044112	—	—	046045	#1/390541	#1/392601	Lg Rfl/095316	—	#9/390951	Large	#7/3921
30/06 ACKLEY IMP	.308	546341	IV	—	—	—	—	046045	#1/390541	#1/392601	Lg Rfl/095316	—	#9/390951	Large	#7/3921
300 H&H	.308	546346	IV	—	—	—	—	046045	#5/390545	#5/392605	Lg Rfl/095316	—	#9/390951	Large	#7/3921
300 OLYMPIC	.308	546355	IV	—	—	—	—	—	#35/390575	#35/392635	Lg Rfl/095316	—	#9/390951	Large	#7/3921
300 REM SA ULTRA MAG	.308	546347	I	046455	044160	—	—	046057	#5/390545	#5/392605	Lg Rfl/095316	—	#9/390951	Large	#7/3921
308 NORMA MAG	.308	546356	IV	—	—	—	—	046045	#5/390545	#5/392605	Lg Rfl/095316	—	#9/390951	Large	#7/3921
300 WIN SHORT MAG	.308	546369	I	046453	044160	—	—	046057	#35/390575	#35/392635	Lg Rfl/095316	—	#9/390951	Large	#7/3921
300 RCM	.308	546353	I	046592	044111	—	—	046045	#5/390545	#5/392605	Lg Rfl/095316	—	#9/390951	Large	#7/3921
300 WIN MAG	.308	546352	I	046353	044112	—	—	046045	#5/390545	#5/392605	Lg Rfl/095316	—	#9/390951	Large	#7/3921
300 WBY	.308	546350	I	046351	044112	—	—	046045	#5/390545	#5/392605	Lg Rfl/095316	—	#9/390951	Large	#7/3921

Rifle Cartridge	Bullet Diameter (inches)	Die Set	Die Series	Full-Length Size Die	Seating Die	Expander Die	Taper Crimp Die Only	Neck Size Die	Shell Holder # / Item No.	Shell Plate # / Item No.	Case Feeder Plate Size / Item No.	Bullet Feeder Die	Trimmer Pilot # / Item No.	Primer Punch	Bullet Puller Collet # / Item No.
EM ULTRA MAG	.308	546365	I	046447	044159	—	—	046057	#5/390545	#5/392605	Lg Rfl/095316	—	#9/390951	Large	#7/392160
8 WBY	.308	546419	IV	—	—	—	—	046057	#14/390554	#14/392614	Lg Rfl/095316	—	#9/390951	Large	#7/392160
OJ	.308	—	—	—	—	—	—	046045	#27/390567	—/—	Lg Rfl/095316	—	#9/390951	Large	#7/392160
39	.308	546424	I	046425	044126	—	—	—	#6/390546	#6/392606	Sm Rfl/095314	—	#9/390951	Large	#7/392160
K CART 22-45 CAL	—	544591	IV	—	—	—	—	—	—/—	—/—	—/—	—	—/—		#7/392160
WIN	.311	546364	III	046365	044113	—	—	—	#7/390547	#7/392607	Sm Rfl/095314	—	#9/390951	Small	#7/392160
ELG	.312	546368	III	046369	044114	—	—	—	#24/390564	—/—	Lg Rfl/095316	—	#10/390952	Large	#7/392160
RITISH	.312	546366	I	046367	044114	—	—	—	#11/390551	#11/392611	Lg Rfl/095316	—	#10/390952	Large	#7/392160
P	.312	546370	III	046371	044114	—	—	—	#1/390541	#1/392601	Lg Rfl/095316	—	#10/390952	Large	#7/392160
WIN	.321	546374	IV	—	—	—	—	—	#2/390542	#2/392602	Lg Rfl/095316	—	#11/390953	Large	#8/392161
N SPL	.321	546372	IV	—	—	—	—	—	#2/390542	#2/392602	Lg Rfl/095316	—	#11/390953	Large	#8/392161
M	.321			—	—	—	—	—	#12/390552	#12/392612	Lg Rfl/095316	—	#12/390954	Large	#8/392161
33 KURZ	.323	546375	III	046376	044137	—	—	—	#1/390541	#1/392601	Sm Rfl/095314	—	#11/390953	Large	#8/392161
MAUS	.323	546382	I	046383	044116	—	—	—	#1/390541	#1/392601	Lg Rfl/095316	—	#11/390953	Large	#8/392161
S	.323	546376	III	046377	044116	—	—	—	#1/390541	#1/392601	Lg Rfl/095316	—	#11/390953	Large	#8/392161
06	.323	546380	IV	—	—	—	—	—	#1/390541	#1/392601	Lg Rfl/095316	—	#11/390953	Large	#8/392161
R LEBEL	.323	546383	IV	—	—	—	—	—	#49/390605	—/—	Lg Rfl/095316	—	#11/390953	Large	#8/392161
SM	.323	546387	IV	—	—	—	—	—	#35/390575	#35/392635	Lg Rfl/095316	—	#11/390953	Large	#8/392161
S	.323	546378	IV	—	—	—	—	—	#30/390570	#30/392630	Lg Rfl/095316	—	#11/390953	Large	#8/392161
REM MAG	.323	546384	IV	—	—	—	—	—	#5/390545	#5/392605	Lg Rfl/095316	—	#11/390953	Large	#8/392161
46R	.324	546386	IV	—	—	—	—	—	#2/390542	#2/392602	Lg Rfl/095316	—	#11/390953	Large	#8/392161
HUNGARIAN-MANN	.329	546385	IV	—	—	—	—	—	#47/390603	—/—	Lg Rfl/095316	—	#11/390953	Large	#8/392161
IN	.338	546388	IV	—	—	—	—	046058	#14/390554	#14/392614	Lg Rfl/095316	—	#13/390955	Large	#9/392162
EDERAL	.338	546397	III	046595	044131	—	—	046058	#1/390541	#1/392601	Lg Rfl/095316	—	#13/390955	Large	#9/392162
ARLIN EXPRESS	.338	546359	I	046597	044131	—	—	046058	#52/390607	#52/392652	Lg Rfl/095316	—	#13/390955	Large	#9/392162
ORMA MAG	.338	—	—	—	—	—	—	046058	#43/390583	—/—	Lg Rfl/095316	—	#13/390955	Large	#9/392162
6	.338	546395	IV	—	—	—	—	046058	#1/390541	#1/392601	Lg Rfl/095316	—	#13/390955	Large	#9/392162
CM	.338	546399	I	046594	044131	—	—	046058	#5/390545	#5/392605	Lg Rfl/095316	—	#13/390955	Large	#9/392162
IN MAG	.338	546390	I	046391	044117	—	—	046058	#5/390545	#5/392605	Lg Rfl/095316	—	#13/390955	Large	#9/392162
BY	.338	546392	IV	—	—	—	—	046058	#5/390545	#5/392605	Lg Rfl/095316	—	#13/390955	Large	#9/392162
LTRA MAG	.338	546389	III	046446	044117	—	—	046058	#5/390545	#5/392605	Lg Rfl/095316	—	#13/390955	Large	#9/392162
APUA	.338	546393	III	046593	044117	—	—	046058	#43/390583	—/—	Lg Rfl/095316	—	#13/390955	Large	#9/392162
78 WBY	.338	546391	IV	—	—	—	—	046058	#14/390554	#14/392614	Lg Rfl/095316	—	#13/390955	Large	#9/392162
IN	.348	546394	IV	—	—	—	—	—	#25/390565	—/—	Lg Rfl/095316	—	#14/390956	Large	#9/392162
M	.358	546398	III	046399	044130	—	—	—	#26/390566	—/—	Lg Rfl/095316	—	#15/390957	Large	#9/392162
IN	.358	—	—	—	—	—	—	046046	#33/390573	—/—	Lg Rfl/095316	—	#15/390957	Large	#9/392162
IN	.358	546408	IV	—	—	—	—	046046	#1/390541	#1/392601	Lg Rfl/095316	—	#15/390957	Large	#9/392162
EM MAG	.358	546402	IV	—	—	—	—	—	#5/390545	#5/392605	Lg Rfl/095316	—	#15/390957	Large	#9/392162
HELEN	.358	546400	III	046401	044119	—	—	046046	#1/390541	#1/392601	Lg Rfl/095316	—	#15/390957	Large	#9/392162
ORMA MAG	.358	546406	IV	—	—	—	—	046046	#5/390545	#5/392605	Lg Rfl/095316	—	#15/390957	Large	#9/392162
7	.366	546410	III	046411	044120	—	—	—	#1/390541	#1/392601	Lg Rfl/095316	—	#20/390962	Large	#9/392162
4R	.366	546414	III	046415	044120	—	—	—	#13/390553	#13/392613	Lg Rfl/095316	—	#20/390962	Large	#9/392162
2	.366	546412	III	046413	044120	—	—	—	#1/390541	#1/392601	Lg Rfl/095316	—	#20/390962	Large	#9/392162
OJ	.375	—	—	—	—	—	—	—	#27/390567	—/—	Lg Rfl/095316	—	#16/390958	Large	#10/392163
WCF	.375	546537	IV	—	—	—	—	—	#2/390542	#2/392602	Lg Rfl/095316	—	#16/390958	Large	#10/392163
IN	.375	546530	IV	—	—	—	—	—	#2/390542	#2/392602	Lg Rfl/095316	—	#16/390958	Large	#10/392163
TEYR	.375	546417	IV	—	—	—	—	—	#15/390555	—/—	Lg Rfl/095316	—	#16/390958	Large	#10/392163
&H	.375	546416	I	046417	044121	—	—	—	#5/390545	#5/392605	Lg Rfl/095316	—	#16/390958	Large	#10/392163
UGER	.375	546415	I	046418	044121	—	—	—	#5/390545	#5/392605	Lg Rfl/095316	—	#16/390958	Large	#10/392163
EM ULTRA MAG	.375	546450	IV	—	—	—	—	—	#5/390545	#5/392605	Lg Rfl/095316	—	#16/390958	Large	#10/392163
BY	.375	546418	IV	—	—	—	—	—	#14/390554	#14/392614	Lg Rfl/095316	—	#16/390958	Large	#10/392163
00 NITRO EXPRESS 3"	.410	546421	IV	—	—	—	—	—	#25/390565	—/—	Lg Rfl/095316	—	#17/390959	Large	#11/392164
IN	.411	546425	II	046456	044162	044571	—	—	#42/390582	—/—	Lg Rfl/095316	—	#17/390959	Large	#11/392164
60	.415	546420	IV	—	—	—	—	—	#25/390565	—/—	Lg Rfl/095316	—	#17/390959	Large	#11/392164
AYLOR	.416	546427	IV	—	—	—	—	—	#5/390545	—/—	Lg Rfl/095316	—	#17/390959	Large	#11/392164
GBY	.416	546428	IV	—	—	—	—	—	#38/390578	—/—	Lg Rfl/095316	—	#17/390959	Large	#11/392164
UGER	.416	546429	IV	—	—	—	—	—	#5/390545	#5/392605	Lg Rfl/095316	—	#17/390959	Large	#11/392164
EM MAG	.416	546426	IV	—	—	—	—	—	#5/390545	#5/392605	Lg Rfl/095316	—	#17/390959	Large	#11/392164
BY	.416	546430	IV	—	—	—	—	—	#14/390554	#14/392614	Lg Rfl/095316	—	#17/390959	Large	#11/392164
EFFERY	.423	546423	IV	—	—	—	—	—	#53/390608	—/—	Lg Rfl/095316	—	#17/390959	Large	#12/392165
ARLIN	.430	546551	II	046552	044149	044553	—	—	#27/390567	#27/392627	Lg Rfl/095316	—	#18/390960	Large	#12/392165
USHMASTER	.452	546452	V	046422	044721	044550	044176	—	#1/390541	#1/392601	Lg Rfl/095316	—	#19/390961	Large	#13/392166
OCOM	.458	546464	III	046424	044190	—	—	—	#1/390541	#1/392601	Lg Rfl/095316	—	#19/390961	Small	#13/392166
GOVT	.458	546566	II	046567	044152	044568	—	—	#14/390554	#14/392614	Lg Rfl/095316	—	#19/390961	Large	#13/392166
ARLIN	.458	546553	II	046587	044152	044568	—	—	#5/390545	#5/392605	Lg Rfl/095316	—	#19/390961	Large	#13/392166
NITRO EXPRESS 3¼"	.458	546433	IV	—	—	—	—	—	#54/390609	—/—	N/A	—	#19/390961	Large	#13/392166
IN MAG	.458	546569	II	046570	044153	044568	—	—	#5/390545	#5/392605	Lg Rfl/095316	—	#19/390961	Large	#13/392166
OTT	.458	546465	II	046457	044153	044572	—	—	#5/390545	#5/392605	Lg Rfl/095316	—	#19/390961	Large	#13/392166
BY	.458	546422	IV	—	—	—	—	—	#14/390554	#14/392614	Lg Rfl/095316	—	#19/390961	Large	#13/392166
TRO EXPRESS	.474	546434	IV	—	—	—	—	—	#55/390610	—/—	N/A	—	#23/390939	Large	—/—
GOVT	.510	546462	IV	—	—	—	—	—	—/—	—/—	Lg Rfl/095316	—	#50/390937	Large	—/—
OWULF	.500	—	—	—	—	—	—	—	#6/390546	#6/392606	Lg Rfl/095316	—	#50/390937	Large	—/—
ASKAN	.510	546586	IV	—	—	—	—	—	#25/390565	—/—	Lg Rfl/095316	—	#50/390937	Large	—/—
NITRO EXPRESS 3"	.510	546435	IV	—	—	—	—	—	#55/390610	—/—	N/A	—	#50/390937	Large	—/—

Pistol Dies & Reloading Essentia

Pistol Cartridge	Bullet Diameter (inches)	Die Set	Die Series	Full-Length Size Die	Seating Die	Expander Die	Taper Crimp Seater Die	Taper Crimp Die Only	Shell Holder # / Item No.	Shell Plate # / Item No.	Case Feeder Plate Size / Item No.	Bullet Feeder Die	Trimmer Pilot # / Item No.	Primer Punch
22 RCFM-JET	.224	546218	IV	—	—	—	—	—	#6/390546	#6/392606	Sm Pstl/095310	N/A	#1/390943	Small
25 AUTO	.251	—	—	—	—	—	—	—	#37/390577	—/—	Sm Pstl/095310	N/A	#4/390946	Small
30 LUGER	.308	546336	IV	—	—	—	—	—	#8/390548	#8/392608	Sm Pstl/095310	N/A	#9/390951	Small
30 MAUSER	.309	—	—	—	—	—	—	—	#8/390548	#8/392608	Sm Pstl/095310	N/A	#9/390951	Small
32 AUTO	.311	546506	II	046507	044113	044508	—	—	#22/390562	#22/392622	Sm Pstl/095310	N/A	#10/390952	Small
32 S&W LONG/H&R/327 FEDERAL	.311	546509	II	046510	044143	044511	—	—	#36/390576	#36/392636	Sm Pstl/095310	N/A	#10/390952	Small
7.5 SWISS ORDEN	.312	546504	IV	—	—	—	—	—	#48/390604	—/—	Sm Pstl/095310	N/A	#10/390952	Small
8MM LEBEL REV	.326	546510	IV	—	—	—	—	—	#48/390604	—/—	Lg Pstl/095312	N/A	#11/390953	Large
380 AUTO	.355	546518	II	046519	044144	044517	—	044170	#16/390556	#16/392616	Sm Pstl/095310	095330	#15/390957	Small
TAPER CRIMP 9MM/9x21	.355	546516	II	046516	044177	044517	044177	—	#8/390548	#8/392608	—/—	N/A	#15/390957	Small
9MM LUGER/9x21	.355	546515	II	046516	044144	044517	—	044170	#8/390548	#8/392608	Sm Pstl/095310	095330	#15/390957	Small
357 SIG	.355	546575	II	046576	044144	044577	—	—	#10/390550	#10/392610	Sm Pstl/095310	N/A	#15/390957	Small
9x23	.355	546532	IV	—	—	—	—	—	#8/390548	#8/392608	Sm Pstl/095310	N/A	#15/390957	Small
38 S&W	.357	546521	IV	—	—	—	—	—	#28/390568	#28/392628	Lg Pstl/095312	N/A	#15/390957	Large
38 SUPER AUTO	.357	546524	II	046525	044144	044526	—	—	#8/390548	#8/392608	Sm Pstl/095310	N/A	#15/390957	Small
357 HERRETT	.357	546396	IV	—	—	—	—	—	#2/390542	#2/392602	Lg Pstl/095312	N/A	#15/390957	Large
357 B&D/44	.358	546404	IV	—	—	—	—	—	#30/390570	#30/392630	Lg Pstl/095312	N/A	#15/390957	Large
38 SPECIAL	.357	546527	II	046528	044145	044523	—	—	#6/390546	#6/392606	Lg Pstl/095312	095331	#15/390957	Small
357 MAGNUM	.357	546527	II	046528	044145	044523	—	—	#6/390546	#6/392606	Lg Pstl/095312	095331	#15/390957	Small
357 REM MAX	.357	546527	II	046528	044145	044523	—	—	#6/390546	#6/392606	Lg Pstl/095312	095331	#15/390957	Small
COWBOY 38-357-357 MAX	.357	546528	III	046528	044169	044591	—	—	#6/390546	#8/392608	Lg Pstl/095312	N/A	#15/390957	Small
9x18 MAKAROV	.364	546512	II	046513	044154	044514	—	—	#8/390548	#8/392608	Sm Pstl/095310	N/A	#15/390957	Small
40 S&W	.400	546533	II	046534	044146	044535	—	044171	#10/390550	#10/392610	Lg Pstl/095312	095332	#21/390941	Small
TAPER CRIMP 40 S&W	.400	546534	II	046534	—	044535	044178	044171	#10/390550	#10/392610	Lg Pstl/095312	N/A	#21/390941	Small
10MM AUTO	.400	546533	II	046534	044146	044535	—	044171	#10/390550	#10/392610	Lg Pstl/095312	095332	#21/390941	Large
TAPER CRIMP 10MM	.400	546534	II	046534	—	044535	044178	044171	#10/390550	#10/392610	Lg Pstl/095312	N/A	#21/390941	Large
38/40 WIN	.400	546536	IV	—	—	—	—	—	#9/390549	#9/392609	Lg Pstl/095312	N/A	#21/390941	Large
400 COR-BON	.400	546538	IV	—	—	—	—	—	#45/390606	#45/392645	Lg Pstl/095312	N/A	#21/390941	Large
41 AE	.410	546539	II	046540	044147	044541	—	—	#9/390549	#29/392629	Lg Pstl/095312	N/A	#17/390959	Small
41 REM MAG	.410	546539	II	046540	044147	044541	—	—	#29/390569	#29/392629	Lg Pstl/095312	N/A	#17/390959	Large
COWBOY 44/40 WIN	.429	546543	III	046460	044166	044593	—	—	#9/390549	#9/392609	Lg Pstl/095312	N/A	#18/390960	Large
44 AUTO MAG	.430	546545	IV	—	—	—	—	—	#1/390541	#1/392601	Lg Pstl/095312	095333	#18/390960	Large
44 REM MAG	.430	546548	II	046549	044148	044544	—	—	#30/390570	#30/392630	Lg Pstl/095312	N/A	#18/390960	Large
44 SPECIAL	.430	546548	II	046549	044148	044544	—	—	#30/390570	#30/392630	Lg Pstl/095312	095333	#18/390960	Large
COWBOY 44 SPCL	.430	546549	III	046549	044166	044592	—	—	#30/390570	#30/392630	Lg Pstl/095312	N/A	#18/390960	Large
445 SUPER MAG	.430	—	—	—	—	—	—	—	#30/390570	#30/392630	Lg Pstl/095312	N/A	#18/390960	Large
45 AUTO	.451	546554	II	046555	044151	044556	—	044172	#45/390606	#45/392645	Lg Pstl/095312	095334	#19/390961	Large
45 AUTO RIMMED	.451	546554	II	046555	044151	044556	—	044172	#31/390571	#31/392631	Lg Pstl/095312	095334	#19/390961	Large
45 WIN MAG	.451	546554	IV	046555	044151	044556	—	044172	#1/390541	#1/392601	Lg Pstl/095312	095334	#19/390961	Large
TAPER CRIMP 45 AUTO	.451	546555	II	046555	044179	044556	044179	—	#45/390606	#45/392645	Lg Pstl/095312	095334	#19/390961	Large
COWBOY 45 COLT	.452	546581	III	046583	044168	044594	—	—	#32/390572	#32/392632	Lg Pstl/095312	095334	#19/390961	Large
45 COLT	.452	546582	II	046583	044151	044556	—	—	#32/390572	#32/392632	Lg Pstl/095312	095334	#19/390961	Large
45 SCHOFIELD	.452	546546	IV	—	—	—	—	—	#41/390581	—/—	Lg Pstl/095312	095334	#19/390961	Large
454 CASULL	.452	546584	V	046584	044151	044556	—	044588	#32/390572	#32/392632	Lg Pstl/095312	095334	#19/390961	Small
460 S&W	.452	546583	V	046720	044721	044719	—	044722	#46/390602	#46/392646	Lg Rfl/095316	095334	#19/390961	Large
455 WEBLEY	.455	—	—	—	—	—	—	—	#51/390601	—/—	Lg Pstl/095312	N/A	#19/390961	Large
480 RUGER/475 LINB	.475	546547	V	046585	044158	044586	—	044174	#14/390554	#14/392614	Lg Pstl/095312	N/A	#23/390939	Large
50 ACTION EXP	.500	546580	II	046581	044155	044582	—	—	#40/390580	—/—	Lg Rfl/095316	N/A	#50/390937	Large
500 S&W	.500	546585	V	046699	044700	044701	—	044702	#44/390584	#44/392644	Lg Rfl/095316	N/A	#50/390937	Large
500 LINEBAUGH	.510	546587	IV	—	—	—	—	—	#25/390565	—/—	Lg Rfl/095316	N/A	#50/390937	Large

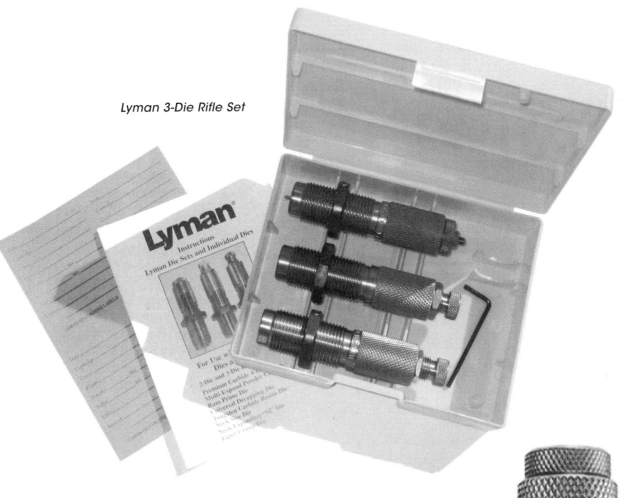

Lyman 3-Die Rifle Set

Lyman Precision Dies

I had my first experience with Lyman Dies as a young reloader, when I bought a set of used Lyman dies for my .375 H&H at a gun show. You could tell they had been used quite a bit, but they cleaned up nicely and made thousands of rounds of ammunition for me. Lyman makes a quality set of dies, which will last nearly forever if you take care of them.

Lyman also makes one of the most useful dies ever: The Universal Decapping Die.

I don't like sticking dirty brass into my resizing dies, and I don't like to clean brass with the old primers still in place, because I want the primer pockets to be cleaned in either the ultrasonic cleaner or vibratory tumbler. The solution? The Universal Decapping Die. It doesn't touch your brass other than to pop out the old primer. Brilliant idea.

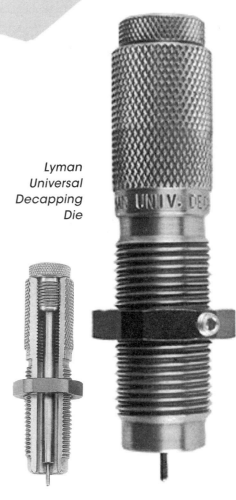

Lyman Universal Decapping Die

*Lyman
Classic Black
Powder Dies*

Lyman also makes a great set of dies, at a very affordable price, for the larger black powder cartridge guns, like 40-65, 45-120-3-¼", and 50-90, all on the ⅞"-14 thread size, so there's no adapter needed.

Forster Products

Forster offers their own line of proprietary rifle dies, with three different resizing models to choose from and two different seater dies. They offer a standard full-length resizing die, and Shoulder Bump Neck Sizer – which resizes the neck for bullet tension and moves the shoulder into its specified SAAMI location for proper headspacing – and a neck-sizing die, that only resizes the neck for bullet tension.

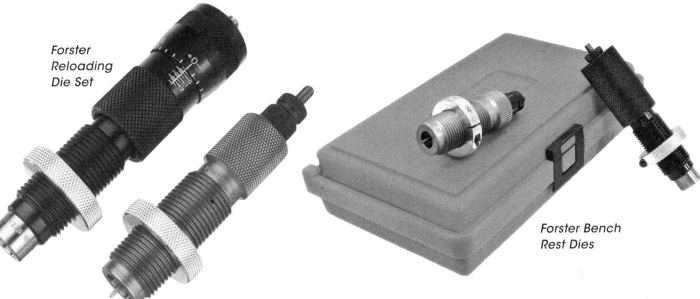

Forster Reloading Die Set

Forster Bench Rest Dies

The standard Bench Rest Seater die features a sliding die chamber that holds the bullet, case and seating stem in perfect alignment while the bullet is seated. The Ultra Micrometer Seating Die uses the same features as the Bench Rest Seater, but comes with a micrometer adjustable seating depth.

Dillon Precision

Dillon makes a set of dies with some unique, and very useable, features. When you set them up properly, especially with their progressive presses, you see that some serious thought went into the design. Well known for their pistol die sets, Dillon uses a spring-loaded floating decapping rod, which throws the primer downward. This is especially useful when resizing military brass, or any brass that has a primer crimp.

Their dies have a quick-disassemble design, which is especially useful when they need to be cleaned. Any residue, shavings or debris that accumulates from the bullet seating procedure can easily be cleaned out without taking the die out of adjustment. One of the coolest features is the 'flip-flop' bullet seater; by simply removing a pin and turning the bullet seater over, you can switch from a semi-wadcutter bullet seater to a roundnose seater.

Dillon .45ACP dies

Dillon Bullet Seater

The Dillon rifle dies are equally cool. The full-length resize is the equivalent of other companies small-base dies, in that the Dillon dies will resize rifle brass so that it can easily be used in an autoloading rifle without the jamming issue that has been known to exist with other full-length sizer dies.

They feature a carbide expander ball to minimize the amount of pressure needed to resize, a great feature if you're prepping a whole bunch of brass at one sitting. They also have a taper crimp rifle die available, which works very well with the autoloading rifles also.

RCBS

The industry standard, and has been for years. RCBS came to define proper loading equipment, and they still make a fantastic product. There are few things that can't be loaded with a set of RCBS dies; and I'm not really certain what they are, south of 105mm Howitzer shells. Wait, I think they're available from the Custom Shop…

RCBS dies feature steel body construction, threaded decapping rods with replaceable decapping pins, knurled lock nuts, and lock rings with brass set screws so they don't mat the threads.

RCBS breaks down their die sets into groups, organized by popularity. The rarities are well represented, as well as some of the wildcat cartridges and older British safari cartridges. And, even better, if RCBS doesn't stock it – they can make it for you.

Their shellholders are an industry standard as well, interchangeable with most common reloading presses and/or priming tools. I probably own and use more sets of RCBS dies than anything else, so that's a testimony to their durability and value.

*RCBS Small Base Dies
for autoloading rifles*

I like their carbide pistol die sets, as the carbide sizer ring eliminates the need for case lubrication. They give an excellent roll crimp for the revolvers that I like to shoot, and if you order a set for the autoloading pistols, i.e. 9mm Luger, .40 S&W, .45 ACP and the like, RCBS supplies a taper crimp die with the set. Good stuff!

RCBS .50BMG Dies

RCBS Cowboy Action Reloading dies

Redding Reloading.

I've saved the best for last. When you handle a set of Redding Dies, you can feel the difference immediately. The threads are cut precisely, the little details have been paid attention to; the knurled adjustment knobs, the blued steel heavy duty parts, the tiny piece of lead shot that sits between the lock ring screw and the threads on the body. These little things make for an excellent package.

Working with a set of Redding dies seals the deal. You can feel the difference in the way your reloading press interacts with the dies on the first stroke of the ram. It's a positive feel, you can actually tell when the brass is being sized, in a different manner than other dies. The Bushing dies I've described above have become a favorite of mine, and I'm slowly adding a set to my die library, as money allows, for any rifle caliber that shows a potential for great accuracy.

The Master Hunter die series offers a simple, yet very effective set of reloading dies. The resizing die is full-length, so there's no getting hung up when trying to work the bolt for a necessary second shot, yet the bullet seating die has the micrometer adjustment that I find so handy, to assure you produce uniform ammunition every time you sit at the bench.

The Redding Dual Carbide pistol dies are a bit of genius, giving the pistol reloader exactly what he or she needs without overworking the pistol brass. The first carbide ring resizes the case body to a dimension that will allow smooth chambering in the cylinder, and the second ring works that portion of the case which holds the bullet. In this manner, the brass in the case body doesn't get overworked, and the area that holds the bullet gets the proper amount of attention.

Hell, Redding even offers a micrometer adjustable taper crimp die, so you don't have to keep removing the die when space is tight on a progressive!

*Redding Dual
Ring Set*

The adjustment changes the crimp depth at .001" intervals with the turn of a knob, allowing you to dial in the perfect amount of crimp without removing the die. The guys at Redding are thinking all the time, and I like the way they think.

*Redding
Micro Crimp
adjustable die*

METALLIC HANDLOADING TOOLS: POWDER MEASURING

Powder Measuring

This is one area where the game has changed, and changed for the better. The digital scales - which were sketchy at best 15 years ago - have become very precise instruments. When combined with an automated powder dispenser, you can really speed up the measuring process. The balance beam scales that have given stellar results for over a century are still with us, and better than ever. The powder throwers are also much improved, giving the most consistent results that we've ever achieved.

No matter which method you choose, you must choose one, because weighing powder is one of the most important steps in the assembly of a cartridge. I really like the ease and convenience of the modern digital scales, but I routinely check my charges on my favorite balance beam scales. I guess I subscribe to the theory that 'gravity never wears out!'

The powder throwers that make our lives much easier when dispensing powder have improved greatly as well. There are smaller models, designed for handgun and small rifle loads, as well as models that throw well over 100 grains of powder – damned accurately – that are available to the lovers of the Ultra Magnum series and other large cartridges like the .338 Lapua.

We reloaders use our scales not only for measuring powder, but for weighing brass cases and bullets as well, when extreme accuracy is the goal. If there's an area where a larger investment is warranted, it would be in a good digital and balance beam scale, as both will come in handy.

Editor's Picks:
Balance Beam Scales

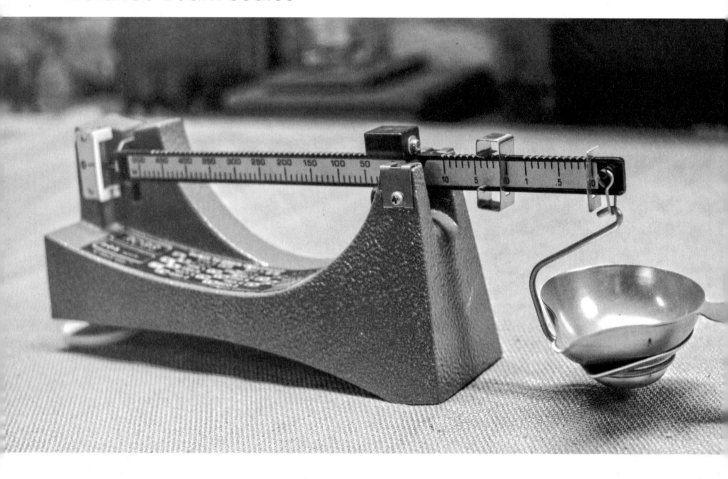

1. The Redding No. 2 Powder & Bullet Scale. – Part No. 02000

This is a serious machine! The beam swings on stainless steel bearing seats, using knife-edge, hardened pivot points, and is also magnetically dampened for speed. Handling up to 505 grains, and hand-calibrated to the U.S. Government's standards, the Redding No. 2 is the kind of precision machine that you'll be able to hand down to your grandchildren. It makes a good value for those that appreciate tools that will last a lifetime.

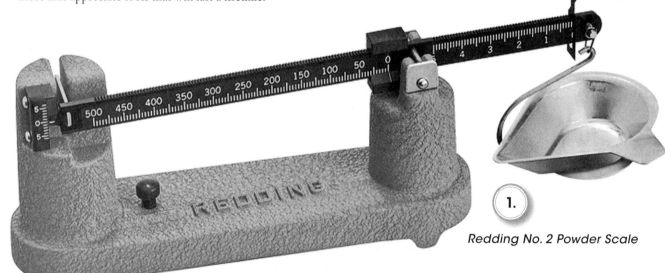

1.

Redding No. 2 Powder Scale

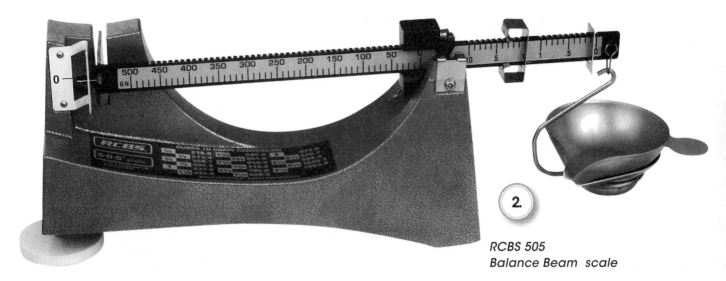

2

RCBS 505
Balance Beam scale

2. The RCBS 5·0·5 Scale. Part No. 9071

This was the scale I was raised on; ol' Grumpy Pants had purchased one when I was an infant. The 5·0·5 is easy to use, and measures very accurately, up to 511 grains, so weighing bullets for the bigger safari calibers isn't a problem. The balance bar is incremented to 1/10 grain, and features magnetic dampening to help settle the scale quickly. An adjustment wheel under the left side of the scale allows the user to zero the unit easily, so whether or not your bench is perfectly level, the scale can be used. If you already own a good five-oh-five, you really don't need another scale.

Other Powder Scales

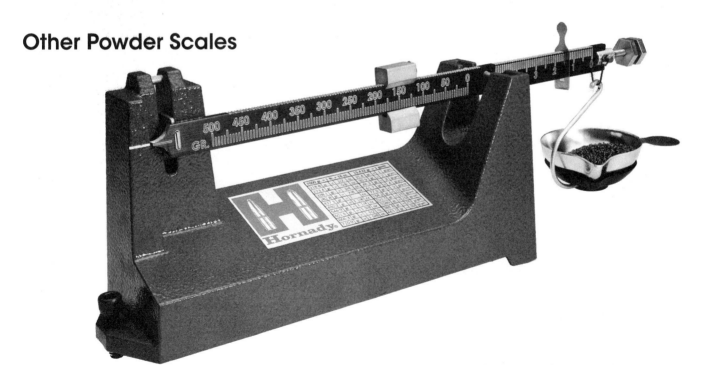

Hornady Balance Beam Powder Scale – Part No. 050109

Cast aluminum frame, 500 grain capacity, magnetic damping. Pivot pins and bearings are hardened for long term use. Balance beam features laser engraved, white on black labeling. Accurate to +/- 0.1 grains.

RCBS M500 Magnetic Powder scale – Part No. 98915

505-grain measuring capacity, die cast metal base with leveling foot, ambidextrous design. RCBS magnetic damping system for quick readings. Tip proof metal pan. Accurate to +/- 0.1 grains

Lyman Pro 1000

Lyman Pro 1000 Magnetic Power Scale – Part No. 7752218

High Impact Styrene base, 1005-grain capacity, counterweight included for weighing objects over 500 grains.

Dillon Eliminator Balance Beam Scale- Part No. L11-13480

511 grain capacity, leveling wheel, magnetic damping. Manufactured by Ohaus. Accurate to +/- 0.1 grains

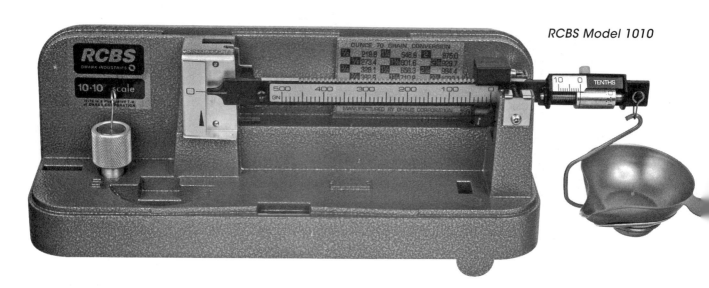

RCBS Model 1010

RCBS Model 1010 Balance Beam Scale – Part No. 9073

Metal alloy base and beam, steel pivot points. Magnetic dampening, accuracy to +- 0.1 grains.

Editor's Picks:
Digital Scales

1. The Lyman Pro Touch 1500 digital scale

Lyman's new scale for 2015 has proven to be a winner, being very accurate and easy to use. It gives the user the ability to measure up to 1,500 grains, and the high contrast digital display makes it easy for even my aging eyes to see without squinting. I've used this scale for a few months now, checking it against balance beam loads (I have a digital scale complex; I'm always waiting for them to screw up), and it has been spot on, without exception. So long as you zero the scale prior to use, check it with the provided scale weights, and keep it in a vibration-free environment, you'll be happy with this convenient little scale.

The Lyman
Pro Touch 1500

The RCBS
ChargeMaster
1500

2. The RCBS ChargeMaster 1500

The ChargeMaster was the first digital scale I owned that really worked out well for me. It holds a special place on the bench, and I enjoy the design. Giving accurate readings out to 0.1 grains, it comes with a set of weights to keep it well calibrated, and zeroes itself at the touch of a button. The best feature of the RCBS ChargeMaster 1500 is that it is simple to mate it to the ChargeMaster Dispenser, giving you an automated powder thrower that delivers charges accurately to 0.1 of a grain of powder, time after time.

You can store your favorite loads, which is great for those who only reload for a few different calibers, but the feature I like best is the auto dispense. Simply punch in the desired charge weight, and once the first is accurately thrown and the audible 'beep' is sounded, the dispenser waits until you replace the pan, and the scale registers 'zero', and it automatically dispenses another load of the same weight. This machine, once running correctly, saves the reloader a whole lot of time.

Other Digital Scales

Hornady Lock-N-Load Bench Scale – Part No. 050108

1500-grain capacity and large LCD display. Two calibration weights, AC adapter and metal powder pan included. Accurate to +/- 0.1 grains

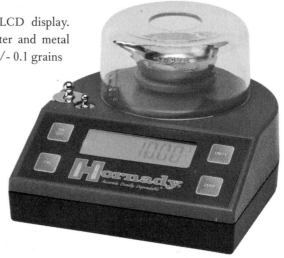

Hornady Lock-N-Load Bench Scale

Hornady GS-1500 Grain Electronic Scale – Part No. 050107

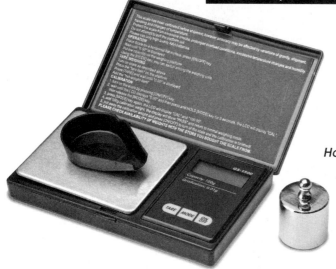

Compact design, powered by two AAA batteries. 1500 grain capacity. Not intended for use with a powder trickler.

Hornady GS-1500

RCBS RangeMaster 2000 Electronic Powder Scale – Part No. 98945

A great all-around digital scale, the RangeMaster 2000 features a backlit LCD display, touch screen operation, and is able to operate on either AC or DC power, making it completely portable. Accurate to +/- 0.1 grains, capacity of 2,000 grains.

RCBS Range Master

Frankford Arsenal Platinum Series Precision Electronic Scale – Part No. 909672

LCD display, blue backlit screen, 1500 grain capacity. Digital scale comes with two calibration weights, powder pan, clear dust cover, 110V power supply and storage case. Accurate to +/- 0.1 grains

Lyman Accu-Touch 2000 Electronic scale- Part No. 7751558

Touch screen controls, LCD display and 2000 grain capacity are among the features of the Accu-Touch 2000. Ambidextrous powder trickler, powder brush (for easy cleanup), storage tray and plastic dust cover are all included. Accurate to +/- 0.1 grains.

Lyman AccuTouch 2000

Dillon D-Terminator Electronic Scale – Part No. L11-10483

900 grain capacity, runs on four AA batteries or AC adapter, LCD display, scale weights for calibration included. Accurate to +/- 0.1 grains

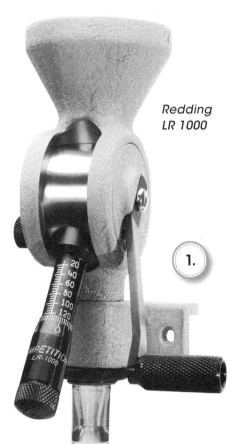

Redding LR 1000

Powder Dispensing

Whether you scoop, throw, or employ an electronic device to dispense your powder, it must be an accurate measurement, rather close to what you need for your chosen cartridge. I've used all three methods, and all work well. The powder scoop, which I learned on, takes the longest. The latter two methods are much quicker, and much more accurate.

Editor's Picks:

1. The Redding LR-1000 Powder Measure

I load for quite a few of the larger calibers, which run on 70 to 90 grains of powder, and the LR-1000 works out perfectly for these big guys. This model gives charges up to 140 grains of powder. It has Redding's famous hemispherical powder chamber, scaled up to hold the larger powder charges. I love mine, and it has worked very well for me for years now.

2. The RCBS ChargeMaster 1500 combination powder dispenser

ChargeMaster 1500 Combo

This modern day wonder took a while to convince me of its accuracy and dependability, but despite my suspicions regarding modern electronic doo-dads, this device has proved itself time and time again. Simply put the powder in the hopper, punch the charge weight on the keyboard, and the machine will dispense that exact charge, delivering an audible 'beep' when the amount of powder has been dispensed. The LCD display will indicate whether that charge is lighter or heavier than you've punched in, and it even has the capability of automatically dispensing another charge of the same weight when the pan is replaced.

Easy to zero, the ChargeMaster 1500 can store some of your favorite loads, and the hopper is easily emptied through a powder drain on the side. One note – don't forget to close the powder drain when using a new powder, or you'll spill it all over the reloading bench. Not that that's ever happened to me...

2

Mechanical Powder Measurers

Redding Match Grade 3BR Powder Measure – Part No. 03700

With the capability of throwing the smaller pistol charges as well as the medium rifle charges, the Model 3 Bench Rest powder measure will give years of good service. A powder baffle keep your charges uniform, and the micrometer-adjustable chamber will stay where you set it.

RCBS Uniflow Powder Measure

The Uniflow Powder Measure is an industry standard. It can throw powder weighing 0.5 grains to 50 grains with the small chamber, or 5 to 110 grains with the large chamber, making it a rather universal choice no matter what you're loading. As an added bonus, the Uniflow measure can be screwed into a standard die hole on any reloading press, for even more flexibility.

RCBS Uniflow

Redding Model 3BR

Hornady Lock-N-Load Powder Measure – Part No. 290524

The Hornady Lock-N-Load powder measure will offer quite a bit of flexibility also. Like the Uniflow, it can be mounted into any standard 7/8"-14 threaded hole, and will throw a wide variety of powder accurately. A wide selection of metering inserts will allow the user to customize their powder requirements. Aluminum and steel body, with a plastic hopper.

Hornady Lock-N-Load

RCBS Little Dandy Handgun Powder Measure

A great choice for the smaller capacity cases, the RCBS Little Dandy offers a powder measure that works with multiple rotors (sold separately), allowing for easy change over for different powder charges.

RCBS Little Dandy

RCBS Competition Powder Measure

The RCBS Competition Powder Measure – Part No. 98908

Designed for pistol and smaller rifle cartridges, the Competition Powder Measure will accurately dispense charges from .5 to 40 grains. The folks at RCBS have added a powder baffle for uniform metering, and the UPM Micrometer Adjustment Screw so you can accurately adjust the charge thrown. You can also use the micrometer reading to save your often-used powder charges and quickly adjust the screw to change loads.

Lyman #55 Powder Measure – Part No. 7767783. With a 2,400 grain reservoir and a baffle that resists chemical reactions with smokeless powder, the #55 is threaded to work with your press, or any 7/8"-14 hole. Comes with powder baffle, and a three slide adjustable powder cavity. Throws powder charges up to 200 grains.

Electronic powder measures

The Lyman Gen 6 Compact Touch Screen Powder Scale – Part No. 7750550 A really cool combo machine, with some serious features. A touch screen allows full use of the controls and parameters, and the Anti-Static/Anti-Drift feature will minimize the hassled associated with the electronic scales. Another nice feature of the Gen 6 is that it's a compact unit, taking up less space on your bench.

The Hornady Lock-N-Load Auto Charge Powder Scale – Part no. 050068

Hornady has entered the electronic dispenser game with Lock-N-Load Auto Charge Powder Scale. Complete with a large, backlit screen with keypad, the Lock-N- Load has a 1,000 grain scale, and precision down to 0.1 grains. The Hornady unit also has a trickle function and over-charge protection.

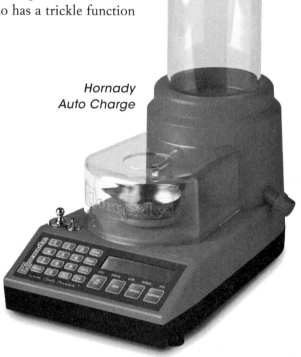

*Hornady
Auto Charge*

Powder Tricklers

Sometimes you need to fine-tune your powder charge, and the trickler is just the tool for that job. They use a worm-screw mechanism that you spin to deliver small amounts of powder into the pan to get your charge just right.

Redding #5 Powder Trickler – Part No. 05000

An all-steel design, made to the proper height to work well with almost all powder scales.

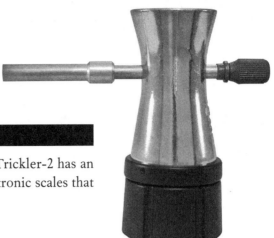

RCBS Powder Trickler-2 – Part No. 09089

Cast aluminum body, adjustable base height. The Powder Trickler-2 has an extended tube, so it will work with even the most difficult electronic scales that have a pan situated in a difficult area to reach.

Hornady Powder Trickler – Part No. 050100

Plastic body design and brass spout, wide base design for stability.

Lyman Powder Dribbler – Part No. 419297

Plastic body, aluminum tube, extended base for stability.

Frankford Arsenal Powder Trickler – Part No. 903535

All-steel construction, with knurled handle for positive grip. Comes with rubber dust cover that doubles as a non-skid base.

METALLIC HANDLOADING TOOLS:
CASE TRIMMERS &
CASE PREPERATION

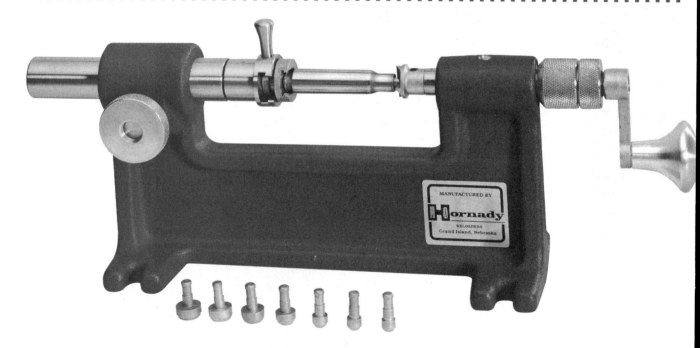

Case Trimmers & Preperation

The brass case stretches upon firing; it's just a simple fact. We, as handloaders, must be able to trim that brass case back to the proper SAAMI dimension. Trimming brass can be handled with a variety of tools; from the simplest (yet genius) designs, to the motor-driven, collet-guided, all-in-one machines.

Cases must also be prepared for reloading, i.e. case mouths must be chamfered and de-burred, primer pockets must be cleaned, cases must be

lubricated for resizing, etc. There are many different tools on the market for this, and in this section we will list some of the more popular items that our staff has had good experiences with. Whether or not you have the most expensive, electric-motor driven device, or one of the simple tools that requires more elbow grease than investment, there is one simple fact that remains: we need a means to keep our brass trimmed and uniform. Once you find a setup that works for you, you'll see your accuracy improve and your end product more satisfying.

Cases must also be kept clean. I prefer to clean my brass before running it into my resizing dies. For years, cleaning brass meant using a tumbler or vibratory cleaner and some form of cleaning media, such as crushed walnut shells or ground corn cobs. Now we have stainless steel tumbling media and fantastic ultrasonic cleaners. The solutions for these ultrasonic cleaners can do wonderful things: the inside of our brass cases are cleaner than they ever have been, and that helps us to keep things uniform.

There are all kinds of doo-dads and gadgets to clean, trim and prep your brass, of which we'll list the latest and greatest.

Editor's Picks:
Case Trimmers

*Top of Case
Prep Center*

1. *The RCBS Universal Case Prep Station*

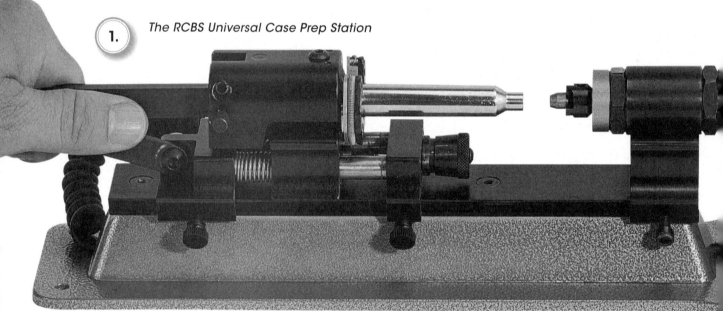

1. The RCBS Case Prep Station – Part No. 90370

This is what I refer to as "The Cadillac" as it can save your wrists a lot of wear and tear. Plugging into the wall, the Case Prep Station has a six-station rotating top, with chamfer, deburring and several brush attachments.

The on/off switch in the rear allows the user to 'dial in' the speed of the unit by adjusting the rpms. The trimmer section uses a carbide steel cutter and pilots of specific caliber, and a spring-loaded jaw system to hold the case to be trimmed. This jaw system holds almost any brass case (the only case I've found that it won't hold is the huge 50-90 Sharps).

There are two set screws that lock down the trimming mechanism once you get in close to the cutter, and properly aligned by the pilot, and a dial micrometer allows you to trim to the precise length that you need. The motor is interrupted when you depress the lever that opens the spring-loaded jaws, allowing you to remove the trimmed cartridge and install a case in need of trimming. Once trimmed to length, the case can be chamfered, and de-burred with the attachments that thread into the rotating receptacles in the top of the unit. Brushes are available for large and small primer pockets, and before you know it your case is ready for loading. In my opinion, The RCBS Case Prep Station is a very worthwhile investment.

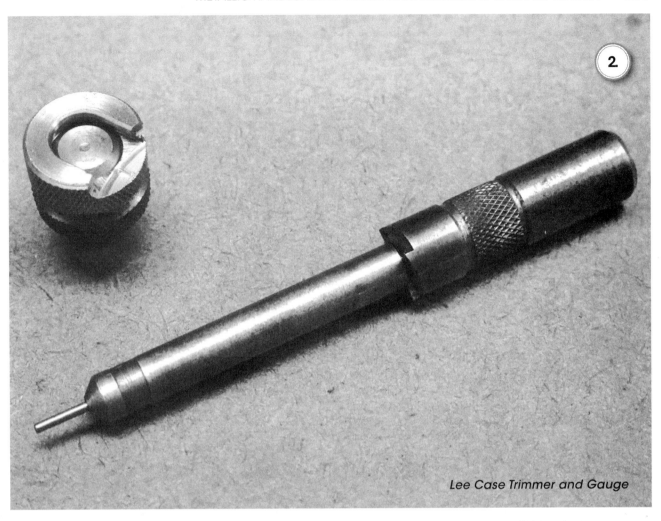

Lee Case Trimmer and Gauge

2. The Lee Case Length Gauge and Cutter - Part No. 90110

At the opposite end of the spectrum is the simple and inexpensive Lee Case Length Gauge and Cutter.

This little wonder makes all the sense in the world, especially if you don't need to produce a ridiculous amount of ammo at a sitting. It uses a threaded base with a hexagonal stud – for chucking into a drill – that screws into a case head holder (with dimensions of the proper shell holder) to secure the base of the case.

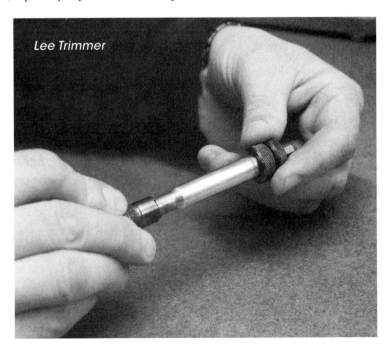

Lee Trimmer

The other half consists of a threaded cutter, knurled for a firm grip, and a case-specific gauge of hardened steel, that uses a pin which goes through the flash hole and stops on the base that holds the case. If the case exceeds the SAAMI specified length (the dimension to which the gauge is made), with several twists of the wrist, the cutter will handily remove the necessary amount of material. If you use a drill to spin the base, the process goes much quicker, and you'll avoid blisters.

I've used this wicked tool for decades, in a multitude of calibers, for both rifles and pistols. If you are reloading on the cheap, this is your baby. One good cutter and base, and you can pick up gauges and case holders for all the calibers you want to reload.

3. The Trim-It II Case Trimmer

This is another bit of genius, from the folks at Trim It. This design uses a micrometer-adjustable housing and a carbide cutter, in conjunction with a 'die' that uses the cartridge shoulder dimensions to set the trimming length, for bottleneck cartridges, or a base that sets the proper depth for the straight-walled cases. The mechanism requires a bit of getting used to, but once I got the hang of it, I was getting nicely trimmed cases. The carbide cutter gives a chamfer angle of 15° inside and a 45° outside bevel. When loading pistol bullets with a light copper plating, or when using the sleek, high B.C. target bullets in your rifle, this angle works out very well, making bullet seating easy as pie. If you're serious about uniform cases, give the Trim-It II a try.

Redding 2400
Case Trimmer

4. Redding 2400 Match Precision Case Trimmer – Part No. 24000

A cast iron frame that uses a universal collet and six pilots (in calibers .22, 6mm, .25, .270, 7mm and .308), the Redding 2400 Trimmer will trim cases up to 3-1/4" long. Adjustable micrometer will fine-tune your case length to 0.001". Like most Redding products, the 2400 is built to last a lifetime.

5. Lyman Universal Trimmer Power Pack – Part No. 7862003

The Lyman Universal uses a patented chuckhead to hold any case head diameter from the diminutive .17s up to the .458 Winchester Magnum. Includes nine collets in popular calibers and features an adjustment ring for dialing in the proper trim length.

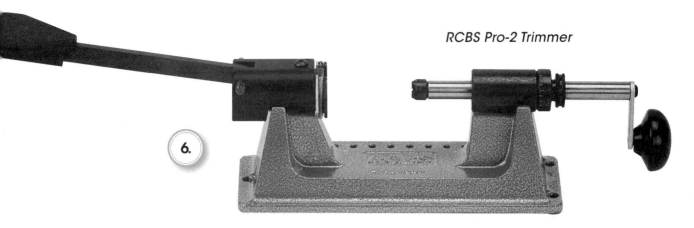

RCBS Pro-2 Trimmer

6.

6. The Hornady Lock-N-Load Case Prep Center – Part No. 050012

An all-in-one case preparation center, the Hornady Lock-N-Load machine will trim your cases to length, deburr, chamfer, and clean the primer pockets. Uses standard shell holders in lieu of a collet device to hold the cases, and comes with seven different pilots for trimming.

7. The RCBS Pro-2 Manual Case Trimmer – Part No. 90366

If you prefer the personal touch of a crank-style case trimmer, the RCBS Pro-2 may be your baby. Handling cases as long as the .338 Lapua, the die cast metal body has a universal shellholder that will accept cases with rim diameters from 0.250" to 0.626". The fine adjustment bushing has micrometer marks for adjusting trim length to 0.001". Comes with nine pilots in popular calibers.

*RCBS Pro-2 Manual
Case Trimmer*

7

Editor's Picks:
Case Preparation Tools

1. The L.E. Wilson Chamfer/Deburring tool

Shaped like a 1950s-era space rocket, this gem of a tool is constantly on my reloading bench. The nose of the tool will nicely chamfer any case mouth from .17 caliber to .45 caliber and the rear section will deburr equally well any case mouth. For under twenty bucks, this is a worthy tool to keep close at hand, should you ding or nick a case mouth on a die body during bullet seating.

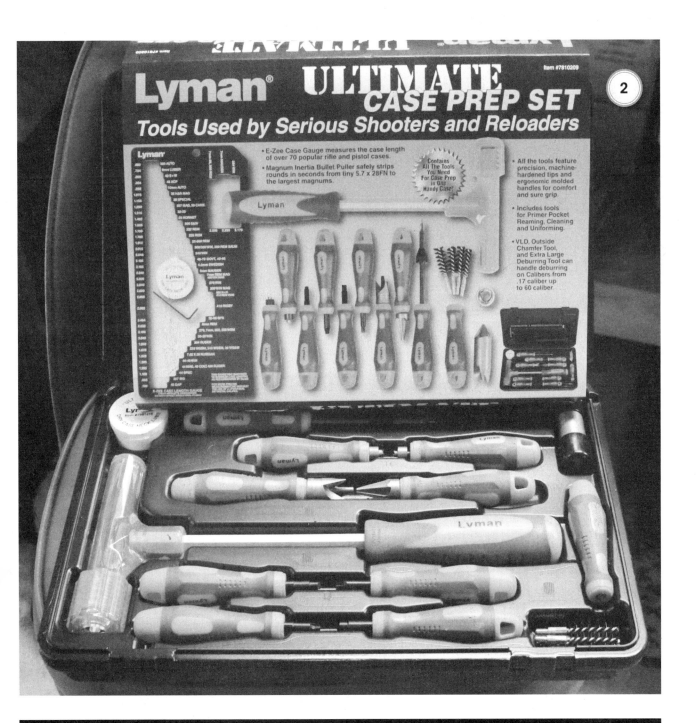

2. The Lyman Ultimate Case Prep Set

This little plastic brief case full of goodies solves a heck of a lot of problems. A deburring tool, a chamfer tool, flash hole uniformer, primer pocket cleaners, reamers and uniformers in both large and small sizes, nylon neck cleaning brushes, an inertia hammer for pulling bullets, and a case gauge for measuring case lengths. Quite the value in one concise package.

Lee Chamfer/Deburring Tool

3. Lee Chamfer and Deburring Tool – Part No. 90109

A hardened steel design, the Lee Chamfer and Deburring Tool will quickly and easily take good care of your case mouths, at a fraction of the cost of similar tools. Can also be used to remove a primer crimp from military brass.

4. RCBS Chamfer Tool VLD – Part No. 9352

A special tool for putting a 22° chamfer on the case mouth, for seating the VLD (Very Low Drag) bullets. Will chamfer cases of .17 caliber up to .45 caliber. Can be used independently, with an accessory handle or mounted on the Trim Mate Case Prep Center.

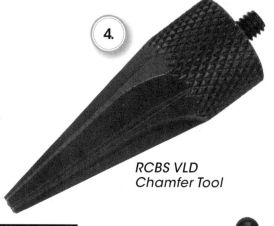

RCBS VLD Chamfer Tool

5. Lyman Flash Hole Uniformer Tool – Part No. 7777760

When you need consistent ignition in your handloads, a uniform flash hole is imperative. The Lyman Tool will uniform the flash holes in your cases, removing any and all burrs and giving the repeatable results you're after.

6. RCBS Bench Mounted Primer Pocket Swager – Part No. 9474

When you have military brass with a primer crimp, it must be removed before you can install the new primer. The RCBS unit will do exactly that, for both small and large primer pockets. Hardened steel rod supports and swaging heads.

RCBS Primer Pocket Swager

7. Lee Primer Pocket Cleaner – Part No. 90101

A dual-sided, knurled steel tool featuring a screwdriver-type blade, for scraping clean the primer pockets of both large and small primer pockets.

Lyman Cleaning Solutions

Editor's Picks:
Case Cleaners and Tumblers

1. The Lyman Turbo Sonic 2500 Ultrasonic Cleaner – Part No. 7631700

1.

In the new age of liquid cleaning, the Lyman Turbo Sonic 2500 can do a lot for a little. This modern age wonder will hold 900 cases of 9mm Luger, 400 .223s, and 250 '06 cases, and will clean them inside and out in less than 20 minutes. It can also be used to clean your dies, shellholders, and even smaller handguns! Want to degrease a rifle bolt for a sub-zero hunt? No problem. Ultrasonic cleaning does a much better job at cleaning the inside of cases than a regular tumbler, and the Lyman 2500 is a good machine.

There are special solutions available for cleaning brass, steel, and other items.

Lyman UltraSonic
2500 Case Cleaner

RCBS Vibratory Case Cleaner

2. The RCBS Vibratory Case Cleaner – Part No. 87088

As much as I love the ultrasonic cleaners, I still like to have a vibratory tumbler in the shop. While I feel the ultrasonic cleaners will do a better job of cleaning the inside of a case, the vibratory cleaners will actually polish the cases so they feed easier into your chamber. So, I use them together for a clean, polished case. The vibratory cleaners use some type of tumbling media – ground corn cobs, crushed walnut shells, or even little bits of stainless steel – to surround your cases and the electric motor vibrates the media to polish your cases to a nice shine. Be careful to clean all the media out of the case and primer pocket before loading. The RCBS Vibratory Case Cleaner will hold around 400 .38 Special or 9mm Luger cases, or 180 30-'06 cases.

3. Hornady Lock-N-Load Sonic Cleaner 2L – Part No. 043320

An 80-watt ceramic heater and Hornady's One-Shot cleaning solution will clean your cases quickly. The two-liter tank holds 300 .223 Remington cases or 150 .308 Winchester cases, in addition to other small metal items that require cleaning.

4. Lyman Turbo Sonic Power Professional Ultrasonic Case Cleaner – Part No. 7631734

A huge cleaner, measuring 38.5"x10.75"x14", for cleaning a huge amount of cases or entire handguns. The cleaner will heat up 175 degrees F, and can handle the barreled action of most rifles.

5. Thumler's Tumbler Model B High Speed Rotary Case Tumbler – Part No. 140HS

A heavy-duty tumbler with an all-steel hexagonal barrel, Thumler's Tumbler rotates your cases at 40rpm. Will work with liquid media, or dry media, including stainless steel. Built to last a lifetime.

6. Frankford Arsenal Platinum Series Rotary Case Tumbler – Part No. 909544

A voluminous tank, capable of holding 1,000 rounds of .223 Remington, Frankford Arsenal's tumbler has a timer that can be set for up to three hours of running time. Includes sifting caps on the end for separating your media.

7. RCBS Sidewinder Rotary Case Tumbler – Part No. 87000

With a drum set on its side, the Sidewinder Case Tumbler has a timer, for setting automatic shut-off, and a drum capable of holding 150 .30-'06 cases or 300 .38 Special cases. Can use wet or dry media.

Sidewinder Case Tumbler

Other Goodies.

RCBS Universal Case Loading Block

With two different sized holes for holding most cartridge cases, the RCSB Case Block will neatly hold your cases and prevent them from rolling off the bench and onto the floor, potentially dinging the case mouth. Simple, yet effective tool.

Redding Case Lube Kit

A pad for rolling out cases, lubricating them with Redding's Bio Green case lubricant. Allows the even distribution of lube, without over-lubricating, which can cause dents in the cartridge shoulder.

RCBS Universal Case Block

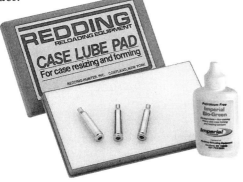

Redding Case Lube Kit

Hornady One-Shot Case Lube

An aerosol spray that won't contaminate powder or primers, One-Shot case lube can lubricate an entire case block at a single time. Easy to apply, with little risk of over-lubrication.

METALLIC HANDLOADING TOOLS:
BULLET PULLERS & OTHER ERASERS

Bullet Pullers & Other Erasers

We all make mistakes. It's just part of being human. But when we seat a bullet a bit too deep, or something else goes wrong that we didn't expect, a bullet puller can help save the other valuable components. Some of these bullet pullers are press-mounted, while others are simple inertia hammers that work in conjunction with the case head to pull a bullet out of a case.

Eventually, you'll stick a case in a resizing die, and rip the rim off the case. There are tools for fixing that as well. Your reloading gear should definitely include these tools, as it can save a reloading session, as well as your stomach lining.

Knowing how to get out of a jam is just as important as knowing how not to get into one, and the ability to save components that may otherwise need to be discarded is equally important. I've had customers with obsolete calibers, that had old ammunition with primers that were questionable at best, or bullets that were so oxidized that they didn't want to fire them. I used the press-mounted bullet puller to (carefully) disassemble the ammunition, and reload them with modern components.

Editor's Picks:

1. The RCBS Collet Bullet Puller

Resembling a reloading die, this tool threads into any reloading press that accepts 7/8-12 threads, and uses an expandable collet of specific caliber to firmly grab the projectile when the ram is extended upward. Once the bullet is firmly in place, you tighten the screw on the top of the puller to lock it down, and by lowering the ram you simply pull the cartridge apart, leaving the bullet in the collet and the case in the shellholder Very simple procedure, and unlike the inertia hammers, more than likely you won't damage the bullet, or spill powder all over your floor.

The RCBS Collet Bullet Puller

Lyman Magnum Impact Bullet Puller

2. Lyman Magnum Impact Bullet Puller

The inertia hammers are the simplest of tools to disassemble ammunition. They resemble a plastic hammer with a hollow cavity and a threaded receptacle on the uphill side. The user can choose from one of three collets, depending on case head size. You simply screw the cap over the loaded cartridge, and whack the hammer against a block of wood. The resulting inertia sends the bullet out of the cartridge case, and you can reclaim your metallic components. It also feels really good to beat the snot out of something once you realize you've screwed up your ammunition! I've found that some rifle cartridges with a lot of neck tension can require some brute force to pull apart, and sometimes softer bullet will have a deformed meplat after being disassembled. All in all, a good and inexpensive way to undo your mistakes.

3. The Redding Stuck Case Remover

If you haven't done it, you will one day. Everybody has; whether it's too-little lubrication, or a faulty case rim, it'll happen if you load enough ammunition. I once stuck a nickel-plated .375 H&H case in a resizing die so bad that I threw the die and case into the woods as far as I possibly could (total temper tantrum!), but I really wish I'd known about this handy little tool kit.

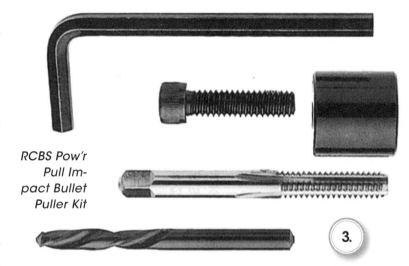

RCBS Pow'r Pull Impact Bullet Puller Kit

3.

You'll need a small vice to hold the die, and a drill to use the supplied bit. Here's the how: place the die and stuck case in the vice, and back the expander ball out until it is free from the flash hole. Using the proper size drill bit from the kit, drill a hole through the web of case, centered on the flash hole. The kit comes with a tap, and you next thread the hole you drilled with the provided tap. A steel cap mates up to the lip of the die, and an allen-headed bolt screws into your threaded hole. Turn the bolt with the allen-key, and voila! You will back the stuck case right out of the resizing die.

You can then smash the stuck case to little bits if that relieves the stress, or simply crush it with a pair of pliers so it won't end up in the mix again.

One more tip: always thoroughly inspect your resizing die and expander ball, to make sure that no part of the case ripped off inside the die body, and to make sure that the drilling process didn't break your decapping pin or mangle the expander ball.

Redding Stuck Case Remover Kit

4.

5.

RCBS Pow'r Pull Impact Bullet Puller Kit

4. RCBS Pow'r Pull Impact Bullet Puller Kit – Part No. 9412

A simple, yet effective impact hammer, with two collets to fit most cartridges.

5. Hornady Cam-Lock Bullet Puller – Part No. 050094

Using a cam lever and a series of collets, which are caliber specific, the Hornady Cam-Lock Bullet Puller will quickly and effectively pull the bullet from a cartridge. Mounts to your reloading press.

METALLIC HANDLOADING TOOLS:
PRIMING TOOLS

Priming Tools & Accessories

Seating your primers to the proper depth is a very important step in constructing your ammunition. If a primer is left out too far, a risk of accidental discharge may exist in certain firearms (at worst) or your ammunition won't feed properly (at best).

I like to set my primers perfectly flush, or slightly recessed – 0.003" or 0.004" deep at most – and I use several tools to achieve that measurement.

Many times I will use the priming cup mounted on the press, be it my old RCBS RockChucker or my Redding T7, but there are those who feel that priming from the press uses the tons of leverage generated to rob you of the feel of priming by hand.

When Kent Sakamoto of RCBS showed me the Summit press at the SHOT show in '14, I immediately asked why such a cool design wouldn't include a priming arm; Kent looked at me deadpan and replied "Because you should be priming by hand!"

Hornady Hand Priming Tool – Part No. 0500021

Lyman E-ZEE Prime

In my opinion, Kent's not wrong, but he's not entirely right either. I have, through the process of priming tens of thousands of rounds on a press, developed a feel for it. That aside, I also use several hand-priming tools when I'm developing precision ammunition. The choice is ultimately up to you as to which method will work best for you, but I'd be willing to wager that before all is said and done you'll end up owning and using both methods, at least to see if there is any difference is the end product. The priming tool on your press is rather self explanatory, so let's look at the hand primers.

Editor's Picks:
Priming Tools

1. Lyman E-ZEE Prime Universal Hand Priming tool – Part No. 7777810

Using standard shellholders, the ergonomic design of the E-ZEE Prime allows you to comfortably install primers, both small and large. Unit has small and large priming trays, which slide into the handle, and have an integral primer punch. A collar snaps into place once the shellholder is installed, and you can begin priming. Each tray has a shut-off gate to keep the primers in the tray when you've finished. Gives a good feel for precision priming.

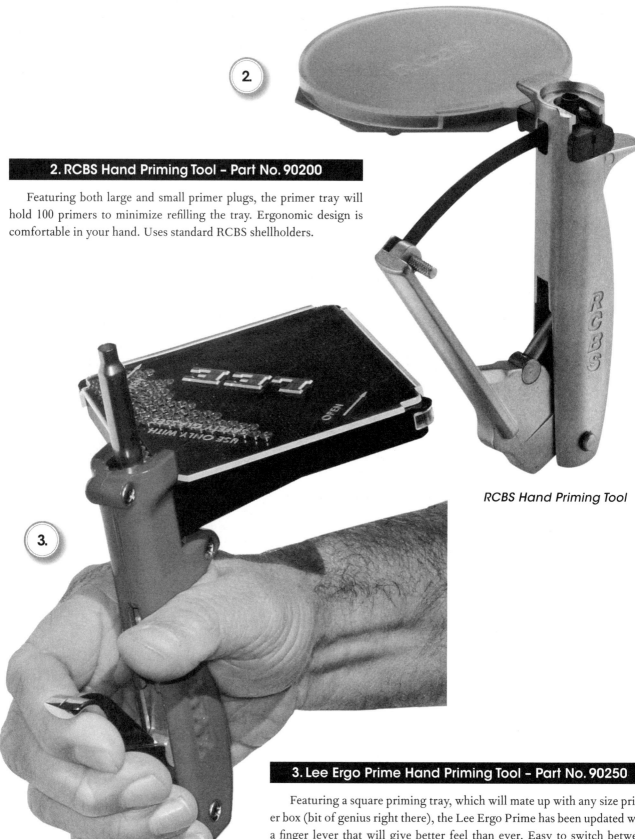

2. RCBS Hand Priming Tool – Part No. 90200

Featuring both large and small primer plugs, the primer tray will hold 100 primers to minimize refilling the tray. Ergonomic design is comfortable in your hand. Uses standard RCBS shellholders.

RCBS Hand Priming Tool

3. Lee Ergo Prime Hand Priming Tool – Part No. 90250

Featuring a square priming tray, which will mate up with any size primer box (bit of genius right there), the Lee Ergo Prime has been updated with a finger lever that will give better feel than ever. Easy to switch between large and small primers. Note: The Ergo Prime system uses the Lee Auto Prime shellholders, and will not work with standard shellholders. Auto Prime shellholders are sold separately.

Lee Ergo Prime Hand Priming Tool

4. Hornady Hand Priming Tool – Part No. 0500021

With a handle designed to feel like a pair of pliers, The Hornady Hand Priming Tool will work with both large and small primers. The round priming tray has large and small primer cups, set on opposite ends of the tray. Will work with Hornady shellholders, and comes with an adapter for using RCBS-style shellholders.

Editor's Picks:
Priming Accessories

1. RCBS Primer Turning Tray – Part No. 9480

This genius little device comes in very handy when priming from a single-stage or turret press. If you've ever been on your hands and knees picking up a box of spilled primers, you'll see why a simple tool like this should be on your bench. Square shape, so you can easily empty the box of primers into the tray.

RCBS Primer Turning Tray

RCBS APS Priming Strip loader

2. RCBS APS Primer Strip Loader – Part No. 88505

If you have a press that uses the APS priming system, you know how mundane it can be trying to refill the primer strips. This tool flips the primers to the proper position, and with a single squeeze will install 25 primers into the strip.

3. Lyman Primer Turning Tray – Part No. 7728053

A 4" diameter grooved tray. Simply dump primers into the tray, shake gently and they'll turn anvil side up.

METALLIC HANDLOADING TOOLS:
RELOADING MANUALS

The reloading manual is the cookbook for reloaders. It gives us the recipe we need to create safe ammunition, without resulting in dangerously high or low pressures. In years past, we owned only one manual: an early 1970s Sierra book that we would use for loading everything. Now, mind you, there wasn't the wide selection of bullet types when I started to reload – most bullets were of cup-and-core design – but simply put, I didn't know any better.

I was lucky in that I always started at the bottom of the data chart and worked up, but I wouldn't do that today. Monometal bullets, banded bullets, uber-thick jackets, bullets with more bearing surface, less bearing surface, etc; all these construction differences equal a great variance in load data. I'd highly recommend that you purchase, or at least obtain, the specific data for the bullet you're loading.

This will result in owning a multitude of reloading manuals, or keeping many different company's websites marked as a favorite on your computer. I use many different bullets, so I am familiar with some of the general variances, but I'd advise that you do your homework when loading a different bullet.

Most bullet companies offer a manual for their bullets (North Fork and Cutting Edge Bullets are two that, to my knowledge, don't produce a manual, but are working on them) and many put load data on their website. Powder companies offer load data as well, but you need to look carefully to see which brand or type of bullet was tested to arrive at the data.

Not all powders that are applicable to a particular cartridge are tested in every manual. The modern books do their best, but as you've seen

throughout the catalog section of this book (which is abbreviated, at best), there is a ton of gear on the market. A word of advice: if you don't see a powder tested, call the bullet company. Ask if the powder you're interested in is a viable choice for the cartridge in question, and secondly ask if they have any load data for you. You'll be surprised how eager they can be to help you out; after all, they're reloading geeks like us!

I'll admit to a bit of geekdom here: I enjoy reading reloading manuals. There is plenty of cartridge history, and little tidbits of information that I've relied on for decades. I especially like to read the anecdotal stuff, like Nosler has long provided, where different writers and hunters share their experiences and tips regarding each different cartridge.

Some of the powder companies will test with more than one company's bullet, but the Lyman Reloading Manual is an example of a company that doesn't make a bullet or powder, but provides a broad spectrum of load data, including data for the cast bullets. I've used Lyman data as a load source, or as a source of affirmation, when I think I may have found a typo in a manual (yes, they do exist, so it pays to double check). The 49th Edition is current for Lyman, and I look forward to the 50th.

Powder, cartridges and bullets continue to evolve, and new models are introduced, so as time moves along be certain to get the latest edition of the manual which covers the bullets you love best.

1.

Swift Reloading Manual No. 2

Editor's Picks:
Reloading Manuals

1. Swift Reloading Manual No. 2

Updated to cover the expanded line of bullets, as well as cover newer cartridges and powders, I've used Swift bullets in six different countries, and their products and data have never let me down.

2.

Hornady's 9th Edition

2. Hornady Handbook of Cartridge Reloading, 9th Edition

Hornady makes many different bullets, of different construction. They do a fantastic job of covering the spectrum of powders, both pistol and rifle. I use Hornady bullets quite often, and rely on their data.

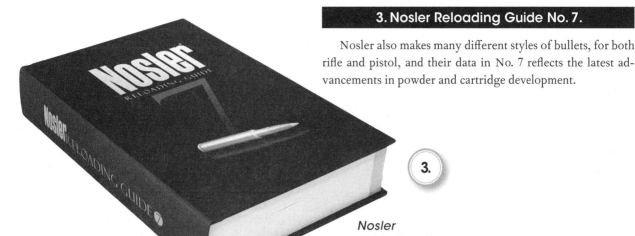

3. Nosler Reloading Guide No. 7.

Nosler also makes many different styles of bullets, for both rifle and pistol, and their data in No. 7 reflects the latest advancements in powder and cartridge development.

3.

Nosler Reloading Guide No. 7

4. Berger 1st Edition Reloading Manual

Berger is one of those companies who make bullets in a non-traditional manner, in that they are often long-for -caliber, due to the sweeping ogives and sleek boat tails. This construction changes the data, as the bearing surface changes. I'm glad Berger has come out with their first manual; they have a great team of ballisticians.

Berger 1st Edition

4.

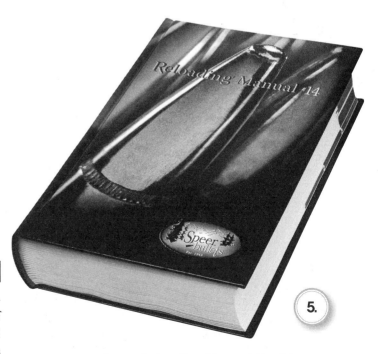

5. Speer Reloading Manual No. 14

You don't get to your 14th reloading manual without knowing a bit about what you're doing. Speer has a long history of dependable bullets, and Speer No. 13 was the first manual I purchased on my own. The data is very reliable, and the means of testing is well explained.

5.

Speer Reloading Manual No. 14

Sierra's 5th Edition

6.

6. Sierra 5th Edition Rifle and Handgun Reloading Manual

I have always loved Sierra bullets, and I can tell you they have a fantastic team of people who are very dedicated to their job. Sierra has taken the pains to extensively research their data, including many powder/bullet combinations in their book. The Sierra manuals have been something I've always relied on.

7. Lyman Reloading Handbook 49th Edition

As I outlined above, Lyman tests with many different bullets, of different construction, from different companies. They cover most American and European powders. Their test data is clear and concise, and includes load data for the cast bullets from Lyman moulds. Rifle and pistol cartridges are covered extensively.

Lyman 49th Edition

8. Norma Reloading Manual Vol. 2

The folks at Norma have produced a good reloading manual for their lineup of smokeless powders. Norma's fine component bullets are included, in addition to popular bullets from the major manufacturers. Load data is for Norma powder only.

Norma Reloading Manual Vol.2

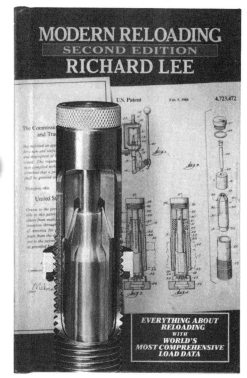

9. Lee Modern Reloading, 2nd Edition, Revised

A good basic manual, for both beginners and experienced reloaders. Updated to include load data for newer cartridges such as the WSSM series and the 6.5 Creedmoor, which didn't appear in the original 2nd Edition.

Lee Modern Reloading 2nd Edition

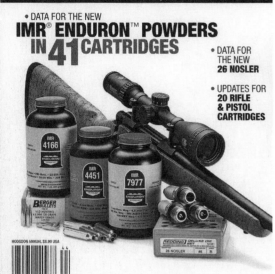

10. Hodgdon 2015 Reloading Manual

Hodgdon, IMR and Winchester powder are all covered in this complete manual, including the CFE series of Hodgdon powder and the new Enduron line from IMR. A relatively inexpensive must-have manual.

11. Barnes Reloading Manual No. 4

Another great job by the Barnes company, providing safe and accurate load data for the monometal bullet that they are famous for. Published in 2008, I'd expect No. 5 isn't all that far away.

12. Woodleigh Bullets Loading Manual

I happen to be buddies with Geoff McDonald, of Woodleigh Bullets, and I can attest as to how dedicated he is to his line of bullets. I've relied on Woodleigh as a source for the more obscure calibers, like the .318 Westley Richards, and I had great success using their load data for my .404 Jeffery on two recent safaris to South Africa and Zimbabwe. The Woodleigh Loading Manual contains modern loading data for all the Woodleigh bullet line – including the new Hydro-statically Stabilized Solids – as well as a section for the older British cartridges for double guns and repeaters, all at safe pressures for the older guns. A great resource for safari guns.

Woodleigh Bullets Loading Manual

13. Alliant Powder 2015 Reloader's Guide

A reloading manual for Alliant's sweet lineup of powders, including rifle, pistol and shotgun data. Includes data for the newer Reloder powders, like Reloder 23, 26 and 33, in addition to Power Pro 200-MR and Power Pro 4000-MR.

*Alliant 2015
Reloader's Guide*

METALLIC HANDLOADING COMPONENTS:
BULLETS

U ndoubtedly, the bullet we use in our cartridges certainly doesn't get the respect it deserves, for no matter the intended target, the bullet, and only the bullet, is the one part of the equation that makes contact. Circassian walnut, European optics, tritium night sights, bobtailed hammers; all these are merely efforts in aiding the attempt to put that single bullet where we want it. Simply put: the bullet does the work.

Tracking the history of bullet development is quite an undertaking; I did my best to outline and explain bullet performance and construction in my book "Understanding Ballistics: Complete Guide to Bullet Selection" – available through Gun Digest. For the reloader, there are probably more good bullet choices on the market today than we have time to experiment with. These developments have truly changed the game as we knew it, however all of our old favorites are still with us and as dependable as always.

Polymer-tipped boattails, all-copper pistol bullets with crazy-deep hollowpoints, bonded-core semi-spitzers, solids with little cups on their nose to create a shockwave of destruction without expanding beyond caliber – these are some of the new developments in recent years that have opened my eyes and sent me scurrying back to the bench like a child at the sight of a piñata.

I said earlier "the game as we knew it", and by that I was referring to the classic bullet/cartridge idioms that we have held dear since the days of O'Connor v. Keith, and these newer style of bullets really call for a revision of those ideas. Hopefully by now you've obtained a copy of Understanding Ballistics to aid in the choice of proper projectile.

The cast lead bullets and cup-and-core classics of yesteryear still account for a huge portion of the market share, and rightfully so. These are time-proven winners, which at the proper velocities will still give us the performance we've come to expect. Names like Speer, Hornady, Sierra, Remington, and Nosler have been a part of the hunting and shooting world for the better part of 70 years, and while their product lines have evolved to include some of the radical designs that changed the game, the Grand Slams, InterLocks, Match Kings, Core-Lokts and Partitions are still getting the nod from shooters around the world.

That said, there are also the Deep Curls, GMXs, Tipped Match Kings, Accu-Tip and AccuBonds that represent the respective updates to older product lines. The new bench research ultimately falls to you. I use old and new bullets, simple designs as well as high-tech, and I love them all.

The 'boutique' bullet companies, like North Fork, Cutting Edge Bullets, Woodleigh Bullets, Barnes, and Swift Bullets have a respectable product line as well, and many of these products are only available in component form. We reloaders have the ballistic world at our fingertips; reach out and grab something cool!

Editor's Picks:
(I'll try to be brief, but I love them all!)

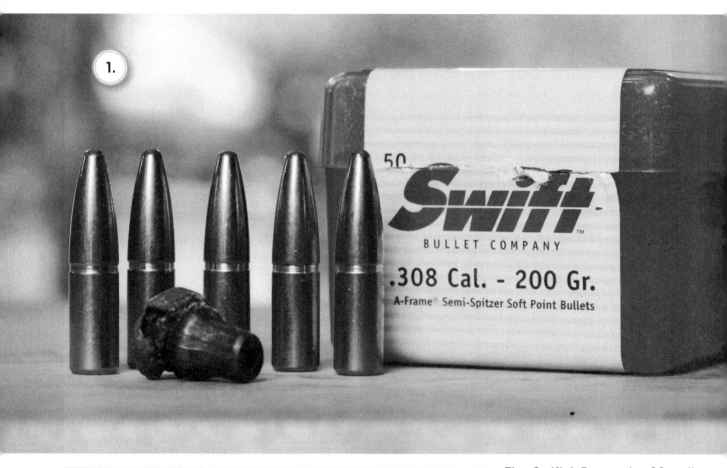

1.

The Swift A-Frame.

The Swift A-Frame, in .30 caliber 200-grain, shown unfired and recovered from an ostrich!

I consider this to be one of the finest hunting bullets on the market. Its cross section resembles the famous Nosler Partition, except the A-Frame has a thicker jacket, and that jacket is chemically bonded to the front core, resulting in a very tough bullet that will give ultra-reliable penetration as well as good expansion, even at the lower velocities. I've used this bullet in 6.5mm caliber, .308" caliber, .375" caliber and .416" caliber; in addition to the great field performance, they have proven to be wonderfully accurate.

When I need a bullet that will perform under any and all circumstances (save elephant), I know I can reach for a box of Swift A-Frames and hunt confidently. Available in most bullet diameters from .257" to .509"

The Swift A-Frame, in .375 caliber 300-grain, Semi-Spitzer Soft Point Bullets

The Sierra Tipped Match King

Well, I really didn't think that the incredible Sierra Match King could be improved upon. I mean, seriously, these things have been an industry standard for decades, and the tiny cloverleaf groups they print are a force to be reckoned with in the benchrest world.

However, while I was at the SHOT show in Vegas in January of '15, my buddy Carroll Pilant from Sierra saw me in the hallway and said "stop by the booth, I've got something to show you." The something was the Tipped Match King, and I couldn't wait to get my hands on them.

The Sierra-green polymer tip not only increases the B.C., but prevents the tip from being damaged easily. Mark Nazi and I had a chance to test these out: they're every bit as accurate as the original MKs, and although we haven't had a chance to stretch out the yardage, I'm sure the higher B.C. will help flatten the trajectory a bit. Available in .224 caliber, 69 & 77 grains; .308 caliber, 125, 155, 168 and 175 grains.

Sierra Tipped Match King, with signature green polymer tip

Cutting Edge Bullets Handgun Raptor

I was introduced to Cutting Edge Bullets at the Great American Outdoor Show in Harrisburg, Pennsylvania, and upon inspecting their lineup of Handgun Raptor bullets, I was immediately intrigued. Monometal construction, deep hollowpoints, an ogive that breaks into little 'blades' upon impact; these things look like fun! Being all-copper, they are lighter for caliber when of the same length as their cup-and-core counterparts, so velocities climb quickly. After the break-up, the remainder of the bullet stays at caliber dimension, to drive deep into the target. Available in 9mm, .400 and .45 calibers

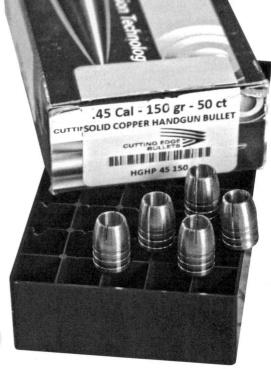

3.

Cutting Edge Handgun Raptors, .45 caliber 150 grain

North Fork Semi-Spitzers

Founded in Wyoming, now working in Oregon, North Fork bullets just plain work. There's a simple genius here: a pure lead core, in the front-half of the bullet only, is chemically bonded to a pure copper jacket and base, in a semi-spitzer design which keep the bullet weight forward for straight line penetration and organ-wrecking expansion. The shank of the bullet – the bearing surface – is grooved, so that the part of the bullet engages the rifling almost looks threaded (but certainly isn't).

This reduces pressures, and actually helps to keep the bore clean. What I like best is the accuracy and terminal performance. They shoot well in all my guns, and they offer some bullets that are problem solvers. My good buddy Dave deMoulpied loves his .350 Remington Magnum, a stubby little belted affair that doesn't have the magazine length or case capacity for the longer .35-caliber bullets.

However, the 200-grain North Fork semi-spitzer worked like a charm, fitting perfectly in the Remington Model 700 Classic's magazine (most bullets, when seated to the necessary COL, sit with the case mouth on the ogive – something you never want to do – but the 200-grain North Fork, with its weight forward, is perfect), and the bonded-core construction allows Neighbor Dave to use a light-for-caliber bullet and still take game cleanly, from any angle. A big-bodied Maine whitetail was less than pleased with our chosen load, dropping to the 250-yard shot, not unlike a stone. Available in 6.5mm up to and including the big safari calibers.

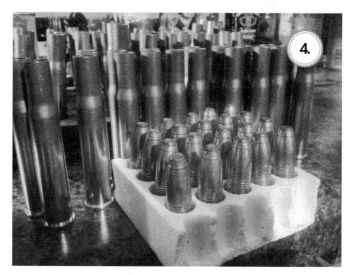

4.

North Fork Percussion Point Semi-Spitzer, 400-grain for the 450/400 NE

Falcon Bullets Fal-Coated .45ACP 230-grain hard-cast lead bullets

Cast lead is the friend of those who play the gun games, as well as those pistol shooters who enjoy expending a high volume of ammunition on the weekends. Casting your own can be quite time-consuming, and the cost of purchasing jacketed bullets continues to rise. Enter Falcon Bullets, from the great State of Tennessee. Mr. David Moore delivers an affordable, accurate and clean bullet. The bullet profile mirrors the 230-grain FMJ military ball ammo profile, so it will run well in your 1911 and all of the clones, and the proprietary Fal-Coating prevents your barrel from leading too quickly, as well as helping to keep the reloading dies on the progressive presses cleaner. I've had nothing but good results with this bullet, along with the entire Falcon line. If you're on a budget and you need a large supply of projectiles, Falcon is the answer.

Falcon Fal-Coated 230-graqin roundnose .45 bullets

Woodleigh Hydrostatically Stabilized Solids

In the world of bullets for African safaris, the need for a non-expanding, deep penetrating bullet – referred to as a 'solid' – has always existed. These bullets will smash through the thickest hide and bone, often penetrating the entire animal; an important point when dealing with the likes of elephant, buffalo and hippo. The problem is that the solids offer no expansion, or the tissue destruction associated with it. Woodleigh has changed that with the Hydrostatically Stabilized Solid.

It is an all brass bullet with shallow grooves on the shank, to keep pressures down, and a funky little 'dish' depression on the meplat. That dish creates a 'low-cavitation bubble', which aids in deeper penetration. The feature that I like best about the Woodleigh Hydro is the shockwave of destroyed tissue it creates throughout the game animal, while still only leaving a caliber-sized exit wound. I recently used this bullet in South Africa and Zimbabwe, on animals of widely differing sizes.

My rifle was a .404 Jeffery, in a Heym Express bolt-action, and the .423" diameter bullets weighed 400 grains. They were handloaded to 2,280 fps, and printed 1" groups at 100 yards. I took an impala ram and a blue wildebeest bull in South Africa, both falling quickly to the shot, running no more than 35 yards. As advertised, the exit wound was of caliber dimension, but the vitals were ruined. The Zimbabwean bull elephant, weighing the better part of six tons, fell in the same manner – lungs destroyed, with full body penetration on both shots. I'm convinced this bullet makes a good choice as a universal safari bullet.

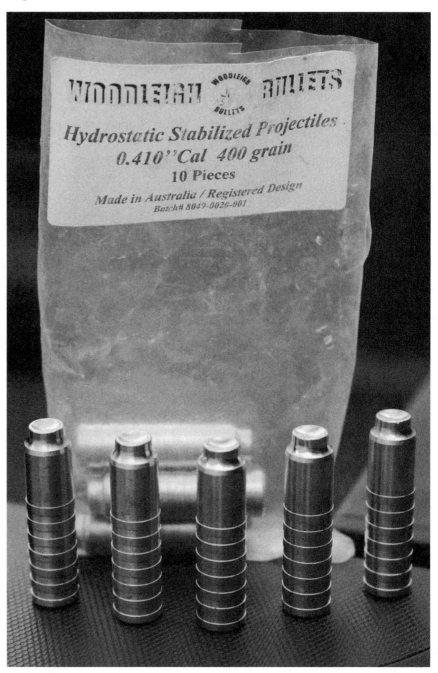

the Woodleigh Hydrostatically Stabilized Solid

The Big Guys

Sierra Bullets

Undoubtedly, Sierra has been onto something wonderful for decades now, and they continue to be innovative. I've probably launched more Sierra bullets at game than any other, simply because they work so well. Our deer season here in New York is three weeks long, and our shots are definitely on the close end of the spectrum, so a .308 Winchester or the like makes a ton of sense.

I absolutely love hunting with Sierra's 165-grain hollowpoint boattail Game King in .308" caliber; the thick jacket gives me the field performance I like, and the design of the bullet approximates the performance of the 168-grain Match King. For our coyote season, I break the rules a bit and use the 52-grain Match King flat-base hollowpoint in my .22-250, as the thin-skinned predators don't require a tough bullet at all, and they shoot so well that 400-yard shots aren't out of the question.

I know, Sierra says not to use the Match King on game animals, but these bullets dump 'em in their tracks. The 180-grain Game King boattail has worked wonderfully in my .300 Winchester Magnum, and I love the 300-grain .375" bullet for distant plains game. Sierra's jacketed handgun bullets have worked splendidly in my .45 Colt revolver, and I wouldn't hesitate to use the 300-grain .452" slugs during our early black bear season. If you're a fan of cup-and-core bullets, Sierra has a bullet for you.

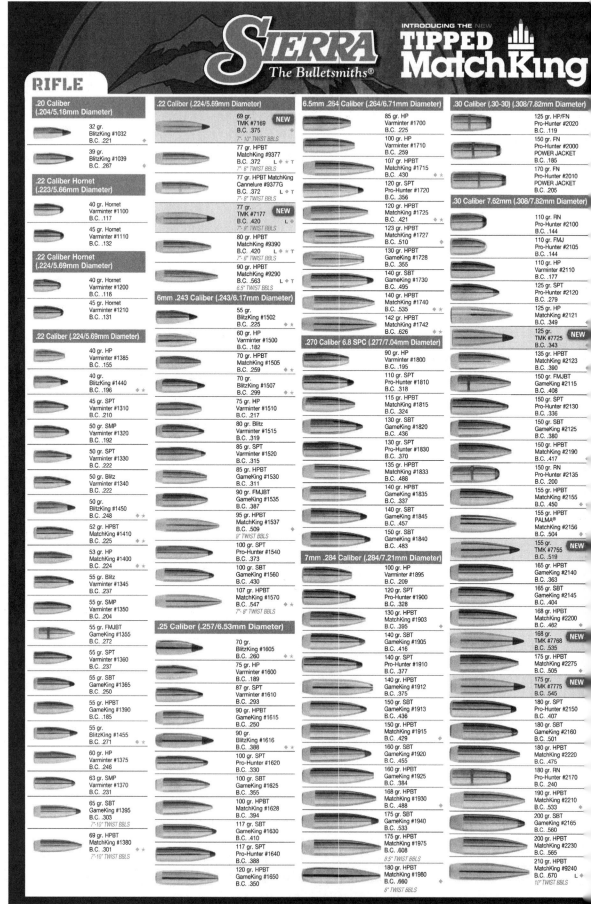

Sierra
The Bulletsmiths®

INTRODUCING THE NEW TIPPED MatchKing

RIFLE

.20 Caliber (.204/5.18mm Diameter)

32 gr. BlitzKing #1032 B.C. .221	
39 gr. BlitzKing #1039 B.C. .287	

.22 Caliber Hornet (.223/5.66mm Diameter)

40 gr. Hornet Varminter #1100 B.C. .117	
45 gr. Hornet Varminter #1110 B.C. .132	

.22 Caliber Hornet (.224/5.69mm Diameter)

40 gr. Hornet Varminter #1200 B.C. .116	
45 gr. Hornet Varminter #1210 B.C. .131	

.22 Caliber (.224/5.69mm Diameter)

- 40 gr. HP Varminter #1385 B.C. .155
- 40 gr. BlitzKing #1440 B.C. .196
- 45 gr. SPT Varminter #1310 B.C. .210
- 50 gr. SMP Varminter #1320 B.C. .192
- 50 gr. SPT Varminter #1330 B.C. .222
- 50 gr. Blitz Varminter #1340 B.C. .222
- 50 gr. BlitzKing #1450 B.C. .248
- 52 gr. HPBT MatchKing #1410 B.C. .225
- 53 gr. HP MatchKing #1400 B.C. .224
- 55 gr. Blitz Varminter #1345 B.C. .237
- 55 gr. SMP Varminter #1350 B.C. .204
- 55 gr. FMJBT GameKing #1355 B.C. .272
- 55 gr. SPT Varminter #1360 B.C. .237
- 55 gr. SBT GameKing #1365 B.C. .250
- 55 gr. HPBT GameKing #1390 B.C. .185
- 55 gr. BlitzKing #1455 B.C. .271
- 60 gr. HP Varminter #1375 B.C. .246
- 63 gr. SMP Varminter #1370 B.C. .231
- 65 gr. SBT GameKing #1395 B.C. .303
  7"-10" TWIST BBLS
- 69 gr. HPBT MatchKing #1380 B.C. .301
  7"-10" TWIST BBLS

.22 Caliber (.224/5.69mm Diameter)

- 69 gr. TMK #7169 B.C. .375 **NEW**
  7"-10" TWIST BBLS
- 77 gr. HPBT MatchKing #9377 B.C. .372 L ♦ T
  7"-8" TWIST BBLS
- 77 gr. HPBT MatchKing Cannelure #9377G B.C. .372 L ♦ T
  7"-8" TWIST BBLS
- 77 gr. TMK #7177 B.C. .420 L ♦ **NEW**
  7"-8" TWIST BBLS
- 80 gr. HPBT MatchKing #9390 B.C. .420 L ♦ ♦ T
  7"-8" TWIST BBLS
- 90 gr. HPBT MatchKing #9290 B.C. .563 L ♦ T
  6.5" TWIST BBLS

6mm .243 Caliber (.243/6.17mm Diameter)

- 55 gr. BlitzKing #1502 B.C. .225 ♦ ★
- 60 gr. HP Varminter #1500 B.C. .182
- 70 gr. HPBT MatchKing #1505 B.C. .259 ♦ ★
- 70 gr. BlitzKing #1507 B.C. .299 ♦ ★
- 75 gr. HP Varminter #1510 B.C. .217
- 80 gr. Blitz Varminter #1515 B.C. .319
- 85 gr. SPT Varminter #1520 B.C. .315
- 85 gr. HPBT GameKing #1530 B.C. .311
- 90 gr. FMJBT GameKing #1535 B.C. .387
- 95 gr. HPBT MatchKing #1537 B.C. .509 ♦
  8" TWIST BBLS
- 100 gr. SPT Pro-Hunter #1540 B.C. .373
- 100 gr. SBT GameKing #1560 B.C. .430
- 107 gr. HPBT MatchKing #1570 B.C. .547 ♦ ★
  7"-8" TWIST BBLS

.25 Caliber (.257/6.53mm Diameter)

- 70 gr. BlitzKing #1605 B.C. .260 ♦ ★
- 75 gr. HP Varminter #1600 B.C. .189
- 87 gr. SPT Varminter #1610 B.C. .293
- 90 gr. HPBT GameKing #1615 B.C. .250
- 90 gr. BlitzKing #1616 B.C. .388 ♦ ★
- 100 gr. SPT Pro-Hunter #1620 B.C. .330
- 100 gr. SBT GameKing #1625 B.C. .355
- 100 gr. HPBT MatchKing #1628 B.C. .394
- 117 gr. SBT GameKing #1630 B.C. .410
- 117 gr. SPT Pro-Hunter #1640 B.C. .388
- 120 gr. HPBT GameKing #1650 B.C. .350

6.5mm .264 Caliber (.264/6.71mm Diameter)

- 85 gr. HP Varminter #1700 B.C. .225
- 100 gr. HP Varminter #1710 B.C. .259
- 107 gr. HPBT MatchKing #1715 B.C. .430 ♦ ★
- 120 gr. SPT Pro-Hunter #1720 B.C. .356
- 120 gr. HPBT MatchKing #1725 B.C. .421 ♦ ★
- 123 gr. HPBT MatchKing #1727 B.C. .510 ♦
- 130 gr. HPBT GameKing #1728 B.C. .355
- 140 gr. SBT GameKing #1730 B.C. .495
- 140 gr. HPBT MatchKing #1740 B.C. .535 ♦ ★
- 142 gr. HPBT MatchKing #1742 B.C. .626 ♦ ★

.270 Caliber 6.8 SPC (.277/7.04mm Diameter)

- 90 gr. HP Varminter #1800 B.C. .195
- 110 gr. SPT Pro-Hunter #1810 B.C. .318
- 115 gr. HPBT MatchKing #1815 B.C. .324
- 130 gr. SBT GameKing #1820 B.C. .436
- 130 gr. SPT Pro-Hunter #1830 B.C. .370
- 135 gr. HPBT MatchKing #1833 B.C. .488
- 140 gr. HPBT GameKing #1835 B.C. .337
- 140 gr. SBT GameKing #1845 B.C. .457
- 150 gr. SBT GameKing #1840 B.C. .483

7mm .284 Caliber (.284/7.21mm Diameter)

- 100 gr. HP Varminter #1895 B.C. .209
- 120 gr. SPT Pro-Hunter #1900 B.C. .328
- 130 gr. HPBT MatchKing #1903 B.C. .395 ♦
- 140 gr. SBT GameKing #1905 B.C. .416
- 140 gr. SPT Pro-Hunter #1910 B.C. .377
- 140 gr. HPBT GameKing #1912 B.C. .375
- 150 gr. SBT GameKing #1913 B.C. .436
- 150 gr. HPBT MatchKing #1915 B.C. .429
- 160 gr. SBT GameKing #1920 B.C. .455
- 160 gr. HPBT GameKing #1925 B.C. .384
- 168 gr. HPBT MatchKing #1930 B.C. .488 ♦
- 175 gr. SBT GameKing #1940 B.C. .533
- 175 gr. HPBT MatchKing #1975 B.C. .608
  8.5" TWIST BBLS
- 180 gr. HPBT MatchKing #1980 B.C. .660 ♦
  8" TWIST BBLS

.30 Caliber (.30-30) (.308/7.82mm Diameter)

- 125 gr. HP/FN Pro-Hunter #2020 B.C. .119
- 150 gr. FN Pro-Hunter #2000 POWER JACKET B.C. .185
- 170 gr. FN Pro-Hunter #2010 POWER JACKET B.C. .205

.30 Caliber 7.62mm (.308/7.82mm Diameter)

- 110 gr. RN Pro-Hunter #2100 B.C. .144
- 110 gr. FMJ Pro-Hunter #2105 B.C. .144
- 110 gr. HP Varminter #2110 B.C. .177
- 125 gr. SPT Pro-Hunter #2120 B.C. .279
- 125 gr. HP MatchKing #2121 B.C. .349
- 125 gr. TMK #7725 B.C. .343 **NEW**
- 135 gr. HPBT MatchKing #2123 B.C. .390
- 150 gr. FMJBT GameKing #2115 B.C. .408
- 150 gr. SPT Pro-Hunter #2130 B.C. .336
- 150 gr. SBT GameKing #2125 B.C. .380
- 150 gr. HPBT MatchKing #2190 B.C. .417 ♦
- 150 gr. RN Pro-Hunter #2135 B.C. .200
- 155 gr. HPBT MatchKing #2155 B.C. .450 ♦
- 155 gr. HPBT PALMA® MatchKing #2156 B.C. .504
- 155 gr. TMK #7755 B.C. .519 **NEW**
- 165 gr. HPBT GameKing #2140 B.C. .363
- 165 gr. SBT GameKing #2145 B.C. .404
- 168 gr. HPBT MatchKing #2200 B.C. .462
- 168 gr. TMK #7768 B.C. .535 **NEW**
- 175 gr. HPBT MatchKing #2275 B.C. .505 ♦
- 175 gr. TMK #7775 B.C. .545 **NEW**
- 180 gr. SPT Pro-Hunter #2150 B.C. .407
- 180 gr. SBT GameKing #2160 B.C. .501
- 180 gr. HPBT MatchKing #2220 B.C. .475
- 180 gr. RN Pro-Hunter #2170 B.C. .240
- 190 gr. HPBT MatchKing #2210 B.C. .533
- 200 gr. SBT GameKing #2165 B.C. .560
- 200 gr. HPBT MatchKing #2230 B.C. .565
- 210 gr. HPBT MatchKing #9240 B.C. .670 L ♦
  10" TWIST BBLS

TOLL-FREE TECH SUPPORT
1.800.223.8799

HANDGUN

.30 Caliber 7.62mm (.308/7.82mm Diameter)

- 220 gr. HPBT MatchKing #2240 B.C. .629 ♦
- 220 gr. RN Pro-Hunter #2180 B.C. .310
- 240 gr. HPBT MatchKing #9245 B.C. .711 L ♦ T
  9" TWIST BBLS

.303 Caliber 7.7mm (.311/7.90mm Diameter)

- 125 gr. SPT Pro-Hunter #2305 B.C. .274
- 150 gr. SPT Pro-Hunter #2300 B.C. .344
- 174 gr. HPBT MatchKing #2315 B.C. .499 ♦
- 180 gr. SPT Pro-Hunter #2310 B.C. .411

8mm .323 Caliber (.323/8.20mm Diameter)

- 150 gr. SPT Pro-Hunter #2400 B.C. .336
- 175 gr. SPT Pro-Hunter #2410 B.C. .381
- 200 gr. HPBT MatchKing #2415 B.C. .520
- 220 gr. SBT GameKing #2420 B.C. .521 ○

.338 Caliber (.338/8.59mm Diameter)

- 215 gr. SBT GameKing #2610 B.C. .485
- 225 gr. SPT Pro-Hunter #2620 B.C. .462 ○
- 250 gr. SBT GameKing #2600 B.C. .565 ○
- 250 gr. HPBT MatchKing #2650 B.C. .587 ○ ♦
- 300 gr. HPBT MatchKing #9300 B.C. .768 L ♦ T
  10" TWIST BBLS

.35 Caliber (.358/9.09mm Diameter)

- 200 gr. RN Pro-Hunter #2800 B.C. .148 ○
- 225 gr. SBT GameKing #2850 B.C. .370 ○

.375 Caliber (.375/9.53mm Diameter)

- 200 gr. FN Pro-Hunter #2900 POWER JACKET B.C. .195
- 250 gr. SBT GameKing #2950 B.C. .353 ○
- 300 gr. SBT GameKing #3000 B.C. .475 ○
- 350 gr. HPBT MatchKing #9350 B.C. .805 L ♦ T
  12" TWIST BBLS

.45 Caliber (.45-70) (.458/11.63mm Diameter)

- 300 gr. HP/FN Pro-Hunter #8900 B.C. .120 ○

.30 Caliber 7.62mm (.308/7.82mm Diameter)

- 85 gr. RN Sports Master #8005 B.C. .102
  For use in handguns only

.32 Caliber Mag. (.312/7.92mm Diameter)

- 90 gr. JHC Sports Master #8030 POWER JACKET B.C. .125

9mm .355 Caliber (.355/9.02mm Diameter)

- 90 gr. JHP Sports Master #8100 POWER JACKET B.C. .095
- 95 gr. FMJ Tournament Master #8105 B.C. .0935
- 115 gr. JHP Sports Master #8110 POWER JACKET B.C. .127
- 115 gr. FMJ Tournament Master #8115 B.C. .107
- 125 gr. FMJ Tournament Master #8120 B.C. .115
- 125 gr. JHP Sports Master #8125 POWER JACKET B.C. .124

.38 Caliber (.357/9.07mm Diameter)

- 110 gr. JHP Blitz Sports Master #8300 POWER JACKET B.C. .120
- 125 gr. JSP Sports Master #8310 B.C. .133
- 125 gr. JHP Sports Master #8320 POWER JACKET B.C. .133
- 140 gr. JHP Sports Master #8325 POWER JACKET B.C. .0776
- 158 gr. JSP Sports Master #8340 B.C. .100
- 158 gr. JHC Sports Master #8360 POWER JACKET B.C. .100
- 170 gr. FMJ Match Tournament Master #8350 B.C. .175
- 180 gr. FPJ Match Tournament Master #8370 B.C. .147

10mm .400 Caliber (.400/10.16mm Diameter)

- 135 gr. JHP Sports Master #8425 POWER JACKET B.C. .105
- 150 gr. JHP Sports Master #8430 POWER JACKET B.C. .120
- 165 gr. JHP Sports Master #8445 POWER JACKET B.C. .130
- 180 gr. JHP Sports Master #8460 POWER JACKET B.C. .140

.41 Caliber (.410/10.41mm Diameter)

- 170 gr. JHC Sports Master #8500 POWER JACKET B.C. .123
- 210 gr. JHC Sports Master #8520 POWER JACKET B.C. .165

.44 Caliber (.4295/10.91mm Diameter)

- 180 gr. JHC Sports Master #8600 POWER JACKET B.C. .130
- 210 gr. JHC Sports Master #8620 POWER JACKET B.C. .160
- 220 gr. FPJ Match Tournament Master #8605 B.C. .180
- 240 gr. JHC Sports Master #8610 POWER JACKET B.C. .185
- 250 gr. FPJ Match Tournament Master #8615 B.C. .213
- 300 gr. JSP Sports Master #8630 B.C. .230

.45 Caliber (.4515/11.47mm Diameter)

- 185 gr. JHP Sports Master #8800 POWER JACKET B.C. .100
- 185 gr. FPJ Match Tournament Master #8810 B.C. .110
- 200 gr. FPJ Match Tournament Master #8825 B.C. .120
- 230 gr. JHP Sports Master #8805 POWER JACKET B.C. .145
- 230 gr. FMJ Match Tournament Master #8815 B.C. .140
- 240 gr. JHC Sports Master #8820 POWER JACKET B.C. .150
- 300 gr. JSP Sports Master #8830 B.C. .192 ○

.50 Caliber (.500/12.7mm Diameter)

- 350 gr. JHP Sports Master #5350 POWER JACKET B.C. .155
- 400 gr. JSP Sports Master #5400 POWER JACKET B.C. .185 ○

LEGEND:

- ○ = 50 per box.
- ✶ = Moly-coated bullets available in boxes of 500.
- ♦ = Available in boxes of 500.
- L = Long Range Specialty Bullets
- T = Trial Pack Available (50)

ABBREVIATIONS:

SBT	-	Spitzer Boat Tail
SPT	-	Spitzer
JHP	-	Jacketed Hollow Point
HP	-	Hollow Point
JHC	-	Jacketed Hollow Cavity
FN	-	Flat Nose
RN	-	Round Nose
JSP	-	Jacketed Soft Point
HPBT	-	Hollow Point Boat Tail
FMJ	-	Full Metal Jacket
FPJ	-	Full Profile Jacket
SMP	-	Semi-Pointed
FMJBT	-	Full Metal Jacket Boat Tail
TMK	-	Tipped MatchKing

The Hornady Interlock .358" 200-grain spitzer

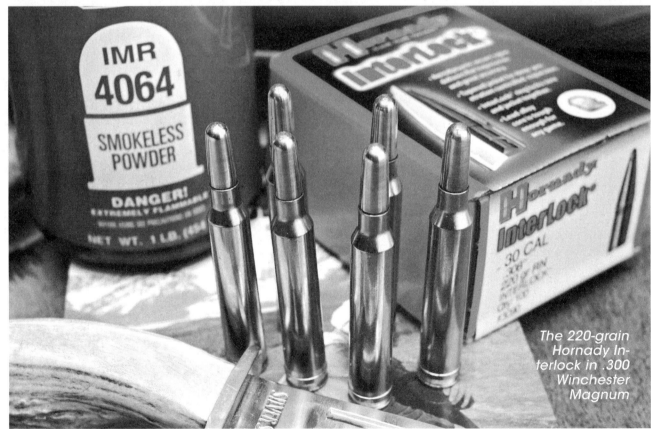

The 220-grain Hornady Interlock in .300 Winchester Magnum

Hornady

The folks at Hornady are one of the few companies that can produce just about any style of bullet, and do it right. I was introduced to Hornady when I caught a bunch of 165-grain .308" boattails on sale in the early 90s; back when a .308 Winchester was my only rifle. I loved the way they printed, and the way they put deer down. The InterLock remains a great bullet to this day, performing perfectly at any sane velocity.

Having an appreciation for classic bullets as well as cartridges, I love the InterLock roundnose bullets, and I still use them in my 6.5-284 Norma (160-grain RN), .300 Winchester (220-grain RN) and my .375 H&H (300-grain RN), although I've that learned the .375" 300 grainer has been discontinued, to my dismay. It has been replaced by the DGX/DGS (Dangerous Game eXpanding/Dangerous Game Solid) combination of safari bullets, and that is a great consolation prize.

Hornady's dynamic duo performs so well that many companies are using them to regulate their double rifles. My own Heym Express bolt gun loves the 400-grain .423" DGX and DGS, and I wouldn't hesitate to use them on buffalo and elephant. They have a nice cannelure so we can get a good roll crimp when we handload them, and their ogive makes feeding a dream even in finicky rifles.

Hornady's FlexTip technology single-handedly changed the lever-action rifle game, making those cartridges that gave 'rainbow' trajectory – and were relegated to the back of the closet or hung on a wall – a viable option once again.

Using a squishy polymer tip, the FlexTips eliminate all danger of loading spitzer bullets nose-to-tail in a tubular magazine, and make Grandpa'a .30-30 a 200+ yard gun. Now that changes the game! And furthermore, the MonoFlex bullet has the same squishy tip on an all-copper bullet if that's your thing.

If you like the modern bullet technology, the GMX (Gilding Metal eXpanding) is Hornady's take on the monometal bullets. Using an all-copper design, with a red polymer tip stuffed into a deep hollowpoint – to ensure consistent expansion – the GMX is a sound design.

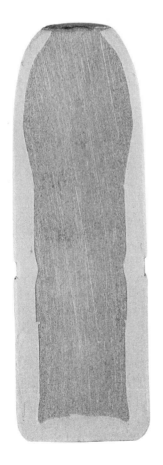
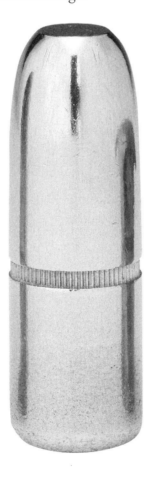

Hornady's DGX

The InterBond uses a thick jacket that is chemically bonded to the lead core to prevent premature bullet breakup, even from the hard-hitting magnum cartridges. I like this design, especially when hunting with a fast cartridge, in a situation where a close shot may present itself. If you like the polymer tip, but prefer traditional style cup-and core construction, look long and hard at the SST. A sleek ogive will help to give flat trajectories, and the polymer tip will ensure expansion, even at long distances when the velocities have dropped off.

Hornady makes one of my favorite handgun bullets ever: the XTP (eXtreme Terminal Performance). Thick jacket for penetration, deep hollowpoint for expansion, and good cannelure for crimping, the XTP works very well in revolvers. My Ruger Blackhawk in .45 Colt likes these bullets best of all. If you prefer the really hard-hitting revolvers, like the .460 S&W or .500 S&W, the XTP Mag has been beefed up accordingly.

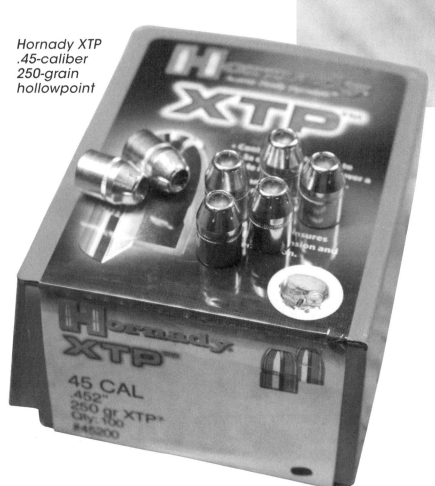

Hornady XTP .45-caliber 250-grain hollowpoint

The Hornady InterBond

Hornady hasn't forgotten the target crowd either. The Match bullets, and A-Max line both pander to the paper-rippers, and have worked very well for me, in calibers from .22 to the big-honkin' .338 Lapua.

Nosler

This is the company that put premium bullets on the map. The story is no secret: John Nosler + .300 H&H with pansy bullets + iron-sided moose = the premium bullet industry. Mr. Nosler took a section of copper rod, drilled both ends – leaving the famous Partition – squeezed the nose into an ogive, and created a bullet that we hunters have come to depend on for almost 70 years. I've gone on record as saying that the Partition isn't the most accurate bullet in the world, but if you weigh them out and load them properly I've seen them produce some impressive groups. The field performance is well worth that effort; a Partition in a suitable caliber, placed in the right spot, will always work.

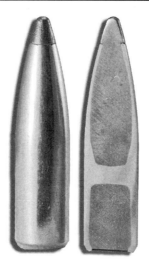

The Original Premium bullet: The Nosler Partition

The Nosler Ballistic Tip was a groundbreaking bullet, and was the first to effectively use the polymer tip. The jacket is tapered, thickening at the base, to give controlled expansion, and a nice boattail bucks the wind well. The color- coded tips indicate caliber, and the bullet weights are very useful. The Ballistic Tip is, well, to be honest, a bit on the frangible side, but if they are of sufficient weight for the velocity, they will work perfectly on deer-sized game. There are some offshoots, like the Ballistic Tip Varmint, and the lead-free Ballistic Tip. Ballistic Tip Hunting bullets are available in calibers from 6mm up to 8mm, inclusive.

The Nosler AccuBond takes the concept and profile of the Ballistic Tip a bit farther by bonding the lead core to that thick, tapering jacket. Using a white polymer tip to easily identify the bullet, the AccuBond has proven the value of bonding the core and jacket, as even the ridiculously huge-cased magnums will deliver this bullet without the worry of jacket/core separation.

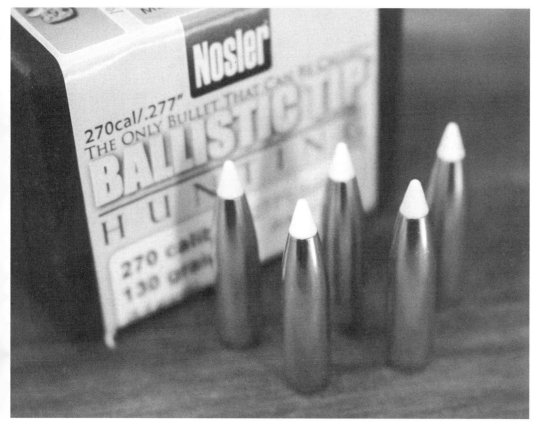

.270-caliber Nosler Ballistic Tips

I've seen this bullet print some seriously tight groups from hunting rifles with barrels resembling pencils. I also like the fact that Nosler had the wisdom to produce this bullet in 9.3mm and .375" caliber, as the AccuBond can make a great long-range load for both of those rifle calibers. The AccuBond LR (Long Range) has been designed for a higher B.C., by streamlining the ogive and boattail to make long-range work a bit easier, and my experiences show that these are a solid choice for those who hunt the wide open spaces where long shots are the norm.

In the recent years, the move to ban lead-core ammunition has unfortunately been gaining ground, and in a certain ocean-front state in the southwest of the United States, lead-core projectiles have been banned. Nosler retorted with the E-Tip, an all-copper bullet with a profile similar to the Ballistic Tip and AccuBond, but with an O.D. Green tip for identification. The E-Tip will give fantastic weight retention – often well into the 90 percent range, and if the last thirty years have taught us anything, it's that the monometals will work very well if loaded to proper specs.

For the benchrest boys and girls, the Nosler Custom Competition is a very worthwhile bullet. We spent some time experimenting with this bullet in a .308 that is known to shoot very well, and the 168-grain Nosler Custom held its ground very well. Give 'em a try!

If you're an Africa junkie, like me, Nosler also offers a brass solid for the thickest-skinned animals. I've used it in my .404 Jeffery, and they shoot as good as any other I've tried.

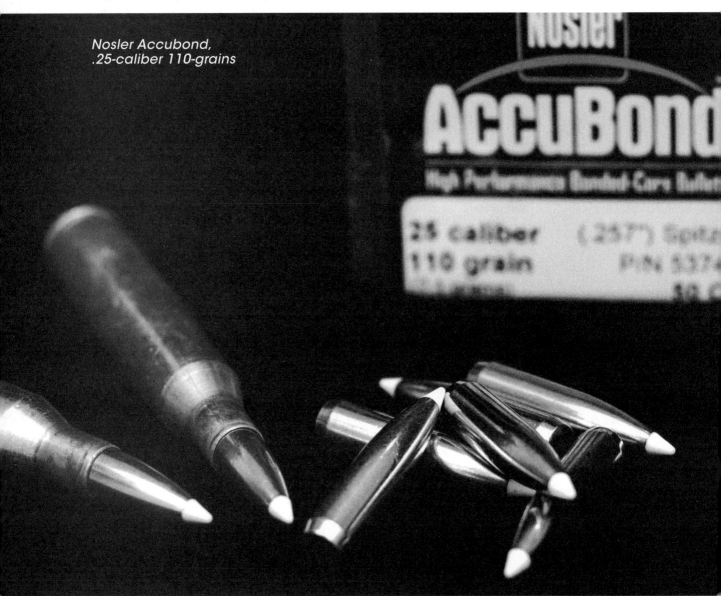

Nosler Accubond,
.25-caliber 110-grains

The updated Barnes TSX – Triple Shock X bullet

Barnes Bullets

Fred Barnes had a vision in the early 1930s, and made a dream come true. Because Mr. Barnes wasn't satisfied with the bullets available, he started making his own in his basement, and Barnes Bullets was born. Fast forward through a major war or two, and you'd see the company sold to Mr. & Mrs. Randy Brooks. Now, I've had the pleasure of speaking to Randy Brooks on the phone on more than one occasion, and I must say he's a gentleman as well as an innovator.

He was the man who took the lead out of our bullets, creating the Barnes X, the pioneer all-copper expanding bullet. Randy and I have had this conversation, but it warrants telling you, dear reader: the first generation of Barnes X bullets gave me fits, and probably cost me my hair. Though I absolutely loved the concept, they just didn't shoot in my guns, and I tried all sorts of tricks. I actually imposed an embargo on monometal bullets for over a decade, but the Barnes TSX brought me back into the fold. Actually, it was several clients of Massaro Ballistic Laboratories that forced me to try them again. When I did, I was amazed. Not only did Barnes solve the copper fouling issue, the grooves cut into the shank of the bullets drastically improved accuracy.

Now there are also those who've reported that the original Barnes didn't give reliable expansion, sometimes acting like a solid.

The Barnes TTSX in .458 SOCOM

That issue has also been resolved, with the Barnes TTSX, a polymer tipped affair that will guarantee expansion, as well as increase the bullet's B.C., and I've found the TTSX to be a very accurate bullet. Barnes TSX line often gives the handloader the option of confidently using what would traditionally be considered light-for-caliber. They shoot fast, flat, and will hold together, making my .375 H&H into a long-range elk rifle.

To compliment the capabilities of the Barnes TSX expanding monometal, the Barnes Banded Solid will engender all sorts of confidence if you're pursuing the biggest creatures Africa has to offer.

Their legendary performance makes Professional Hunters smile when they see them, as they know they can end an argument quickly.

Another Barnes product – that you've read about earlier in this tome – is the Barnes XPB pistol bullet. These neat little gems can really make a hunting revolver shine, giving unprecedented performance from your fetchin' iron.

The Original line of bullets are of cup-and-core design, and like Fred Barnes original designs, they usually run heavy-for-caliber. They make a great choice for the purist, and have saved my bacon as a handloader by providing some rather obscure diameters, when I needed to revive an obsolete caliber.

Barnes Banded Solids

Speer Bullets

The Speer line is smaller than it used to be, but still contains some fantastic bullets. The Grand Slam rifle bullet continues to be a great choice for an all-around big game bullet; it holds together well and expands reliably. I especially like the .30-caliber 180-grain Grand Slam for a deer/black bear bullet here in New York, when the game could easily vary from a 120-pound whitetail buck to a bruin in excess of 500 pounds.

Speer's Hot-Cor bullets are a great value as well, but I'll have to honest here: if impact velocities are too fast these bullets can be downright explosive. The 235-grain .375" Hot-Cor makes a great tool for teaching a new shooter how to properly shoot a safari gun without pounding the snot out of them. Push them to 2,800 fps in a .375 H&H and you've got a low-recoiling, inexpensive teaching tool. We've tried them on whitetail, however, and they make a bit of a mess.

Speer's Gold Dot pistol bullet is a fantastic choice for self-defense loads. Available in most common pistol calibers from .25 up to .45ACP, they give reliable performance time after time. The Gold Dot hunting bullet has been reborn with the Deep Curl moniker. Designed for revolvers, these bullets will give fantastic performance in the game fields and also when loaded for a self defense bullet. I've liked these bullets for years, and will continue to use them.

Of course, the TNT varmint bullets, as well as the FMJ and Target bullets are still in the Speer line; if you haven't had the opportunity to hunt woodchucks or prairie dogs with a TNT, you're missing out on a highly accurate, and highly frangible bullet, fully capable of creating the red mist.

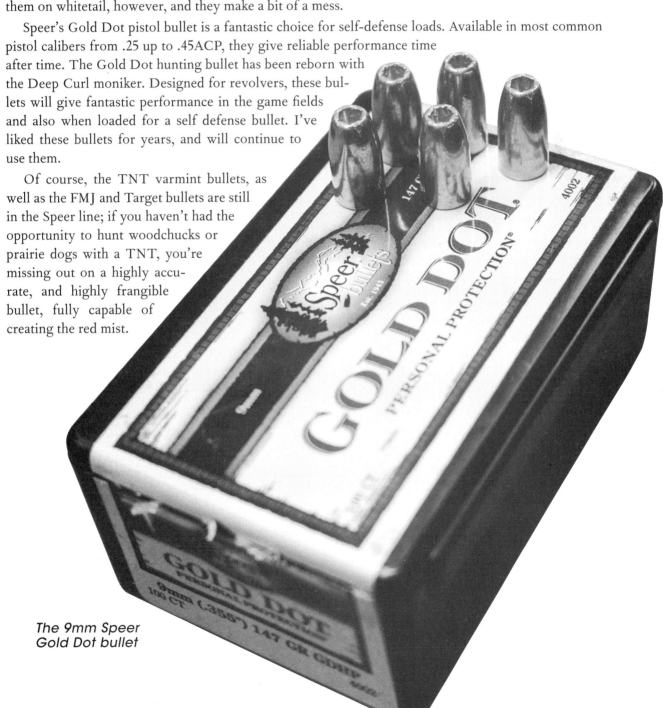

*The 9mm Speer
Gold Dot bullet*

Remington

While Big Green produces a whole bunch of loaded ammunition, they are still producing component bullets. For rifle bullets, the time-tested Core-Lokt is still with us, and Remington makes two premium component bullets. I've handloaded a whole bunch of Core-Lokt bullets over the years, and when used in a moderate velocity rifle, they perform very well, especially on deer sized game.

In the premium bullet lineup, the Accu-Tip features a polymer tip and boattail, and is designed for a flat trajectory. The Premier Core-Lokt Ultra Bonded bullet is a flat-based, bonded-core bullet capable of withstanding high impact velocity. Calibers from 6mm to .338". Remington also offers FMJ pistol bullets for reloading, available in most popular pistol calibers.

Winchester

Winchester still offers some component bullets, including the Power Point softpoint rifle bullet and the SilverTip HollowPoint pistol bullet, as well as other soft point and FMJ pistol and rifle bullets.

The Specialty Shops

Swift Scirocco II, loaded in .300 Winchester Magnum

Swift Bullet Company

I absolutely love Swift's bullets, there's no denying it. Bill Hober, owner of Swift Bullets, is a friend of mine. I knew his bullets long before I knew Bill, and I got to know him based on his products. He only makes two bullets: The Swift A-Frame, and the Swift Scirocco II. I'm ok with that fact, because they are two of the best bullets available.

As I stated in the Editor's Picks, I'd be OK using a Swift A-Frame on any game animal in the world but elephant. They hit like a sledgehammer, penetrate for days, and are accurate to boot. I'll continue to use them for years to come, primarily because I've got all of my rifles to shoot them and the load development is done, but secondly because they work so well. The partitioned cross section has the front core chemically bonded to the thick jacket, and if (not when) the bullet is retrieved from a game animal, the A-Frame develops a 'rivet' just behind the partition. Weight retention, from the handful of bullets that I've actually recovered, has been above 95 percent.

I like to described the A-Frame as "meat-resistant", in that these bullets, especially in the larger safari calibers, will open up to twice caliber dimension on the heavyweights like eland and buffalo, but not as much on the smaller antelope like impala or bushbuck. I really like the A-Frame as a choice for all-around big game hunting.

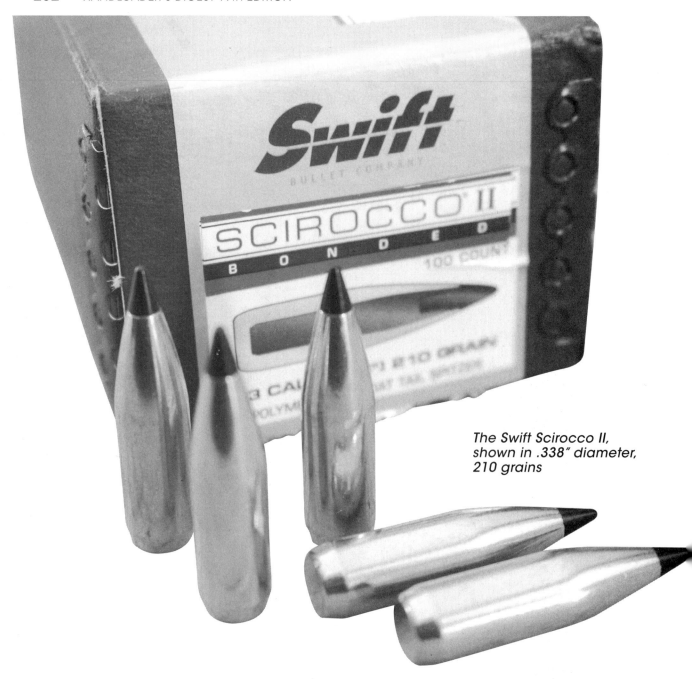

The Swift Scirocco II, shown in .338" diameter, 210 grains

The Swift Scirocco II is a horse of a different color.

While the A-Frame is a flat-base semi-spitzer, the Scirocco II is a boattailed, polymer-tipped bullet, with a very thick jacket that is bonded to the lead core. That black polymer tip and boattail keeps the B.C. high, while the bonded core allows these bullets to be launched from the fastest magnums. They shoot very well, giving sub-MOA in most of my rifles. I've used them to take black bear, whitetail deer, and pronghorn antelope, very neatly I might add. I wouldn't hesitate to use these bullets on elk or moose, or for African plains game. They make a great feral hog bullet, easily penetrating the toughest gristle plate. I you're looking for a great long-range hunting bullet, the Scirocco may just be for you.

For the lever-gun lovers and handgun hunters, Swift has modified the A-Frame to suit your needs; you may enjoy the A-Frame experience with your chosen weapon, whether a .30-30 WCF or .500 S&W.

North Fork Technologies

Oregon's North Fork Technologies puts out a wicked quartet of bullets, filling the bill for all of your big game hunting needs. The flagship of their fleet is their Soft Point semi-spitzer, which has a lead core in the front half of the bullet, while the rear section is solid copper. That lead core is chemically bonded to the copper jacket/shank, to ensure deep penetration, and the shank of this bullet, and all North Fork bullets has a multitude of grooves cut into it, to reduce pressure along the bearing surface. The design thought is to keep the bullet's weight forward, for straight-line penetration, and it works. What these bullets give up in B.C. – they are a semi-spitzer with a flat base – they make up for in terminal performance.

The North Fork Soft Point is designed to pass through an animal, leaving a good blood trail after destroying the vitals. Available in calibers 6.5mm through .509"

For those animals that require a bit more hydraulic shock, like the great cats of Africa, North Fork has modified the Soft Point design to create the Percussion Point. A bit softer up-front, the Percussion Point will give more expansion, yet still penetrate very well, an ideal choice for lion or leopard.

North Fork Semi-Spitzers, 7mm caliber, 140 grains

The North Fork Cup Solid is excellent buffalo medicine.

The Flat Point Solid will work perfectly on large game animals with thick hides, like buffalo, hippo and elephant. The flat meplat makes a larger wound channel than the hemispherical-nosed solids, and penetration is no issue at all.

North Fork's Cup Solid is a cool design – the bullet resembles the Flat Point Solid but it features a small cup at the nose. That cup gives the slightest amount of expansion, creating hydraulic shock and yet still giving the straight line penetration that the Flat Points do. Hunters are using the Cup Solid for all sorts of African Game; I like to load them for a backup bullet while hunting Cape buffalo.

Berger Bullets

Mr. Walt Berger is a member of the Benchrest Hall of Fame; he knows what it takes to make a bullet that shoots well. His company's motto is: All bullets will be of Match Grade quality. Walt achieved that goal, and now has enlisted the help of Mr. Brian Litz, a very talented ballistician and bullet designer.

Berger has four categories of bullets: Varmint, Target, Hunting, and Tactical. In addition to being very specialized designs, Berger bullets feature the proprietary J4 jacket. These jackets are held to some of the tightest tolerances in the industry; the J4's concentricity runs at 0.0003" or less, and that's seriously uniform. The Berger bullets are about not only precision, but about long-range performance.

The Hybrid bullets feature a combination of tangent and secant ogives, to balance the attributes that make a bullet engage the rifling in the best manner, as well as those attributes that buck the wind and best resist air drag. I guess you could say that these guys speak in mathematical formulae. If you're into the long-distance game, take a good long look at the Berger lineup of bullets, you'll be happy you did.

Berger Bullets

Woodleigh Bullets

Hailing from Australia, Woodleigh Bullets makes some serious hunting projectiles. They gained quite a bit of popularity by producing bullets that mimicked the profile of the Kynoch ammunition for the British doubles and bolt-action safari guns. The Weldcore series are round-nosed, with quite a bit of lead exposed at the nose. The core is fused to a jacket of increasing thickness, as you go down the shank, and this controls expansion to balance expansion/penetration. They've been a success story for decades and will continue to be so.

The Woodleigh Protected Point has the same Weldcore jacket/core fusion, but in a semi-spitzer design with much less exposed lead at the meplat.

The Full Metal Jacket lines compliment the Weldcore line, to create the classic African soft/solid duo. Thick steel jackets are covered in a copper alloy to take the rifling yet penetrate the thickest hide and toughest bone.

Woodleigh's Hydrostatically Stabilized Solid, as I've outlined in Editor's Picks, will be a bullet you'll be reading about often in the near future. I think these are an amazing design, and Woodleigh is currently working on a stainless steel tipped Hydro Solid!

HG SOLID HANDGUN SOLID

357 165GR | 40 190GR | 41 220GR | 44 240GR | 45 300GR | 475 340GR | 500 400GR

HG RAPTOR HANDGUN HOLLOW POINTS

22 30GR | 22 32GR | .355 75GR | .355 90GR | 357 105GR | 357 140GR | .400 120GR | .400 150GR | .41 135GR | .41 180GR | .44 150GR | 44 200GR | .45 150GR | .45 240GR | 475 220GR | 475 280GR | 500 340GR

MTH MATCH/TACTICAL/HUNTING

224 40GR ZBC .200 | 224 55GR BC .250 | 224 65GR BC .310 | 243 77GR BC .370 | 243 88GR BC .445 | 257 100GR BC .420 | 257 115GR BC .460 | 264 120GR BC .500 | 264 130GR BC .550 | 264 130GR MAX BC .550 | 264 140GR MAX BC .600 | 277 120GR BC .460 | 277 130GR BC .540 | 277 140GR MAX BC .590 | 284 130GR BC .450 | 284 145GR BC .495 | 284 155GR BC .610 | 284 160GR MAX BC .585 | 284 170GR MAX BC .620 | 308 140GR BC .440 | 308 150GR BC .450 | 308 165GR BC .510 | 308 180GR MAX BC .570 | 308 180GR BC .600 | 308 190GR MAX BC .624 | 308 200GR MAX BC .610 | 338 200GR BC .570 | 338 225GR BC .650 | 338 252GR BC .750

SAFARI SOLID

264 130GR | 264 155GR | 308 180GR | 308 210GR | 366 280GR | 375 300GR | 409 400GR NE | 411 350GR | 411 400GR | 416 350GR | 416 400GR | 423 350GR | 423 400GR | 457 480GR NE | 458 325GR | 458 450GR | 458 500GR | 474 350GR | 474 450GR BM | 474 500GR NE | 500 375GR | 500 405GR | 500 450GR | 500 550GR

SAFARI RAPTOR

366 255GR | 375 275GR | 375 275GR TSG | 411 325GR | 411 375GR | 416 225GR TSG | 416 300GR | 416 325GR | 416 370GR | 423 325GR | 423 375GR | 457 450GR NE | 458 295GR SS | 458 420GR | 458 470GR | 474 320GR SS | 474 420GR BM | 474 460GR NE | 500 410GR | 500 450GR | 505 485GR | 550 650GR | 585 600GR NE | 585 700GR NE

LAZER

308 165GR BC .458 | 308 180GR BC .545 | 308 180GR MAX BC .545 | 308 200GR MAX BC .585 | 338 225GR BC .630 | 338 250GR MAX BC .690 | 338 275GR MAX BC .773 | 338 300GR MAX BC .790 | 375 325GR BC .870 | 375 350GR MAX BC .900 | 375 375GR MAX BC .930 | 375 400GR MAX BC .960 | 375 425GR MAX BC .960

COPPER RAPTOR

22 30GR | 224 45GR BC .220 | 224 60GR BC .263 | 243 60GR BC .270 | 257 90GR BC .360 | 264 110GR BC .393 | 277 115GR BC .405 | 277 90GR BC .330 | 284 120GR BC .436 | 284 135GR BC .470 | 308 135GR BC .352 | 308 150GR BC .393 | 338 185GR BC .445 | 338 225GR BC .550 | 358 180GR BC .335

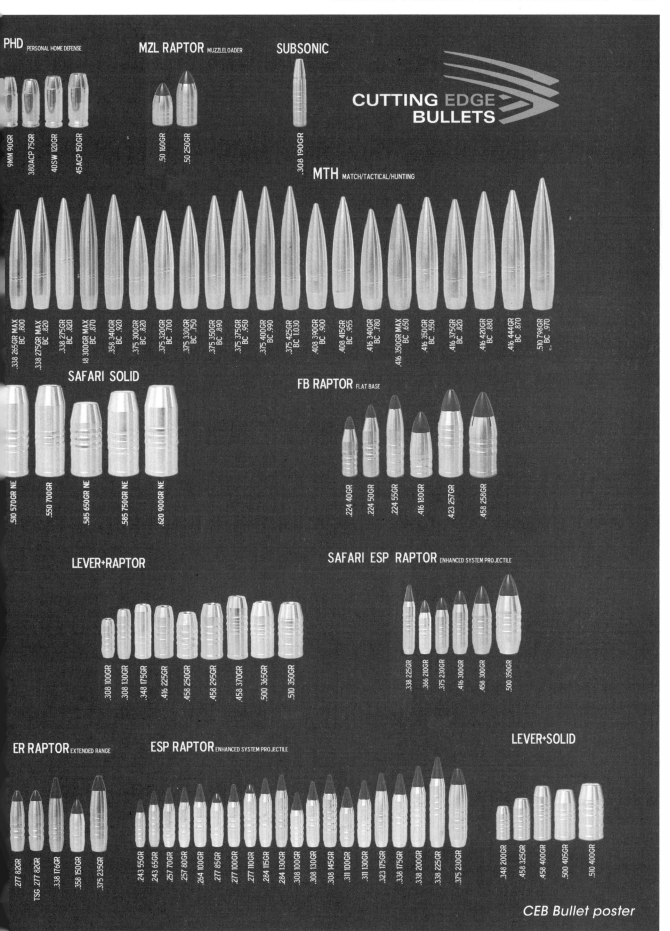

PHD PERSONAL HOME DEFENSE

9MM 90GR
380ACP 75GR
40SW 120GR
45ACP 150GR

MZL RAPTOR MUZZLELOADER

.50 160GR
.50 250GR

SUBSONIC

.308 190GR

CUTTING EDGE BULLETS

MTH MATCH/TACTICAL/HUNTING

.338 265GR MAX BC .800
.338 275GR MAX BC .820
.338 275GR BC .820
.8 300GR MAX BC .870
.358 340GR BC .920
.375 300GR BC .820
.375 320GR BC .700
.375 330GR BC .750
.375 350GR BC .890
.375 375GR BC .950
.375 400GR BC .990
.375 425GR BC 1.030
.408 390GR BC .900
.408 415GR BC .955
.416 340GR BC .780
.416 350GR MAX BC .650
.416 350GR BC .550
.416 375GR BC .820
.416 420GR BC .880
.416 444GR BC .870
.510 796GR BC .970

SAFARI SOLID

.510 570GR NE
.550 700GR
.585 650GR NE
.585 750GR NE
.620 900GR NE

FB RAPTOR FLAT BASE

.224 40GR
.224 50GR
.224 55GR
.416 180GR
.423 257GR
.458 258GR

LEVER+RAPTOR

.308 100GR
.308 130GR
.348 175GR
.416 225GR
.458 250GR
.458 295GR
.458 370GR
.500 365GR
.510 350GR

SAFARI ESP RAPTOR ENHANCED SYSTEM PROJECTILE

.338 225GR
.366 210GR
.375 230GR
.416 300GR
.458 300GR
.500 350GR

ER RAPTOR EXTENDED RANGE

.277 82GR
TSG .277 82GR
.338 176GR
.358 150GR
.375 235GR

ESP RAPTOR ENHANCED SYSTEM PROJECTILE

.243 55GR
.243 65GR
.257 70GR
.257 80GR
.264 100GR
.277 85GR
.277 100GR
.277 110GR
.284 115GR
.284 130GR
.308 100GR
.308 130GR
.308 145GR
.311 100GR
.311 130GR
.323 175GR
.338 175GR
.338 200GR
.338 225GR
.375 230GR

LEVER+SOLID

.348 200GR
.458 325GR
.458 400GR
.500 405GR
.510 400GR

CEB Bullet poster

The Cutting Edge Bullets ER Raptor

Cutting Edge Bullets

Pennsylvania's Cutting Edge Bullets uses a new design that caught my eye immediately. Their bullets are constructed of either solid copper or brass, and with the exception of the Solid bullets for dangerous game, they feature a deep hollowpoint. That hollowpoint is scored along the long axis of the bullet, so that it will break into small 'blades', causing massive trauma on the entrance of the wound channel, while the remainder of the bullet penetrates at caliber dimension.

This theory applies not only to their rifle bullets, but their pistol bullets as well. Cutting Edge Bullets feature 'driving bands' to engage the rifling, a principal similar to the projectiles of naval guns. Some models use CEB's Seal Tite band, which seals gasses and spins the bullet within the rifling.

They have long-range bullets, with polymer tips that can be inserted to increase the B.C. (like the ESP Raptor or Lazer model), they have a Match/Tactical/Hunting bullet for accuracy freaks, and a Safari Raptor for the big guns that I like so much. These Safari Raptors have proven to be a great bullet; I had excellent accuracy and field performance from this bullet in a .416 Rigby and my .404 Jeffery. Both bullets were 325 grains, and some of the tougher African plains game species fell quickly to it (See Chapter 4 – Life in the .40s).

CEB also makes a Safari Solid – a solid brass design – to compliment the hollowpoints.

CEB also offers the Handgun Raptor (see Editor's Picks) for self-defense, as well as the Raptor bullet for lever guns. Oh, and for the .300 Blackout crowd, there's a 190-grain flat-base Raptor designed to operate at sub-sonic velocities!

Cutting Edge Bullets Lazer

The Rest of The Herd

Rainier Ballistics

Rainier's specialty is lead-core, copper plated bullets. And they do that well. Their projectiles are twice-swaged lead wire, which are then copper plated so that there is no exposed lead. This makes them perfectly safe for those indoor ranges that don't allow exposed lead due to the lead vapors created when a lead bullet is fired. Rainier's projectiles are perfect for the gun games or the weekend plinker.

308 Win, Norma Oryx

Norma

Known for its fantastic factory ammunition and reloader-loved brass, Norma has a really good bullet on the market. The Oryx bullet is a flat-base semi-spitzer, with the lower section of the jacket bonded to the core. This allows for quick expansion upon impact, yet guarantees that you'll get all the penetration you'll need. I've used this bullet – factory loaded – in my 6.5-284 Norma, and it resulted in a very impressive kill on a large bodied whitetail deer. I'll be using this bullet again.

Lapua

Here's another fine European company, well known for its precision ammunition. Lapua produces the Scenar, Scenar-L, Mega and Naturalis bullets for reloading. The Scenar and Scenar-L are target bullets; they are hollowpoints with a severe boattail. The Scenar actually holds a couple serious benchrest records. The Scenar-L is supposed to be a bullet with even tighter tolerances, but I haven't had an opportunity to try them.

The Mega and Naturalis are Lapua's hunting bullets. The Mega is a roundnose bullet with a staggered jacket to stop expansion at about halfway down the bullet. The jacket of the Mega leaves very little exposed lead, protecting the meplat. The Naturalis is an all-copper, roundnose bullet with a pliable tip to initiate expansion.

Falcon Bullet Company

Cast lead bullets is all that Falcon Bullets does, and they do them well. Both availability and affordability are on Falcon's side, and they make suitable bullets for most handguns. Roundnose, semi-wadcutter, conical nose, round nose flat point; the usual bullet profiles are here. Falcon also has a proprietary red coating, called FalCoat-

Falcon Bullets .40-caliber truncated cone

ing, which will prevent the lead bullets from fouling your barrel quickly. I like the coated bullets, as they don't dirty up my reloading dies as quickly either. Available in calibers from .380 to .45.

If you're a fan of shooting cast bullets in your rifle, Falcon offers a 165-grain roundnose flatpoint in .30 caliber, which works very well in the .30-30 WCF, .300 Savage and other lever favorites.

Berry's Manufacturing

Offering a full line of plated handgun bullets, hard-cast lead bullets and self defense handgun projectiles.

Oregon Trail Bullet Company

Hard cast lead bullets for pistols and lever-action rifles.

Hawk Precision Bullets

Roundnose jacketed rifle bullets, with annealed copper jackets to prevent jacket breakup upon impact, over a harder than normal lead core. Hawk bullets have a great reputation, and although I haven't had the opportunity to use them, many of my colleagues have great things to say about them. Hawk bullets give 2-3x expansion, while holding together. Available in calibers from 6.5mm up to and including the big .700 Nitro.

Hawk also offers premium handgun hunting bullets, in revolver calibers from .357" up to the .500s.

METALLIC HANDLOADING COMPONENTS:
POWDERS

Smokeless powder is one of the greatest inventions of the last century. It has allowed us to develop cartridges that will push bullets to unprecedented velocities, in an even and repeatable manner. The volatility of the cordite of the early 20th century has been resolved, and our modern powders make our job as reloaders much easier, and quite interesting. Our powders come in three main grain shapes: spherical, flake and stick. The black powder of the 19th century is still available for those who prefer the vintage weapons, along with modern black powder substitutes that burn much cleaner.

1.

IMR4350

2.

*Hodgdon's
Titegroup*

*Alliant
Reloder 25*

3.

4.

*Ramshot
TAC*

Editor's Picks:

This is a rough one, as there are so many powders that work so well. Here are four of my favorites:

1. IMR4350

A stick powder with a burn rate on the slow side of the middle, IMR4350 has proven to be extremely useful in many rifle cartridges. .243 Winchester, .30-'06 Springfield, .300 Winchester Magnum, and even the .375 Holland & Holland Magnum; all can be fueled by good ol' 4350. It gives good velocities, and the standard deviation on velocity is usually quite low.

2. Hodgdon's Titegroup

If you're looking for one pistol powder to feed almost any pistol caliber, Titegroup is your friend. It works well in the smaller 9mm Luger and .380 ACP cases, as well as the bigger revolver cases like the .357 Magnum and .45 Colt.

3. Alliant Reloder 25

When the rifle cases get big, like .300 Remington Ultra Magnum or .416 Rigby big, you need a slow burning powder that will develop the pressures that push the bullet as fast as the cases are capable of. Feeding these cases any other powder is a disservice. Reloder 25 has filled that role for me many times, delivering hair-splitting accuracy and consistently high velocities in cases from the .300 Winchester Magnum to the huge .30-378 Weatherby Magnum

4. Ramshot TAC

A spherical powder with a burn rate slightly faster than IMR4064, Ramshot TAC works just about perfectly in the .223 Remington, but saved my bacon one day when I was loading for a Savage Model 99, in .300 Savage that wouldn't shoot factory ammo well at all. A Sierra Pro-Hunter loaded over TAC showed accuracy that would make the bolt crowd drool. It's a very good powder for the smaller capacity cases.

Other Powders

Hodgdon Extreme Powders

H4198 - This Extreme Extruded propellant has gone through some changes since its inception, all the time maintaining the same important burning speed of the past. The kernels were shortened for improved metering and necessary elements were added to make it extremely insensitive to hot/cold temperatures. H4198 is outstanding in cartridges like the 222 Remington, 444 Marlin and the 7.62 X 39. Available in 1 lb. & 8 lb. containers.

H322 - This Extreme Extruded powder has won more bench rest matches than all other propellants combined. It provides match grade accuracy in small and medium capacity cartridges like the 223 Remington, 6mm PPC and the 7mm TCU. As a fine extruded powder, it flows through powder measures with superb accuracy. Available in 1 lb. & 8 lb. containers

Benchmark - As the name implies, this Extreme Extruded propellant was developed for precision cartridges. As such, it is ideally suited for benchrest and small varmint cartridges like the 6mm PPC, 22 PPC, 6mm BR, 223 Rem. and 222 Rem. Additionally, it performs superbly in the 204 Ruger and with light match bullets in 308 Winchester. With small, easy metering granules, competitors will love how it flows through progressive presses. Available in 1 lb. & 8 lb. containers

H4895 – This is a most versatile rifle powder. This member of the Extreme Extruded line powder is great for 17 Remington, 250-3000 Savage, 308 Winchester and 458 Winchester, to name just a few. It is amazingly accurate in every cartridge where it is listed in our data. It had its origin in the 30-06 as a military powder and was the first powder Bruce Hodgdon sold to the loading public. Available in 1 lb. & 8 lb. containers.

VARGET – The first of Hodgdon's revolutionary Extreme Extruded Powders, VARGET features small extruded grains for uniform metering, insensitivity to hot/cold temperatures and higher energy for improved velocities over other powders in its burning speed class. Easy ignition and clean burning characterize other features that translate into superb accuracy, higher scores and more clean, one shot kills. The perfect powder for competitive Match shooting 223 Remington and Heavy bullets. Outstanding performance and velocity can be obtained in such popular cartridges as the 223 Remington, 22-250 Remington, 308 Winchester, 30-06, 375 H&H and many more. Available in 1 lb. & 8 lb.

H4350 - This Extreme Extruded propellant is a burning speed that has been known to shooters for decades. During that time, Hodgdon has modernized H4350 by shortening the grains for im-

H4895

VARGET

proved metering and making it insensitive to hot/cold temperatures. H4350 is ideal in the WSM family of calibers (270, 7mm, 30, 325). H4350 is the standard in such cartridges as the 243 Winchester, 6mm Remington, 270 Winchester, 338 Winchester Magnum and many more. For magnums with light to moderate weight bullets, it can't be beat! Available in 1 lb. & 8 lb. containers.

H4831 & H4831SC – It is probably safe to say more big game has been taken with H4831 than any other powder. Bruce Hodgdon was the first supplier to introduce this popular burning rate in 1950. Since that time it has become a favorite for cartridges like the 270 Winchester, 25-06 Remington, 280 Remington and 300 Winchester Magnum. As an Extreme Extruded propellant it shares the fine quality of insensitivity to hot/cold temperatures, as well as superb uniformity from lot to lot.

H4831SC - Ballistically, this Extreme Extruded powder is the exact copy of H4831. Physically, it has a shorter grain size, therefore, the designation SC or short cut. The shorter, more compact kernels allow the powder to flow through the powder measures more smoothly, helping to alleviate the constant cutting of granules. With the smoother flow characteristics comes more uniform charge weights, while the individual grains orient more compactly, creating better loading density. Available in 1 lb. & 8 lb. containers.

H1000 - This very slow burning Extreme Extruded powder is perfect for highly overbored magnums like the 7mm Remington Magnum, 7mm STW and the 30-378 Weatherby. In addition, with heavy bullets, H1000 gives top velocity and performance in such cartridges as the 6mm-284, 257 Weatherby, 270 Winchester, and 300 Winchester Magnum. In a short period of time this powder has achieved considerable notoriety among long range match shooters. Available in 1 lb. & 8 lb. containers.

RETUMBO - This magnum powder was designed expressly for the really large overbored cartridges such as the 7mm Remington Ultra Magnum, 300 Remington Ultra Magnum, 30-378 Weatherby Magnum, etc. RETUMBO adds 40-100 fps more velocity to these cartridges when compared to other normal magnum powders. In addition, it is an Extreme Powder, making it perfect for big game hunting under all types of conditions. Available in 1 lb. & 8 lb. containers

H50BMG - As the name implies, this new generation Extreme Extruded rifle propellant is a clean burning powder designed expressly for the 50 caliber BMG cartridge. Because it shares the same technology as VARGET, H50BMG displays a high degree of thermal stability in temperature extremes. Tests have conclusively proven that H50BMG yields very low extreme spreads in velocity and pressure. All this translates into small groups at extended ranges! Available in 1 lb. & 8 lb. containers.

H4831 & H4831SC

Hodgdon Spherical Powders.

CFE223 - Introduced in January 2012, this versatile spherical rifle propellant incorporates in its formula CFE, Copper Fouling Eraser. This ingredient, originally used in military propellant, greatly deters copper fouling. It contributes to longer periods of top accuracy with less barrel cleaning time. Being a spherical powder, metering is superbly accurate. CFE 223 yields top velocities in many cartridges such as the 204 Ruger, 223 Remington/5.56mm NATO, 22-250 Remington and the 308 Winchester/7.62mm NATO, plus many, many more. Match, Varmint and AR shooters will love this one!

H335 – Originated as a military powder, used for the 5.56 NATO, or 223 Remington as handloaders know it. Obviously, it sees endless use in the 222 Remington, 223 Remington and other small cartridges. In particular, prairie dog shooters will find this a favorite, as J.B. Hodgdon has for years! Available in 1 lb. & 8 lb. containers.

BL-C(2) - A spherical powder that began as a military powder used in the 7.62 NATO, commonly known as the 308 Winchester. When it was first introduced to the handloader, benchrest shooters and other target shooters made it an instant success. BL-C(2) works extremely well in the 204 Ruger, 223 Remington, 17 Remington, 22 PPC and of course, the 308 Winchester, plus many more. Available in 1 lb. & 8 lb. containers.

LEVERevolution - Hodgdon® Powder Company and Hornady® Manufacturing have teamed together to answer the frequently asked reloading question; "Can I buy the powder used in Hornady LEVERevolution factory ammunition?" Yes, this is the same spherical propellant used in Hornady's innovative and award winning high performance factory ammunition. This fabulous propellant meters flawlessly and makes lever action cartridges like the 30-30 Winchester yield velocities in excess of 100 fps over any published handloads, with even greater gains over factory ammunition. Other cartridges include the 35 Remington, 308 Marlin Express, 338 Marlin Express and the 25-35 Winchester. The list of cartridges and bullets is limited with this highly specialized powder, but where it works, it really works!

H380 – This was an unnamed spherical rifle propellant when the late Bruce Hodgdon first used it. When a 38.0 grain charge behind a 52 grain bullet gave one hole groups from his 22 caliber wildcat (now called the 22-250), he appropriately named the powder H380. H380 is also a superb performer in the 220 Swift, 243, 257 Roberts and other fine varmint cartridges. Available in 1 lb. & 8 lb. containers.

H414 - This spherical powder has an extremely wide range of use. From the 22-250 Remington to the 375 H & H, it will give excellent results. It is simply ideal in the 30/06. As with all of our

H335

H380

spherical powders, it delivers incredibly consistent charge weights through nearly any type of powder measure. H414 yields similar results to H4350 in most cartridges, although charge weights will vary. Available in 1 lb. & 8 lb. containers.

US869 - Hodgdon Powder Company leads the way again by developing an outstanding 50 BMG propellant that offers significant advantages in many magnum rifle applications! US869 is a true magnum Spherical rifle powder that is superb with heavy bullets in big, overbore rifle cartridges. US869 is a dense propellant that allows the shooter to use enough powder to create maximum velocities in cartridges such as the 7mm Remington Ultra Magnum, 300 Remington Ultra Magnum, 30-378 Weatherby Magnum and others. US869 is superior in the 50 Caliber BMG where it yields high velocity and great accuracy with 750 to 800 grain projectiles. This is a fine 1000-yard match propellant! In addition, US869 is effected minimally by varying temperatures, a key feature for top competition and hunting accuracy.

HYBRID 100V - This powder is the result of combining the technologies of spherical powders and extruded propellants. The chemistry of a spherical powder is combined with the geometry of an extruded propellant, creating a smooth-metering, super short granule extruded shaped propellant with high energy. HYBRID 100V has a burn speed between H4350 and H4831, yielding superb performance in such popular calibers as 270 Winchester, 243 Winchester Super Short Magnum, 7mm Remington Magnum, 300 Winchester Magnum and dozens more.

SUPERFORMANCE - This is another of the spherical powders Hodgdon® Powder Company and Hornady® Manufacturing introduced to answer the frequently asked reloading question: "Can I buy the powder used in the Hornady Superformance factory ammunition?" Superformance delivers striking velocities in cartridges like the 22-250 Remington, 243 Winchester and 300 Winchester Short Magnum. Velocities well in excess of 100 fps over the best published handloads and even larger gains over factory ammunition! Because this propellant is tailored for specific applications, the number of cartridges and bullets is limited, but where it works, it really works!

Hodgdon Shotgun & Pistol Powders

CFE Pistol – This excellent spherical pistol propellant utilizes our CFE formula, Copper Fouling Eraser, virtually eliminating copper fouling, plus providing top velocities with clean burning and minimal muzzle flash. For competitive shooters and hand loaders seeking the perfect powder for target or self-defense loads, CFE Pistol provides optimum performance in cartridges like the 9mm Luger, 38 Super, 40 S&W, the venerable 45 ACP and many more.

TITEWAD - Through advanced technology, Hodgdon Powder Co. has produced a superior flattened spherical shotgun powder. Unlike spherical propellants in the past, TITEWAD features low charge weights, mild muzzle report, minimum recoil and reduced residue for optimum ballistic performance. This outstanding propellant designed for 12 gauge only, meters superbly and is ideal for 7/8, 1 and 1 1/8 ounce loads. As the name implies, "a little goes a long way!" Available in 14 oz., 4 lb. & 8 lb. containers.

CLAYS - Introduced in January, 1992, CLAYS gunpowder has "taken the clay target world by storm". It is the cleanest burning , most consistent 12 ga. 7/8., 1 oz. and 1 1/8 oz. powder available today, the preferred choice of competitive target shooters.. The superb burning characteristics of this powder produce soft, smooth recoil and excellent patterns. These features transfer directly to handgun applications where target shooting is the main goal. 45 ACP and 38 Special are only two of the cartridges where CLAYS gunpowder provides "tack driving" target accuracy with flawless functioning. Available in 14 oz., 4 lb. & 8 lb. containers.

INTERNATIONAL - INTERNATIONAL gunpowder is the second in the "CLAYS" gunpowder series of powders, bringing this technology to the 20 gauge reloader. It also works in 12 ga., 2 3/4" light, medium and heavy 1 1/8 oz. loads, and high velocity 1 oz. As with CLAYS gunpowder, clean burning and flawless functioning is the rule. Available in 14 oz., 4 lb. & 8 lb. containers.

TITEGROUP - As the name implies, this spherical propellant was designed for accuracy. Because of the unique design, this powder provides flawless ignition with all types of primers including the lead-free versions. Unlike pistol powders of the past, powder position in large cases (45 Colt, 357 Magnum and others) has virtually no effect on velocity and performance. Cowboy Action, Bullseye and Combat Shooters should love this one! TITEGROUP has it all, low charge weight, clean burning, mild muzzle report and superb, uniform ballistics. Available in 1 lb., 4 lb. & 8 lb. containers

HP38 - HP38 is a spherical powder that is great for low velocity and mid-range target loads in the .38 Special, .44 Special, and 45 ACP. This high energy powder provides economy in loading. Available in 1 lb., 4 lb. & 8 lb. containers.

UNIVERSAL - UNIVERSAL gunpowder handles the broadest spectrum of cartridges for both pistol and shotgun. This is the Clays gunpowder technology designed for 28 gauge shooters. From the 25 ACP to the 44 magnum and 28 gauge to 12 gauge, UNIVERSAL CLAYS gunpowder provides outstanding performance. As with all the "CLAYS" gunpowder series powders, clean burning and uniformity are part of its attributes. Available in 1 lb., 4 lb. & 8 lb. containers

HS-6 - HS-6 is a fine spherical propellant that has wide application in pistol and shotshell. In pistol, 9mm, 38 Super, 40 S&W and 10mm Auto are some of the cartridges where HS-6 provides top performance. In shotshell HS-6 yields excellent heavy field loadings in 10 ga., 12 ga., 20 ga., and even the efficient and effective 28 ga. HS-6 is truly an outstanding spherical propellant. HS-6 is identical to Winchester's discontinued 540. Available in 1 lb. & 8 lb. containers.

LONGSHOT - This spherical powder is the most versatile shotshell heavy field propellant Hodgdon has ever produced. Great loads in 10 ga., 12 ga., 16 ga., 20 ga., and 28 ga. are shown in Hodgdon's Reloading Data Center. This propellant provides true magnum velocities with superb patterns. In addition, LONGSHOT is the best choice for those competitors shooting games such as "Buddy", "Annie Oakleys" and more. LONGSHOT is the high velocity pistol choice in 38 Super, 40 S&W, and 357 SIG at lower than usual operating pressures. Available in 1 lb., 4 lb. & 8 lb. containers.

H110 is the spherical powder that screams "no wimps, please!" It delivers top velocities with top accuracy in the 44 Magnum, 454 Casull, 475 Linebaugh and the 460 and 500 S&W magnums. Silhouette shooters claim it is the most accurate 44 powder they have ever used. In addition, H110 is "the" choice for 410 Bore shotgun, especially among top competitive skeet and sporting clays shooters. It handles all 2 1/2", 1/2 oz. loads,

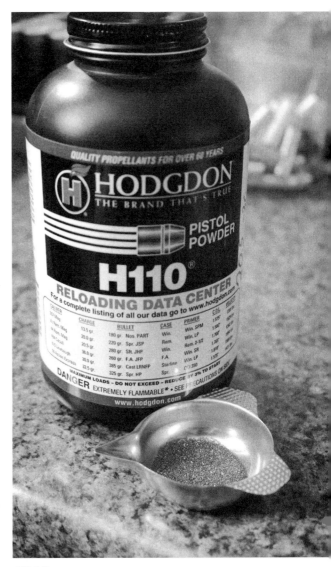

H110

as well as all 11/16 oz. loads for the 3" version. Available in 1 lb., 4 lb. & 8 lb. containers.

LIL' GUN - Advanced technology propellant design just for the 410 BORE. The 410 shotshell has long been difficult to load due to shortcomings in powder fit, metering, and burning characteristics. Not any more! LIL'GUN was designed to fit, meter and perform flawlessly in the 410 BORE. No more spilled shot or bulged cases. In addition, LIL'GUN has many magnum pistol applications and is superb in the 22 Hornet. Available in 1 lb., 4 lb. & 8 lb. containers.

Hi-Skor 700-X -This extruded flake powder is ideally suited for shotshells in 12 and 16 gauge where clay target and light field loads are the norm. It doubles as an excellent pistol target powder for such cartridges as the 38 Special and 45 ACP and many more.

TRAIL BOSS – Trail Boss was designed specifically for low velocity lead bullets suitable for Cowboy Action shooting. It is primarily a pistol powder but has some application in rifles. It is based on a whole new technology that allows very high loading density, good flow through powder measures, stability in severe temperature variation, and, most importantly, additional safety to the handloader.

PB - PB is great for Trap, Skeet, and Sporting Clays where heavy 1 ounce and 1-1/8 ounce loads are needed. In pistol it yields top performance in target and plinking loads for such cartridges as the 40 S&W, 45 Auto, etc. The small extruded grains deliver metering that is always super uniform.

Hi-Skor 800-X - This large-grained flake powder is at its best when used in heavy field loads from 10 gauge to 28 gauge. In handgun cartridges 800-X performs superbly in cartridges like the 10mm auto and 44 Remington Magnum. Excellent velocity and uniformity translate into top accuracy.

IMR Powder

IMR Rifle Powders

IMR 4166

This fine, extruded propellant is the first in the series of Enduron Technology powders. The main features of the Enduron series are copper fouling eliminator, insensitivity to temperature changes, ideal loading density and being environmentally friendly. IMR 4166 is the perfect burn speed for cartridges like the 308 Win/7.62mm NATO, 22-250 Remington, 257 Roberts and dozens more. Positively, a versatile, match grade propellant.

IMR 4451

Another new Enduron extruded powder, IMR 4451, gives top performance in the venerable 30-06, 270 Winchester and 300 Win-

TRAIL BOSS

chester Short Magnum, to name just a few. This propellant is ideally suited for many, many mid-range burn speed cartridges. Simply scroll through the list of cartridges on the Hodgdon Reloading Data Center, and see how many of your favorite cartridges are covered with this fine powder. Once the shooter tries this one in that favorite cartridge, his search is over!

IMR 7977

The slowest burn rate Enduron Technology extruded powder is IMR 7977, and is a true magnum cartridge propellant. It yields outstanding performance in such cartridges as the 300 Winchester Magnum, 7mm Remington Magnum, 338 Lapua and a host of others. Loading density is perfect for magnums, nicely filling the case at maximum charges, contributing to superb uniformity and accuracy. The 7mm Remington Magnum "never had it so good"!

IMR 4198

This fast burning rifle powder gives outstanding performance in cartridges like the 222 Remington, 221 Fireball, 45-70, and 450 Marlin. Varmint shooters with small-bore cartridges love it. Proven metering and necessary elements were added to make it extremely insensitive to hot/cold temperatures. IMR 4198 is outstanding in cartridges like the 222 Remington, 444 Marlin and 7.62 X 39.

IMR 3031

A propellant with many uses, IMR 3031 has long been a favorite of 308 Match shooters using 168-grain match bullets. It is equally effective in small-capacity varmint cartridges from 223 Remington to 22-250 Remington, and it's a great 30-30 Winchester powder.

IMR 8208 XBR

The latest in the versatile IMR line of fine propellants, this accurate metering, super short grained extruded rifle powder was designed expressly for match, varmint, and AR sniper cartridges. Ideally suited for cartridges like the 223 Remington/5.56mm, 308 Winchester/7.62mm NATO and the 6mm PPC, shooters will find IMR 8208 XBR totally insensitive to changes in temperature, while yielding max velocities and "tack driving" accuracy. Clearly, the competitor's "choice" and the Varmint Hunter's "dream powder".

IMR 4895

Originally a military powder featured in the 30-06, IMR 4895 is extremely versatile. From the 17 Remington to the 243 Winchester to the 375 H&H Magnum, accuracy and performance are excellent. In addition, it is a longtime favorite of Match shooters.

IMR 4064

One of the most versatile propellant in the IMR line, used for 223 Remington, 22-250 Remington, 220 Swift, 6mm Remington, 243 Winchester Super Short Magnum, 308 Winchester, 338 Winchester Magnum, and the list goes on and on. Versatility with uniformity and accuracy.

IMR 4320

Short granulation, easy metering, and perfect for the 223 Remington, 22-250 Remington, 250 Savage, and other medium burn rate cartridges. Long a top choice for the vintage 300 Savage cartridge as well.

IMR 4007 SSC

Super Short granulated powder with a burn speed that falls between 4320 and 4350. Ideally suited for varmint cartridges like the 220 Swift, 22-250 Remington and 243 Winchester. Additionally, well suited for the venerable 30-06, the 300 Winchester Short Magnum, and the Super Short Magnums 243 and 25 Winchester.

IMR 4350

The number one choice for the new short magnums, both Remington and Winchester versions. For magnums with light to medium bullet weights, IMR 4350 is the best choice.

IMR 4831

Slightly slower in burn speed than IMR 4350, IMR 4831 gives top velocities and performance with heavier bullets in medium-sized magnums.

IMR 7828

The BIG magnum powder. This slow burner gives real magnum performance to the large over-bored magnums, such as the 300 Remington Ultra Magnum, the 30-378 Weatherby Magnum, and the 7mm Remington Ultra Magnum. This powder is highly regarded by most magnum afficionados.

IMR 7828 SSC

This magnum rifle powder has exactly the same burn rate as standard IMR 7828 and uses the same data. However, due to the super short kernels, metering is virtually as good as a spherical powder. This allows up to 4% more powder space in the case and in many loads yields more velocity than standard 7828. Such loads are marked with an asterisk in the data to show where standard 7828 will not fit.

IMR Pistol & Shotgun Powder

SR 7625

SR 7625 covers the wide range of shotshells from 10 gauge to 28 gauge in both target and field loadings. The versatile powder is equally useful in a large array of handgun cartridges for target, self-defense, and hunting loads.

SR 4756

This fine-grained, easy-metering propellant has long been a favorite of upland and waterfowl handloaders. Top velocities with great patterns are legendary. Like 800-X, SR 4756 performs extremely well in the big handgun cartridges. Always a top choice.

SR 4759

This bulky powder really shines as a reduced load propellant for rifle cartridges. Its large grain size gives good loading density for reduced loads, enhancing velocity uniformity.

IMR 4227

This is the Magnum Pistol Powder in the IMR lineup. If it says Magnum, IMR 4227 is the choice for true magnum velocities and performance. In rifles this powder delivers excellent velocity and accuracy in such cartridges as the 22 Hornet and 221 Fireball.

Winchester Powder

Winchester Rifle Powder

748

This is the powder of choice for 223 Remington ammunition. The low flame temperature extends barrel life compared to other similar speed powder. It is ideal for a wide variety of centerfire rifle loads, including 222 Remington, 30-30 Winchester, 30 Winchester, and up to 485 Winchester Magnum.

760

Combine Winchester components with 760 to duplicate 30-06 Springfield factory load ballistics. 760 has ideal flow characteristics that give it an advantage over other propellants with similar burn rates. 760 in recommended as an excellent choice for 22-250 Remington, 300 Winchester Magnum, as well as 300 WSM.

Winchester Pistol Powder

AUTOCOMP

AUTOCOMP is extremely fine in the 38 Super, 9mm, 45 ACP and 40 S&W race guns. It's just the perfect burning speed to feed the compensators with a higher volume of gas. With AUTOCOMP competitors get off faster shots with minimal muzzle flash, it's a winner.

231

One of the most popular reload propellants, 231 is a pistol powder ideally suited to the 38 special, 45 Auto, and 9mm standard loads. Consistency, clean burning, low flash, and a broad range of applications make this powder a choice for any pistol cartridge reloader.

296

This propellant was developed for Winchester factory-loaded ammunition for 357 Magnum, 444 Magnum, and 410 Bore. Its high loading density provides optimal velocity. 296 is recommended by Winchester for 410 Bore AA loads.

Winchester Shotgun Powder

WST

The choice for 12 gauge AA duplicate handloads and standard velocity handgun loads. Ideal for use in 45 Auto match applications. Consistent, clean, low flash and smoke are benefits to the shooter.

SUPER HANDICAP

Super Handicap is the same propellant used in Winchester's Super Handicap ammunition. This slow-burning, high energy propellant gives the shooter great handicap or long range sporting clays loads at up to 1250 fps with a 1-1/8 ounce shot charge. Great velocity with excellent patterns!

WSF

Super-Field propellant is the propellant of choice for Winchester 20 gauge AA Target loads. WSF is an ideal choice to maximize velocities in 12 gauge 1-1/8 ounce and 1-1/4 ounce loads. Super-Field also performs well in 38 Super, 9mm, and 40 S&W pistol loads. Excellent propellant for action pistol applications.

Alliant Powder

Alliant Rifle Powders

AR-Comp™

Smokeless rifle powder suitable for all semi-automatic and bolt-action rifles.
Ideal for heavy 223 and 308 match bullets. Very consistent across temperature extremes.

Power Pro 1200-R

Smokeless double base spherical powder. Designed for .223 progressive loading. Meters well. Double base formulation. Lot to lot consistency. Made in the U.S.A.

Power Pro 2000-MR (Medium Rifle)

Smokeless spherical medium rifle powder. Improved velocity and density for more efficient metering and loading. Excellent performance in heavy .223 and .308 loads. Enables reloaders to duplicate certain factory loaded ammunition.

Power Pro 4000-MR (Magnum Rifle)

Smokeless spherical magnum rifle powder. Improved velocity and density for more efficient metering and loading. Superior performance in the 7mm and .300 Win. Mag. cartridges. Enables reloaders to duplicate certain medium rifle heavy bullet factory loads.

Power Pro Varmint

Smokeless spherical light rifle powder. Improved velocity and density for more efficient metering and loading. Enables reloaders to duplicate certain factory loaded ammunition. Excellent performance in the standard varmint cartridges.

Reloder 7

Smokeless small rifle powder. Small caliber varmint loads. Meters consistently. Great for .45-70 and .450 Marlin.

Reloder 10x

Smokeless small bore rifle powder. Excellent for bench rest cartridges. Great in 223 and 22-250 with light bullets. Optimum velocity in small cal varmint loads.

Reloder 15

Smokeless medium rifle. Broad caliber range. Consistent at all temperature. High velocity varmint loads.

Reloder 17

Smokeless medium rifle. Designed for short magnum case capacity. Meters easily and consistently. Consistent maximum velocity in extreme weather conditions.

Reloder 19

Smokeless heavy rifle. Powder of choice for .30-06 and .338 calibers. Excellent metering. Accurate and consistent.

Reloder 22

Smokeless magnum rifle. Powder of choice for 7mm Mag and .300 Win Mag. Excellent metering. Accurate and consistent.

Reloder 23

Smokeless magnum rifle powder. TZ® technology provides exceptionally consistent velocities across temperature extremes. Contains proprietary de-coppering additive. Ideal for long-range target shooting.

Reloder 25

Smokeless heavy magnum rifle. Ideal for over bore magnums. Contains proprietary de-coppering additive. Made in Sweden to Alliant Powder specifications.

Reloder 26

Smokeless magnum rifle powder. EI® technology produces extremely high velocities in magnum cartridges. Contains proprietary de-coppering additive. Controlled temperature stability.

Reloder 33

Smokeless magnum rifle powder. Specifically designed for the .338 Lapua. Also suited for a variety of large magnum rifle cartridges. Superior lot to lot consistency.

Reloder 50

Smokeless powder for .50-caliber rifle. Clean burning with less residue. Density designed for application. Superior velocity.

Alliant Handgun Powders

2400
Smokeless magnum handgun. High velocity. Great for 357 and 44 mag. Shooter's choice for .410 bore.

BE-86
Smokeless pistol. Improved flow. Contains flash suppressant. Versatile.

Bullseye
Smokeless pistol. Fast burning and consistent. Economical and accurate.

Power Pistol
Smokeless pistol. Designed for high performance semi-autos. Maximum velocity. Economical and efficient.

Power Pro 300-MP (Magnum Pistol)
Smokeless spherical magnum pistol powder. Improved velocity and density for more efficient metering and loading. Maximum velocity and performance in magnum handguns. Enables reloaders to duplicate certain factory loaded ammunition.

Unique
Smokeless. Most versatile powder made. Good in all popular pistol calibers. Great for 12, 16, 20 and 28 gauge loads.

Alliant Shotshell Powders

20/28
Smokeless Shotshell Powder. Powder of choice for 20 and 28 gauge target loads. Designed for Skeet and Sporting Clays. Competition-grade performance.

410
Smokeless Shotshell Powder. Clean burning. Optimum loading characteristics. Superior performance.

American Select
Ultra-clean smokeless shotshell. Designed for 12 gauge target loads. Optimal recoil and patterns. Great pistol powder, too.

Blue Dot
Smokeless magnum shotshell & handgun. Powder of choice for magnum loads. Consistent. Accurate.

Clay Dot
Smokeless Shotshell Powder. Optimum load for light and standard 12 gauge target loads. Duplicates the performance of Hodgdon Clays at an economical price. Proudly made in America.

e3
Smokeless target shotshell. Clean burning. Low charge weight efficiency. Consistent performance.

Extra-Lite
Smokeless Shotshell Powder. Powder density allows use of standard available components (wads and cases. Pressure level assures complete combustion across temperature ranges. Made in the USA.

Green Dot
Smokeless shotshell. Lower felt recoil. Superior patterning. Versatile for target and field.

Herco
Smokeless heavy shotshell & handgun. Excellent hi-base hunting loads. Great for magnum handguns. Versatile.

Pro Reach
Smokeless shotshell. Specially formulated for long distance 12 gauge shooting. Ideal for games such as Back Porch, Annie Oakley, Protection and Buddy. For use in 12 gauge hunting loads.

Promo
Smokeless shotshell. Full target load performance at an economy price. Reliable. Consistent and easy loading.

Red Dot
Smokeless target shotshell. America's number one choice. Lot-to-lot consistency. Economical and efficient.

Steel
Smokeless shotshell for steel shot. Consistent at all temperatures. Maximum velocity. Proven performance.

Unique
Smokeless. Most versatile powder made. Good in all popular pistol calibers. Great for 12, 16, 20 and 28 gauge loads.

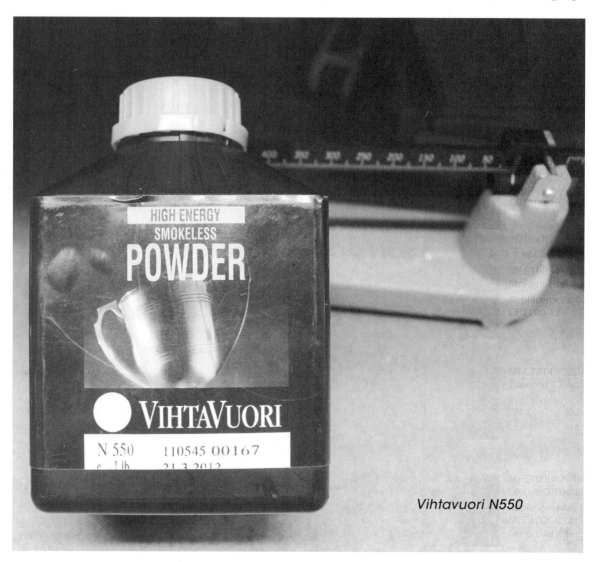

Vihtavuori N550

Vihtavuori Powders

N500 Family of Rifle Powders

N530 - This is the fastest burning powder in the N500 series and its burning rate is close to Vihtavuori N135 and Hodgdon BL-C(2). Developed especially for the 5.56 mm NATO-cartridges and it gives excellent performances in many .45-70 Government loads and also in .308 Winchester loads with bullet weight less than 10 grams (155 grains).

N540 – Faster burning powder with a burn rate like N140 and close to Hodgdon H414 and Winchester 760. For situations where more powder is needed, especially for .223 Remington, .308 Winchester and .30 -06 loads with heavier bullets.

N550 - Burn rate is similar to N150 and close to IMR4350 and Reloder 19. Good choice for the more powerful loads for 6.5x55 Swede, .308 Winchester, .30-06 Springfield and many others.

N560 - Burning rate is between N160 and N165 and close to Norma MRP and Reloder 22. Powder especially for Magnum cartridges to get out the best power for example from .270 Winchester, 7 mm Remington Magnum, 7 mm Weatherby Magnum, .300 Winchester Magnum, .300 Weatherby Magnum and .338 Lapua Magnum.

N570 - This is the newest member of the N500 series powders and also the slowest burning. The burning rate of N570 is near to N170 and it is faster burning than 24N41. The characteristics of this high energy powder with large grain size bring out the best in most of the large volume cases like for example in 6,5-.284 Norma, .300 Winchester Magnum, .300 Remington Ultra Magnum, .338 Lapua Magnum and .30-378 Weatherby Magnum

Vihtavuori Powders for the .50BMG

For .50 BMG there are two special Vihtavuori reloading powders available: 24N41 and 20N29. They are, like N100 series, single base surface treated powders. Their burning rate is slower and grain size larger than that of the N100 series rifle reloading powders. The renewed relative burning rate of the 24N41 is 39 and that of the 20N29 respectively 36, when N110 is given the index 100, and therefore 24N41 is slightly faster burning than 20N29. There is reloading data available also for some other magnum rifle calibers with these powders and 20N29 has gained reputation also when used eg. in .338 Lapua Magnum and in .30-378 Weatherby Magnum.

N100 Rifle Powders

N110
The fastest burning rifle powder from Vihtavuori. Similar to Hodgdon H110 and Winchester 296. N110 can be used in small rifle cases like .22 Hornet and .30 Carbine but also in magnum pistol and revolver cartridges like .357 S&W Magnum, .41 Magnum, .44 Magnum, .454 Casull and .500 S&W.

N120
Slower burning powder for small capacity rifle cases and for lighter bullets in many .22 caliber loads. N120 needs higher pressure than N110 in order to optimize burning. Burning rate is near to Accurate 1680, IMR 4198 and Reloder 7. N120 is suitable also for 7,62x39, .30-30 Winchester and .444 Marlin.

N130
This powder is used in many factory loaded caliber .22 and 6 mm PPC cartridges. Suitable also for lighter bullets in caliber .223 Remington and for straight-wall rifle cases like .45-70 Government and .458 Winchester Magnum. Burning rate is close to Hodgdon H322 and Accurate 2230.

N133

A choice of many bench rest and standard rifle shooters who are using 6 mm PPC. Used also in many loads of .222 Remington, .223 Remington and as well in other applications where a relatively fast burning powder is needed, like in .45-70 Government. Similarly burning powders are Norma 201, Hodgdon H335 and Vectan SP10

N135

An excellent powder for .308 Winchester loads with bullet weight less than 10 grams (155 grains). It will fit applications similar to IMR4064, Hodgdon H4895 or Accurate 2520. Capability for various loads ranging from .222 Remington to .458 Winchester Magnum.

N140

A true multipurpose powder, which can usually be used in place of IMR4320, Reloder 15 or Hodgdon H380. Good choice also for .223 Remington, .22-250 Remington, .308 Winchester, .30-06 Springfield, 8x57 IS (8 mm Mauser) and .375 H&H Magnum.

N150

This powder burns a bit slower than N140 and works as well as Hodgdon H414 and Winchester 760. Typically used with heavier bullets in accuracy and hunting loads of cartridges with middle case volumes, like .308 Winchester, 6,5x55 SE and .30-06 Springfield.

N160

slow burning powder for Magnum cartridges and calibers with large case volume and comparatively small bullet diameter. Burning speed of N160 is close to Reloder 19, Winchester WMR and the various 4831´s. For example some ideal applications are: .243 Winchester, 6,5-.284 Norma, 7 mm Weatherby Magnum, .300 Winchester Magnum, .338 Winchester Magnum and all the Winchester Short Magnums.

N165

A very slow burning powder for Magnum cartridges with heavy bullets. N165 offers performance equal to Norma MRP and Reloder 22. To be used with heavy bullets in calibers ranging from 6,5x55 SE all the way to .416 Rigby.

N170

The slowest burning N100 series rifle powder from Vihtavuori and one of the slowest canister reloading powders generally available from any manufacturer. It will fit applications similar to Hodgdon H1000 and Accurate 8700. Good performances in most of the belted Magnum cartridges like .300 Weatherby Magnum and suitable also for .300 Remington Ultra Magnum and .338 Lapua Magnum. Premium N100 Powders The N100 series powders are primarily rifle powders with different burning rates to optimize your loads.

N300 Handgun Powders

N310

Very fast burning and competitive with Alliant Bullseye, Hodgdon HP38 and Vectan Ba 10. It has applications in a very wide range from .32 S&W Long Wadcutter up to .45 ACP.

N320

A comparatively fast burning multipurpose handgun powder with burning rate about the same as Winchester 231 or Alliant Red Dot. Currently available reloading data for 9 mm Luger, .38 Super Auto, .38 Special, .357 Magnum, .40 S&W, .44 S&W Special, .44 Remington Magnum, .45 ACP and .45 Colt.

Tin Star (N32C)

Special powder developed for Cowboy Action Shooters shooting lead bullets with revolvers and single-action rifles. It has low bulk density (less free space in the case) and it burns very clean without residues with a burning rate between N320 and N330. Reloading data is currently available for .38 Special and .44 Magnum.

N330

Burning rate is a bit slower than with N320 and corresponding to Alliant Unique and Vectan Ba 9. Especially designed for 9 mm Luger but also suitable for .38 Special, .40 S&W, .44 S&W Special and .45 (Long) Colt.

N340

An excellent multipurpose handgun powder with burning rate generally about like Accurate No.5 or Alliant Herco. Wide application area covers the following handgun cartridges: 9 mm Luger, 9x21 mm, .357 SIG, .38 Super Auto, .38 Special, .357 Magnum, .40 S&W, 10 mm AUTO, .44 S&W Special, .44 Remington Magnum, .45 ACP and .45 Colt.

N350

This is the slowest burning N300 series handgun powder, which can usually be used instead of Accurate No.7, IMR Hi- Skor 800-X and Alliant Blue Dot. Appropriate choice for many powerful handgun loads, for example in calibers 9 mm Luger, 10 mm AUTO and .45 ACP.

3N37

Originally developed for .22 rimfire cartridges but has proven to be very versatile and desirable within all competitive handgun shooting disciplines. The burning speed of this small grain powder is near to N350 and Vectan A0. Reloading data available for all popular handgun cartridges.

3N38

This specially designed powder for competitive handgun shooting is recommended for high velocity loads of 9 mm Luger, .38 Super Auto and .40 S&W with moderate bullet weight. Burning rate is corresponding to Vectan SP 2.

N105 Super Magnum

Slow burning handgun powder filling the gap between N350 and N110. Especially developed for handgun cartridges with heavy bullets and/or large case volume. Reloading data is currently available for the following cartridges: 9x21 mm, .38 Super Auto, .357 Magnum, 357 Remington Maximum, .40 S&W, 10 mm AUTO, .41 Remington Magnum, .44 Remington Magnum, .45 Colt, .45 Winchester Magnum and .454 Casull.

WESTERN POWDERS

The firm of Western Powders is responsible the Accurate, Ramshot, BlackHorn and Norma brands.

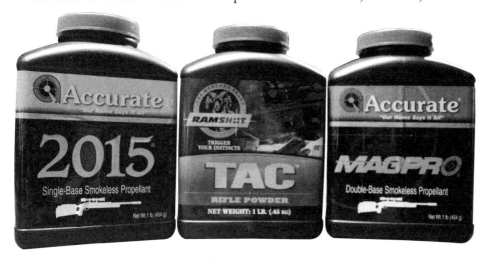

■ Rifle Powders

MAGNUM is the ultimate high performance magnum rifle powder. It provides outstanding performance from the popular 7mm Rem Mag and 300 Win Mag through the Remington Ultra Mags and 338 Lapua. It is a double-base spherical propellant that is the number one choice for high performance "overbore" magnum cartridges. Made in Belgium.

BIG GAME is the ultimate 30-06 Springfield powder. Outstanding velocities and optimum case-fill result in excellent shot to shot consistency. These properties also allow it to outperform the competition in the popular 22-250 Remington and other calibers in this range. It's an extremely clean burning, double-base spherical powder with outstanding metering properties

HUNTER is a double-base, clean burning, high performance propellant that is perfect for elk country cartridges such as the 270 Winchester, 300 WSM and 338 Win Mag. It's the only spherical powder in the popular 4350 burn range making it an ideal powder for a wide range of cartridges. The excellent flow characteristics allow accurate metering and consistent shot-to-shot results.

TAC is a double-base spherical propellant that sets the standard for extreme accuracy and reliability with heavy bullets in the 223 Remington and match applications in 308 Winchester. Excellent flow characteristics ensure consistent metering and charge weights for repeatable results with progressive loading equipment. It is the choice for shooters who demand precision and accuracy.

X-TERMINATOR is a double-base spherical powder designed for the high volume 223 varmint hunters who demands a clean burning, accurate powder. Excellent flow characteristics and small grain size allow trouble-free loading in small diameter case necks. It performs extremely well with light to medium weight bullets in the 223 Remington. It is also an excellent choice for 17 Remington, 20 caliber cartridges, 222 Remington and the 45-70 Government.

■ Handgun Powders

ENFORCER is the best choice for high performance, full power loads in magnum handgun cartridges. It is ideally suited for the 44 Magnum, 454 Casull, 460 S&W, and the 500 S&W. It's is a double-base spherical powder with excellent metering qualities that meets the performance expectations of serious magnum handgun shooters.

SILHOUETTE is the choice for competitive shooters in IPSC, IDPA and USPSA. A double-base high performance spherical powder, it's is an excellent choice for 9mm, 38 Super, 40 S&W and 45 ACP. It has a low flash signature, high velocity, and clean burn-

ing properties which also make it the perfect choice for indoor ranges and law enforcement applications.

TRUE BLUE is the perfect powder for classic calibers such as the 38 Special, 44 Special, and 45 Long Colt. Its a double-base, spherical powder with great metering properties that make it an ideal choice for consistent results using high volume, progressive reloading equipment. It works well with cast bullets and is also an excellent choice for 9mm law enforcement rounds.

ZIP is a clean burning, double-base propellant designed for a wide range of handgun calibers. Low charge weights make it the most economical and versatile choice for high volume shooters with the added benefit of low recoil, low flash and minimum residue. 9mm, 40 S&W, and 45 ACP are just a few of the cartridges that are well-matched with this powder

■ Shotshell Powders

COMPETITION is an extremely clean burning powder for 12 gauge target shooters. A double-base modified (flattened) spherical propellant, It is designed for the 12 gauge competitive clay target shooter who demands a clean burning powder with low recoil and consistent performance. It is a low bulk density powder that is also well suited for many low pressure, low velocity Cowboy Action loads.

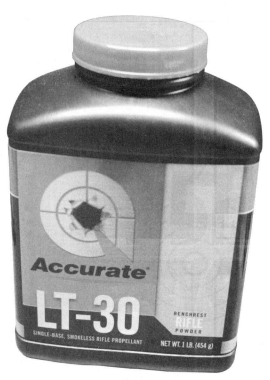

ACCURATE LT-30.

ACCURATE 2015.

ACCURATE POWDERS

■ Accurate Rifle Powders

ACCURATE 5744. Accurate 5744 is an extremely fast burning, double-base, extruded powder. This unique powder can be used in a wide range of rifle calibers and magnum handguns. 5744 is characterized by excellent ignition and consistency over a very wide performance range. Low bulky density and superior ignition characteristics make 5744 an excellent choice for reduced loads in many rifle calibers and in large capacity black powder cartridges such as the 45-70 through 45-120 and 50-90 through 50-120.

ACCURATE 1680. Accurate 1680 is an extremely fast burning, double-base, spherical rifle powder that is well suited for large capacity, high performance handgun cartridges such as the 454 Casull, 460 S&W and 500 S&W. 1680 is also an excellent choice for the 22 Hornet and 7.62 x 39, as well as other low capacity rifle cartridges.

ACCURATE LT-30.

The second in Accurate's line of benchrest-grade Light Target powders, LT-30 is optimized for use in the .30 BR cartridge. While still in its development phase, LT-30 was used to win numerous matches, even claiming a world record along the way. With a burn rate similar to 4198, this double-base fine grained powder is at home in many smaller capacity cartridges including the 6.5 Grendel and .222 Remington.

ACCURATE LT-32. LT-32 is a fine-grained extruded powder that was developed for 6mm PPC benchrest competitors. Already a proven match winner, LT-32's excellent shot-to-shot consistency and low standard deviations provide the ultimate competitive edge. Due to its small grain size, LT-32 flows like a spherical powder and allows for very precise handloading. It also offers outstanding accuracy in varmint and tactical cartridges, including the .223 Rem and .308 Win. LT-32 is the perfect choice for extreme accuracy.

ACCURATE 2015. Accurate 2015 is a fast burning, single-base, extruded rifle powder that performs very well in small to medium varmint calibers (223 Rem, 204 Ruger). 2015 is a popular choice for first-class performance in benchrest calibers and is also recommended for use in large bore straight wall cartridges (45-70, 458 Win Mag). 2015 offers excellent ignition characteristics and shot-to-shot consistency.

ACCURATE 2200. Accurate 2015 is a fast burning, single-base, extruded rifle powder that performs very well in small to medium varmint calibers (223 Rem, 204 Ruger). 2015 is a popular choice for first-class performance in benchrest calibers and is also recommended for use in large bore straight wall cartridges (45-70, 458 Win Mag). 2015 offers excellent ignition characteristics and shot-to-shot consistency.

ACCURATE 2230. Accurate 2230 is a fast burning, double-base, spherical rifle propellant. This versatile powder was designed around the 223 Remington, but can be used in many small and medium caliber cartridges including the 308 Winchester. 2230 also works well in big bore straight wall cartridges such as the 458 Winchester. The excellent flow characteristics and grain size of 2230 make it ideal for progressive loading.

ACCURATE 2460. Accurate 2460 is a fast burning, double-base, spherical rifle powder that is a slower derivative of the AA2230 powder. It is suitable for small and medium sized caliber applications but with slightly higher loading densities than AA2230. It provides an additional option for shooters to fine tune and optimize loads and combinations with calibers ranging from the 223 Rem, 308 Win and for light bullets in the 30-06 Springfield. 2460 is within the threshold limit for M14 systems.

ACCURATE 2495. Accurate 2495 is a single-base, extruded rifle powder that was developed for the 308 Win and can be used over a wide range of rifle calibers. It is a very popular powder for 308 Win. NRA High Power shooting disciplines, as well as heavy bullet 223 Rem target applications. 2495 is a versatile powder with excellent ignition characteristics that provides excellent shot-to-shot consistency.

ACCURATE 2520. Accurate 2520 is a medium burning, double-base, spherical rifle propellant designed around the 308 Winchester. 2520 is our "Camp Perry" powder and is extremely popular with many service shooters. 2520 also performs extremely well in 223 Remington with heavy match bullets (62 to 80 grain). This versatile powder has superb flow characteristics and is well within the threshold limit for the M14 systems.

ACCURATE 2700. Accurate 2700 is a medium burning, double-base, spherical rifle powder that is ideally suited for the 30-06 Springfield and other medium capacity calibers such as the 22-250 Remington, 220 Swift, and the 243 Winchester. 2700 provides excellent velocities and performance in the Winchester Super Short Magnum cartridges.

ACCURATE 4064. Accurate 4064 is an intermediate burning, single-base, short cut extruded rifle powder designed around the 30-06 Springfield. This versatile powder works extremely well in calibers such as 22-250, 220 Swift, 243 WSM, 7×57 Mauser and the 325 WSM. 4064 is a popular choice for High Power shooters using the M1 Garand.

ACCURATE 4350. Accurate 4350 is a short cut, single-base, extruded rifle powder in the extremely popular 4350 burn range. A highly versatile powder, 4350 can be used in a wide range of cartridges from the popular 243 Win to the 338 Win Mag with excellent results. Accurate 4350® is an exceptional choice for the 6mm Rem, 270 Win, 280 Rem and 300 WSM. This short cut extruded powder meters accurately, resulting in excellent shot-to-shot consistency.

ACCURATE MAGPRO. Accurate MAGPRO is a slow burning, double-base, spherical rifle powder developed specifically for the Short magnums of both Winchester (WSM) and Remington (SAUM). This powder excels in the 6.5 x 284, 270 WSM and the 7mm WSM. MAGPRO is an excel-

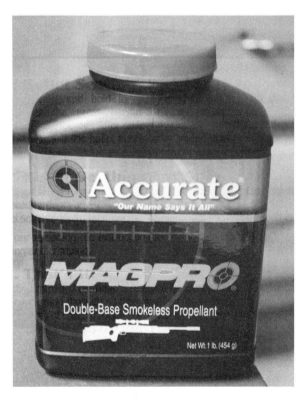

ACCURATE MAGPRO.

lent choice for belted cartridges such as the 300 Win Mag. Consistent performance can be expected from the excellent metering properties of MAGPRO.

■ Handgun Powders

ACCURATE NO. 2. Accurate No. 2 is an extremely fast burning, double-base, spherical handgun powder suitable for use in a wide range of handgun calibers. Low recoil and low flash make No. 2 well suited for use in short barrel, concealed carry applications. No. 2 is a non-position sensitive powder and low charge weights make it an economical and versatile choice for high volume handgun shooters.

ACCURATE NO. 5. Accurate No. 5 is a fast burning, double-base, spherical handgun propellant. This powder is extremely versatile and can be used in many handgun calibers. No. 5 offers a wide performance range from target and Cowboy Action applications to full power defense loads. This powder meters well and strikes a good balance between ballistics and cost efficiency.

ACCURATE NO. 7. Accurate No. 7 is an intermediate burning, double-base, spherical powder suitable for a wide range of handgun calibers. No. 7 is an excellent choice for high performance semi-auto handguns such as the 357 Sig, 38 Super, and 40 S&W. No. 7 is also a cost effective solution in larger magnum handgun calibers.

ACCURATE NO. 9. Accurate No. 9 is a double-base, spherical powder that is ideal for high power loads in traditional magnums such as the 357 Mag, 41 Rem Mag and 44 Rem Mag. It is particularly well suited to the 357 Sig and 10mm Auto, providing high velocities and excellent case-fill. No. 9 can also be used with large magnums such as the 460 S&W and 500 S&W for economical target loads.

ACCURATE 4100. Accurate 4100 is a double-base, slow burning spherical powder with exceptional metering characteristics. 4100 is an excellent choice for high performance, full power loads in magnum handgun cartridges. It is ideally suited for the 357 Mag, 41 Mag, 44 Mag, 454 Casull, 460 S&W and the 500 S&W.

■ Shotshell Powders.

ACCURATE NITRO 100 NF. Nitro 100 New Formulation is a fast burning, flattened spherical, double-base shotshell powder that is a clean burning, cost-effective choice for all 12 gauge target applications.

NOTE: The reformulated Nitro 100 has been optimized to improve flow and ignition characteristics. Always use the most current load data. We are in the process of developing loads for Nitro100 – "New Formulation". For shotshell please use load guide version 2.1 or later. For centerfire metallic cartridges please use load guide version 3.5 or later.

ACCURATE SOLO 1000. Accurate Solo 1000 is a fast burning, single-base, flake shotgun powder. Solo 1000 was the pioneer in the clean burning revolution and is an excellent choice for trap, sporting clays, and skeet shooting. Solo 1000 is an ultra clean burning powder that is well suited for target handgun loads in 45 ACP and Cowboy Action cartridges

NORMA POWDERS.

NORMA 200. Norma 200 is a fast burning rifle powder intended for small bores like the .222 and .223 Remington. Accurate and easy to meter, it is also a great choice for low pressure big bores like the .45-70 Government.

NORMA 201. Norma 201 was optimized for the .223 Remington and is proven to be a top performer across a wide spectrum of cartridges. Accuracy in the 6mm BR with lighter bullets is superb, while its versatility in older military calibers makes it ideal in service rifles from around the world.

Norma Powders

NORMA 202. Norma 202 was developed for the .308 Winchester and delivers superior performance in most medium capacity cartridges including the .22-250 Remington and .220 Swift.

NORMA 203B. Norma 203B was designed for heavy match bullets in the .308 Winchester. Its versatility brings fine performance to favorites like the .220 Swift and .30-06, as well as the powerful .338 Winchester Mag.

NORMA 204. Norma 204 is a slow burning powder that delivers outstanding performance in a wide range of cartridges including the .243 Winchester, .300 WSM and 7mm Remington Mag.

NORMA 217. Norma 217 is a slow burning magnum powder that maximizes performance in large magnum cartridges. Created for the .30-.378 Weatherby, .338 Lapua Mag and the Remington Ultra Magnums, Norma 217 offers unparalleled velocity and accuracy.

NORMA MRP. Norma MRP is a magnum rifle powder that deserves a place on every handloader's shelf. It was created to win 1000-yard competitions and power long range hunting rifles. A winner in cartridges like the 6.5X284, the .270 Winchester and the .300 Winchester Mag, MRP is an extremely versatile magnum powder.

NOMRA URP. Norma URP is the "hunter's powder". It was designed for the range of cartridges hunters typically use in search of deer and elk. Ideal for the .30-06 Springfield, it also works perfectly in cartridges as diverse as the 6.5X55 Swede and the .338 Winchester Mag. If you are serious about hunting, you need Norma URP.

BLACKHORN POWDERS

Blackhorn 209 is a low residue, high performance propellant for muzzleloaders and black powder cartridges that consistently shoots at higher velocities and with greater accuracy than all other muzzleloader powders. In fact, if you compare our benefits with other powders, you will quickly see that Blackhorn 209 absolutely smokes the competition.

Blackhorn Powders

METALLIC HANDLOADING COMPONENTS:
BRASS

The brass cartridge case radically changed the firearms industry, giving the shooter a quick, efficient and reliable means of reloading the gun. It created a uniform load that worked safely within the firearm of choice, eliminating the highly dangerous double charge, and giving much more reliable ignition. The establishment of SAAMI – the Sporting Arms and Ammunition Manufacturers Institute – gave uniform dimensions and pressure limits to our cartridges; eliminating the dangers of cartridge dimension variations and blown-up guns.

Our modern brass cases are better than they've ever been: better manufacturing techniques, a more uniform and consistent product, and innovations like nickel-plated cases to best resist corrosion and oxidation, and match-grade brass that will give fantastic accuracy right out of the box.

The cartridge case is an important part of the accuracy equation. Being a combustion chamber, the dimensions must be uniform in order to generate consistent pressures, which will directly affect your accuracy. The dimensions of the case, which are controlled by your reloading dies, can also dramatically affect the accuracy. If the cartridge doesn't sit uniformly in the firearm's chamber, the results will be disappointing.

As reloaders, we have the advantage of reusing the brass case, but must be careful to rigorously inspect the cases for signs of failure. Essentially, the lower the pressures, the more times the brass can be reused. We scour the ground for spent cases, hoarding them for future use.

*Norma .375
H&H brass*

Editor's Picks:

1. Norma Brass

Unequivocally, Norma brass is my favorite. The Swedish firm is famous for its precision ammunition, but I love the component brass. I've had the best results using Norma as the basis for my handloads, and while it certainly isn't the most economical brass available, the results are well worth the investment. Unlike other brands of component brass, they usually come ready to load, right out of the box. They are held to very tight tolerances, and the dimensions are uniform.

Variances in volume are among the least that I've tested. I love the fact that Norma produces brass for not only the most popular calibers, but for the big safari guns as well, and it's all good stuff. If you're looking for a good source of brass for the Weatherby cases, Norma is it. Much of Norma's brass is annealed at the factory, to ensure long case life. Norma makes rifle cases only.

*Hornady
6.5-284
cases*

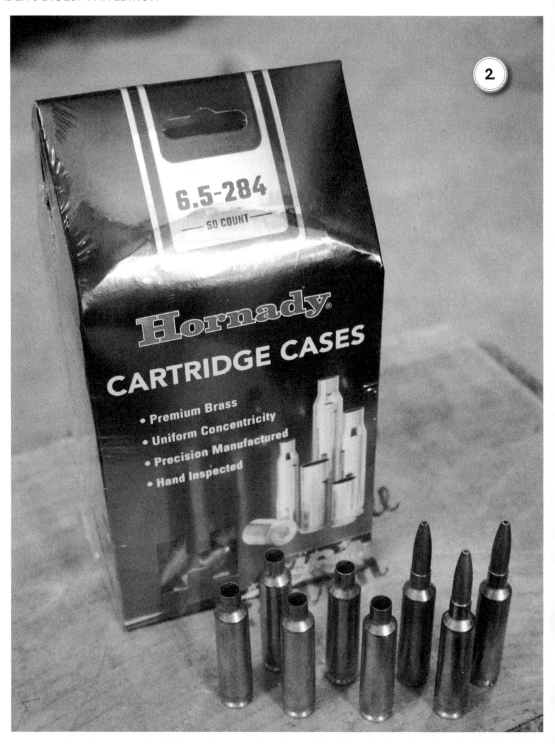

2. Hornady Brass

The big H brand comes on component brass as well, and you should be glad it does. Hornady has really stepped up their game in the brass department, offering a wide choice of rifle and pistol calibers, which should suffice most of your loading needs.

Hornady has embraced many of the more rare cartridges, such as the 7x64 Brenneke, .275 Rigby (properly headstamped!) and the .32 Winchester Special. The safari guns are also on the menu, including the .450/400 3" NE, the .470 NE and the behemoth .500 NE. Pistol cases run from the .380 Auto up to the cavernous .500 S&W.

3. Starline Brass

The famous *-* headstamp has been the basis of many accurate shooting sessions with my Ruger Blackhawk, in .45 Colt, and with good reason.

Starline makes some of the best pistol brass on the market. It is very consistent, and can last for many loadings, even in a progressive press. The .38 Special, .357 Magnum, .40 S&W and .45ACP that we all love so much are well represented in the Starline lineup, as well as some of the straight-walled rifle calibers of yesteryear like the .38-55 Winchester and the .45-100 WCF. If you are after pistol accuracy, give Starline a try.

The .45 Colt Starline brass that my Blackhawk loves so much

4.

4. Lapua Brass

Another fantastic source of rifle brass, Lapua's component cases are on par with the Norma stuff, with the exception of limited caliber choices. The Lapua .308 Winchester brass has given stellar results in my wife's rifle, helping to arrive at 1/4MOA groups. If Lapua is available in your chosen rifle caliber, you won't be sorry for choosing it.

*Lapua .308
Palma brass*

5. Nosler Custom Brass

Nosler, long famous for its fantastic component bullets, has entered the component brass game. In addition to providing the popular rifle calibers, Nosler has offered some rarities, like the 8mm Remington Magnum and .350 Remington Magnum.

*Nosler
Custom brass*

5.

8mm Remington Magnum brass

When you order Nosler Custom brass, it requires very little preparation, as it arrives nearly perfect. The brass is already chamfered for you, making loading bullets that much easier.

6. Federal Brass

While Federal has diminished its brass production lately, their brass is, and always has been, good stuff. Soft enough to last quite a long time, Federal brass offers a great choice for the rifle and pistol reloader.

7. Winchester Brass

Offering a full run of pistol and rifle brass, Winchester has always been a good source of component brass. Whether the headstamp has read W-W Super, Super Speed, or Winchester, I've always been happy using Winchester brass. Some calibers available in nickel plated brass.

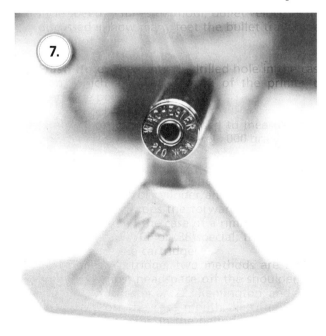

Winchester brass in .270 WSM

Remington brass in .280 Remington

8.

8. Remington Brass

Big Green makes a full complement of component brass, for both pistol and rifle. Their catalog includes some seasonal runs of nearly obsolete stuff, like the .30-40 Krag, 6.5 Remington Magnum and .25-20 WCF. Yes the 9mm, .45ACP and .30-'06 stuff is there, but it's nice to know that the bigger companies still think about those of us who like the more rare choices of caliber.

9. Swift Brass

Yes, you read that correctly. Swift has entered the brass market, producing match brass for the .223 Remington and .308 Winchester. I haven't had an opportunity to hold the Swift stuff in my hands, but if it is held to the same rigid tolerances that the Swift bullets are, it should prove to be a winner.

Quality Cartridge brass in 8.15x46R

10. Quality Cartridge

When you can't find brass for your .351 Winchester Self-Loader, .41 Action Express or .318 Westley-Richards, you want to call Quality Cartridge. I've used their services for reloading 8.15x46R cases, 7-30 Waters and other obscurities. For some of the wildcats, Quality Cartridge will create properly dimensioned, and properly headstamped cases, which can help you avoid a whole bunch of hassles when travelling abroad. This company offers a huge service to the reloader.

11. Bertram Brass

Another specialty brass company, Bertram can fill your needs for the obsolete rifles and pistols. Whether it's a .43 Spanish or a .577-.450 Martini-Henry, Bertram has the oddballs taken care of. Need 8mm Nambu brass? No problem. Your .461 Gibbs No. 2 ammo running low? Bertram has you covered. Reliable brass cases, made and stamped to the proper dimension and name.

12. Jamison International Brass

Here's another problem-solving company, giving the handloader the goods needed to produce ammunition for the cartridges that the major manufacturers have dropped. Jamison has long been a reliable source of obsolete brass. If you can't find brass for your oddball, give Jamison a try.

13. Buffalo Arms Brass

A great source of blackpowder cartridge cases, as well as obscure smokeless cartridges, Buffalo Arms offers a selection of properly headstamped cases, as well as basic and parent cases from which your cartridge can be made. Keep the phone number for Buffalo Arms in your phone; you'll be reaching for them before you know it, if you load enough cartridges.

|||||||||||||||||||||||||||||||||||||||||||||||||||||||||||||||||||||||||||

METALLIC HANDLOADING COMPONENTS:
PRIMERS

|||||||||||||||||||||||||||||||||||||||||||||||||||||||||||||||||||||||||||

O f all the components of a reloaded cartridge, the primer is the most important. We reloaders can re-use a case, cast our own bullets, and, if we needed to get all scientific, more than likely create our own black powder. Now this wouldn't be the ideal scenario, but it would work. Without a healthy supply of primers, we'd be sunk. Ironically, the primer remains the one component that, second only to the cartridge case, remains unchanged over the last sixty or so years.

There are two types of primers for our purposes: Rifle primers and Pistol primers. Each variety comes in large and small sizes and each size has a hotter spark "magnum" variation. Rifle primers have a thicker metal cup, due to the higher pressures at which they operate. Pistols operate at much lower pressures and the primer cups are thinner. Large rifle and Large Pistol primers are 0.210" in diameter, while Small Rifle and Small Pistol primers are 0.175" in diameter.

Editor's Picks:

1. The Federal GM215M Large Rifle Magnum Primer

I shoot quite a few magnum cartridges, especially in the big safari calibers. I've used the GM215M with great results, and have staked my life on their reliability when facing dangerous game on both the continent of Africa and North America. They work for me, whether in the .300 Winchester Magnum and .338 Winchester Magnum, or the big .404 Jeffery and .416 Remington Magnum.

2. The CCI200 Large Rifle Primer

This primer was part of the equation that became my first handload - a 165-grain Hornady spire point over 44.0 grains of IMR4064 - so it holds a nostalgic place in my reloading history. That aside, I've used that CCI200 in many of my medium-sized rifle cartridge loads, including .30-'06 Springfield, .270 Winchester, .22-250 Remington and .35 Whelen. It has never let me down.

	CCI	Federal	Remington	Winchester
Large Rifle:	CCI 200	Federal 210	Remington 9 ½	Winchester WLR
Large Rifle Magnum:	CCI 250	Federal 215	Remington 9 ½ M	Winchester WLRM
Small Rifle:	CCI 400	Federal 205	Remington 6 ½	Winchester WSR
Small Rifle Magnum:	CCI 450	Federal 250M	Remington 7 ½	
Large Pistol:	CCI 300	Federal 150	Remington 2 ½	Winchester WLP
Large Pistol Magnum:	CCI 350	Federal 155	Winchester WLPM	
Small Pistol:	CCI 500	Federal 100	Remington 1 ½	Winchester WSP
Small Pistol Magnum:	CCI 550	Federal 200	Remington 5 ½	Winchester WSPM

There are also several varieties of "Match" primers available, giving the most consistent results, which are readily embraced by the target shooting community. The Federal Gold Medal Match line is one example.

Several companies produce "military primers", which have the thickest cups; these are designed for use in the AR platform and other military-type rifles, and are made to military specifications. The CCI 34 (large rifle) and CCI 41 (small rifle) are two examples. These primers are designed to avoid a "slam fire" infrequently associated with the military firearms' protruding firing pins.

It may take some experimentation with different primer brands within a certain type to find the accuracy and consistency we're all after, but once you've found that combination, stock up on a good supply of primers so you can create all the ammo you need.

SHOTSHELL RELOADING:
PRESSES & ACCESSORIES

Whether you are the scourge of the trap course or a weekend bird hunter, reloading your own shotshells can be an economical endeavor, as well as the gateway to a new hobby. Unlike the centerfire ammunition presses for rifle and pistol, shotshell presses are usually gauge-specific, meaning you'll need one for each different gauge you'll be loading for.

Some companies offer conversion kits, which are very useful if you have multiple gauges of shotgun. There are single-stage presses, performing a single operation per stroke of the handle, and the progressives, which handle multiple operations at once. Either choice is fine, depending on your level of experience, and reloading shotshells is a relatively simple process which will have your scouring the ground for spent hulls before you know it.

My earliest reloading memory is as a very young man, maybe five or six years old, watching my Dad make rabbit loads for his 12 gauge on an old Lee Load-All. Apparently, that event sparked something in my psyche, for nearly forty years later in, I'm still measuring powder and cobbling ammunition together. Thanks Dad!

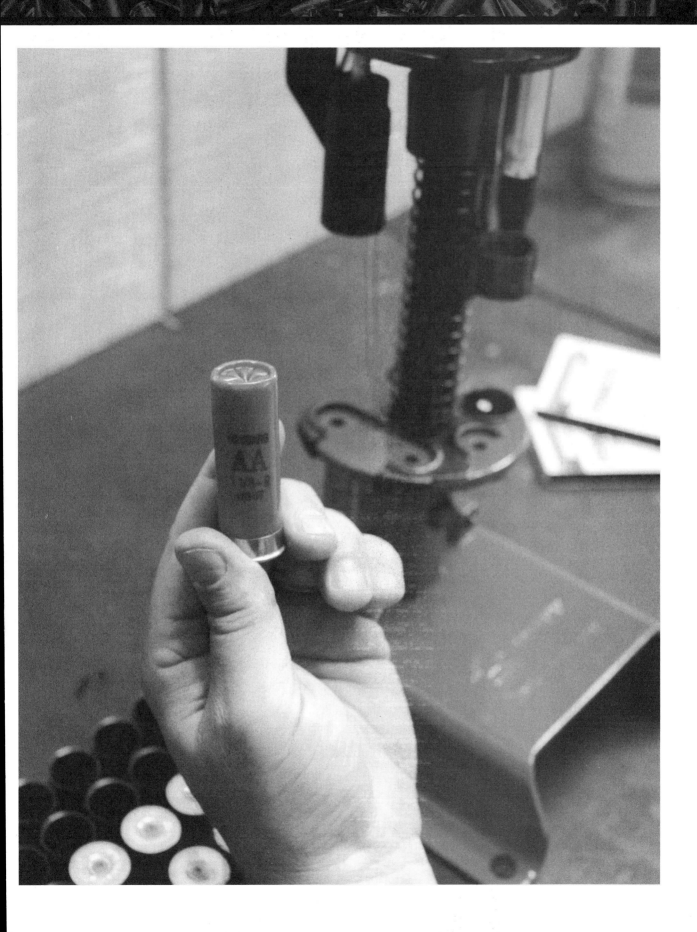

Editor's Picks:

1. MEC Sizemaster – Part no. 812012

MEC is very well known for their fantastic shotshell presses, and the Sizemaster is one of the simplest and most effective among their product line. You can see the Sizemaster in action is Chapter 12, where Dave deMoulpied puts it to work. If you're looking for a good value in a shotshell press, look no further. It comes set up for 12 gauge, 2-3/4" shells, but can be adjusted for 3" shells. It will resize the shell base back to factory dimensions, whether made of steel or brass, high or low base, for easy feeding in the pumps and autoloaders.

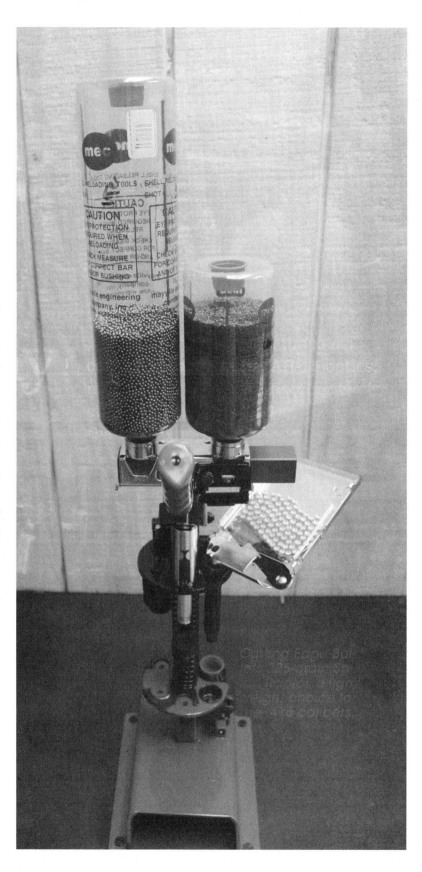

2. Lee Load-All II – Part No. 90011

The Lee Load-All II is a simple, yet effective machine, giving the loader complete control over each stage of the reloading operation. All-steel construction with a plastic base, the Load-All 12 gauge model comes with eight shot bushings for different charge weights and 16 powder bushings, as well as six and eight-point crimp starters and safety charge bar. Can easily be adjusted from 2-3/4" to 3" without needing a conversion kit.

3. MEC 600 Jr – Mark V Single Stage Press – Part No. 844712

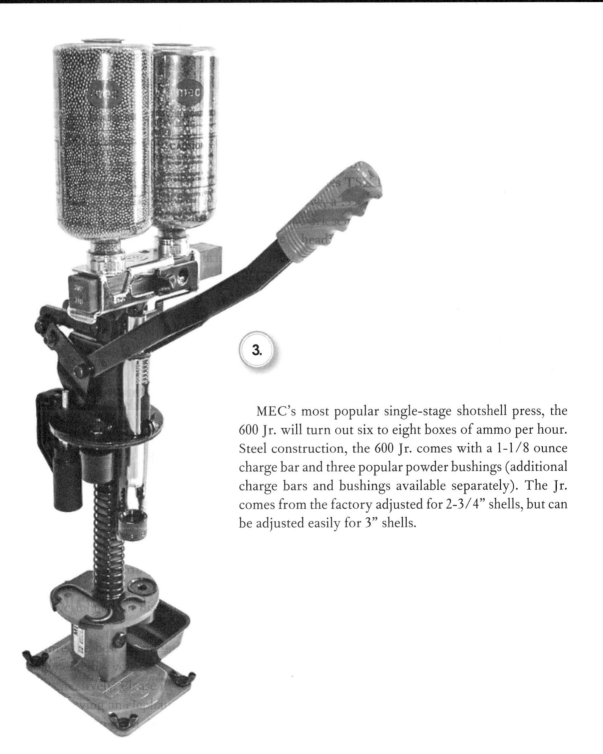

3.

MEC's most popular single-stage shotshell press, the 600 Jr. will turn out six to eight boxes of ammo per hour. Steel construction, the 600 Jr. comes with a 1-1/8 ounce charge bar and three popular powder bushings (additional charge bars and bushings available separately). The Jr. comes from the factory adjusted for 2-3/4" shells, but can be adjusted easily for 3" shells.

4. RCBS The Grand Progressive Shotshell Press – 12 ga. – Part No. 89001

Made of high-grade cast aluminum, The Grand Progressive is a sound design, with many convenient features. Powder and shot dispensing is case activated, which virtually eliminates the risk of spillage. The steel sizer will return high and low base hulls back to factory dimensions. Auto-indexing, yet easily switched to manual indexing. The huge shot hopper holds 25 lbs. of shot, and the powder hopper holds a full pound of powder. Includes a bushing for 17 grains of Alliant Red Dot, and for 1-1/8 oz. of 7-1/2 shot.

The Grand Progressive

5. Dillon Precision SL900 Shotshell Reloader

As with Dillon's fine metallic reloading machines, the SL900 will make great shotshells. Comes adjusted for the Winchester AA hulls – an industry standard – the SL900 is an auto indexing progressive, with dual-action crimping and case-activated powder and shot dispensing. Optional automatic case feeder available, as well as low powder sensor.

6. MEC 650N Progressive Press – Part No. 650N12

6.

A fully progressive press, with three-stage crimping. Six shells are worked on simultaneously, however I'd recommend you purchase the "Power Ring Collet Sizer", as the 650N won't resize the shell bases. Comes with E-Z Prime Primer Feed, so you don't have to handle each primer individually.

7. MEC 9000E Electronic Progressive Shotshell Press – Part No. 9000E12

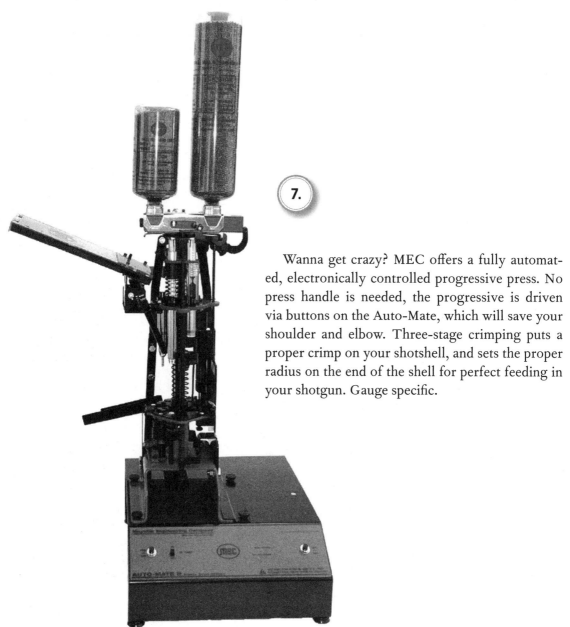

7.

Wanna get crazy? MEC offers a fully automated, electronically controlled progressive press. No press handle is needed, the progressive is driven via buttons on the Auto-Mate, which will save your shoulder and elbow. Three-stage crimping puts a proper crimp on your shotshell, and sets the proper radius on the end of the shell for perfect feeding in your shotgun. Gauge specific.

Accessories

Multi-Scale Universal Charge Bar with Powder Baffle

A fully adjustable charge bar which can replace 42 powder bushings and 23 charge bars; can be used with lead shot, steel shot and bismuth. Throws loads of lead-shot from ½ ounce to 2-1/4 oz., for steel shot 7/8 oz to 1-1/2 oz. Includes powder baffle.

MEC E-Z Pak

A neat little metal bin that allows finished shotshells to be stacked for easy placement into cardboard boxes. Available in 12, 16, 20, and 28 gauges, as well as .410 bore.

SUPER-SIZER: The Super-Sizer can update conventional reloaders with MEC's exclusive Power-Ring collet resizing device. Eight steel fingers encircle the base and apply even pressure until the base is reshaped back to its original size. Available in 10, 12, 16, 20, 28 gauge and .410 bore. Item #8119 (specify gauge)

E-Z PRIME SINGLE STAGE: These completely automatic primer feeds eliminate the time consuming bother of handling individual primers. Not available for .410 bore single stage reloaders. Item #285CA (specify gauge)

E-Z PAK: The MEC E-Z Pak neatly stacks reloaded shells and fills an entire box in one easy step. Not available in 10 gauge. Item #15CA (specify gauge)

DUST COVER: Keeps MEC Reloaders clean and dust-free. E-Z on, E-Z off form fitting cover secures with Velcro™ strip. Attractive MEC shotgun shooter logo draws attention to your favorite past-time. Durable canvas construction. Made to fit MEC Grabber, Hustler, Sizemaster, and 9000 series equipped with 12" shot bottles. Made of long-lasting, machine washable, color-fast canvas duck material. Tapered fit measures: Base -11 1/2" x 13 1/2", Top- 7 1/2" x 11", Height- 31 1/2" tall. Item #8807

STEEL SHOT CHARGE BAR for Single Stage and Progressive Reloaders. Available to load from 7/8 oz. to 1 1/2 oz. of shot and BB sizes down to #6.

SHOTSHELL CHECKER: Now you can easily measure the precision of your reloaded shells to be sure they will chamber properly. This durable, stainless steel tool accommodates 10, 12, 16, 20, 28 gauges, plus .410 bore. Item #8486

MEC EZ-FILL FUNNEL: The perfect way to fill bottles. There's no need to hold onto the funnel while pouring because the funnel fits securely over the bottles. Item #8994

MAINTENANCE KIT: The perfect tools to keep your MEC Reloader running smoothly and efficiently. Includes: Anti-Seize Collet Lubricant, Pick, Brush, Column Spring Lifter, Closure Nut Wrench. Item #8948

COLLET LUBRICANT: Used to extend the life of the collet and smoothness of operation on MEC Sizemaster, Super Sizer, Grabber, and 9000 Series. Item #8925

BOTTLE SUPPORT: For use on Progressive and Single Stage models, the heavy duty support holds bottles steady and eliminates any movement while reloading. It also holds bottles securely when tipping back to change bars or bushings.
Item #8938 Progressive/ #8939 Single Stage

POWDER BUSHING
CHART
and Charge Bar Selection Information

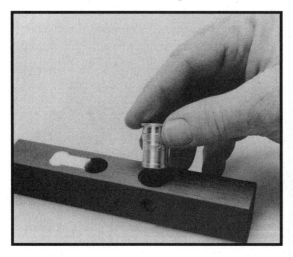

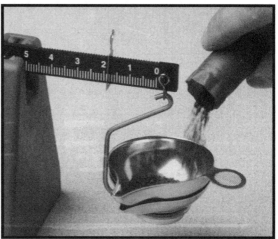

This brochure is meant to supply you with the information needed to select the right bar and bushing insert to safely load the shotshell of your choice.

The MEC charge bar determines the amount of shot that will be dropped and the MEC bushing determines the amount of powder. The ratio for powder is determined by the recipe you select and the brand name powder you wish to use.

WARNING!

The use of an accurate scale is strongly recommended with the use of this powder bushing chart. Many things can cause a variation from the weight listed on the chart. They include but are not limited to:

#1 Powder density. The manufacturers tolerance can cause a slight variation from the weight shown on the chart, and may even vary from lot to lot.

#2 Individual operators give varying amounts of vibration to the machine causing the powder to pack. All loads should be checked during the actual reloading cycle. Do not just throw a powder charge and expect it to be the same as during the reloading cycle. Even the amount of powder in the reloader's bottle may cause a slight variance.

#3 Powder exposed to the atmosphere can pick up moisture and weigh heavy.

#4 The larger the flake size, the lighter the charge tends to be.

#5 A machine that is not solidly mounted will usually not throw charges as uniform as one that is.

#6 Single stage machines will usually throw heavier charges than progressive reloading machines.

 # CHARGE BARS

LEAD CHARGE BARS

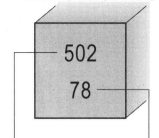

STEEL CHARGE BARS

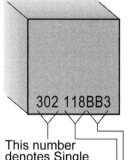

ars bored for powder bushings are designated 502 eries for progressive tools and 302 series for single tage tools. The number below either series indicates the mount of shot the bar will dispense. Example: A 302-18 is a single stage charge bar and will drop 1-1/8 oz. of hot. **POWDER HOLES ONLY** are bored to accept ushings. It is mandatory that your order for bars cludes both the series number and weight of the shot harge. Powder bushings are selected by number from e bushing chart (see inside spread).

CAUTION: Lead Shot Bars and Steel Shot Bars are not interchangeable.

This number denotes Progressive Reloaders

Number 78 denotes 7/8 oz. shot load

This number denotes Single Stage Reloaders

Number indicates 1-1/8 oz. shot load

BB3 denotes shot sizes BB thru 3

POWDER BUSHINGS ARE AVAILABLE FOR THE FOLLOWING CHARGE BARS

PROGRESSIVE STEEL SHOT BARS AVAILABLE

50207814	$^7/_8$ oz.	#1 thru #4 Shot
50207856	$^7/_8$ oz.	#5 thru #6 Shot
502100BB2	1 oz.	BB thru #2 Shot
50210036	1 oz.	#3 thru #6 Shot
502118BB3	$1^1/_8$ oz.	BB thru #3 Shot
50211846	$1^1/_8$ oz.	#4 thru #6 Shot
502114BB2	$1^1/_4$ oz.	BB thru #2 Shot
50211436	$1^1/_4$ oz.	#3 thru #6 Shot

ntact the factory for information regarding steel shot conversion for the hydraulic presses. Both 302 and 2 charge bars have a soft insert to prevent the shearing of shot. With this insert it is no longer necessary use a grommet under the shot bottle. If the insert ever requires replacing, it is Part #8440.

SINGLE STAGE STEEL SHOT BARS AVAILABLE

30207814	$^7/_8$ oz.	#1 thru #4 Shot
30207856	$^7/_8$ oz.	#5 thru #6 Shot
302100BB2	1 oz.	BB thru #2 Shot
30210036	1 oz.	#3 thru #6 Shot
302118BB3	$1^1/_8$ oz.	BB thru #3 Shot
30211846	$1^1/_8$ oz.	#4 thru #6 Shot
302114BB2	$1^1/_4$ oz.	BB thru #2 Shot
30211436	$1^1/_4$ oz.	#3 thru #6 Shot
302138BB2	$1^3/_8$ oz.	BB thru #2 Shot
30213836	$1^3/_8$ oz.	#3 thru #6 Shot
302112BB2	$1^1/_2$ oz.	BB thru #2 Shot
30211236	$1^1/_2$ oz.	#3 thru #6 Shot

MISCELLANEOUS LEAD SHOT BARS AVAILABLE

Bar Number	Oz. Shot	Bar Number	Oz. Shot
214	$2^1/_4$	114	$1^1/_4$
200	2	1316	$1^3/_{16}$
178	$1^7/_8$	118	$1^1/_8$
134	$1^3/_4$	100	1
158	$1^5/_8$	78	$^7/_8$
112	$1^1/_2$	34	$^3/_4$
138	$1^3/_8$	1116	$1^1/_{16}$
		58	$^5/_8$
		12	$^1/_2$

SKEET SPECIAL

Single Stage Bar No.	Oz.	Progressive Bar No.	Oz.	Shell Size
302118SS	$1^1/_8$	502118SS	$1^1/_8$	12GA
30278SS	$^7/_8$	50278SS	$^7/_8$	20GA
30234SS	$^3/_4$	50234SS	$^3/_4$	28GA
30212SS	$^1/_2$	50212SS	$^1/_2$	410GA

Note To Skeet Shooters
When using soft #9 shot with our standard bar, it is possible that your charge weight will exceed that which is allowed by the NSSA. By using our "SKEET SPECIAL" charge bar, you will stay within the limits set by the NSSA.

MEC charge bars with soft inserts help minimize shearing of shot.

CHILLED SHOT CONVERSION TABLE

Weight Ounces	$^1/_2$	$^5/_8$	$^3/_4$	$^7/_8$	1	$1^1/_8$	$1^1/_4$	$1^3/_8$	$1^1/_2$	$1^5/_8$	$1^3/_4$	$1^7/_8$	2	$2^1/_8$
Weight Grains	219	273	328	383	438	492	547	602	656	711	766	820	875	930
Loads per Lb.	32	26	21	18	16	14	13	12	11	10	9	9	8	8
Size Dia. In.	Approximate No. of Pellets per load (lead shot only)													
BB .18	25	21	38	44	50	56	63	69	75	81	88	94	100	106
2 .15	44	55	66	77	88	99	110	121	132	143	154	165	176	187
4 .13	68	85	102	119	136	153	170	187	204	221	238	255	272	289
5 .12	86	108	129	151	172	194	215	237	258	280	301	323	344	366
6 .11	112	139	167	195	223	251	279	307	335	362	390	418	446	474
7 .10	150	187	224	262	299	336	374	411	449	486	523	561	598	635
$7^1/_2$ .095	173	216	259	302	345	388	431	474	518	561	604	647	690	733
8 .09	205	256	301	358	409	460	511	562	614	665	716	767	818	869
$8^1/_2$ .085	240	300	360	420	480	540	600	660	720	780	840	900	960	1020
9 .08	293	366	439	512	585	658	731	804	878	951	1024	1097	1170	1243

MAYVILLE ENGINEERING CO., INC.
An Employee Owned Company
800 Horicon Street, Suite 1 • Mayville, WI 53050 • Phone (920) 387-4500 • Fax (920) 387-5802
Website: www.mecreloaders.com • E-mail: support@mecreloaders.com

The bushing chart does not represent recommended weights of charge. It is intended as a guide only to show the relationship of the volumetric capacity to the various bushings.

SHOTSHELL POWDERS / RAMSHOT / ACCURATE / ALLIANT

BUSHING #	COMPETITION	BUSHING #	ACCURATE NO. 5	SOLO 1000	ACCURATE NO. 2	NITRO 100	SOLO 1250	BUSHING #	AMERICAN SELECT	RED DOT	GREEN DOT	HERCO	2400	BLUE DOT	UNIQUE	BULLSEYE	e3	20/28	EXTRA-LITE	PRO REACH	BUSHING #	410
10	7.2	10	13.7	7.0	9.2	7.5	7.0	10	6.9	6.3	6.7	7.9	11.8	10.8	7.5	8.6	6.6	9.1	6.6	9.9	7	10.2
11	7.6	11	14.6	7.6	9.8	7.9	7.4	11	7.3	6.7	7.2	8.3	12.5	11.3	7.9	9.1	7.0	9.4	6.9	10.3	8	10.5
12	8.1	12	15.4	8.2	10.3	8.3	7.9	12	7.7	7.1	7.6	8.8	13.3	11.9	8.4	9.6	7.2	10.1	7.4	10.9	9	11.1
12A	8.5	12A	16.3	8.8	10.9	8.8	8.3	12A	8.2	7.5	8.0	9.3	14.0	12.5	8.9	10.1	7.5	10.8	7.9	11.6	10	11.7
13	9.0	13	17.2	9.3	11.5	9.2	8.8	13	8.6	7.9	8.4	9.8	14.8	13.1	9.4	10.6	8.0	11.3	8.3	12.3	11	12.1
13A	9.5	13A	18.1	9.8	12.2	9.7	9.3	13A	9.1	8.3	8.9	10.4	15.6	13.7	9.9	11.2	8.3	11.9	8.6	12.9	12	13.0
14	10.0	14	19.0	10.3	12.8	10.2	9.7	14	9.6	8.7	9.3	10.9	16.4	14.4	10.4	11.7	8.9	12.5	9.0	13.5	12A	13.6
15	10.5	15	20.0	10.8	13.3	10.8	10.1	15	10.1	9.2	9.8	11.4	17.2	15.0	10.9	12.3	9.2	13.0	9.5	14.2	13	14.5
16	11.0	16	21.0	11.4	14.0	11.2	10.6	16	10.6	9.6	10.3	12.0	18.1	15.7	11.4	12.9	9.9	13.8	9.9	14.9	13A	15.1
17	11.5	17	22.0	12.0	14.7	11.7	11.1	17	11.1	10.1	10.8	12.6	18.9	16.3	12.0	13.5	10.5	14.5	10.5	15.8	14	15.7
18	12.1	18	23.0	12.5	15.2	12.3	11.6	18	11.7	10.6	11.3	13.2	19.8	17.0	12.6	14.1	11.0	15.1	11.0	16.7	15	16.6
19	12.6	19	24.1	13.1	15.9	12.8	12.2	19	12.2	11.1	11.8	13.8	20.7	17.7	13.1	14.8	11.7	15.7	11.6	17.5	16	17.4
20	13.2	20	25.1	13.8	16.5	13.4	12.8	20	12.8	11.6	12.4	14.4	21.7	18.4	13.7	15.4	12.3	16.3	12.0	18.2	17	18.4
21	13.8	21	26.2	14.4	17.3	14.0	13.4	21	13.3	12.1	12.9	15.0	22.6	19.2	14.5	16.1	12.8	17.1	12.7	19.1	18	19.2
22	14.4	22	27.4	15.0	18.2	14.6	14.0	22	13.9	12.6	13.5	15.7	23.6	20.1	15.1	16.8	13.4	18.0	13.3	19.9	19	20.2
23	15.0	23	28.5	15.7	18.8	15.2	14.6	23	14.5	13.1	14.0	16.3	24.6	21.0	15.8	17.5	13.8	18.8	13.7	20.7	20	21.1
24	15.6	24	29.7	16.2	19.6	15.7	15.2	24	15.1	13.7	14.6	17.0	25.6	21.9	16.4	18.2	14.2	19.6	14.4	21.5	21	22.1
25	16.2	25	30.9	16.7	20.4	16.3	15.7	25	15.7	14.2	15.2	17.7	26.6	22.8	17.1	18.9	14.8	20.5	14.8	22.3	22	23.1
26	16.9	26	32.1	17.2	21.0	17.0	16.4	26	16.4	14.9	15.8	18.4	27.7	23.7	17.7	19.6	15.3	21.3	15.2	23.1	23	24.4
27	17.5	27	33.4	17.9	21.7	17.7	16.9	27	17.0	15.7	16.4	19.1	28.8	24.6	18.4	20.4	15.9	22.1	15.8	23.5	24	25.6
28	18.2	28	34.6	18.6	23.1	18.3	17.8	28	17.7	16.4	17.0	19.8	29.9	25.5	19.1	21.2	16.4	23.0	16.6	24.2	25	26.1
29	18.9	29	35.9	19.3	23.8	19.0	18.3	29	18.3	17.1	17.7	20.6	31.0	26.4	19.8	21.9	16.9	23.8	17.2	25.3	26	26.9
30	19.6	30	37.3	20.0	24.7	19.8	19.1	30	19.0	17.8	18.3	21.3	32.1	27.3	20.5	22.8	17.4	24.5	17.9	26.7	27	28.0
31	20.3	31	38.6	20.7	25.6	20.6	19.7	31	19.7	18.5	19.0	22.1	33.3	28.2	21.1	23.7	17.9	25.4	18.5	27.5	28	29.5
32	21.0	32	40.0	21.5	26.4	21.3	20.6	32	20.4	19.2	19.6	22.9	34.5	29.1	21.7	24.6	18.5	26.3	19.1	28.2	29	30.3
33	21.7	33	41.4	22.2	27.5	21.8	21.2	33	21.1	19.9	20.3	23.7	35.7	30.5	22.5	25.5	19.5	26.8	19.6	29.2	30	31.4
34	22.5	34	42.8	22.9	28.5	22.5	22.0	34	21.8	20.6	21.0	24.5	36.9	31.6	23.2	26.4	20.5	27.6	20.2	30.5	31	32.4
35	23.2	35	44.2	23.8	29.3	23.2	22.7	35	22.6	21.3	21.7	25.3	38.1	32.7	24.0	27.3	21.0	28.8	20.9	31.2	32	33.6
36	24.0	36	45.7	24.5	30.2	24.0	23.5	36	23.3	21.9	22.4	26.2	39.4	33.8	24.8	28.2	21.8	29.9	21.6	32.1	33	34.7
37	24.8	37	47.1	25.3	31.4	24.8	24.2	37	24.1	22.7	23.2	27.0	40.7	35.0	25.6	29.1	22.3	31.2	22.5	33.5	34	35.9
38	25.6	38	48.7	26.1	32.4	25.6	25.1	38	24.9	23.3	23.9	27.9	42.0	36.1	26.5	30.1	22.8	32.4	23.3	34.5	35	37.0
38A	26.4	38A	50.2	27.2	33.4	26.4	25.9	38A	25.7	24.1	24.7	28.8	43.3	37.3	27.3	31.0	23.2	33.2	23.9	35.5	36	38.1
39	27.2	39	51.7	28.1	34.3	27.2	26.7	39	26.5	24.7	25.4	29.7	44.6	38.5	28.2	31.9	23.8	34.0	24.6	36.2	37	39.3
39A	28.0	39A	53.3	28.9	35.3	28.0	27.5	39A	27.3	25.2	26.2	30.6	46.0	39.7	29.0	32.8	24.5	35.1	25.3	37.4	38	40.6
40	28.9	40	54.9	29.9	36.2	28.8	28.4	40	28.1	25.9	27.0	31.5	47.4	40.9	29.9	33.7	25.4	36.2	26.1	38.6	38A	42.0
40A	29.7	40A	56.6	30.8	37.3	29.6	29.2	40A	28.9	26.6	27.8	32.4	48.8	42.2	30.8	34.7	26.0	37.5	26.7	39.8	39	43.3
41	30.6	41	58.2	31.9	38.3	30.5	30.1	41	29.8	27.3	28.6	33.4	50.2	43.4	31.7	35.7	26.6	38.8	27.4	41.0	39A	45.0
41A	31.5	41A	59.9	32.8	39.2	31.4	31.1	41A	30.7	27.9	29.4	34.3	51.6	44.7	32.6	36.9	27.0	39.9	28.2	42.1	40	46.7
42	32.4	42	61.6	33.7	40.3	32.2	31.9	42	31.5	28.4	30.3	35.3	53.1	46.0	33.5	38.1	27.5	41.1	29.0	43.4	40A	48.0
42A	33.3	42A	63.3	34.8	41.2	33.1	32.8	42A	32.4	29.3	31.1	36.3	54.6	47.4	34.5	39.4	28.8	42.4	29.8	44.2	41	49.2
43	34.2	43	65.0	35.8	42.3	34.0	33.7	43	33.3	29.9	32.0	37.3	56.1	48.7	35.4	40.7	30.0	43.7	30.7	45.2	41A	50.4
43A	35.1	43A	66.8	36.9	43.4	34.9	34.6	43A	34.2	30.8	32.8	38.3	57.6	50.1	36.4	42.0	31.1	45.0	31.6	46.7	42	51.7
44	36.1	44	68.6	37.9	44.3	35.9	35.6	44	35.2	31.5	33.7	39.3	59.2	51.5	37.4	43.3	32.2	46.2	32.6	48.0	42A	53.0
44A	37.0	44A	70.4	38.8	45.4	36.9	36.5	44A	36.4	32.1	34.6	40.4	60.7	52.9	38.4	44.6	33.1	47.1	33.0	49.4	43	54.8
45	38.0	45	72.3	39.9	46.4	37.8	37.5	45	37.0	32.7	35.5	41.4	62.3	54.3	39.4	46.0	33.9	48.1	33.8	51.0	43A	56.3
45A	39.0	45A	74.1	40.8	47.3	38.7	38.5	45A	38.0	33.4	36.4	42.5	63.9	55.7	40.4	47.4	34.8	48.9	34.6	52.3	44	57.4
46	39.9	46	76.0	41.9	48.3	39.7	39.4	46	39.0	34.1	37.4	43.6	65.6	57.2	41.4	48.8	35.9	49.9	35.3	54.4	44A	58.0

HANDLOADER GUIDES FURNISHED FROM:

Alliant Techsystems
Route 114 • P.O. Box 6
Radford, VA 24141-0006
(800) 276-9337
www.alliantpowder.com

Ramshot
Western Powders
P.O. Box 158 • Yellow Stone Hill
Miles City, MT 59301
(406) 234-0422
www.ramshot.com

Hodgdon Powder Co., Inc.
6231 Robinson Street
Shawnee Mission, KS 66202
(913) 362-9455
www.hodgdon.com

Accurate Arms
Western Powders
P.O. Box 158 • Yellow Stone Hill
Miles City, MT 59301
(406) 234-0422
www.accuratepowder.com

IMR Powder Co.
6231 Robinson Street
Shawnee Mission, KS 66202
(913) 362-9455
www.imrpowder.com

Winchester Powder
6231 Robinson Street
Shawnee Mission, KS 66202
(913) 362-9455
www.wwpowder.com

COMPATIBLE COMPONENTS: Primers, wads, powder charge and weight of the shot charge must be in accordance with manufacturers specifications. Handloader guides are available from component manufacturers or possibly from your source of reloading components. We recommend that you use the data listed in the handloader guides. Because we have no control over the type, quality, or quantity of components used, we assume no responsibility relative to your reloading or finished shells.

	IMR							HODGDON											WINCHESTER				
BUSHING #	800-X	700-X	PB	SR7625	SR4756	4227	BUSHING #	HS6	HS7	H110	CLAYS	INTERNATIONAL CLAYS	UNIVERSAL CLAYS	LONGSHOT	TITEWAD	BUSHING #	LIL GUN	BUSHING #	SUPER HCP	WAA LITE	SUPER TARGET	296	SUPER FIELD
	6.4	6.0	7.5	9.2	9.3	11.8	10	12.6	13.4	14.2	6.3	7.2	8.3	11.8	7.9	7	12.1	10	10.5	7.5	7.9	13.7	10.9
	7.0	6.4	8.0	9.7	9.8	12.5	11	13.4	14.2	15.0	6.7	7.6	8.8	12.5	8.3	8	12.6	11	11.2	8.0	8.3	14.6	11.5
	7.6	6.8	8.4	10.2	10.3	13.3	12	14.2	15.0	15.8	7.0	8.1	9.3	13.3	8.8	9	13.1	12	11.8	8.4	8.8	15.4	12.2
	8.0	7.2	8.8	10.7	10.8	14.0	12A	15.0	15.8	16.7	7.4	8.6	9.9	14.0	9.3	10	13.6	12A	12.5	9.1	9.3	16.3	12.9
	8.6	7.6	9.3	11.2	11.3	14.8	13	15.8	16.7	17.6	7.8	9.1	10.4	14.8	9.8	11	14.5	13	13.3	9.8	9.8	17.2	13.6
	9.2	8.0	9.8	11.8	11.9	15.6	13A	16.7	17.6	18.5	8.2	9.6	11.0	15.6	10.4	12	15.3	13A	14.0	10.2	10.4	18.1	14.3
	9.8	8.4	10.3	12.3	12.4	16.4	14	17.6	18.5	19.5	8.6	10.1	11.6	16.4	10.9	12A	16.2	14	14.7	10.6	10.9	19.0	15.0
	10.4	8.9	10.8	12.8	13.0	17.2	15	18.5	19.5	20.4	9.1	10.6	12.2	17.2	11.4	13	17.1	15	15.5	11.2	11.4	20.0	15.8
	11.0	9.5	11.3	13.6	13.7	18.1	16	19.5	20.4	21.4	9.5	11.1	12.9	18.1	12.0	13A	18.0	16	16.2	11.8	12.0	21.0	16.6
	11.6	10.1	11.8	14.2	14.3	18.9	17	20.4	21.4	22.4	9.9	11.7	13.5	18.9	12.6	14	18.9	17	17.1	12.3	12.6	22.0	17.4
	12.2	10.7	12.4	14.9	14.9	19.8	18	21.4	22.4	23.4	10.4	12.3	14.2	19.8	13.2	15	19.9	18	18.0	12.7	13.2	23.0	18.2
	12.8	11.3	13.2	15.5	15.5	20.7	19	22.4	23.4	24.5	10.9	12.8	14.8	20.7	13.8	16	20.9	19	18.8	13.3	13.8	24.1	19.0
	13.5	11.9	13.6	16.3	16.2	21.7	20	23.4	24.5	25.6	11.4	13.4	15.5	21.7	14.4	17	21.9	20	19.6	13.9	14.4	25.1	19.9
	14.2	12.5	14.1	16.9	16.9	22.6	21	24.5	25.6	26.7	11.8	14.0	16.2	22.6	15.0	18	22.9	21	20.7	14.6	15.0	26.2	20.8
	15.0	13.1	14.7	17.6	17.7	23.6	22	25.6	26.7	27.8	12.3	14.6	17.0	23.6	15.7	19	24.0	22	21.7	15.4	15.7	27.4	21.6
	15.7	13.7	15.3	18.2	18.4	24.6	23	26.7	27.8	28.9	12.9	15.3	17.7	24.6	16.3	20	25.0	23	22.5	15.9	16.3	28.5	22.6
	16.3	14.3	15.9	18.9	19.1	25.6	24	27.8	28.9	30.1	13.4	15.9	18.4	25.6	17.0	21	26.1	24	23.2	16.5	17.0	29.7	23.5
	17.0	14.9	16.4	19.5	19.8	26.6	25	28.9	30.1	31.3	13.9	16.6	19.2	26.6	17.7	22	27.3	25	24.1	17.2	17.7	30.9	24.4
	17.5	15.6	17.1	20.4	20.7	27.7	26	30.1	31.3	32.5	14.5	17.2	19.7	27.7	18.4	23	28.4	26	25.0	17.9	18.4	32.1	25.4
	18.2	16.2	17.7	21.1	21.4	28.8	27	31.3	32.5	33.8	15.0	17.9	20.8	28.8	19.1	24	29.6	27	25.9	18.6	19.1	33.4	26.4
	18.8	16.9	18.4	21.9	22.1	29.9	28	32.5	33.8	35.0	15.6	18.6	21.6	29.9	19.8	25	30.8	28	26.7	19.3	19.8	34.6	27.4
	19.4	17.5	19.1	22.6	22.8	31.0	29	33.8	35.0	36.3	16.2	19.3	22.4	31.0	20.6	26	32.0	29	27.8	20.0	20.6	35.9	28.4
	20.2	18.2	19.8	23.5	23.7	32.1	30	35.0	36.3	37.6	16.7	20.0	23.3	32.1	21.3	27	33.3	30	28.8	20.7	21.3	37.3	29.5
	20.9	18.9	20.5	24.3	24.5	33.3	31	36.3	37.6	38.9	17.3	20.8	24.1	33.3	22.1	28	34.5	31	30.0	21.4	22.1	38.6	30.5
	21.6	19.9	21.3	25.4	25.6	34.5	32	37.6	38.9	40.3	17.9	21.5	25.0	34.5	22.9	29	35.8	32	31.2	22.1	22.9	40.0	31.6
	22.3	20.3	21.9	26.2	26.4	35.7	33	38.9	40.3	41.7	18.6	22.3	25.9	35.7	23.7	30	37.2	33	31.9	22.7	23.7	41.4	32.7
	23.1	21.0	22.7	27.1	27.3	36.9	34	40.3	41.7	43.1	19.2	23.0	26.8	36.9	24.5	31	38.5	34	32.6	23.3	24.5	42.8	33.8
	24.0	21.8	23.4	28.0	28.1	38.1	35	41.7	43.1	44.5	19.8	23.8	27.7	38.1	25.3	32	39.9	35	33.9	24.3	25.3	44.2	35.0
	24.8	22.5	24.2	29.0	29.2	39.4	36	43.1	44.5	45.9	20.5	24.6	28.6	39.4	26.2	33	41.3	36	35.2	25.4	26.2	45.7	36.1
	25.7	23.3	25.0	29.8	30.1	40.7	37	44.5	45.9	47.4	21.1	25.4	29.6	40.7	27.0	34	42.7	37	36.7	26.3	27.0	47.1	37.3
	26.5	24.1	25.8	30.9	31.2	42.0	38	45.9	47.4	48.9	21.8	26.3	30.6	42.0	27.9	35	44.1	38	38.3	27.3	27.9	48.7	38.5
	27.3	24.9	26.6	31.8	32.2	43.3	38A	47.4	48.9	50.4	22.5	27.1	31.5	43.3	28.8	36	45.6	38A	39.4	28.1	28.8	50.2	39.7
	28.1	25.7	27.3	32.7	33.1	44.6	39	48.9	50.4	52.0	23.2	28.0	32.5	44.6	29.7	37	47.0	39	40.6	28.9	29.7	51.7	40.9
	28.9	26.5	28.1	33.6	34.1	46.0	39A	50.4	52.0	53.5	23.9	28.8	33.5	46.0	30.6	38	48.6	39A	41.7	29.7	30.6	53.3	42.2
	29.7	27.3	29.0	34.6	35.1	47.4	40	52.0	53.5	55.1	24.6	29.7	34.5	47.4	31.5	38A	50.1	40	42.8	30.6	31.5	54.9	43.4
	30.4	28.1	29.7	35.5	36.0	48.8	40A	53.5	55.1	56.7	25.3	30.6	35.4	48.8	32.4	39	51.6	40A	44.1	31.6	32.4	56.6	44.7
	31.6	29.0	30.7	36.4	37.0	50.2	41	55.1	56.7	58.4	26.0	31.5	36.6	50.2	33.4	39A	53.2	41	45.5	32.7	33.4	58.2	46.0
	32.5	29.9	31.3	37.1	38.1	51.6	41A	56.7	58.4	60.0	26.8	32.4	37.7	51.6	34.3	40	54.8	41A	46.8	33.7	34.3	59.9	47.4
	33.5	30.7	31.9	37.9	39.0	53.1	42	58.4	60.0	61.7	27.5	33.3	38.8	53.1	35.3	40A	56.5	42	48.1	34.8	35.3	61.6	48.7
	34.8	31.6	32.5	38.9	40.0	54.6	42A	60.0	61.7	63.4	28.3	34.3	39.9	54.6	36.3	41	58.1	42A	49.6	35.6	36.3	63.3	50.1
	35.7	32.5	33.1	39.9	41.0	56.1	43	61.7	63.4	65.1	29.1	35.2	41.0	56.1	37.3	41A	59.8	43	51.1	36.5	37.3	65.0	51.5
	36.3	33.4	33.7	40.9	42.0	57.6	43A	63.4	65.1	66.9	29.9	36.2	42.1	57.6	38.3	42	61.5	43A	52.5	37.3	38.3	66.8	52.9
	36.9	34.4	34.3	42.0	42.9	59.2	44	65.1	66.9	68.6	30.7	37.2	43.2	59.2	39.3	42A	63.2	44	54.0	38.2	39.3	68.6	54.3
	37.5	35.6	34.9	43.0	43.8	60.7	44A	66.9	68.6	70.4	31.5	38.2	44.4	60.7	40.4	43	64.9	44A	55.3	39.2	40.4	70.4	55.7
	38.1	36.2	35.5	44.1	44.7	62.3	45	68.6	70.4	72.3	32.3	39.2	45.6	62.3	41.4	43A	66.7	45	56.6	40.2	41.4	72.3	57.2
	38.7	37.2	36.1	45.2	45.6	63.9	45A	70.4	72.3	74.1	33.1	40.2	46.8	63.9	42.5	44	68.5	45A	57.8	41.2	42.5	74.1	58.6
	40.3	38.2	36.7	46.4	46.5	65.6	46	72.3	74.1	75.1	33.9	41.2	48.0	65.6	43.6	44A	70.3	46	59.1	42.2	43.6	76.0	60.1

mount of powder
y bushings
ulated using
age reloaders.
sive reloaders
hrow a lesser
Please verify by
accurate scale.

POWDER CONVERSION TABLE

GRAINS PER LOAD	LOADS PER POUND	GRAINS PER LOAD	LOADS PER POUND	GRAINS PER LOAD	LOADS PER POUND	GRAINS PER LOAD	LOADS PER POUND	GRAINS PER LOAD	LOADS PER POUND	GRAINS PER LOAD	LOADS PER POUND
12	583	18	388	24	291	30	233	36	194	42	166
13	538	19	368	25	280	31	225	37	189	43	162
14	500	20	350	26	269	32	218	38	184		
15	466	21	333	27	259	33	212	39	179		
16	437	22	318	28	250	34	205	40	175		
17	411	23	304	29	241	35	200	41	170		

LET'S LOOK INSIDE A SHOTSHELL...

A. **CRIMP:** Seals all components tightly inside the hull. May be 6 or 8 point.

B. **HULL:** The outer case that holds the components. May be plastic or paper.

C. **SHOT:** Comes in variety of sizes and types for different shooting situations.

D. **SHOT CUP:** Plastic cup holds shot in the pattern as it leaves gun muzzle.

E. **WAD:** Confines powder for uniform ignition and separates powder from shot. (Most used is a one piece shot cup and wad called a "wad column".)

F. **POWDER CHARGE:** When ignited by primer, powder charge, burning at a controlled rate, generates gas pressure which, with the aid of a wad column, propels shot out of the gun barrel.

G. **PRIMER:** Gun firing pin detonates component in primer, which ignites the main powder charge.

H. **BASE:** Holds primer and securely anchors shell in gun breech. May be brass or steel.

I. **PRIMER POCKET:** Opening in metal base into which primer is inserted.

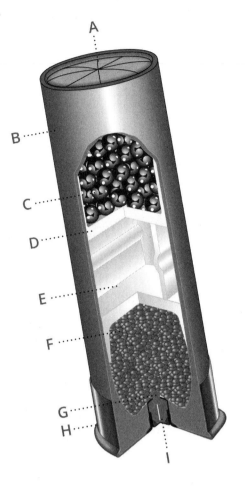

WADS

The wad is an important piece of the shotshell because it confines the powder for uniform ignition and separates the powder from the shot. Experienced shooters know the difference that quality components make and a good wad is an integral part of your reloading experience.

MEC's wads are made of high-grade material right here in the USA, and shooters appreciate the better shot pattern and reduced cleaning that is required. Our wads are also made with a one-piece column for easier reloading and the color-coded system makes it easy for everyone to select the right component for their shot weight.

If you want a quality shot with consistent pattern that will help you improve your shooting, look no further than MEC!

 MEC118T4 - 12GA 1 1/8OZ Tapered 4 Pedal Wad
Replacement: WAA12, CB1118-12, CBO118-12, Blue Duster

MEC100T4 - 12GA 1OZ Tapered 4 Pedal Wad
Replacement: WAASL12, CB1100-12, Green Buste

 MEC118S8 - 12GA 1 1/8OZ Straight Hull Wad
Replacement: 12S3, CB2118-12, DRF3

 MEC100S4 - 12GA 1OZ Straight Hull Wad
Replacement: 12S0, CB2100-12

 MEC118T8 - 12GA 1 1/8OZ Tapered 8 Pedal Wad
Replacement: Remington Figure 8, CB3118-12A, DRRF8

MEC78T4 - 12GA 7/8OZ Tapered 4 Pedal Wad
Replacement: WAA12L, CB0178-12, XXL Pink

 MEC118BIOT4 - 12GA 1 1/8OZ OXO-BIO Tapered 4 Pedal Wad
Replacement: WAA12, MEC118T4, CB1118-12, CBO118-12, Blue Duster

 MEC100BIOT4 - 12GA 1O OXO-BIO Tapered 4 Ped
Replacement: WAA12SL MEC100T4, CB1100-12, Green Duster

LET'S START RELOADING

On the next few pages you will find a general description of the steps involved in shotshell reloading. This discussion is not intended as a substitute for the instructions provided with your particular reloading equipment. Always read carefully the instructions provided by the manufacturer of your reloader.

EXAMINE THE HULL - The first step in reloading is to inspect your empty hulls to see that they are clean and dry, have no split ends, no cracked or split metal bases, and have no other visible damage. Also, be sure that all hulls have the same capacity and crimp (6 or 8 point). Don't mix paper and plastics hulls.

DEPRIME - With manual reloading tools, the spent primer is removed with a punch and hammer. With a semi-automatic reloader the initial pull of the handle pushes out the spent primer. On some reloaders, such as the MEC 600 Jr. Mark V, Sizemaster, 8567 Grabber and 9000 Series, this same pull of the handle resizes the metal base.

RESIZING - Almost all shotshell heads are made of brass or steel. Anytime one of these is fired in any gun, the head tends to expand to the size of the chamber in which it is fired. If the shell is continually fired in the same gun, chances are you would never have to resize, but if fired shells are from a
erent gun you most likely will have to resize the metal. The most common resizing method is to force
ardened steel ring of the proper diameter down over the metal base, forcing it back to original size.
noted earlier, the newest method of resizing is the Power Ring collet resizer found only on the MEC
master, Grabber, and the 9000 Series models. Advantages of this method are that you never scratch

the metal base, you don't increase the rim diameter, and you don't have to force the resized base out of a resizing ring (the collet fingers open so the shell may be freely removed). Although hull sides usually do not require resizing, you will sometimes find that paper hulls are oversize. This is because they swell when they absorb moisture. They must be brought back to size by drying them out before reloading.

REPRIMING - After the spent primer has been removed, a new primer must be inserted in the primer pocket. With a manual tool, this must be done by hand. With most semi-automatic reloaders, a pull of the handle forces the shell down over the new primer. Not all primers are interchangeable. Be sure the primers you are using are compatible with the other components you are using.

CHARGING WITH POWDER - Your next step is to put powder into the empty sh[ell]. There are several ways to measure powder. The least accurate is hand dipping with a manual reloading tool. Next comes the standard volumetric measure. T[he] most accurate method is weighing each charge. Hand dipping relies complete[ly] on the ability of the operator to measure uniform charges and pour the powd[er] without spilling. The volumetric measure common to all MEC and most other semi-automatic reloaders consists of a bar containing a hole of a given volum[e]. Powder falls into the hole, and is then dropped into the hull. This is the quicke[st] method of measuring powder and is also much more accurate than hand dip[ping]. The disadvantage is that it measures volume, which may cause variations in the load due to differences in various powder densities. Undue agitation of th[e] reloader also causes the powder to compact, resulting in heavier powder load[s]. By following your instruction manual you should always get uniform loads an[d]

good performance. Of course, weighing each individual charge is the most accurate method. Obviously, it is also the slowest of the three methods. We do recommend, however, that when reloading you periodically check your charges on an accurate powder scale.

INSERTING THE WAD COLUMN - Regardless of what system of reloading you use, the wad must be handled manually. The modern one-piece wad column is the most commonly used. You must, of course, use only the wad column of the proper height to match your other components.

ADDING THE SHOT - The last item to be added to the shell is the shot. This can be done several way[s]. With a manual reloader the shot must be carefully dipped, measured, and poured (without spilling). Most semi-automatic reloaders use a built-in volumetric measure or "charge bar". This bar contains two holes: one for powder (discussed above) and one for shot.

THE CHARGE BARS on all MEC reloaders are equipped with a soft insert to help eliminate shearing when larger shot sizes and hard lead shot are used.

CRIMPING THE SHELL - After all the new components have been inserted in the shell, the last operation is to close the mouth of the shell. Almost all modern reloaders seal the shell with a "star" [or] folded crimp. The crimp usually takes from two to four operations. In most cases the first operation starts the crimp. Plastic hulls may require a 6 or 8 point "crimp starter", depending on the number o[f] folds in the original hull. Paper cases are usually closed with a 6 point crimp. Usually, paper cases ar[e]

best closed with a smooth cone to start the crimp. With most MEC reloaders, closing the hull is a two-step operation. First, a self-aligning "crimp starter" partially closes the hull, following the original folds of the shell. The shell is then tightly closed with a patented cam-actuated crimping die.

Wad too short
or too little
powder or shot

Wad too long
or too much
powder or shot

Proper crimp - correc[t]
wad, & powder and
shot charges*

* Note that a properly crimped shell has a slight inward taper similar to original factory loads.

HOW TO SELECT COMPONENTS

SHOT SIZES
(Shown Actual Size)

Lead Shot		Buckshot	
No.	Dia.	No.	Dia.
9	.08"	4	.24"
8½	.085"		
8	.09"	3	.25"
7½	.095"		
7	.10"	1	.30"
6	.11"		
5	.12"		
4	.13"	0	.32"
2	.15"		
Air Rifle	.175"	00	.33"
BB	.18"		

A shotshell is made up of several different components. There are many different variations of each component. Packed with every MEC reloader are brochures supplied by leading component manufacturers. A study of this literature will show you numerous combinations of primer, powder charge, and the wad and shot you should use with each empty hull, for waterfowl, small game, trap, skeet, or sporting clays. Each combination of components has been carefully tested by ballistic experts for maximum effectiveness and safety. Experimenting with combinations that are not recommended by a component manufacturer is extremely dangerous!

CHOOSING THE HULL: Proper choice of empty hulls is one of the most important choices you must make to keep your reloading simple. The problems encountered by trying to use any and all of the hulls you may find are usually quite discouraging. Not all hulls have the same capacity. Not all hulls have the same crimp. Each time that you use a hull with a different capacity (usually caused by different base wad height) you must assemble a different set of components to properly fill this case. We recommend that when starting to reload, you choose the most popular of the low brass trap, skeet, or sporting clays hulls in your area and choose a set of components to fit this hull. Usually, these hulls can be purchased for a nominal amount, and when you consider that a modern plastic case can be reloaded many times, it will add very little to the cost of your reloads. We are not recommending that you throw away all the non-standard hulls that you have but are advising you keep it simple until you have gained the experience necessary to assemble the different components. With the proper choice of components, all your loads from the heaviest magnum down to the lightest skeet, trap, or sporting clays load may be loaded in the same low brass hull.

THE SHOT: There are two kinds of shot – lead and non-toxic. Warning: Although lead and non-toxic shot are both easy to reload, it is absolutely essential that instructions for each are followed to the letter. For instance, never, ever substitute non-toxic shot for lead shot. This could result in chamber pressure high enough to burst the gun causing injury or death to the shooter or bystander. Wads that work fine with lead shot will not work with some non-toxic shot. When loading non-toxic shot, it is important that proper components are used and according to directions furnished by the manufacturer. As the size of the shot increases, fewer pellets can be loaded into the hull. The smaller sizes are used for trap, skeet, and sporting clays, doves, small game, etc. The larger shot sizes are for heavier game—ducks, geese, turkey, etc.

SELECTING THE RIGHT WAD: The wad is the part of the shotshell between the powder and the shot. A tight seal permits the expanding gas from the burning powder to push the shot column out of the gun barrel with maximum velocity. Modern "wad columns" combine both the shot cup and the wad in one piece. These one-piece wad columns are the easiest to reload, and therefore are the most popular. Use only the specific wad column recommended for the other components you are using.

RCBS - "Reloading a Cartridge Step by Step"

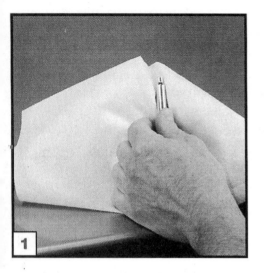
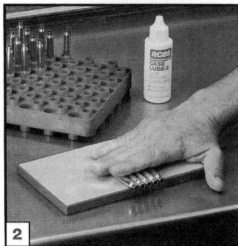
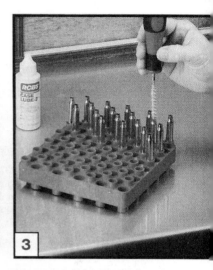
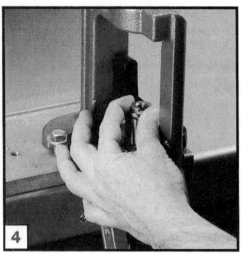

Follow this step-by-step guide using the tools from the Rock Chuck Supreme Master Reloading Kit and you'll soon be reloading like a

1. Clean and Check

Using a soft cloth, wipe each case clean to prevent dirt from scratching the case and the sizing die. Inspect the case for anything that would keep it from being safely reloaded, such as split case mouths, case head separations, excessive bulges and other case defects. Any case found to be defective should be thrown away.

2. Lubricate the Cases (Part 1)

Because of the force involved, you'll need to lubricate the cases before they go into a sizer die. Spread some lube on the pad and lubricate the body of the case. Make sure not to lube the neck of your cases as this can cause dents. If you're using a carbide sizer die for reloading straight-wall pistol cases, you can eliminate this step. The carbide ring in the sizer die is so smooth that cases simply can't get stuck in the die.

3. Lubricate the Cases (Part 2)

Clean dirt and powder residue from inside case necks and simultaneously add a light coating of case lube with a case neck brush. This will reduce the sizing effort and prevent excess working of the brass. Roll the brush across the after every three or four cases for just the right amount.

4. Install the Shell Holder

Snap a shell holder into the press ram with a slight twisting motion. holder will securely grip the head of the cartridge case. Check out catalog or see your local dealer for help in selecting the correct shell holde Reference Table on page 11 lists shell holder numbers for our top 30 cali

5. Install the Sizer Die

Thread the sizer die into the press until the die touches the shell ho the ram is at the top of the press stroke. Raise the press handle and tu down another one-eighth to one-quarter of a turn and set the large lo you're using a carbide sizer die, leave a 1/16" gap between the bottom and the shell holder.

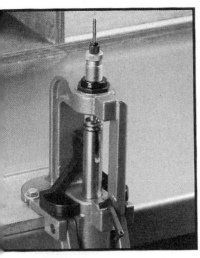
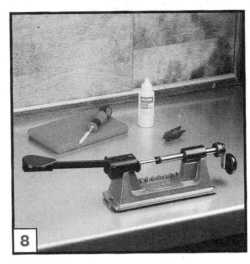
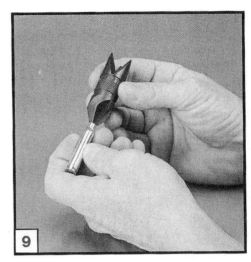

sert the Case
press handle in the up position, slide a case into the shell holder.

ze the Case
ut firmly lower the press handle all the way to the bottom and run the
the way into the sizer die. This will size the case to the proper dimension
h the fired primer out of the case. Next, raise the press handle. This will
e case and expand the case mouth (on bottle-neck cartridges), correctly
he case neck diameter to hold the bullet tightly.

eck the Case Length and Trim if Necessary
everal firings, cases sometimes stretch and become longer
ie specified maximum length. These cases must be trimmed
w for proper chambering and for safety reasons. The
works like a small lathe and can be used to trim most cases up
45-caliber. Check the Speer Reloading Manual for maximum case
nd trim length.

iamfer and Deburr
that have been trimmed need to also be chamfered and
d. This will remove any burrs left on the case mouth after trimming

and will allow a new bullet to be easily seated into the case. Insert the pointed
end of the Deburring Tool into the case to remove burrs and chamfer the case
mouth interior. Fit the other end over the case mouth to remove exterior burrs.

10. Expand the Case Mouth (applies only to straight wall cases)
Because of their design, straight-wall cases need to be expanded in a separate
expander die. Install the expander die in the press, place a sized case in the
shell holder and run it into the die. The expander should be adjusted so the case
mouth is belled outward just enough to accept the new bullet.

11. Prime the Case (Part 1)
Use the Primer Tray—2 for fast, easy primer handling. To use, first scatter primers
onto the grooved surface of the tray. Then, shake the tray horizontally until all the
primers are positioned anvil side up.

12. Prime the Case (Part 2)
Place a fresh primer, anvil side up, into the cup of the primer arm and insert a
case into the shell holder.

STEPS 13-23 CONTINUED ON NEXT TWO PAGES.

RCBS -"Reloading a Cartridge Step by Step"

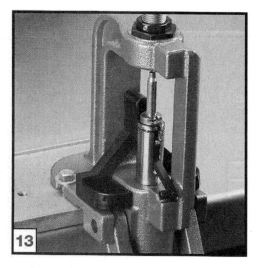

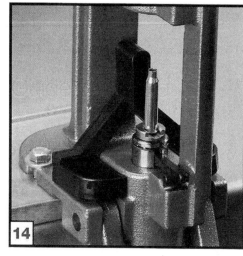

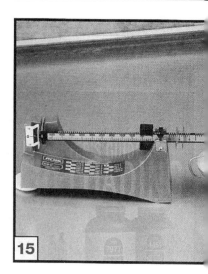

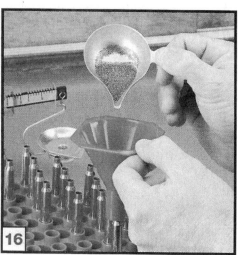

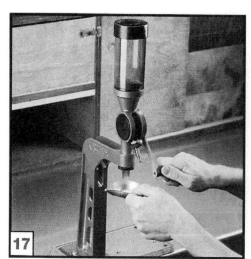

13. Prime the Case (Part 3)
Lower the handle and flip the primer arm into the slot in the shell holder ram.

14. Prime the Case (Part 4)
Now, gently and slowly raise the press handle. As the case is drawn out of the die it will be lowered onto the fresh primer which will be seated into the primer pocket. Push the handle all the way up. Inspect the primer to make sure it is properly seated. In order to gain optimum primer sensitivity, the primer must be seated firmly to the bottom of the primer pocket.

Tip for Priming the Case
For a faster way to prime cases, use the Hand Priming Tool that is included with your Rock Chucker Supreme Reloading Kit or purchase separately the Rock Chucker Supreme Auto Prime. Primers drop one at a time into the primer arm on the press.

15. Powder Charging (Part 1)
Consult the Speer Reloading Manual to learn what kind of powder, a how much is recommended to reload your cartridge. Then v recommended charge on your scale.

16. Powder Charging (Part 2)
After accurately weighing the powder charge, pour it into the case powder funnel.

17. Powder Charging (Part 3)
You can dispense a precise charge, without weighing every charge o Fill the measure with powder and dispense several charges to establis settle the powder in the hopper. Return this powder to the hopper. reloading scale to adjust the powder measure. Weigh every charge ur consecutive charges show the desired weight. Re-check the weight a 10 cases.

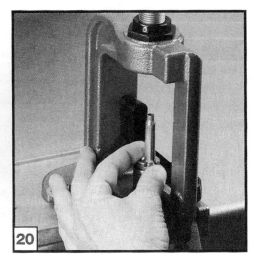

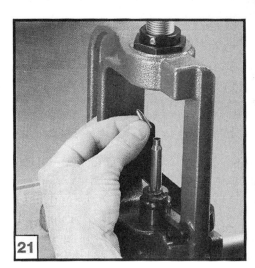

Bullet Seating (Part 1)
the seater die a few turns into the press. Put a case in the shell holder
ver the press handle, running the ram with the case to the top of the
roke. Turn the die body down until it stops. The crimp shoulder in the die
pressing against the top of the case mouth. Back the die out one turn,
the crimp shoulder above the case mouth. Secure the die in position with
lock ring.

Bullet Seating (Part 2)
nscrew the seater plug enough to keep the bullet from being seated
ply.

Bullet Seating (Part 3)
e handle in the up position, insert a properly primed and charged case
shell holder.

21. Bullet Seating (Part 4)
Take a bullet and hold it over the case mouth with one hand while
you lower the press handle with the other, easing the case and
bullet up into the die. After raising the handle, note the seating depth of the
loaded round. If the bullet needs to be seated deeper into the case, turn the
seater plug down.

22. Bullet Seating (Part 5)
Run the loaded round back up into the die, raise the press handle and check
the seating depth again. A few more adjustments may be needed for the proper
bullet seating depth; then, you simply tighten the small seater plug lock ring.

See our reloading die instructions for more detailed information about bullet
seating and crimping.

23. That's It!
Your first reloaded cartridge is ready to be fired. Of course, we've described only
one case going through all the reloading steps. When actually reloading, you'd
take a batch of cases through each operation before moving on to the next step.

SHOTSHELL RELOADING:
COMPONENTS

The basic components for a shotshell aren't difficult to assemble. A hull needs to be re-shaped, a new primer installed, the hull must be charged with powder, a wad and shot installed, and the end crimped.

As reloaders, we can only reuse the hull, all other components must be new. The Winchester "AA" hull has become an industry standard, being able to be reused many times. However, there are many different manufacturers of quality hulls, and like shotshell wads, the choice is up to you. I'll direct you to the metallic reloading section for a list of applicable shotgun powders; they are all listed there. Rather than compile a list of boring part numbers, let's highlight the companies that produce shotshell components and their best products!

Shotshell Hulls

Fiocchi

The famous Italian company produces a line of component hulls in 12, 16, 20 and 28 gauge. They will accept both six and eight-point crimping.

BPI

BPI offers a lineup of primed shotshell hulls in 12, 16, 20 and 28 gauges, as well as .410 bore.

Cheddite

A full selection of primed hulls in 10, 12, 16, 20, and 28 gauges and .410 bore, as well as 12 gauge 2-3/4" paper hulls, for the vintage enthusiast.

Magtech

If you're into the military-style full brass shotshells, Magtech provides a valuable resource. All brass construction, in 12, 16, 20, 24 (yes, that's right!), 28 and 32 gauges, as well as .410 bore.

209 Shotshell Primers

The 209 primer is the spark plug of any good shotshell. They are available from the following companies: Fiocchi, Winchester, Remington, Federal and CCI (CCI also offers the 209M Magnum Shotshell primer.

209 Primers

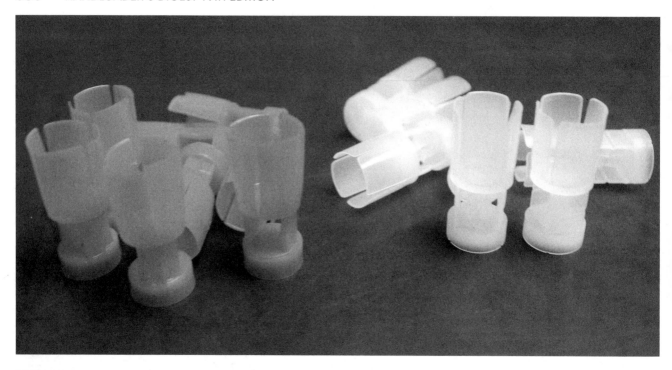

Wads

The shotgun wad holds the payload of shot, and can help control the shape of your shot pattern, as well as protect the shot from becoming deformed

[SC 03 - Wads]

Federal

The Champion wad from Federal is a proven winner. Available in different shot sizes for 12, 20, and 28 gauge and ,410 bore.

Winchester

Winchester has long been a leader in the shotshell game, and continues to provide wads in 12, 20, and gauges as well as .410 bore.

Remington

Big Green offers a compliment of wads in 10, 12, 16, 20 and 28 gauge, and .410 bore.

BPI

A rather extensive lineup of shotshell wads, well researched and well designed. If you'd really like to cook up something different, take a look at the BPI selection of wads. Available in 10, 12, 16, 20, 28 and 32 gauges and ,410 bore.

Claybuster

A company dedicated to precision component wads. Numerous designs in 12, 20 and 28 ga, and ,410 bore.

Downrange Technologies

Offering numerous designs in 12, and 20 ga, and ,410 bore. Downrange makes some wads that work especially well with 12 gauge 00 buckshot loads.

Shot

The shot column is the only part of the equation that touches the intended target, so you want to use the best you can.

Lawrence Brand Shot

Lawrence is a familiar name in the lead shot industry, offering chilled lead shot, magnum lead shot, copper-plated lead shot and hard cast buckshot, in addition to #2 and BB steel shot.

Eagle Shot

Offering chilled lead shot, magnum lead shot, nickel-plated lead shot, copper-plated lead shot, and nickel-plated lead buckshot. Eagle has a type and size of shot for all your reloading needs.

Hornady

Hornady offers five-pound boxes of 000, 00 and #4 buckshot in component form.

A Compendium of Contacts:
Your Electronic Rolodex

Hodgdon Powder
www.hodgdon.com
913-362-9455

IMR Powder
www.imrpowder.com
913-362-9455

Winchester Powder
www.wwpowder.com
913-362-9455

Alliant Powder
www.alliantpowder.com
800-256-8685

Ramshot Powder
www.ramshot.com
406-234-0422

Accurate Powder
www.accuratepowder.com
406-234-0422

VihtaVuori Powder
www.vihtavuori-lapua.com
800-683-0464

American Pioneer Powder
www.americanpioneerpowder.com
888-756-7693

Precision Ballistics
www.precisionballisticsllc.com
702-331-1337

MTM Molded Products
www.mtmcase.gard.com
937-890-7461

CCI Primers
www.cci-ammunition.com
800-256-8685

Rainier Ballistics
www.rainierballistics.com
800-638-8722

Cutting Edge Bullets
www.sitecuttingedgebullets.com
814-345-6690

Berger Bullets
www.bergerbullets.com
714-441-7200

Lee Precision
www.leeprecision.com
262-673-3075

Hornady
(Bullets and Reloading)
www.hornady.com
800-338-3220

Lyman Products
www.lymanproducts.com
800-22LYMAN

RCBS
www.rcbs.com
800-533-5000

Redding Reloading
www.redding-reloading.com
607-753-3331

Whidden Gun Works
www.whiddengunworks.net
229-686-1911

Forster Products
www.forsterproducts.com
815-493-6360

Dillon Precision Products
www.dillonprecision.com
800-762-3845

Swift Bullet Company
www.swiftbullets.com
785-754-3959

Barnes Bullets
www.barnesbullets.com
435-856-1000

Sierra Bullets
www.sierrabullets.com
888-223-3006

North Fork Technologies
www.northforkbullets.com
541-929-4424

Nosler Bullets
www.nosler.com
800-285-3701

Speer Bullets
www.speer-bullets.com
800-256-8685

Remington Reloading Components
www.remington.com
800-243-9700

Downrange Manufacturing
www.downrangemfg.com
(402) 463-3415

Winchester
(Bullets and Brass)
www.winchester.com
No phone available

Woodleigh Bullets
www.woodleighbullets.com.au
+61 3 5457 2226

Federal Premium
www.federalpremium.com
800-379-1732

Norma USA
www.norma-usa.com

Lapua
www.lapua.com
800-683-0464

Lazzeroni Arms
www.lazzeroni.com
888-492-7247

TulAmmo
www.tulammousa.com
888-317-5810

MagTech Ammunition
www.magtechammunition.com
800-466-7191

Fiocchi
www.fiocchiusa.com

Bullseye Camera Systems, LLC
www.bullseyecamera.com
541-357-7035

Lawrence Brand Lead Shot
www.lawrencebrandshot.com
(866) 618-7468

MEC
(Mayville Engineering Company, Inc.)
www.mecshootingsports.com
(800) 797-4632

Quality Cartridge
www.qual-cart.com
(301) 373-3719

Jamison International
www.custombrassandbullets.com
(928) 387-2222

Buffalo Arms
www.buffaloarms.com
(208) 263-6953

Starline
www.starlinebrass.com
(800) 280-6660

Falcon Bullets
www.falconbullets.com
(931) 339-7010

Berry's Manufacturing
www.berrysmfg.com
(800) 269-7373

Oregon Trail Bullet Company
www.oregontrailbullet.com
(800) 811-0548

Hawk Precision Bullets
www.hawkbullets.com
(856) 299-2800

Sinclair Internantional
www.sinclairintl.com
(800) 741-0015

Glossary:

Some real-world definitions of common reloading terms

Ballistic Coefficient (B.C.): the measure of a bullet's ability to resist the effect of air drag. The number is derived from highly complex mathematical formula, involving S.D. and a direct comparison of shape to a standard model of bullet, and is also represented by a three digit decimal. The higher the B.C. is, the better the bullet can "slip" through air. B.C. is a debatable figure, and is dependent upon velocity. If the physics intrigues you, have at it, but for our purposes it is only necessary to know that higher B.C bullets will resist wind drift better and have a much flatter trajectory than low B.C. bullets.

Brass: a common term for cartridge cases. When someone says "I picked up some brass for my .45ACP...", it means they have acquired cases for the firearm.

C.O.L.: Short for Cartridge Overall Length. It is a standardized measurement of the long axis of a loaded cartridge, represented by inches and decimal portions of an inch. There are maximum dimensions allowed by SAAMI, and for the handloader it is important to adhere to these dimensions.

Decapping: the act of removing a primer. Common primers are a derivation of percussion caps, and the term has carried over.

Feet Per Second: abbreviated fps, or FPS, it is a measure of a bullet's velocity. Just like your vehicle speed in miles per hour, bullet velocities are discussed in how many feet the bullet travels per second of time.

Flash Hole: The centrally drilled hole in the case web, which allows the spark of the primer to reach the powder charge.

Grains: a unit of weight, used to measure both powder and bullets. There are 7,000 grains in one pound.

Headspace: the distance between the face of the bolt, breech or cylinder and that part of the chamber which stops the forward motion of the cartridge case. In the case of a rimmed cartridge, like the .30-30 WCF or .38 special, the rim serves to headspace the cartridge.
In a rimless cartridge, two methods are usually employed: most headspace off the shoulder, like the .308 Winchester or .223 Remington; and a few headspace off the case mouth, like the .45ACP or .450 Bushmaster. In the belted magnum case, the original design used the belt for headspacing. This still holds true in the .375 Holland & Hol-

land Magnum and the .300 Holland & Holland Magnum. They have a minimal, sloping shoulder, which isn't pronounced enough to use for accurate headspacing. The more modern belted magnums, while still retaining the belt of the H&H cases, usually headspace on the shoulder of the case. The .300 Winchester Magnum, 7mm Remington Magnum and .338 Winchester Magnum are all examples of this situation.

Headspacing is very important to a firearm. If it is too short, the cartridges will not fit properly. If it is too long, dangerous gases can escape upon firing. There are several good headspace gauges available, and if there's any question you should invest in one for your firearm.

Heavy-for-caliber: a term used to describe the longer bullets for a given diameter. In any caliber, the bullet diameter must remain constant, so for a bullet to have more weight, it must be made of a constant diameter, yet made longer.

MOA or Minute of angle: An arc defined as 1/60th of a degree. Used in shooting terms to represent a group of shots with an extreme spread no greater than the sine of one minute of angle at the particular distance to the target. At 100 yards (a common shooting distance) one MOA = 1.04".

Ogive: The curved nose section of a bullet. Some are hemispherical, some based on secant or tangent curves. Almost all bullets have some sort of an ogive, save the wadcutters and semi-wadcutters.

Sectional density (S.D.): the ratio of a bullet's mass to its cross sectional area (caliber). Represented by a three digit decimal, the higher the S.D. is, the heavier the bullet is. The number is derived by dividing the weight of the bullet (in pounds) by the bullet diameter squared. For example, a .375" diameter 300-grain bullet will have a S.D. of 0.304. Here's the math: 300 grains/7,000 (the number of grains in a pound) = 0.042857. Square the bullet diameter (0.375 x 0.375) to get 0.140625. Divide the first number (0.042857) by the second (0.140625) to arrive at a Sectional Density of 0.304

Softpoint: a jacketed bullet with an area of exposed lead at the nose.

Solid: a bullet designed for the largest game animals, originally designed as a copper-clad steel jacketed bullet with a lead core, and no exposed lead at the nose. Today they are often constructed as a homogenous metal alloy.

"Understanding Ballistics"

By Philip P. Massaro

BOOK EXCERPT: DANGEROUS GAME RIFLES

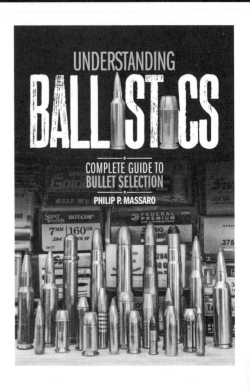

When we speak of dangerous game, my ears prick up like a spaniel at the mention of a car ride. The mere fact that the entire hunt could end in loss of limb (or worse, life) is not only exciting, but defines the 'man v. nature' premise of so many adventure stories. Grizzly bears, with jowls flapping and teeth bared, lions roaring in the predawn darkness, the manner in which a leopard seemingly floats into a baited tree, the Cape buffalo, whose nickname "Black Death" is well deserved, and the mighty African elephant, weight measured in tons: these animals both frighten and excite.

It takes a hunter with great confidence in his or her field skills to pursue these creatures, and a healthy dose of respect for the possible outcome. This category of game animal certainly warrants the best hunting gear available, but no hand-rubbed walnut stock or fancy engraving has ever made the difference in life or death; it is the bullet - and only the bullet - that decides in whose favor the scales will tip.

Cartridges for this type of game extend from the 6.5mm and .270 class, for leopard alone, through the .300 and .338s for grizzly bears, and then from the 9.3mms well up into the .500s and above, for lion, buffalo and elephant. Rather than handle the idea by caliber, let's look at suitable bullets for each game animal, with some reasons for the recommendation.

Leopard: The Golden-Spotted Wraith

The lightest of the dangerous cats, the leopard, does not require a huge bore to kill effectively. I've touched on the idea in the medium game chapter, but I believe some more light needs to be shed on the topic. A leopard is no tougher than any deer, and the same calibers and bullets that perform well on deer will effectively kill a leopard, with one little asterisk: Once a leopard is wounded, the entire game changes. They will usually seek ridiculously thick cover, and charges from wounded leopards are the stuff of nightmares.

That said, I'd pick your favorite deer bullet (and rifle), make sure you have the accuracy necessary to put that bullet exactly where your Professional Hunter tells you to, and practice, practice, practice.

The one area that I think is important is the sectional density of the bullet. Although you can kill a leopard cleanly with a light-for-caliber bullet, I like things on the heavy side of the scale, to absolutely guarantee destruction of the vitals. For example, I've cleanly killed deer with 125-grain Nosler Ballistic Tips from my little .308 Winchester, but I wouldn't venture across the pond with that load and a leopard in mind. I would however, do so with 165-grain Ballistic Tips, and quite confidently I might add.

Bullets like the Sierra Game King hollowpoint boat-tail, available in sensible weights in 6.5, .270, 7mm and .308, would make a great leopard bullet. The jacket is thickened to give good weight retention, but the hydrostatic shock from the expansion of the hollowpoint is plenty sufficient to switch the nervous system of Mr.

Spots to the 'off' position. Check with the PH about caliber minimums; Tanzania for example requires a minimum of .375" diameter to hunt any dangerous game, yet Zimbabwe allows anything above .270" diameter.

The traditional softpoints, like a Hornady InterLock or Remington Core-Lokt, if of suitable weight, can make for a good leopard bullet, but in the cartridges that deliver a higher-than-normal impact velocity, there can be excessive hide damage. Now, a taxidermist can do wonderful things, but we should avoid putting softball sized holes in the leopard skin if we can help it.

Some of the heavier cup-and-core bullets will fit the bill perfectly, and there are no flies on a good round-nose. You want good expansion for hydraulic shock, but not so much that penetration suffers.

A lineup of expanded .30-'06 bullets, showing different levels of expansion and weight retention.

In a recent trip to the Federal Premium factory in Anoka, Minnesota, I had the opportunity to punch some good .30-'06 bullets into blocks of ballistic gelatin, to get a feel for the balance of expansion and penetration, and this demonstrates well what we're after in a leopard bullet. The Nosler Partition, after almost 70 years, proved to me in the lab what I'd always found in the field: that the softer nose section would open like a true softpoint and the rear core hung together for good penetration.

The Trophy Bonded Tipped gave great performance as well. It provided a huge wound channel and the bullet expanded nicely, to over two times the original diameter, while retaining weight into the 80 percent

range. The Trophy Copper gave similar performance, with its copper petals well expanded, while giving a large wound channel.

Federal's 150-grain softpoint did exactly what I thought it would: radical expansion with a much lower retained weight. Now, that bullet didn't 'fail' because it expanded so much, but it might make a bit

more of a mess than would a 165 or 180-grain soft-point.

Oh, and by the way, when folks like Sierra warn us hunters not to shoot big game with match-grade bullets, they mean it. The 168 Match Kings broke to pieces in the gel, and pieces of jacket and core went all over the place, sending a shower of glass down from the ceiling. Federal, I'm sorry, and I'll replace that fluorescent light bulb.

The goal with a leopard is to have a rifle that you shoot the most accurately, as shot placement is paramount. Whether it's a 7mm Remington Magnum, .30-'06 Springfield, or some variety of .300 Magnum, putting that bullet into the vitals has never been more important.

Should you want a good leopard bullet for your 9.3mm, .375 or .416, stay away from the premium bullets altogether, and opt instead for a good cup-and-core bullet for more rapid expansion. The premiums will often punch a caliber-sized hole through the cat, which will kill him in the end, but in the meantime he may enjoy his last minutes on earth gnawing upon your person. In the 9.3mm cases, I like the Hornady 286-grain InterLock.

The Sierra 250-grain boat-tail is a good choice in .375 bore, as is the Hornady InterLock 270-grain spitzer and the 300-grain InterLock roundnose. Even a Remington Core-Lokt or Winchester Power Point will do the job well; you're after expansion here, yet you can feel confident knowing a bullet of that size and weight will clearly penetrate the entire leopard and ruin his day quickly. Same goes for the .416s and .404s: look for a classic cup-and-core roundnose or soft-point spitzer to give the hydrostatic shock that you're after, and if you put that bullet through the vitals your cat will be in the salt.

Lion: Teeth And Muscle Covered In Tawny Fur

The largest of African cats is a totally different character than the leopard, weighing two to three times that of that spotted ninja. They also have canine teeth that can crush your skull with one bite. They are an apex predator, and have intrigued mankind from the dawn of history. Regal, brutal, terrible, magnificent, triumphant; the lion has been the stuff of wondrous tales and family crests for thousands of years.

The hunting of lion is now a political hotbed, but if you're well-heeled enough to book a safari for Simba, bullet choice is paramount. Caliber-wise, the lion demands a heavy bullet, though many have been taken (with varying degrees of success) with 6.5mm, 7mm and .30-caliber bullets. Most African countries prohibit the use of bore diameters less than .375", and that makes much sense, but some permit the use of lesser calibers. The tough, corded muscles that a lion is built of will give a bullet of lighter weight and caliber a run for its money, but there are sensible choices.

I think the 9.3mm cartridges are on par with the .375s, when it comes to good lion medicine. They can use bullets of .366" diameter from 250 to 300 grains, with the 286-grain being a good blend of speed and bullet weight. There are many 9.3s, from the 9.3x62mm and 9.3x64mm, to the .370 Sako Magnum, to the venerable and relatively sedate 9.3x74R designed for single shots and double rifles.

Were I pursuing Panthera Leo with a 9.3, I'd probably opt for the 9.3x62 in a handy rifle, or the newer .370 Sako, for its speed and hydraulic shock. Hornady's Dangerous Game series offers a 9.3x62 load featuring the 286-grain InterLock spitzer at a muzzle velocity of 2,360 fps. That bullet is heavy enough to penetrate, yet the cup-and-core design will expand very well to create a nasty wound channel.

The Federal Premium Safari line loads the .370 Sako Magnum with the 286-grain Barnes TSX and Swift A-Frame. This is one instance where I think the Swift A-Frame is a bit too good, or better put, there isn't enough lion to get that bullet to expand well. Penetration with an A-Frame is never an issue, especially at the relatively short distances at which lions are hunted. I would opt for the hollowpoint TSX in the factory load, delivered at 2,550 fps, which should open up and switch that lion to the off position.

The long, lean 9.3x74 operates at the same muzzle velocity as the 9.3x62, so the same bullets can be recommended. Were I handloading for any one of the 9.3mm for a lion hunt, I'd opt for the 250-grain North-Fork semi-spitzer, as the higher velocity would open the bullet up a bit more, creating a larger wound channel.

The .375 Holland & Holland Magnum, pushing a 300-grain bullet at 2,550 fps, is just about the perfect lion rifle. Like the leopard, you'll want a stout bullet, but not too tough. Bullet profile really doesn't matter here, as the shots on lion are generally over bait, and mostly at less than 100 paces. I like the 270 and 300-grain .375s, like the Sierra 300-grain Game King, with a tough jacket, but still a nose soft enough to give good expansion.

Norma loads the 300-grain Oryx bullet, which should prove to be a fantastic lion load. Hornady's Superformance .375 H&H load is built around the

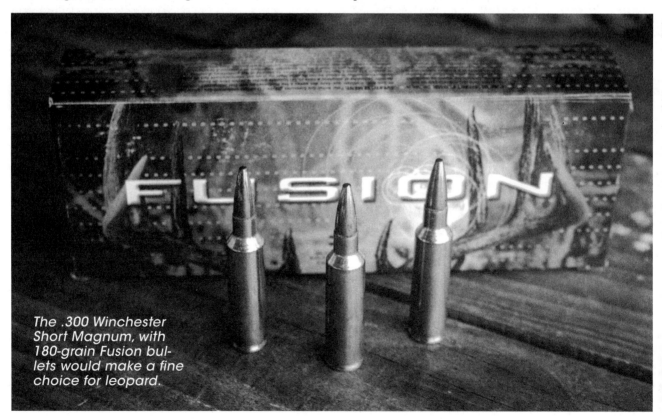

The .300 Winchester Short Magnum, with 180-grain Fusion bullets would make a fine choice for leopard.

Sierra 220-grain spitzer boat-tail, 8mm caliber, a good leopard bullet.

270-grain InterLock bullet, and is just about a perfect lion bullet. A-Square made a frangible softpoint specifically for Mr. Leo: the Lion Load. It was the same size and shape as their Dead Tough, but was easily mistaken for the tougher bullet, with disastrous results. You definitely don't want to shoot a buffalo with the Lion Load. Remember, most of the premium bullets designed for dangerous game are a bit too tough to open up enough to do the kind damage you'll want to do on a lion.

I say most, because some are soft enough to do the job properly. A Nosler Partition in .375", weighing 260 grains, should give a good blend of hydrostatic shock and deep penetration, as the Partition has a reputation of being soft, up front. North Fork makes a special bullet for the cats: the 300-grain Percussion Point. Scored just behind the meplat, it will give rapid expansion in the front end, yet like the Partition, the rear portion will drive deep into the cat's vitals.

A new and different style of bullet, which should work perfect on lion, is the Cutting Edge Bullets Safari Raptor. It is an all-copper spitzer, with a black polymer tip sitting in a hollow point. The bullet's nose, once it impacts, breaks into a set of 'blades' that create severe tissue damage and trauma. The remainder of the bullet, being a solid copper slug, continues to drive through the animal, for deep penetration into the vitals. I have used them in my .300 Winchester Magnum (but not on lion), and they are very accurate. Field reports continue to roll in, with positive results. A 300-grain Safari Raptor in .375, or a .416 in 300 grains or even 325 grains, made of all copper, should handle the king of the jungle quite well.

A 250-grain Barnes TTSX in .375" diameter should work well, when the hollowpoint opens rapidly from the higher velocity of 2,700 fps. This would also make a good choice for a dual-purpose bullet on lion/plains game.

If you like heavy bullets, take a look at Norma's African PH load for the .375 H&H featuring a 350-grain Woodleigh Soft Point. Plenty heavy enough even for shots at the

The trio of North Fork bullets: the Flat Point Solid, the bonded core Semi-Spitzer and the Percussion Point. Shown here in .410" diameter for the .450/400 3" Nitro Express.

Cutting Edge Bullets 325-grain Safari Raptor, a lightweight choice for the .416 calibers.

lion's rear, it should give good expansion and its weight will carry the bullet through the entire length of the cat. All that I have told you about the .375 H&H can be said for the .375 Ruger, as they are so close in performance that the lion will never know the difference.

Jumping up in caliber to the popular .416s, you'll want to be even more careful; the bullets are verily designed for thick-skinned game. Were I grabbing my beloved .416 Remington for a lion hunt, I'd load the 400-grain Hornady InterLock roundnose to an even 2,400 fps and hunt confidently. The Norma African PH load with a 450-grain Woodleigh soft point at 2,150 fps, in either .416 Remington or the epic .416 Rigby would make a close second choice. I like the thought of a heavy, slow bullet tearing large holes in the lion, so the lion doesn't tear large holes in me. I'd avoid the Hornady DGX line of ammunition, because as good as they are for buffalo and grizzly, they are probably a touch too stiff for the lion.

For those who are fans of the .458s, whether a .458 Winchester Magnum, .458 Lott or .450 Nitro Express, I'd recommend the lighter-for-caliber and inexpensive 350 and 405-grain softpoint bullets, to raise the velocity and give better expansion. They can be pushed to right around 2,400 fps from the smallest .45 safari cartridges, and will make good lion medicine. Hornady's 350-grain roundnose Inter-Lock will fit the bill, but avoid the hollowpoint 300-grainers, as they are designed for the slower .45-70 Government, and might not give the necessary penetration for a lion.

Grizzly: Ursus Arctos Horribilus, The Horrible Bear

The second largest carnivore on earth (the polar bear is bigger), these popular game animals roam the northern reaches of Canada and Alaska, with a presence in Montana, Wyoming and Idaho. Even the smallest of the subspecies can weigh between 400 and 800 lbs., with the coastal brown bears tipping the scales at over 1,500 lbs. That, my friend, is an animal that will get your attention in a heartbeat. With claws that will open you like a box cutter, and teeth to match, you'll not want to save money on discount ammunition for this hunt.

They require the best expanding bullets available, and I'll recommend that you carry the biggest bore that you can shoot effectively. Please re-read the last half of that sentence; carrying an elephant rifle that you can't shoot well does you no good. You must be able to put the bullet in the bear's vitals. Ol' Grumpy Pants and

I go around and around about the sensible minimum caliber for a grizzly bear. He feels that a heavy 7mm 175-grain or 220-grain .30 would work very effectively in the hands of a good shot, while I feel that heavier bullets and bigger calibers are the best tools for the job. In truth, we are both correct.

The bullets of today have changed the game, and a 7mm Remington Magnum loaded with 175-grain Swift A-Frames, or a .30-'06 Springfield with a 220-grain Nosler Partition will indeed kill a grizzly, even a coastal brown. They penetrate well, carry a good payload of energy and can be an effective tool. However, there are better choices, and I feel that when your life is on the line, not to mention the huge sums of money involved in hunting the great bears, it's worthwhile to pick a larger caliber.

I like what the .338 Winchester Magnum and .340 Weatherby do with 250-grain Swift A-Frames and Barnes TSX bullets, or for those who are recoil sensitive, a .35 Whelen with 250-grain Partitions or North Fork semi-spitzers would work good also. But if I were heading north to Alaska, I'd consider my .375 H&H a good choice, and my .416 Remington even better.

The 300 and 400-grain bullets will stop a charge of a wounded grizzly bear in the thick alders or willow flats better than any lesser bullet. I like the way both these rifles shoot those Swift A-Frame bullets, and the Hornady DGX and Woodleigh Weldcore would be on the menu as well. Those DGX bullets have a copper-clad steel jacket, and a core of lead with high antimony content. These bullets will break the heavy bones and tear through the huge muscles that shroud the grizzly's vitals. Hornady's DGX load in a .416 Rigby will have a dramatic effect on even the largest coastal grizzly.

The .375 H&H, loaded with a 300-grain bullet at 2,550 fps will deliver over 4,000 ft.-lbs. of energy at the muzzle, while both the .416 Remington and its older brother the .416 Rigby give 5,000 ft.-lbs. when shooting the 400-grain bullets at 2,400 fps. You'll notice that the classic dangerous game calibers usually run at a muzzle velocity of 2,100 to 2,500 fps. This is due to the fact that most soft-point bullets perform best against large slabs of mammal at those velocities, but we'll discuss this further in the Cape buffalo section.

The larger-cased .375 bores, like the .378 Weatherby Magnum and the .375 Remington Ultra Magnum, require the best premium bullets, as their velocities are

300 or more fps faster than the .375 H&H. The recoil ramps up dramatically, but for the hunter who can handle it they are effective. Look to the monometals, like the 300-grain Barnes TSX or even the huge 350-grain TSX for an impressive grizzly load.

The .458 Winchester Magnum and .458 Lott, in the hands of the hunter who can hit his mark, will make any grizzly bear guide smile when he meets his hunter in camp. Or, maybe another way to put it is like this:

you'll often see a .375 H&H or Ruger, a .416 of some noble house, or a .458 of some variety in the hands of a bear guide, and with good cause. These rifles can very effectively stop a bear in its tracks. The quick-handling lever-action rifles chambered to the .45-70 Government are a popular choice in the thickets of the Alaskan peninsula.

The 140-year-old cartridge is still viable there, especially when combined with the firepower of the le-

Author's favorite dangerous game caliber, the .416 Remington Magnum, with the Norma load using 450-grain Woodleigh Weldcore bullets.

I would have no hesitation in using that same load on a grizzly or brown bear at under 100 yards, and that handicap is based on the iron sights on the rifle and my old eyes, not the load.

In the .458 Winchester and Lott, I like the 500-grain bullets, at velocities between 2,100 and 2,300 fps. Swift A-Frame, Nosler Partition, Hornady DGX, Barnes TSX, North Fork semi-spitzer; they all will work just fine. Granted, this level of recoil is not for the faint of heart, these are true stopping rifles, capable of handling anything on earth with four feet and a heartbeat, but if you can shoot it, you'll feel a foot taller. And your guide will sleep that much better in camp.

Most grizzly bears are shot at relatively short range, that is, less than 200 yards. This makes it a pretty even playing field between the spitzer and round-nosed bullets, so don't discount the older design. The larger frontal diameter of a round nose generally causes a 'shudder' effect when it strikes a game animal, and often it is visible through the riflescope. I know for sure that if I were following a wounded grizzly into the willow thicket, I'd feel very comfortable with a large-diameter, heavy-for-caliber roundnose in the chamber.

Cape Buffalo: Black Death

There have been volumes of material written about the Cape buffalo: its tenacity, its adrenalin level, and its ability to soak up copious amounts of lead. Stories of hunters being gored, trampled, and thrown are not hard to find. One thing is for sure: you want to put that first bullet perfectly into the buffalo's vital organs, because a wounded Nyati is a very scary thing. There has been an ongoing campfire debate about the proper bullet for hunting buffalo, and it rages on today. Essentially, there are three schools of thought.

The first (and oldest) is that you use only bullets with no exposed lead. These are the full metal jacket, or full patch bullets, and the more modern style are constructed of a homogenous metal, that are commonly referred to as "solids." They offer no expansion, but give fantastic penetration. The second school of thought is to load a premium softpoint bullet for the first shot, and load the remainder of the magazine with solids for any backup shots.

This gives the advantage of an expanded bullet for the initial shot, and then the great penetration of the solids should you have to shoot the buffalo while it is

ver action. The newer rifles, capable of handling much higher pressures than the Springfield Trapdoor and its ilk, can shoot the revved-up loadings offered today. Buffalo Bore Ammunition makes a 400-grain softpoint load that runs at 2,000 fps, which will make a great grizzly load. I've loaded the 400-grain flatpoint Swift A-Frame in GP's 1886 Browning .45-70 for a bison hunt, the velocities were 1,850 fps, and it worked very well on a 1,700 lb. bull.

running away. Shots into a running buffalo's rear are not uncommon, and the solids can penetrate the entire length of a buffalo. The third, and newest, way of thinking is that the premium softpoints of today are so well built that penetration is not an issue.

So which one of these ideas is right? Surely we must examine the shape and construction of the new bullets available to the buffalo hunter to make a proper, informed decision. And let me put this out there before we delve too deeply: consult your professional hunter prior to your safari and find out what he wants to see in your rifle. Ultimately, he must feel as comfortable as possible with what you're shooting, as it's his responsibility to ensure that you come home in one piece, as well as to clean up messes like wounded bovines in the thick stuff.

I think that the historical choice of 'solids only on buff' has its roots in the failure of traditional softpoint bullets.

The .300 Winchester Magnum with 200-grain Swift A-Frame bullets.
J.D. Fielding photography

There have been thousands of buffalo killed with the softpoints made in the early 20th century, and the quality of those bullets has drastically improved over the last half-century. But many PHs still feel more comfortable with more penetration than expansion, and a solid bullet will "let the air out" of any buffalo. This deep penetration can pose a bit of a problem though. If there are animals behind the bull you wish to kill, the solids can (and often will) completely penetrate the entire animal, and exit with enough retained energy to kill or wound unintended targets. So a hunter must be very careful to be sure the path behind his or her buffalo is clear of other buffalo in the herd.

The traditional 'solid' is a bullet with a lead core, and a thick jacket of copper-coated steel. In an ideal world, they do not deform, expand, or bend. If recovered, they will look just as they did before being fired, but with grooves from the rifling engraved into the jacket. They are often of roundnose design; some are tapered and some have parallel sides and a hemispherical nose section. The older model Hornady solid was a fantastic bullet, as was the Kynoch, and often both would hit to the same point of impact as softpoints in my dangerous game rifles. But, like the softpoints, the game has changed with these bullets as well.

The traditional solid still exists, but there have been major improvements made in the technology. The parallel-sided, hemispherical nose solid is still with us, but improved in the form of the monometal homogenous solid. Barnes Banded Solids and the A-Square Monolithic solid are fine examples of this style bullet. They feed without issue from the box magazine of a bolt-action rifle, and are very accurate. The flatpoint solid, with a slightly tapered nose, is a popular model as well.

The Trophy Bonded Sledgehammer was among the first to adopt this design, and it has continued today in the North Fork Flat Point Solid. Made of solid brass, these are among the toughest bullets available. For buffalo, there are some new designs that have combined several new features with the concept of a monometal solid. Firstly, the North Fork Cup Solid is very similar in design to their flatpoint solid, with the exception of a shallow cup in the nose section.

What this does is give just the slightest bit of expansion to the nose of the bullet, creating a wound channel that won't seal as easy as if it were a hemispherical-nosed solid. I really like these bullets for buffalo, and I've seen folks using them on the gamut of plains game as well, with good effect.

The .416 Rigby with suitable premium bullets.

If you like sectional density, here is a winner: The Barnes TSX in .375″ caliber, at a whopping 350 grains.

The 300-grain Fusion load in .45/70 makes a good bear load.

Woodleigh has introduced the Hydrostatically Stabilized Solid, and it is loaded by Federal Premium in their line of safari ammunition. It has a funky-looking sort of nipple on the front of the solid, and that nipple is covered with a blue polymer tip that is hemispherical in shape. This blue 'nipple hat' allows the cartridge to feed perfectly from the magazine of a bolt-action rifle, and I'm very curious to see these recovered from buffalo, and hear the results of the wound channel created.

So, with these great solids available, are they the choice for your buffalo bullet? It depends. The premium softpoints of today have progressed so far that professional hunters are coming to depend on them exclusively. Bullets like the Barnes TSX, Federal's Trophy Bonded, North Fork semi-spitzer and Swift A-Frame have really set the standard for ideal bullet performance when it comes to Nyati.

On both of my buffalo safaris, my professional hunters were younger than I was, and both were huge fans of the Barnes and Swift softpoints. Ironically, both of them also asked me to leave the solids I had brought along in camp; they saw I had 400-grain Swift A-Frames for my .416 Remington and felt completely confident using them for any backup shots that might have been needed.

Some PHs have suggested that the Nosler Partition is a bit too soft in the nose for frontal shots, but if the weight is chosen carefully, that is, heavy-for-caliber, I believe you'll be fine. The old A-Square Dead Tough was (and still is) a favorite of mine, and one of the nice features of that bullet is that it has the same shape and profile as the Monolithic Solids that A-Square makes.

As I promised in the grizzly section, we should discuss dangerous game cartridge velocity. There seems to be a magic number for dangerous game, and for game in general, under traditional circumstances. The velocity number is 2,400 fps. It was not discovered by me, but I first read about the observation in Kevin 'Doctari' Robertson's *The Perfect Shot*, and his observation has merit.

Loosely paraphrased, those cartridges with velocities that range between 2,100 fps and 2,400 fps have been heralded as "the classics", as these will deliver a bullet within the bore diameter with a S.D. of .300 or greater at those velocities. When it comes to the cup-and-core bullet of yesteryear, there were little-or-no premature breakup or penetration problems when this muzzle velocity was adhered to; when things got faster

416 Remington Magnum, with 400-grain Swift A-Frame premium softpoints and 400-grain Hornady solids.
J.D. Fielding photography

The Trophy Bonded Sledgehammer solid, in .375 H&H Magnum.

The classic "T" on the flat meplat of the Federal Trophy Bonded Sledge-hammer.

The 400-grain .416 Swift A-Frame, recovered from a Cape buffalo. Great expansion and penetration, they were resting against the off-side skin.

than 2,400 fps, or the bullets got lighter, penetration became an issue.

This theory holds especially true when the game gets as large as Cape buffalo. The black beasts have overlapping ribs, thick muscle, and huge shoulder bones. The skin of the chest region is loose enough to make traditional softpoints 'upset' too early in the wound channel, compromising penetration. This is one of the reasons that the ultra-fast Weatherby cartridges gained a sketchy reputation early on: the velocity was too high for the strength of the projectiles. I've seen solids that have bent at right angles, and laid eyes upon the softpoints that have just about broken apart.

Now I don't want to sound like I'm picking on the Weatherbys and other cartridges that run at faster velocities, but the classics are classics for a reason. I firmly believe that the super-fast cases are best used for longer shots, where their speed gets a chance to drop off to that of smaller cases at a short velocity. Dangerous game, generally speaking, is taken at relatively short ranges, and today's premium dangerous game bullets make the classics just that much more effective.

That said, I know people who've taken buffalo with traditional softpoints in dangerous game calibers, and I'm certain it could still be done, but when on a hunt of that magnitude, I think you owe it to yourself, your family, and the animal to use the readily available premium bullets of suitable construction and weight.

To answer my own rhetorical question, I personally subscribe to the second scenario, where I carry a premium softpoint in the chamber, and solids in the magazine for backup shots when hunting buffalo. I want to know I can penetrate the length of a buffalo's body from any angle, and I like those North Fork Cup Solids as my buffalo solid. There are still those 'old school' professional hunters who insist on using nothing but solids, but they are becoming fewer and fewer, once they see the performance of the premium softpoints. I suggest you listen to the man to whom you're paying all that money, and use the bullet he asks you too.

There are a couple of points of interest about those blunt-point solids that we should discuss. First, some bolt-action magazine rifles don't like to feed them well from the magazine, and I think this has to do with the rifle's feed ramp. No matter what, you must be absolutely certain that you can feed cartridges into the chamber reliably, every single time, without looking at the rifle. In all sincerity, your life may depend on it. Second, not all solids will hit the same point of aim as their softpoint counterparts.

400-grain North Fork Cup solids, perfect for the follow-up on buffalo.

The Woodleigh Hydrostatically Stabilized Solids.

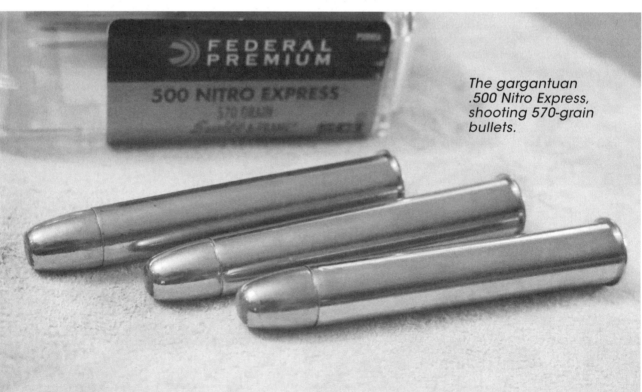

The gargantuan .500 Nitro Express, shooting 570-grain bullets.

It will take some experimentation on your part (read that as time spent at the range with your rifle), but you can find a combination of soft and solid that will work for you. Remember, if you're using solids for backup, odds are that the shot will be on the close side, as most buffalo shots are taken inside of 125 yards.

I like to shoot three-shot groups from my buffalo rifles, using one soft and two solids. I understand there has to be some leeway in the group assessment, but I will say that one of the beauties of the .375 H&H is that it does a fantastic job of putting bullets of different weight, shape, and construction to very near the same point of impact. My .416 Remington does that as well, although it took a little bit of reloading work to get that to happen.

If you choose to get nostalgic and pursue Cape buffalo with a double rifle (which I would love to do!), bullet selection becomes much more critical. A double rifle can be a very finicky creature. It is not easy to get two parallel barrels to hit to the same point of aim. The barrels are soldered together, and are 'regulated' with a certain weight bullet, moving at a particular speed. If you vary too awful far from that, things can get weird. I've done some loading work for guys with doubles that wouldn't regulate well, and with specific powder charges and experimentation with bullet shape, we corrected most of the issue.

It is with the double rifle that you probably need to take the most time and thought into a combination of soft and solid. This is where the folks at Hornady have stepped up to the plate yet again, with their DGX/DGS line of ammunition. The softpoints and the solids have the same nose profile, and they are available in many of the classic double rifles calibers, like .450/.400 3", .450 NE (Nitro Express), .470 NE and the massive 500 NE. Many manufacturers of double rifles are regulating their guns with the Hornady ammunition. Hunting buffalo with a double requires that you get a bit closer than you might need to with a scoped rifle, but the up close experience is worth it.

Should you be a fan of the fast Weatherby cartridges for dangerous game, consider the best premium bullets for use on that which will bite, claw, or stomp you. Traditionally, Weatherby stuff was loaded with good, heavy cup-and-core bullets, but they are better performers with a bullet that can withstand the higher velocities Weatherby cartridges produce. My pal Kraig Kiger has a Mark V Weatherby in the enormous .460 Weatherby, which will certainly generate the ballistics

necessary to cleanly kill any buffalo.

He has a vintage box of Weatherby 500-grain softpoints, which should suffice, but load that giant case with a 500-grain Woodleigh, Barnes TSX or Swift A-Frame and you'll avoid any question of bullet failure. Considering that the .460 pushes a 500-grain bullet at 2,900 fps, it takes a muzzle brake and a pair of brass ones to shoot that cannon accurately, but if you can, you've got a stopping rifle for sure.

There are some good bolt-action rifles on the market, in calibers usually reserved for the professional hunters. If you have a desire to use one, please be sure and practice like crazy with it. The difference in size (although very significant) between the .375 H&H and the .500 Jeffrey's won't make up for poor shooting. A .375 in the right place will kill better than a .500 in the wrong place. And those .500s do kick!

Loxodonta Africana: The African Elephant

Hunting the mighty African elephant is a source of controversy these days, but to help with the overpopulation of the species, and to better manage and keep a healthy herd, hunting is a very effective tool. Controversy aside, if you are lucky enough to be able to pursue a Jumbo with rifle in hand, you'll be shooting a solid for sure.

The most popular shot on an African elephant is the brain shot, which puts the animal down quickly and cleanly, but requires that you penetrate over two feet of honeycombed bone if you take the frontal shot.

Now, our premium softpoints are fantastic, but for this kind of work we want the penetration that only a solid can deliver. Furthermore, I personally like the idea of the monometal solids, which have much less of a chance to bend, break or deform than the copper and steel coated lead models.

The flatpoint monometal solids have been giving incredible results when the autopsy is performed on a hunted elephant. They are giving straight-line penetration, and plenty of it at that. Be careful with these, because as good as they penetrate on the frontal shot, if you take a side-on brain shot the bullet can exit the skull and kill or wound animals behind your target.

It is pretty well accepted that the .375 H&H is the minimum accepted cartridge for hunting elephant, and I'd tend to agree with that. Many lesser cartridges have killed elephant cleanly (the .318 Westley Richards and

The .460 Weatherby Magnum is not for the recoil sensitive.

The .500 Jeffery's, with 535-grain Swift A-Frame softpoints.

9.3x62mm come to mind), but there have been many wounded elephant and many wounded hunters from trying to use too small a rifle.

In the .375 H&H and other cases with that bore diameter, I like the 300-grain monometal solids, like the North Fork flatpoint solid, the Trophy Bonded Sledgehammer, Woodleigh Hydrostatically Stabilized, and the Barnes Banded Solid. They all have a fantastic reputation throughout Africa, and just about any PH on the continent will sing the praises of the penetration capabilities of those long 300-grain .375s.

The traditional solids will still work, such as the heavy full metal jackets produced by Woodleigh, but I have heard stories and seen photos of steel and copper-covered lead bullets that bent at right angles, or that were sent on a strange path once that bullet hit the honeycombed skull of the elephant. This has been known to result in an elephant that is knocked out by the shot, but eventually 'comes-to' and is none too happy about your efforts to kill him. One of the features of the .375 bores is that they are relatively easy to shoot, and accuracy is as important - if not more important - than bore diameter. A PH would much rather have a client who can shoot his or her .375 accurately, than a client who carries one of the big .458 cases and has a wicked flinch.

That said, there really is no such thing as "too much gun" when it comes to hunting elephant, and there are some classic choices as well as some new developments. The good old .404 Jefferys was a standard issue for decades to the game scouts of many African countries, and still makes a great elephant cartridge. The .404 shoots a .423" 400-grain bullet, at a sedate velocity of 2,100 fps. Not as impressive as its .416" cousins, but the lack of recoil makes the old gun a winner among elephant hunters, as the shot will definitely be under 50 yards.

Hornady's 400-grain DGS (Dangerous Game Solid), a flat-nosed bullet with lead core and copper-clad steel jacket, is available in their Dangerous Game Series of ammo.

Those .416s (Rigby, Remington and Ruger, and even the wildcat Taylor) are certainly a solid choice (pun intended) when it comes to elephant, as they are much easier to shoot than the .458s, yet deliver a 400-grain slug at 2,400 fps, plenty enough to quickly dispatch the giant pachyderms. My own .416 Remington really likes the North Fork 400-grain flatpoint solid, putting three of them into a group of just about one inch.

The Cutting Edge Safari Solid should make for a most impressive choice on elephant, but for now they

George Gibbs' .505 cartridge, with Cor-Bon and Norma ammunition.

J.D. Fielding photography

must be handloaded. Again, make sure that the flat-point solids will feed reliably in your particular bolt-action, as some of them have been known to hang up in certain feed ramps.

There are plenty of solids to choose from in the factory ammunition, including that wicked cool .416" 400-grain Woodleigh Hydrostatic Stabilized solid in the Federal Premium Safari line. The Ruger, Rigby and Remington are all represented in Hornady's Dangerous Game Series as well, giving an economical option for those who are pursuing Africana Loxodonta.

If you prefer a single-shot or double rifle in .40 caliber, the .450/.400 Nitro Express has seen a resurgence of late, especially in the Ruger No. 1 single shot. Shooting a .411" diameter 400-grain bullet at about 2,050 fps, there are some good choices for the elephant hunter.

Kynoch still produces ammunition loaded with solids, but I like the Hornady DGS for this classic and the Barnes 400-grain Banded Solid will certainly get the job done. The parallel-sided and flatpoint solids create a larger wound channel than do those of a more curved profile, and are well worth the investment should you need to stop a charge on an enraged elephant.

The .458 calibers are probably considered the classic elephant calibers, from the .458 Winchester Magnum and .458 Lott, through the .450 Rigby and .450 Watts, to the .450 Nitro Express and .450 No. 2, designed for the single-shots and double rifles. Using a good 500-grain solid, they run from around 2,100 fps to 2,400 fps, and they deliver over 5,000 ft.-lbs. of energy, and a nice big wound channel. They penetrate

A true elephant stopper, the .505 Gibbs with 600-grain Woodleigh solids.

wonderfully on brain shots, and are good for side body shots as well. The older Kynoch-style solids have been with us forever, but there are better choices on the market today.

The Hornady DGX and the Trophy Bonded Sledgehammer are loaded in factory ammunition, and both are fully capable of taking an elephant cleanly. Woodleigh offers their classic full metal jacket bullet in 500 grains, and they will regulate very well in the many .45-caliber double rifle cartridges, and I firmly believe that they are, structurally speaking, a better choice than the Kynoch bullets while being of the same weight and shape. In .458" diameter, I like the way the parallel-sided and true roundnose solids shoot.

When we headed over to Tanzania on a buffalo safari, I loaded ol' GP some 500-grain A-Square Monolithic solids for his .458 Winchester, and they shot very well. It took a bit of handloading, and experimentation with several different powders, but I got that rifle to match the factory velocity of 2,150 fps. I understand the A-Square trio of Monolithic Solid, Dead Tough and Lion Load are available again this year, and I hope they are as good as they ever were.

Cartridges over .45 caliber, including the veteran .470 Nitro Express, .475 No.2 Jeffreys, .500 NE, .505 Gibbs and .500 Jeffreys, are usually in the hands of

The .458 Winchester Magnum, and its big brother, the .458 Lott.

A good choice for an all-around dangerous game rifle: the .458 Lott with 500-grain softpoints and solids.

a professional hunter, not a client, but lately there seems to be exceptions to that rule. I had the opportunity to spend some time with my buddy Mike McNulty's Montana Rifle Works Model 99DGR in .505 Gibbs, and I wouldn't hesitate to use that rifle on an elephant.

Norma's African PH ammo, with a Woodleigh full metal jacket 600-grain solid at 2,100 fps was surprisingly manageable, and plenty accurate to hit the brain of an elephant. Many of the calibers in the class give the same, or at least very similar, levels of performance. The gist remains the same; when it comes to something as massive as an African elephant, get the best solid you can afford and put that ammo through rigorous testing to make sure it functions perfectly through your rifle. You can't be too prepared for a hunt like this.

The .458 Winchester Magnum, with Federal Trophy Bonded Sledgehammer solids.

"Gun Digest Shooter's Guide to Reloading"
By Philip P. Massaro

BOOK EXCERPT: WHY DIDN'T THIS WORK OUT?

In this chapter, I'm going to delve into some of the problems and pitfalls that come with loading your own ammunition, from the disappointing to the dangerous. Hopefully, this will allow you to learn from the mistakes of others without having to make them yourself.

If you're like me, you've done your best to adhere to all the rules and guidelines that have been outlined so far. You've read the reloading manuals, learned the history and design of your particular cartridge, tumbled the cases until they are shiny, resized them properly, picked out the bullet, primer, and powder that tickle your fancy, and assembled it all to the best of your ability. As you head to the range, you're as giddy as a five-year-old on Christmas Eve. Then, after settling into the bench, stuffing the shiny little fellas into your sweetheart pistol or rifle, and holding and squeezing, the walk to the target shows disappointing results. The groups are much larger than you've expected. This is the most common problem, and here are some of the causes.

Powder Choice

As I've previously outlined, there are many different types of smokeless powder on the market today, for both pistols and rifles. Some have been around for more than 70 years, while others are just a year or two old.

Rifles, to a greater degree than pistols, are finicky creatures. I've owned and loaded for some that would happily and accurately digest just about any powder I stuffed in the case. Those kinds of guns are a joy. Then, there have been some, like Dad's Ruger Model 77, chambered in .300 Winchester, that seemed to be unhappy with everything I brewed up.

The fact of the matter is, every barrel is different. Accuracy comes from one thing, and that is consistent, repeatable barrel harmonics. The same thing applies to pistols.

There will usually be some suggested powders in the overview of your cartridge choice in the major reloading manuals. Listen to the people who wrote these tomes, as they do research for a living. That said, it may take some experimentation to find *your* recipe, that magic combination of components that provide the level of accuracy you're happy with. Don't be afraid to try a different type or brand of powder (if it's listed in your manual), and certainly don't get married in the first place to a particular powder. There are many websites, social forums, and blogs that discuss the best starting points for a particular cartridge, and the reloading manuals, old and new, provide a great resource for choosing powders. A change in powder has many a time resulted in a rifle shooting sub-MOA groups where before it was minute of softball. By the bye, I found the magic recipe for Dad's .300, using Reloder 25 powder and 200-grain Swift A-Frames. He is, finally, a happy moose hunter.

Powder Charge

The reloading manual will give you a range of powder weights for your cartridge, from the start weight (being the lowest) to the maximum. It is always best and safest to start at the lowest weight and slowly increase the load while watching for pressure signs. Finding the sweet spot is usually a matter of diligent trial and error. Sometimes a small adjustment in the powder charge can result in a dramatic change in group size. My .416 Remington printed 2½-inch groups with my initial loading. This was acceptable, the rifle being intended for the large vitals of the Cape buffalo, but I'm not one to settle. An adjustment

Photo courtesy Massaro Media Group & J.D. Fielding Photography

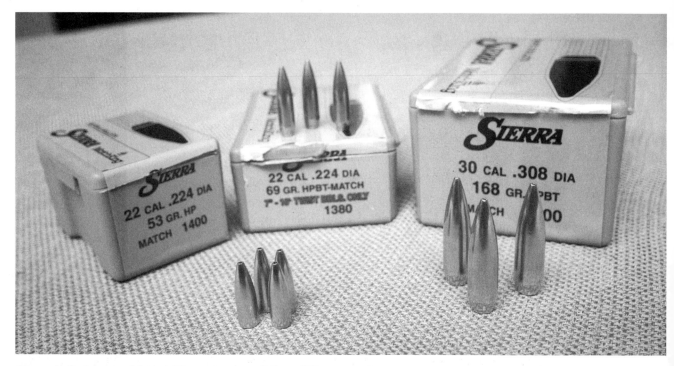

Sierra's flat-base MatchKing made all the difference in the accuracy of the author's .22-250. You have to experiment.
Photo courtesy Massaro Media Group & J.D. Fielding Photography

of one grain of powder brought the 100-yard group size down to about 0.9-inch. Now, to me, that's pretty impressive for a rifle of that caliber and a 5x scope. The same scenario presented itself in my .308 Winchester and, this time, a 0.2-grain adjustment made all the difference.

When I'm getting close to the accuracy I want via the load development process described in the last chapter, what I usually do is make cartridges in groups of six (for two, three-shot groups), with various powder charges in half-grain increments, then fine-tune the load until I find that which the rifle likes.

Bullet Choice

I enjoy using many different bullet makes and models. Some of my rifles prefer long, lean, boat-tailed spitzers, while others prefer flat-based bullets, either round-nosed or spitzer. I spent a lot of time and money (not to mention stomach lining), chasing my tail and wondering why my .22-250 would not print the 52-grain boat-tail hollowpoint match-grade bullets into the tight little groups I wanted. I tried various powders, different cases, human sacrifice (kidding), all with no luck. My colleague and mentor, Col. Le Frogg, overheard my complaining one day and solved the problem immediately.

"Your barrel's crown is a bit imperfect," he said to me. "Switch to the 53-grain flat-base and call me in the morning."

He was spot on. Switching to the flat-base gave me $3/_8$-inch three-shot groups, with the same powder charge I'd been using with the 52-grain bullets. Le Frogg had been right, the crown was (and still is) ever so slightly out of round, and the gasses were affecting the flight of those boat-tail bullets because of that crown imperfection. I could have had it re-crowned, but it shoots those flat-base bullets so well I haven't bothered. Lesson here: If you're unhappy with your rifle's performance with boat-tails, try a flat-base bullet. The difference in long-range trajectory is minimal at most sane hunting ranges, but the accuracy usually improves dramatically.

The same applies to the pistols. Some barrels prefer the jacketed hollowpoints we love so much, while I've also seen some snub-nosed .38 Specials that will print wadcutters into very tight groups. A finicky 1911 .45 ACP I had would only print 230-grain round-nosed ammunition well; no matter how we loaded 185-grain jacketed bullets, it wasn't happy. Bottom line is, it may take some time to find the particular bullet for your rifle or pistol. Let go of "loving" a particular powder or bullet if it's not working though your gun, because why would anyone want to keep barking up that tree and getting crappy results? That just doesn't make sense. Experiment, switch things up. When you get to the load that sings, you'll be a confident and happy shooter.

Mechanical Issues

After hunting moose in Quebec, glassing across those long, wide lakes and finally seeing the sheer size of those Kings of Deer, I promptly headed to my local gun shop and purchased a rifle I felt worthy of *Alces Alces*, the .375 Holland & Holland Magnum. Proud as a peacock, I bought a set of dies, a couple hundred rounds of brass, and some bullets I really liked the look of. But,

no matter what I did, regardless my procedure, I had the same issue: I would put the first shot on paper, the second would hit three inches up and to the right, and the third would land within an inch of the first. Being new to handloading at the time and unwilling to settle for that degree of accuracy, I made a phone call to a custom rifle shop in New Braunfels, Texas, that specializes in fixing these sorts of problems. They told me that my loading wasn't the problem, rather that the barreled action wasn't bedded properly into the stock (an inherent problem with my particular gun model). The rifle was shipped to them and re-bedded and, lo and behold, the problem was solved. That big stick now prints under

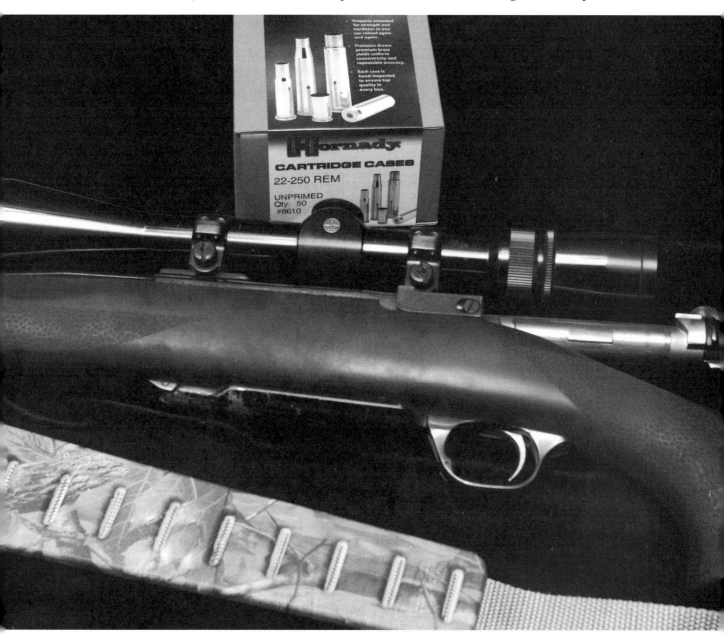

Quality bases, rings, and optics help to evaluate accuracy, taking mechanical issues out of the equation.
Photo courtesy Massaro Media Group & J.D. Fielding Photography

one-inch groups with 250-, 270-, or 300-grain bullets.

Another rifle I had, a military Mauser conversion, wouldn't group below 2 MOA. Different bullets, powders, and primers were used, all with the same results. The culprit? A military trigger. Creepier than an old man in a van, the trigger broke at about eight pounds. It was virtually impossible to keep the rifle on target while getting this trigger to break. The solution? A premium replacement trigger. I ordered one from Timney, took my time installing it, and ended up reducing the groups to minute of angle or better, depending on the load.

Lesser quality optics and/or bases and rings can also be a source of frustration. Bases that loosen from vibration and rings that don't properly hold the scope or are simply improperly installed can drive you crazy. Purchasing the best bases and rings you can afford is worth every penny you spend. If the hardware won't hold zero, the best handloaded ammunition in the world won't make a bit of difference.

Loading Difficulty

At the bench, target all set up, hopes higher than Heaven, you load your firearm—except the bolt won't close, the pistol won't chamber a round, the autoloading rifle won't go into battery. Now what?

It's time to reexamine the cases. Did you properly resize them? A bolt-action rifle has the strength to cam-over on a slightly over-sized cartridge, but pumps, levers, and auto-loaders do not. Full-length resizing, described in Chapter 4, is imperative, when it comes to the pump-action, lever-action, and auto-loading rifles (and pistols). The partially sized case can be the bane of the handloader. You must make sure all your resizing dies are properly adjusted, to ensure the ammunition you've worked so hard to make works properly in your firearm. If loading problems do rear their ugly heads, try switching over to small base sizing dies, which will resize the cases all the way to the base.

Unloading Difficulty

Okay, it loads fine. You take two deeps breaths, let the last one half-way out, hold, and gently squeeze … *bang*! But, the action won't cycle. The bolt won't open. You can't extract the cartridge. What does this mean?

You, my friend, have a pressure problem. Pressure is funny thing. It's also a very, very dangerous thing. It can result in a damaged firearm at best, or loss of life at worst. It works like this: Every cartridge is nothing more than a pressure "chamber." It

The primer on the left shows acceptable pressure. It has the same appearance as a new one, with the exception of the firing pin mark. The primer on the right has been flattened and the firing pin mark appears "cratered," showing signs of excessive pressures.

The author's dad, a.k.a. Grumpy Pants (right), explaining the effects of a canted reticle on long-range shooting. He knows what he's talking about!

is made of brass, a malleable metal, and is designed to hold a specific charge of propellant in order to propel the bullet or shot when ignited. If you exceed that pressure limit for which the cartridge was designed, excessive pressure will show its ugly face. In the revolver, it can result in a cracked cylinder. In a rifle, it becomes a stuck bolt or, perhaps, a broken extractor. I don't ever want you to experience this, so allow me to identify some symptoms.

If you are able to extract the cartridge but with difficulty, examine the struck primer. If the mark left by the firing pin appears to have a raised crater around the edges or the edges of the primer don't have the nice rounded appearance they did when you seated them, the pressure has become excessive. This means that, *for the particular firearm you are holding*, the load is too hot and it has created excessive and unacceptable pressures.

But, wait, Phil. I loaded these .270 Winchester cartridges in accordance with the manual of the bullet manufacturer. Everything should be fine, no?

In theory, yes, but, there are variables you might not be aware of. First, what is the barrel length of your fire-arm in comparison to the barrel length of the firearm used in the test data? For every extra inch of barrel, you gain around 25 fps of velocity and the pressure increases accordingly.

An example: The test data shows the loads for the .270 Winchester were fired in a 22-inch barrel, but you've got a 26-inch barrel. This will result in an increase of roughly 100 fps, so the powder charges that proved safe and acceptable in the test rifle have shown excessive pressure in your rifle. Reduce the charges and work up, carefully, until you have a load that is sufficiently accurate and shows no pressure signs.

Another example: My .357 Magnum had its cases stuck in the cylinder one day at the range. I used an appropriate load for the bullet weight, but was still getting pressure problems. I have a six-inch barrel, but the data was tested in a four-inch barrel. Once again, it is imperative to compare your firearm to the test firearm and be aware of any differences.

Many people contact me wondering why their particular rifle or pistol doesn't measure up to the advertised velocities of the ammunition companies or reloading manuals. Often times, the barrel length is again the issue: the advertised velocities were established in a longer (read higher pressure) barrel, and, for you, having a firearm equipped with a shorter barrel, it is only logical that your velocities should be lower. When dealing with Magnum cartridges, they often reach their potential only in long-barreled rifles and pistols, so keep this in mind when you plan a firearm purchase.

Sometimes, groups delivered to the target aren't what we wish for. We blame the load. We blame the trigger. We blame the wind. We blame the fact that Orion isn't aligned with Cassiopeia. It has happened to me, and I'm sure it will happen to you. We just need to be honest enough to admit the ugly truth to ourselves. Say it with me, "I'm not shooting well right now."

When trying to develop and assess a load you've created, you will need to call upon your best shooting skills. The goal is to try and evaluate whether the rifle or pistol delivers consistent results (group size) and, to do that, we have to remove as much of the human error as possible. Shooting from uncomfortable positions or off a shaky rest will not allow you to obtain the true accuracy potential of your handloads, and it will keep you awake at night wondering if the firearm/load combination is the problem or if it was your shooting. Grumpy Pants taught me the basic shooting mechanics at a very young age.

"When you get the rifle settled," he'd tell me, "take two deep breaths, let the last one halfway out, and slowly squeeze the trigger."

I still hear his voice in my head, as if I were 11 again, whether he's with me at the bench or not. You

A steady, comfortable rest that does not impinge the rifle's fore-end is a must to properly evaluate the accuracy of your handloaded ammunition.

Photo courtesy Massaro Media Group & J.D. Fielding Photography

A .38 Special on sandbags.
Photo courtesy Massaro Media Group & J.D. Fielding Photography

don't want to know when the gun is going to go off, so that you don't tense up and send the shot awry. A slow, smooth trigger pull with "follow-through" (imagine trying to see the bullet rip the paper), will give the best results. Jerking or slapping at the trigger will not give good accuracy.

When developing loads for hard-kicking rifles or pistols, I bring my favorite bolt-action .22 Long Rifle with me. Shooting that rifle in between groups of big-game rifles or pistols helps prevent me from developing a flinch, a tough habit to break once it sets in. With the rimfire rifle, which has virtually no

recoil, you can actually see the bullet hit, so it helps me to keep my shooting skills sharp.

I like to shoot from a comfortable bench, built sturdily, and off of sandbags. The sandbag rest allows the rifle to settle down and is, in my opinion, the best way to eliminate the human element from the equation. Sometimes I use one sandbag under the fore-end of the rifle, other times I'll use one under the fore-end and one under the butt of the stock. When I use only one, I like to hold the rear portion of the stock with my left hand (I shoot right-handed) to help steady the rifle, leaving the fore-end comfortably nestled in the sandbag. The goal is not to impinge the barrel in the fore-end of the stock, thereby allowing it to move freely throughout recoil.

There are vice-type shooting rests available, and they can be a help to hold steady, so long as the fore-end of the rifle is free to move. You never want to put a force on the firearm that won't be there under normal shooting conditions. Doing so will affect the point of impact and group size.

Several shooting friends use a Lead-Sled to absorb the recoil from hard-kicking rifles. I haven't ever used one myself, and I've heard mixed reviews. Some guys swear by them, because the lack of recoil allows them to shoot much better, while other guys tell me about cracked stocks from the way the device holds the firearm. Again, I haven't used them, but if you plan to, please do your research.

The Bullseye Camera System.

Photo courtesy Massaro Media Group & J.D. Fielding Photography

When developing pistol loads, I use the same one-sandbag and two-breath technique described for rifle shooting, put I usually place my left hand under my right, for the steadiest hold. This grip works well for me. The goal in either case is to hold the firearm as steady as possible, to give repeatable results.

Hey, speaking of the shooting bench, I found a new company that makes a rather innovative product. Bullseye Camera Systems has a wireless target camera that you set up about 10 feet away from your target, align the laser pointer to the center of the bull's-eye and, when you switch it on, the device interfaces with your Windows-based laptop computer, iPhone, or iPad. In other words, the target images are delivered to the device you choose, at the bench, and the 100-yard shuffle is a thing of the past! You can isolate individual shots or groups of shots on your device, record group size, etc., out to 600 yards with the basic model and out to 2,000 yards with the extended range version. Now, not only is it really cool to have the group size and image recorded on your phone or laptop, but think about how much time you'll save waiting for your heart rate to slow down after you've walked 100 yards (or more) to the target and then again for the return trip. It *really* pays off at the 300-yard plus ranges. This is a truly ingenious product. I am a bit spoiled, having a personal 200-yard rifle range on premises, but I can imagine that these camera systems will be a hit with just about any rifle or pistol club in America!

Now, let's examine some problems as they occur at the reloading bench.

There's nothing worse than a stuck case. You seat the case in the shellholder, work the press handle, and *bam*! You simply can *not* remove that dirty bugger from the sizing die. Maybe you've even ripped off the case rim trying. Ten seconds ago you had a great new hobby, now you're reaching for the rocks glass and two fingers of bourbon. You're asking yourself, *Why me, Lord, why me?*

Well, friend, we've all done it. In fact, this happens so often that many companies have marketed the solution: *the stuck case remover.* I use an RCBS model. With it I take the provided drill bit to drill through the flash hole and into the case's web, and then I use the provided tap to thread the newly drilled hole. The kit includes a hardened screw that threads into the tapped hole and, one crank at a time, it draws the stuck case out of the resizing die.

FRUSTRATED?!

Follow these simple steps to remove a stuck case

1. *Case rim ripped away, you stare at a case stuck in the resizing die.*

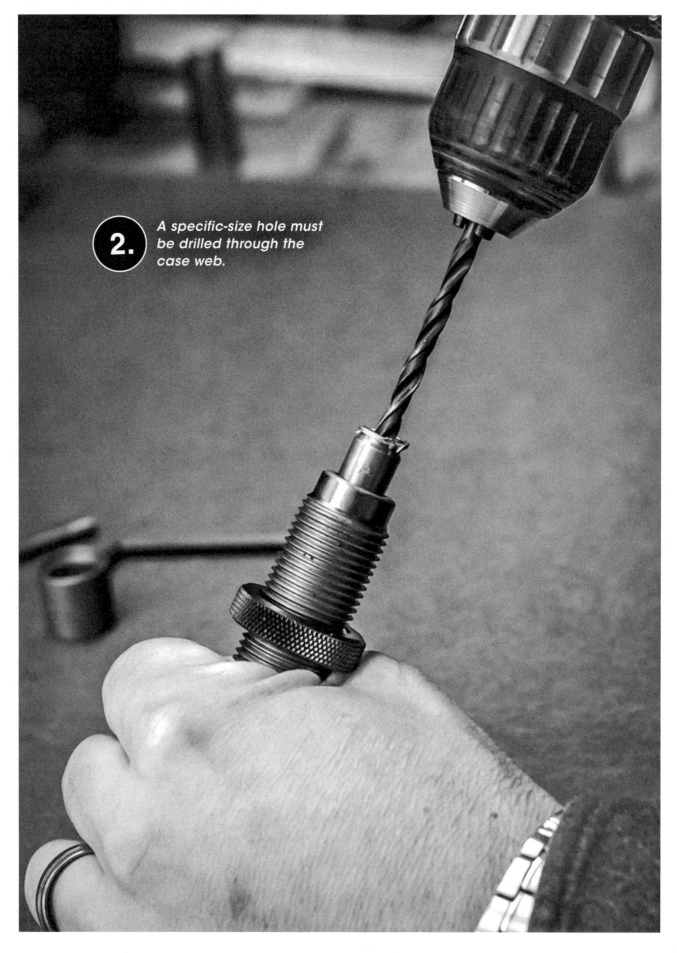

2. A specific-size hole must be drilled through the case web.

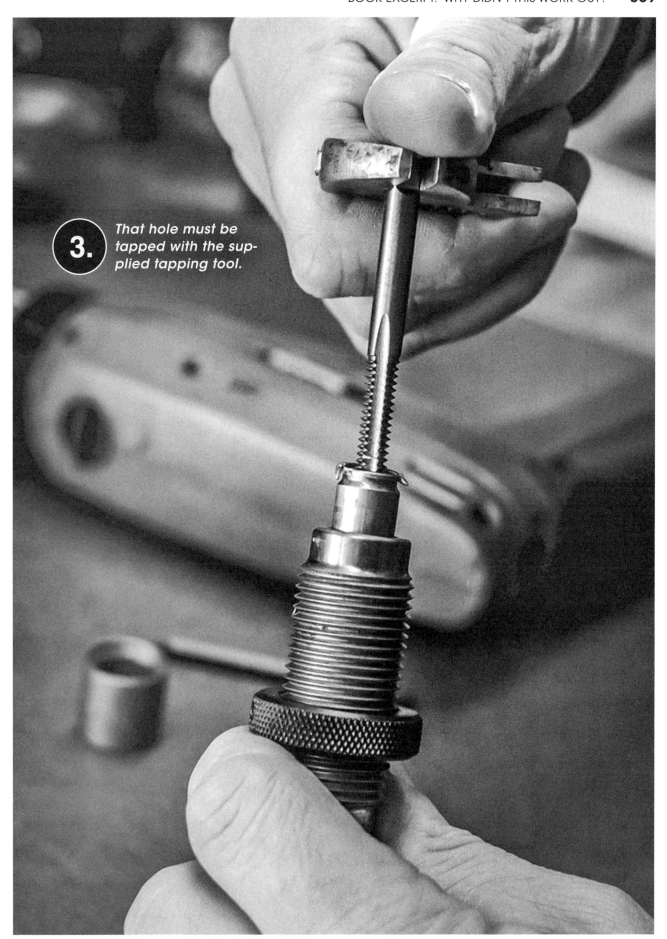

3. *That hole must be tapped with the supplied tapping tool.*

4. The hardened screw is threaded into the tapped hole in the web.

Why did it happen? An insufficient amount of case lube. Lubricating the cases in just the proper fashion is important. Not enough lubrication and the cases will stick in the die like peanut butter to the roof of your mouth. Too much lubricant, and the cases develop those funky little shoulder dents that can ruin the appearance of your shiny, wonderful little creations.

Cartridge cases, as I've said, are generally made of brass or nickel-coated brass. Brass is used primarily because of its malleability, or ability to mold, bend, and flow. It is much less rigid than steel, and the cases can be reused several times. However, they don't last forever. It is important to keep a record of how many times the cases have been fired, resized, and reloaded. When brass cartridge cases have reached the end of their days, they lose their malleability and become brittle. When this happens, they are prone to split in the neck. When you see this symptom, it is crucial that you remove and destroy these cases. *They are not safe.*

The neck of this .22-250 Remington has split from being fired and resized too many times. Toss it away!

Photos both pages courtesy Massaro Media Group & J.D. Fielding Photography

The .458 Winchester Magnum on the right is a victim of too much crimp and not enough flare. That caused the case to crumple.

As expensive as cartridge cases are these days, there is no reason to use unsafe components.

Sometimes, after running the case through a seating die set up to give a roll crimp (e.g., the .45 Long Colt, .357 Magnum, .45-70 Government, and many hard-recoiling safari calibers), you may see that the case appears crumpled or that the shoulder area is bulged or rolled. The problem? The seating die is adjusted too low, giving too much crimp and actually crushing the case as it does so. You don't ever want to try and fire ammunition that is bulged or has a rolled shoulder, as it can be dangerous to the weapon and the shooter.

Obviously, if you have this problem, you need to adjust your seating die. But why not cut to the chase and prevent the problem in the first place? When I'm starting a new load, I often use three or four dummy rounds (bullet and case, no primer or powder) to adjust the dies properly.

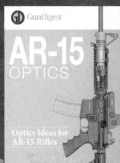
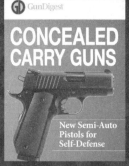

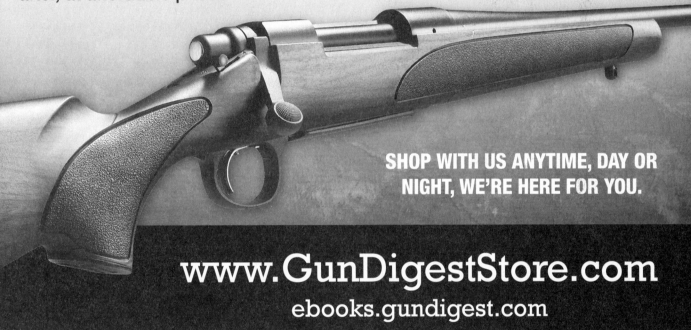

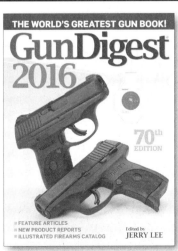

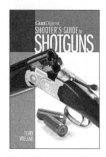

GUN DIGEST SHOOTERS GUIDE TO SHOTGUNS
U2146 • $19.99

GD SHOOTER'S GUIDE TO RIFLES
V6631 • $19.99

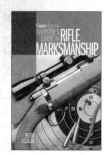

GUN DIGEST SHOOTER'S GUIDE TO RIFLE MARKSMANSHIP
U2928 • $19.99

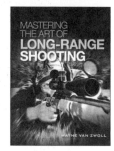

MASTERING THE ART OF LONG-RANGE SHOOTING
U2148 • $29.99

2016 GUN DIGEST
T6948 • $35.99

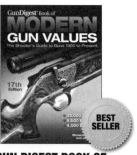

GUN DIGEST BOOK OF MODERN GUN VALUES
U5559 • $34.99

GD BOOK OF THE REMINGTON 870
V8197 • $32.99

GUN DIGEST PRESENTS CLASSIC SPORTING RIFLES
W7930 • $24.99

GUN DIGEST SHOOTER'S GUIDE TO SHOTGUN GAMES
T5657 • $19.99

ABCS OF RIFLE SHOOTING
U8579 • $27.99

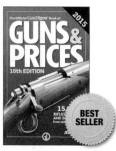

THE OFFICIAL GUN DIGEST BOOK OF GUNS & PRICES 2015
T6947 • $26.99

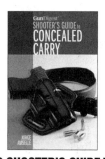

GD SHOOTER'S GUIDE TO CONCEALED CARRY
T2884 • $19.99

GUN SAFETY IN THE HOME
T0031 • $15.99

GUN DIGEST GUIDE TO MAINTAINING & ACCESSORIZING FIREARMS
T0033 • $32.99

GUN DIGEST SHOOTER'S GUIDE TO THE AR-15
U7713 • $19.99

GUN DIGEST GUIDE TO MODERN SHOTGUNNING
U9369 • $32.99

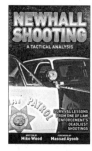

NEWHALL SHOOTING: A TACTICAL ANALYSIS
T1794 • $24.99

To order, go to www.GunDigestStore.com.

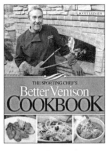

THE SPORTING CHEF'S BETTER VENISON COOKBOOK
U1948 • $24.99

COOKING GAME
U2929 • $9.99

BIG BUCK SECRETS
T4648 • $24.99

WE KILL IT WE GRILL IT
V6707 • $9.99

301 VENISON RECIPES
VR01 • $10.95

ADVENTURE BOWHUNTER
V9708 • $34.99

HUNTING MATURE WHITETAILS THE LAKOSKY WAY
W4542 • $29.99

DEER & DEER HUNTING'S GUIDE TO BETTER BOW HUNTING
V6706 • $9.99

STRATEGIES FOR WHITETAILS
WTLDD • $24.99

TOM DOKKEN'S ADVANCED RETRIEVER TRAINING
U1863 • $22.99

TROPHY WHITETAILS WITH PAT AND NICOLE REEVE
U3680 • $31.99

LEGENDARY WHITETAILS
W7618 • $29.99

GUT IT. CUT IT. COOK IT.
Z5014 • $24.99

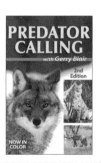

PREDATOR CALLING WITH GERRY BLAIR
Z0740 • $19.99

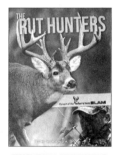

THE RUT HUNTERS
U7573 • $31.99

GAME COOKERY
U7125 • $24.99

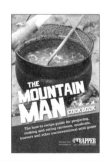

THE MOUNTAIN MAN COOKBOOK
U9370 • $12.99

TOM DOKKEN'S RETRIEVER TRAINING
Z3235 • $19.99

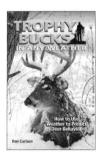

TROPHY BUCKS IN ANY WEATHER
Z1781 • $21.99

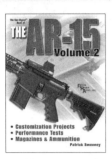

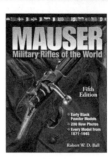
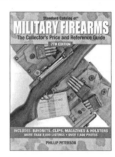
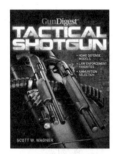
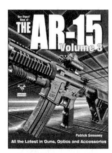
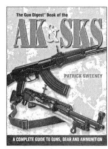

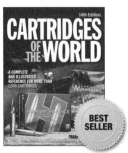
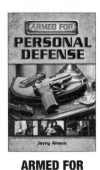

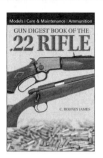

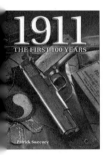
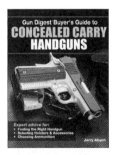
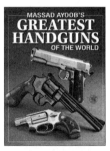
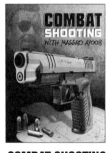
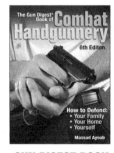
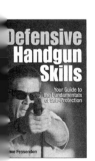

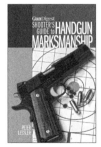
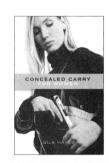

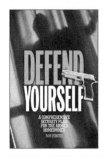

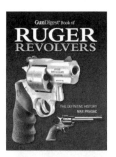
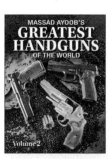
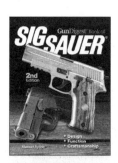
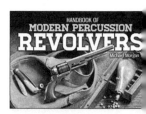
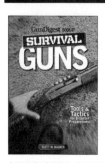

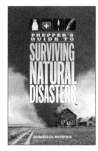

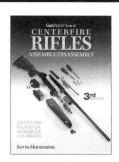

**GUN DIGEST BOOK OF
CENTERFIRE RIFLES ASSEMBLY/
DISASSEMBLY 3RD ED.**
U2620 • $34.99

**GD BOOK OF SHOTGUNS
ASSEM/DISSASEM,
3RD ED.**
V6630 • $36.99

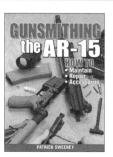

**GUNSMITHING
THE AR-15**
Z6613 • $27.99

**GUN DIGEST BOOK OF
TACTICAL WEAPONS
ASSEMBLY/DISASSEMBLY**
U3671 • $29.99

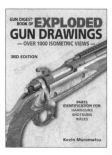

**GUN DIGEST BOOK
OF EXPLODED
GUN DRAWINGS**
T5656 • $41.99

**GUN DIGEST BOOK
OF REVOLVERS
ASSEMBLY/DISASSEMBLY**
Y0773 • $34.99

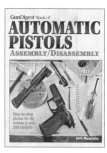

**GUN DIGEST BOOK
OF AUTOMATIC PISTOL
ASSEMBLY / DISSASEMBLY**
W7933 • $39.99

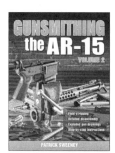

**GUNSMITHING THE AR-15
VOLUME 2**
U7714 • $29.99

**CUSTOMIZE THE
RUGER 10/22**
NGRTT • $29.99

**CUSTOM RIFLES:
MASTERY OF
WOOD & METAL**
V8196 • $59.99

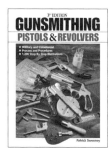

**GUNSMITHING:
PISTOLS & REVOLVERS**
Z5056 • $29.99

**GUN DIGEST BOOK
OF RIMFIRE RIFLES
ASSEMBLY/DISASSEMBLY**
W1577 • $34.99

**GUN DIGEST BOOK
OF THE AR-15**
GDAR • $27.99

To order, go to www.GunDigestStore.com.

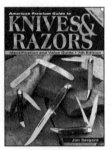
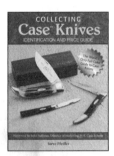
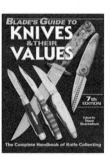

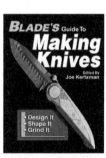